PENETRATING CRITIQUES

Emasculated Empire and Victorian Identity in Africa

LESLIE ALLIN

Penetrating Critiques

Emasculated Empire and Victorian Identity in Africa

UNIVERSITY OF TORONTO PRESS
Toronto Buffalo London

© University of Toronto Press 2020
Toronto Buffalo London
utorontopress.com

ISBN 978-1-4875-0152-5 (cloth) ISBN 978-1-4875-1342-9 (EPUB)
ISBN 978-1-4875-1341-2 (PDF)

Library and Archives Canada Cataloguing in Publication

Title: Penetrating critiques : emasculated empire and Victorian identity in Africa / Leslie Allin.
Names: Allin, Leslie, 1984– author.
Description: Includes bibliographical references and index.
Identifiers: Canadiana (print) 20200231715 | Canadiana (ebook) 20200232029 | ISBN 9781487501525 (cloth) | ISBN 9781487513429 (EPUB) | ISBN 9781487513412 (PDF)
Subjects: LCSH: English literature – 19th century – History and criticism. | LCSH: Masculinity in literature. | LCSH: Imperialism in literature. | LCSH: Africa – In literature.
Classification: LCC PR468.M38 A45 2020 | DDC 820.935309/034–dc23

This book has been published with the help of a grant from the Federation for the Humanities and Social Sciences, through the Awards to Scholarly Publications Program, using funds provided by the Social Sciences and Humanities Research Council of Canada.

University of Toronto Press acknowledges the financial assistance to its publishing program of the Canada Council for the Arts and the Ontario Arts Council, an agency of the Government of Ontario.

Canada Council for the Arts Conseil des Arts du Canada

Funded by the Government of Canada | Financé par le gouvernement du Canada | Canada

Contents

Illustrations

Acknowledgments

I would like to thank everyone who has offered feedback and peer review that underpinned the production of this book, but especially I am profoundly grateful to Danny O'Quinn – your insights, readings, and sound-boarding have been invaluable, as has your enduring encouragement at all stages of this project. For your confidence and the intellectual investment you have made in this work, I am deeply appreciative, and your support has meant more to me than I can say.

To others who have weighed in on various arguments throughout the work – Michelle Elleray, Julie Cairnie, Jennifer Schacker, Jade Ferguson, Susan Brown, Emily Sharpe, Stephen Arata, Pamela Gilbert, Hannah McGregor, and Cindy McMann – thank you each for the generosity with which you offered me your expertise.

Thank you to the editors at University of Toronto Press who have shepherded this book along to production, Richard Ratzlaff and Mark Thompson – I am grateful for your work. I would also like to acknowledge the help of the staff at the National Archives at Kew, the British Library, and the British Museum with accessing the archives explored in this book.

I am very lucky to have had a close network of colleagues, friends, and family who have been a part of my life as I worked on this project. This circle is large, and you know who you are, so with brevity but profound appreciation, I thank you. To my parents, Lise Allin, Jeff Allin, and Lola Reid-Allin, and to my partner, Steve Zuccala, thank you for your abiding respect, confidence, and support.

PENETRATING CRITIQUES

Emasculated Empire and Victorian Identity in Africa

Introduction: Bodies / Spaces / Texts – British Masculinity and the Failure of Colonial Efficacy

Mystery has, for centuries, hung above [the Dark Continent] like a gruesome pall, the wild riot of a boundless superstition has hovered over its strange people until the world has whispered the very name with a feeling of dread and given to it that regard which attaches only to ghostly and ghastly things of distempered fancy. But dark as has been the mantle of dread which enveloped her during the long centuries, Africa has at last been revealed, through the searchlight of bold exploration, and now meets our scrutiny with the interest of a newly discovered world.

– J.W. Buel, *Heroes of the Dark Continent*, 17

This book traces the emergence of a crisis in Victorian modes of imperial masculine authority at the fin de siècle. It aims to show that, in Africa, imperial confrontations with unanticipated martial prowess, environmental hostility, and the ensuing inability of imperial archives to represent adequately and rationalize events in African contact zones destabilized entrenched imperial ideologies about identity and narrative. These confrontations, in challenging established ideas of British martial heroism, laid bare the problem that traditional constructions of masculinity were, in fact, anxiously maintained fantasies. That these fantasies of heroism, authority, and governance were underpinned by notions of impenetrable physicality, territory, and narrative meant that, when penetrations of these constructions occurred at the levels of the body, space, and text, these modes of imperial authority and legitimation started to deteriorate from *within* imperial discourse. Thus this book, tracing pervasive imperial discourses across archival documents, newsprint, and immensely popular fiction, argues that these texts, ostensibly profoundly invested in empire, in fact trouble the imperial tenets of bounded martial bodies, ordered colonial territories, and solid histories. In doing so, these texts begin, to varying degrees, to recognize that the monstrous threat to imperial identity is not the colonial other, as it would often seem, but rather the seductive narrative of imperial legitimacy itself.

This relationship between fantasies of heroic identity and fixation on penetration emerges disquietingly in J.W. Buel's 1889 volume, *Heroes of the Dark Continent*. This text promises to relate "grand achievements," "glorious deeds," and "Heroism and Unparalleled Daring"[1] of British imperialists in Africa, here represented as a site in which "bold exploration" and "scrutiny" work to consolidate imperial manhood. Buel's claims highlight what is generally recognized in Victorian studies – that Africa has often been reduced to a stage for British identity formation. But his claims and their implications also hint at the dynamics structuring the interdependence of physical penetration and narrative authority. In many ways, Buel's heroes (men who performed imperial services to the British government – working to chart and secure order in Africa – while threatened and overwhelmed by the ostensible chaos of Africa itself) came to embody fortitude, endurance, and knowledge production. Such underpinnings of imperial masculinity emerge in the work's illustrations, which indulge voyeuristic fantasies of white (sexualized) dominance, various forms of suffering, and racialized chaos. At one level, this would seem to be business as usual: Buel's is neither the first nor the last text that would associate African people with dangerous beasts, that would treat Africa as a spectacular mise-en-scène or blank territory, that would understand the continent as a homogeneous arena whose complete history can be contained within a single volume, or that would use African space as a foil for defining heroic British masculinity. But Buel's frontispiece (figure 1) is a valuable starting point for this study because it collates the history of myths about the African continent in a way that underscores a seemingly gratuitous sexualization of both figure and ground that in fact configures both nineteenth-century fantasies about martial manhood and anxieties about its limitations. This illustration also employs many of the same mechanisms of representing British bodies within African spaces that this study unearths in a range of archival and popular texts. To these ends, Buel's frontispiece, artist unknown, introduces the foundations on which fin-de-siècle critiques of imperial masculine authority in Africa are based.

This rather bizarre image clinches the long legacy of how power, danger, and relationships between bodies and space in Africa are often encoded sexually in the Western imagination. Importantly, African power is depicted as threatening; simultaneously, this image seeks to contain it. The arrangement of the Cyclops, roc, dwarf, "Blemmyer,"[2]

Figure 1. Frontispiece of *Heroes of the Dark Continent* (1889)

"Sciapodes,"[3] the woman cooking a baby (probably an Amazon boiling a male child), and the unicorn endows these "curiosities" with varying degrees of menace to the British explorer. Indeed, endowment is one of this illustration's central preoccupations: most of the curiosities have some kind of phallic instrument, from the Cyclops's club, the Blemmyer's spear, the dwarf's arrow, and the woman's knife to the unicorn's horn. Yet, each figure is seized within an ethnographic tableau. Power in African space is thus figured as phallic threat, but is then contained through a fantasy of knowledge production as the figures become subject to the viewer's gaze. Alongside this tension between threat and containment, British masculinity, authority, and narrative are often constructed. At the same time, these phallic dangers are augmented by elements of the landscape that are encoded as feminine – the giant central crevice with its highly suggestive unruly vegetation, the indeterminate lake, the splayed fronds in the background (not to mention the yonic cauldron) – which crowd the space imposingly. Finally, danger is also signified as sexualized by the abundance of nakedness, skin, and muscle of the figures presenting phallic weapons amidst the yonic landscape: the boundaries of humanity are pushed in these figures whose size, parts (or lack thereof), and actions transgress Western understandings of what constitutes the human. As we'll see, it is often the simultaneous representation of African power as phallic and yonic, as penetrating and engulfing, that British narratives seem to find most monstrous.[4]

But if Buel's text depicts Africa as a fantastic space, subject to "the search-light of bold exploration,"[5] it also highlights the relationship between the conquest of this space and writing it. In presenting "a history of ancient Africa" according to colonial accounts, Buel argues that he has "been able to follow the advancing lines of conquest and reclamation."[6] His use of "to follow" is ambiguous: first, it suggests tracing and reporting "the advancing lines," and second, it implies imitating, suggesting that Buel himself is enacting this "reclamation" ideologically. In this latter signification, writing itself is figured as a form of conquest, and thus the writer becomes a kind of hero parallel to those chronicled. This study takes up this double meaning of "to follow" by attending not only to actants – both historical and fictional – engaged in the imperial project in Africa, but also to the acts of writing that attempted to capture, however tenuously, complex intercultural encounters in colonial spaces. As this book traces these mechanisms of representation, it engages with both the history of British colonial activity and its continual restructuring of the fantasies that ostensibly secured British masculine identities in the period. In this process of restructuring, the relationships between bodies, spaces, and texts are profoundly co-legitimizing, and thus co-dependent, underpinnings of these fantasies. In turn, when one buttress of imperial masculine authority begins to crumble, the cracks in the others also widen.

Bodies

The relationship between these fin-de-siècle understandings of masculinity and national identity deeply informed social orientations toward empire. Buel's frontispiece exemplifies how imperial projects in Africa become central to British identity, especially through the challenge of sexual threat. The image's unbalanced circular composition, together with the collection of splayed bodies – which are emphasized over faces as shoulders, breasts, and limb muscles are softly lightened, glistening, while faces tend to be darkened, turned away, or subsumed within the body itself – suggests an encompassing danger. At the centre of this encircling mass of bodies appears the unicorn. The unicorn bears a complex relation to Britishness, not only because it appears on Britain's coat of arms. It is differentiated from the other figures in the illustration through its mobility and whiteness. Traditionally, the unicorn symbolized purity and chastity[7] – that is, the preservation of bodily borders. It was also, however, closely associated with Scotland, which was historically colonial in relation to England and thus aligned with the primitive, but which had by this time been reined in, so to speak (hence the unicorn is depicted as chained in the coat of arms), and thus subsumed into British identity. Nevertheless, the unicorn remains a liminal, slippery symbol, which is perhaps why it functions as a suitable avatar for the metropolitan self in the realm of fantasized danger. Indeed, the unicorn in the frontispiece *is* threatened – hunted by the dwarf, dwarfed by the roc, surrounded by a mass of sexually aggressive beings – and its capacity for survival amidst these challenges is its central test. Thus, in this African mise-en-scène, the tension generated between danger and survival sets the stage for the consolidation of British identity.

When we recognize that Britain seems consistently to find itself at the centre of the foreign, it is impossible to understand Britain's fin-de-siècle identities or its domestic culture separately from empire.[8] As the rate of imperialist growth increased in the late-Victorian period, dominant constructions of imperial masculinity were built around the idea of a stable, solid, authoritative masculine identity that was physically and mentally capable, sound of judgment, and trustworthy. To understand the men of empire – whether soldiers, colonial administrators, policy makers, or adventurers who narrated experiences at and beyond colonial frontiers – as efficacious, competent, and reliable was also to conceive of the imperial project as ideologically sound, even necessary. In other words, the capabilities of the men acting for empire were inseparable from the legitimacy of imperial narratives.

Masculine identity was also linked to imperial power more broadly through analogies of boundary transgressions as borders of different kinds of bodies understood to be within male domains were materially and figuratively crossed. Klaus Theweleit has articulated how the experience of the body in physical space informs the inscription of reality: "The relationship of human bodies to the larger world of objective reality grows out of one's relationship to one's own body and to other human bodies. The relationship to the larger world in turn determines the way in which these bodies speak of themselves, of objects, and of relationships to objects."[9] If all narrative is refracted through the body's relationship with its environment, then experiences and conceptions of contact and exchange impinge on cultural understandings of the relationship between the individual and the larger social body. As Jules Law has noted, "the practice of linking the portals of the individual body to the contours and health of the body politic has a long history."[10] My exploration of this relationship between bodies and communities, and more specifically my assertion that conceptions of narrative solidity are profoundly based on stable bodies, draws also on Mary Douglas's suggestion that the image of society itself "has form; it has external boundaries, margins, internal structure. Its outlines contain power to reward conformity and repulse attack ... For symbols of society, any human experience of structures, margins or boundaries is ready to hand."[11] For both national and martial bodies, "all margins are dangerous[;] ... orifices of the body ... symbolise its specially vulnerable points,"[12] which means that bodies that seek to retain the image of solidity must continuously preserve their figurative and analogous borders. Thus, for fin-de-siècle Britain, spiritual as well as physical soundness mattered: "Victorian intellectuals ... all thought physiologically: they adopted the well-knit body as their model for the well-formed mind, and the mind-body harmony as their model for spiritual health, the harmony of the self with external principles of growth and order."[13] An ordered mind with a grounded and informed grasp of reality and a healthy, capable, strong body were thus mutually constituted.

This kind of stable, impermeable, white male body is therefore burdened with the maintenance – physically through its martial capacities and conceptually through its narratives – of stable, impermeable geopolitical and territorial bodies. The psychic space created by both of these boundaries relies on a fantasy of virile, solid, masterful masculinity that can repulse external threat. Although "masculinity" is, at any given point, plural, complex, contradictory, ephemeral, and historically specific, it is, nevertheless, an identity through which "men claim certain kinds of authority, based upon their particular type of bodies."[14] Recognizing, then, that masculinity is nebulous and disunited,[15] this study focuses on the destabilization of hegemonic, martial masculinity, arguing that its own limitations informed its demise. In other words, this book examines how critiques of dominant forms of masculinity undercut the authority of empire.[16]

The ideals of heroic masculinity have been variously described as "the Englishman's 'stiff upper lip,'" "combative masculinity," and "neo-Spartan virility as exemplified by stoicism, hardiness, and endurance."[17] Tending to dominate the public sphere and generally transcending class,[18] these ideals were institutionalized through literature and through the system of public schools. As Joseph Bristow has shown, the reorganization of the school system in the mid-Victorian period facilitated the emergence of a masculinity that drew on upper-class idealization of chivalry and on middle-class values of "competition, independence, and a wilful strength of mind"; the resulting "educated male" became "a much more admirable and moral hero – the kind of man all boys (regardless of class) could try to be."[19] Meanwhile, the broad enthusiasm for team sports that emerged in these public schools in the 1850s influenced late nineteenth-century Britain's interest in athleticism. As empire grew, the physical and mental fitness of men became more central than ever to national defence and imperial prowess. Sports were thought to serve these needs by fostering athleticism and building character, cultivating the qualities of "courage, self-control, stoical endurance, and the subordination of the ego to the team. The requirements of sport, taken in deadly earnest, were perfectly attuned to the 'stiff upper lip' character formation so common among men brought up in conventional middle-class families at this time."[20] In this configuration, manliness was understood through "metaphors of control, reserve, and discipline, that were placed in opposition to images of chaos, excess, and disorder."[21] Indeed, the maintenance and appearance of order was crucial to Victorian manhood, as "the proper regulation of an innate male energy," including sexuality and other forms of desire, determined nineteenth-century practices of masculinity.[22] The values propagated at this time, emerging in part from the doctrine of Muscular Christianity, resonated strongly with Victorian conceptions of chivalry and knighthood; indeed, alongside this veneration of the heroic male body and moral responsibilities, interest in medieval knights revived.[23] This set of values generated mass appeal across the social spectrum and prescribed both physical and psychic regulations.[24]

Yet the excessive force with which this ideology was sustained and replicated points to an extant fragility of this myth of what we might call "hypermasculinity." Again and again in Victorian imperial literature, this fragility is indicated by persistent narratives of rigidity: "In the iconography of chivalry in the nineteenth century, this inscription of maleness and dominance is marked by armour, which transforms the male body into the supreme signifier of masculinity, the permanent erection."[25] The knight's armour, so prevalent in late-Victorian representations of errantry, "is an exaggeration of the phallus, making permanent its erectile state; ... [is] bellicose, aggressive, combative, martial, all qualities distinguishing masculinity; ... explicitly links the masculine with the moral, since it conceals the fallen flesh abhorrent to Christianity; ... [and] protects the genitals against castration and castration anxiety."[26] This logic of the supplement – the need for such complete protection – bespeaks both the male body's vulnerability and its susceptibility to "castration," and the fragility of the idea of martial masculinity itself, which must present itself as impenetrable. This pattern of compensation consistently emerges throughout the fictional and archival texts examined in this book. As this study demonstrates, this "permanent erection" indicates fear of the environment surrounding the body, a desire for the body to remain separate, regulated, and impermeable, and a need to define masculinity as such. In turn, when African prowess and environmental challenges overwhelm the rigid British martial body, imperial masculinity finds itself in crisis.

This masculine ideal that combined morality with toughness, dominance, and patriotism surfaced in the context of rising imperial expansion as warfare became a central social preoccupation. Indeed, by the end of the nineteenth century, British militarism had become a popular movement intrinsic to national pride, values, and identity.[27] This of course meant that a certain degree of violence was acceptable; as Bradley Deane and Merrick Burrow have recently argued, within certain spheres, a kind of imperial barbarianism became embedded in fin-de-siècle conceptions of virile manhood.[28] Insofar as Britain sought to assert prowess in the "contact zone,"[29] this "ideological bulwark of the New Imperialism's aggressive militarism"[30] was, on one hand, an empowering fantasy; I argue, however, that barbaric violence buttressed imperial masculinity only when the image of the imperial barbarian was understood *as* a fantasy. As chapters 1 and 6 especially demonstrate, when this fantasy is indulged and becomes a reality, the image of the British imperial man as barbarian becomes a paralysing anxiety. As Burrow recognizes, this image – its "obscene limit" made visible through "the imperial souvenir" or war trophy – "is imbued with a horror that is intolerable to metropolitan domesticity."[31] But this is precisely where the figure of the knight errant becomes so ideologically useful to the motivations of empire. Tempering the more "carnal impulses"[32] with Christian imperatives, the disciplining code of the heroic knight regulates the violence of martial masculinity. As Michael Paris puts it, "Chivalry … removed the most brutal elements of war by creating a strict moral code for the warrior – the generally accepted 'rules of war.'"[33] As this study demonstrates, however, the impossibility of discursive containment, along with shifts in fin-de-siècle literary form – the emergence in imperial romance of critical distance and ironic inversion, the disruptive blurring of genre during imperial disaster, erotic auto-critique – began to expose these ideals of regulation as fantasies.

Spaces

Understandings of space, landscape, and environment became crucial in the dissolution of these fantasies of regulation and impermeable male bodies. Once again, this relationship emerges in Buel's frontispiece as the threat that African bodies pose to the unicorn is augmented by the landscape. In addition to threatening white purity by guiding our gaze from figure to figure via topographical lines, the ground also forms a reclining body on which the figures are posed. This body's focal feature is the giant vaginal crevice, around which jagged ground, serrated rocks, toothy ferns, and wild vegetation – thinly symbolic pubic hair – appear. Thus emerges the terrifying vagina dentata, pointing menacingly toward the unicorn. Notably, while the black figures are concentrated around the mouth of the crevice, the unicorn is positioned up toward where the body's head would be; thus, the racialized division of sexual impulse and reason and logic is deployed in this fantasy about survival. This imaginary space then establishes titillating danger to the constitution of British identity as the African landscape itself is figured as a sexual threat. At once a seemingly passive, reclining ground over which active bodies walk, it is simultaneously dangerous, engulfing, and consuming, figured as an unknown toothed darkness with which African bodies also become aligned. That these threats to British authority are figured as both yonic and phallic not only emphasizes the monstrosity of the other, but crucially sustains the metaphor of a menace that consumes and then penetrates imperial ideologies.

That this dynamic is set in Africa is no coincidence. As the illustrations and Buel's prose symptomatically demonstrate, Africa, more than any other space in the globe at this time, remained an epistemological vacuum for Victorian Britain and the West. Both the public and the military knew less about it than they did of colonial spaces such as Australia, India, and the Americas, and, most frequently, the term "Africa" was applied to that continent without recognition of manifold differences across its diverse spaces and its complex historical formations. Furthermore, it was a difficult space for the British to colonize – the climate, topography, and ecosystems of many coastal regions in Africa seemed to repel British efforts to establish a foothold and build settlements the way they had in other locations. Thus, very few Britons had direct experience with the continent, and, to a large extent, Africa functioned as an imaginary space in much of the public discourse. This was also the case in terms of attempts to survey the land – maps, especially of interior spaces, were often constructed from conjecture. As a result, understandings both of Africa and of British behaviour within it depended largely on narratives from imperial adventurers or agents. Furthermore, because Africa's environment was understood as physically unforgiving of Europeans, survival "in the wilds" also functioned as a test of manhood: to withstand corporeal and psychic hardships was to prove hardiness and stamina – it was to live to tell the tale. The tale in turn became an artifact of manly achievement, narrating – but also itself an embodiment of – sound judgment, reliability, and provision of reassurance through the imperial man. Thus, this books takes up Edward Said's observation that the cultural power of narrative is "premised on the recording, ordering, observing powers of the central authorizing subject, or ego" to explore not only the relationship between narrative and imperial identity but also the power dynamics of gender, and their corollaries, in imperial contests.[34]

However, if the relationships between the male body, masculine authority, and narrating were codependent and co-legitimizing, they were also potentially mutually destructive; while Douglas's work considers the body as a cultural tool for symbolizing social collectives and their boundaries, this book investigates the impact of understandings of the gendered body on textual authority and national identity. If manliness and masculine prowess are understood in terms of the ability to write, forge, and normalize reality, then larger fractures in conceptions of impenetrable male bodies, authority, and stable narration that together triangulate imperial legitimacy also entail the weakening of the whole frame of governmental power. In the popular and institutional fin-de-siècle texts explored in this study, this is exactly what happens. Representations of masculinity and male domains of the kind outlined here were susceptible to the weakness of their own excess; the fact that imperialism was so reliant on this kind of identity construction meant that narratives figuring it were overwrought and contrived, and therefore fragile. In other words, these texts critiqued the terms on which martial masculinity, masculine authority, and imperial narratives established their legitimacy. This book argues that these narratives ostensibly forging a powerful imperial masculinity not only were remarkably cognizant of their own instability but also exposed this instability through metaphors that countered dominant representations of martial masculinity through tropes, images, and evidence of perforation, penetration, and dissolution of bodies that were typically constructed as being firmly bounded, contained, and unshakeable. Interrogating martial bodies on these specific terms exposed imperial masculinity and imperial legitimacy as unstable fantasies.

In these imperial narratives, the purportedly solid body is threatened by different forms of currents that transgress its borders, dissolve the boundaries separating interior from exterior, and instigate the body's deterioration into monstrosity. For Victorian men whose identity was defined by regulation and impermeability, this became a particularly fearsome prospect. The containment of internal fluids and the repulsion of external forms of fluctuating currents – physical, environmental, ideological – were crucial for the imperial man. This focus on impermeability stems from early Victorian preoccupations with manhood, understood as "the possession of an innate, distinctively male energy … This interior energy was consistently imagined or fantasied in a metaphorics of fluid, suggestively seminal, and in an imagery of flame."[35] The ability to control this hydraulic dynamic determined one's "manliness." By the end of the nineteenth century, this yearning for a bounded, stable body, minimally porous to its environment, was reflected in an anxiety about "spermatorrhoea" (which is exactly what it sounds like): "Loss of semen from masturbation or nocturnal emissions was thought to be a harbinger of insanity, derangement, mental instability or physical debilitation."[36] By contrast, John Ruskin offers an ideal of manhood that embodies the values of heroism, strength, gallantry, and toughness, and that is able to resist these threats of fluidity:

> The man's power is active, progressive, defensive. He is eminently the doer, the creator, the discoverer, the defender. His intellect is for speculation and invention; his energy for adventure, for war, for conquest, wherever war is just, wherever conquest necessary … The man, in his rough work in the open world, must encounter all peril and trial; – to him, therefore, must

> be the failure, the offense, the inevitable error: often he must be wounded, or subdued, often misled; and *always* hardened.[37]

This study draws out how the recurring figuration of disintegration is manifested in the threat of flow.[38] Fluidity, leakiness, and surrounding currents continually menace the bounded male body as they engulf and overpower it. This process signals a loss of masculine prowess, individuality, and autonomy. In the fictional and institutional writings about Africa examined in this book, the threat of flow assumes different forms: crowds of hostile bodies, manifestations of a forbidding environment, a conglomerate of otherness figured through an embodied fantasy, desire in its multiple incarnations, and even narrative itself – the confounding and confusing stream of words that claims to clarify experience, enacts moral assertions, and threatens individual critical freedom. Representations of flow are thus a means of demonstrating weakness in ostensibly bounded bodies, igniting anxieties about the underpinnings of identity, and critiquing dominant discourses of conquest.

When bodies, spaces, and texts are depicted as perforated, unbounded, porous, leaky, or dissolved, their grotesqueness – in the Bakhtinian sense – becomes a mechanism that undermines imperial masculinity and authority. Consistent with what we have seen in Buel's frontispiece, and as the following chapters demonstrate, "the most important of all human features for the grotesque is the mouth. It dominates all else."[39] It is that "through which the world enters to be swallowed up."[40] Because this "wide-open bodily abyss" is a site where internal and external mingle, the mouth, materially and as metaphor, represents a threat to the fortified body. In addition to apertures, the phallus is central to the grotesque, for it "protrudes from the body …[and] seeks to go out from beyond the body's confines."[41] But while Bakhtin emphasizes that "the grotesque ignores the impenetrable surface that closes and limits the body as a separate and completed phenomenon,"[42] the texts explored here indicate rather that the grotesque violently and devastatingly explodes the would-be impenetrable body.

Texts

Since the imperial appropriation of Africa as a space for forging masculine identity and narrative authority crucially impinges on the operations of authorization and legitimation, this investigation also follows a spatial logic. I focus, in three parts and in roughly chronological order, on three major regions in which particular historical events had profound repercussions for masculinity and imperial authority in the metropole and in imperial networks at large: South Africa; Egypt and Sudan; and Sierra Leone and Congo. Each of these sections examines popular fiction alongside institutional and archival writing in order to draw out a pervasive recognition of the limitations of traditional masculinity as a legitimating buttress of imperial projects despite hegemonic ideals. Both modes of writing were undoubtedly invested in constructions of national identity: imperial archives often claimed to present a reality ideologically consistent with accepted models of Britishness, while popular adventure novels often informed imperial identity. As John Kucich puts it, "novels were instrumental in shaping late-century attitudes toward imperialism ... During the last decades of the nineteenth century, as debates over imperial expansion intensified and questions about the rise or fall of the empire seemed to cut to the very heart of the national character, British readers turned increasingly to colonial fiction for coherent models of British identity."[43] Indeed, negotiations of masculine identity and imperial legitimacy traversed forms of cultural production, and penetrating critiques of these narratives operated across and between genres and at different political levels. One narrative mode that pervades each of the texts – popular and institutional – in this study is auto-critique: that is, it is through the very enactment of imperial discourse that these texts illustrate empire's failure to legitimate itself – and this legitimation crisis revolves around the shortcomings of imperial men. In this sense, imperial writing functions to eat itself from the inside out. Although the ethos of this kind of imperial writing often seeks ultimately to bolster imperial efficacy, as it turns out, these archives enact not only penetrations of individual, martial, territorial, and legal boundaries, but also the dissolution of the legitimacy of the British Empire itself. Thus, while writing is a potentially powerful tool for shoring up imperial ideology, the very inscription of strength can shade into profound weakness, can trace the faults and insufficiencies it attempts to conceal, and, even when inadvertently, exposes a porous, gaping body of colonial misrule.

Part 1 begins in South Africa in 1879. The Cape Colony was an important territory in Britain's global network. A key outpost in the trade route between Britain and India, as well as in military deployments to the South Pacific, the Cape was also commercially significant. To protect these interests, the British sought to regulate the regions surrounding the Cape Colony. In 1879, the Anglo-Zulu War profoundly shifted British understandings of martial efficacy in Africa – having strutted overconfidently into the war, the redcoats encountered numerous disasters, most notably the Zulu triumph at

Isandlwana. Chapter 1 traces how during the war the British, despite ultimate victory, registered their own engulfment and penetration by the Zulus. These modes of representation worked to figure the destruction of extant models of impenetrable, self-regulating masculinity. In other words, tropes of penetration and engulfment signified the destabilization of the foundations on which imperial masculine authority was built. Importantly, the landscape itself worked as a figure of resistance, bound up as it was with representations of African men, and seemed to enact both engulfment and penetration of the British martial body. Imperial retribution against Zulus was brutal and savage, and the recognition that the British had come to enact the very barbarism that they claimed characterized their enemies shocked the metropolitan public. Letters and public texts surrounding these events, in their construction of the African landscape, the military body, and the white male body itself, mark the irretrievable fracturing of the traditional image of British martial masculinity, the inversion of imperial discourses about savagery, and the paving of inroads that later texts would pursue in critiquing British imperial identity and narrative authority.

This skepticism regarding imperial identity also crept into popular British fiction, suggesting that the inadequacies of the fantasy of martial masculinity were becoming apparent not only at the peripheries but also in the metropole. The martial failures in South Africa resonate in H. Rider Haggard's early romances. Haggard's most popular works, *King Solomon's Mines* (1885) and *She: A History of Adventure* (1887), illustrate the relationship between masculine prowess and narrative as they deploy auto-critique to enact complex criticisms of imperial manhood. Chapter 2 examines these works to theorize the relationship between different levels of male authority and broader political narratives. While the dominant trend in Haggardian criticism has been to argue various angles of the idea that his texts enact fantasies of masculine recuperation (though this has begun to change), I contend that these works, appearing on the heels of the growing doubt about martial manhood – its efficacy as well as its morality – highlight irredeemable flaws both in traditional conceptions of imperial masculinity and in accounts of Africa: Haggard criticizes dominant narratives of imperial prowess by discrediting his narrators, undermining their authority, and parodying conventional codes of masculine identity. In these manoeuvres, the fearsomeness of the African landscape, as represented during the Anglo-Zulu War, reappears and again functions as both feminized and phallic, with a threatening libido. As Haggard interrogates unbridled imperial desire, he reveals imperial authority to be morally bereft.

Crucially, writing, figuring as the central mechanism of authority, is shown to be inadequate, flawed, and profoundly limited.

Part 2 moves to Egypt and Sudan, both crucial sites of British investment. The Suez Canal was understood as a kind of spinal cord of the British Empire because of its centrality for trade, and thus simultaneously signified imperial wealth and vulnerability. Egypt itself figured in the British metropole in a number of ways, especially as a marker of economic, martial, and cultural capital. Egypt came under threat, however, with General Gordon's death at Khartoum in 1885, which greatly intensified the imperial sense of exposure in the East. Examining the relationships between fluid spatial boundaries, technological inadequacy, and the role of the Gothic in articulating uncertainty and loss, chapter 3 examines Gordon's Khartoum journals and various periodicals announcing the fall of Khartoum, arguing that failures of regulation, demarcation, and epistemology shifted late-Victorian thinking about the ramifications of empire for the British nation: imperial failure had ruptured the image of British martial efficacy; this faltering image profoundly undermined imperial history and identity. As ensuing anxieties surrounding imperial prowess proliferated, generic transgressions materialized – Gothic modes, extra-rational and disruptive, bled into the news – and metropolitan institutional writing became keenly aware of its own limitations in producing imperial knowledge, further destabilizing the validity of authoritative history.

While Egypt, in the British imagination, symbolized a site of heritage, history, plunder, and a gateway to the East, it also connoted fantasy and desire. Richard Marsh's *The Beetle* (1897) engages with British fantasy about Egypt in order to respond to the traumatic loss of Gordon, a fantasy rekindled by the "reconquest" of Sudan that was underway while Marsh was writing and publishing this text. Marsh intensifies Haggard's style of auto-critique in order to thematize and articulate threats to imperial masculinity – this time within the metropole itself. This novel enacts a dark fantasy of male subjugation: as male characters are penetrated in various ways – mesmerized, deprived of autonomy, surveilled, physically assaulted, and humiliated – a sexualized dynamic of control underlines the limitations to their physical and psychic boundaries. The violations to which men's bodies and minds are subject underlie their inability to provide stable narratives; their attempts to make sense of reality are indeed as leaky as the bodies from which they materialize. Like Haggard's works, *The Beetle* parodies traditional codes of manliness to underscore masculinity's failure to live up to late-Victorian fantasies of masculine prowess, but it demonstrates that these failings have still more profound implications than

Haggard's works envisioned. For Marsh, the imperial narrative itself becomes grotesque – nebulous, fluid, and uncontainable. While in Gothic novels the foreign is frequently cast as infiltrating the domestic, in *The Beetle* the domestic itself bears and enacts the violent desires that are often projected onto the foreign. Although, on one level, this novel gestures to the anxiety that Eastern corruption penetrates British culture, on another, it signals that these national imaginations, perversions, and fears are always already circulating within the "bounded" nation. These narrative instabilities interrogate reading practices as narrators' own accounts betray the limitations of their authority. In this sense, the Gothic monster is narrative itself: writing becomes the opposite of a concretizing power; it is confusing, distorting, and mesmerizing as it threatens the reader's understanding of reality, and it enacts transgressions of ostensibly bounded bodies through activating affective registers. The novel itself, then, becomes both an artifact and an enactment of gendered violent fantasy.

This same destabilization of narrative certainty also plagues the colonial archive and institutional writing. Part 3 transitions to West Africa, as chapter 5 zeroes in on Sierra Leonean colonial archives from the 1880s to the early twentieth century. This colony occupied a special place in the narrative of British imperialism because it was originally established under the ostensible project of abolishing the slave trade and promoting "legitimate trade" in 1787. Supposed to reflect Britain's philanthropic identity, Sierra Leone was also intended to be a commercially viable territory. A century later, however, the colonial administration was still attempting to wring a trade economy out of the regions surrounding Freetown while also facing the consequences of subversive indigenous violence. The colonial archive's representation of this violence illustrates the ultimate consequences of the perceived disintegration of the martial body, the fantasy of imperial masculinity, the efficacy of writing, and imperial authority. Two indigenous fraternities, through their rationales, resistance to surveillance, and modes of organization and operation, disrupted physical, geographical, and legal boundaries that the administration had taken for granted. Their violence was a complex, multi-layered disruption of colonial order that could not be contained – and in fact, it highlighted problems with colonial complicity that impinged on regulation, epistemology, and the legitimacy of the project of empire at large. Tracing the distortions of how violence in the contact zone registers in the imperial centre, this chapter explores the investments of metropolitan media in sustaining omissions, sensational fillers, and emphases by examining technologies of narrativizing in colonial reports and dispatches. Unpacking moments of uncertainty, contradiction, failure, and complicity, I explore both the role of fantasy in maintaining colonial power and the impossibility of sustaining it, given the weaknesses and failings that this archive itself betrays, embodies, and enacts. Once again, tropes of flow, engulfment, penetration, the grotesque, and ultimate dissolution reappear across representations of landscape, territory, the military body, and the imperial network – figuring the faults in the foundations of dominant fantasies of imperial masculinity and authority, and thereby fatally impinging on governmental efficacy. Thus, imperial writing, supposedly a tool of surveillance and discipline, is actually the conduit of a crisis in morality and power.

Chapter 6 explores the manifestation of this view of imperial writing in Joseph Conrad's *Heart of Darkness.* My analysis emphasizes this modernist work's engagement with the anxieties, strategies, and failures surrounding imperial identity that this study uncovers. Ultimately, Conrad's text explores the devastating consequences of colonial desire for masculinity and identity: desire and its ramifications are shown to explode extant myths about impenetrable masculinity and philanthropic identity. Read against the crisis in masculine authority confronted in imperial archives and popular texts, *Heart of Darkness* not only underscores how the mechanisms of oppression and control operated through a willing complicity in the lie of the philanthropic cause, but also illuminates how imperial desire becomes an engulfing force, a seductive flow underlying narratives that provide capital and a sense of power at the cost of critical autonomy.

These problems of legitimacy and troubling seduction of engulfing desire that pervaded imperial narratives of the fin de siècle have continued to inhere in the twenty-first century. This book concludes by considering how such narratives of complicity and desire are at work in contemporary imperial ideology. As we'll see, this same effect emerges in similar patterns of imperial violence and complicity in the more contemporary contact zones of Abu Ghraib and Guantánamo Bay, patterns that threaten modern identity and autonomy in our own historical moment.

Reading popular fiction alongside historical archives illuminates how cultural concerns inhere across genres and permeate British society. This book is historically situated, but, in dealing with fantasy and psychic boundaries, it also engages psychoanalytic criticism. Psychoanalysis's argument "that the gap separating consciousness from unconsciousness, and thus distinguishing agency from psychic drives, throws awry the very idea of coherent individualism" addresses the fact that impulses and ideas are often complex and contradictory, incoherent and incomplete.[44] Since this project studies fantasies by tracing the language and imagery that expresses and constitutes them, it draws at times on this theoretical framework that accounts for non-material aspects of experience, such as repression, which "exists *regardless of the historical and cultural conditions in which it occurs*," even while its forms and mechanisms "are contingent on social forces."[45] As this study explores this history of representation and the private anxieties that impinged on the politics of narrativization, it converses with the large body of scholarship on imperialism in Africa. However, since this book illuminates the nuances of late nineteenth-century gender construction and the complexity of the fraught perspectives on empire in Africa at the fin de siècle, it also engages with Victorian studies more broadly. Understanding these historically and geographically specific dynamics between narration and identity offers insight not only into economies of desire, capitalism, and governmentability, but also into how Victorian fictional and archival texts work both to produce and unmake knowledge. While this study does not investigate the deterioration of the myth of British martial manhood through the lens of African history, it nevertheless demonstrates the recognition of illegitimacy from within the ranks of the ostensible proponents, agents, and figures of imperial masculinity. To that end, this work is about the history of the construction – or more specifically, the failings of the construction – of patriarchal imperialism in British Africa at the end of the nineteenth century. Finally, such a history has consequences: these particular weak points in imperial ideology resonate with our present moment; as this discourse of imperial decay illuminates the fault lines of imperial narratives, it begs for the recognition that similar discourses of masculinity, authority, and philanthropy have underpinned Western liberal humanist identities that have inhered across time, and also have continued to legitimize violence, colonial desire, and complicity into the twenty-first century.

PART I

Ruptures in Adventure Romance

Chapter One

Permeable Boundaries: Violence and Fantasy in Zululand

It grieves us to write these things; but the alternative ... is a wretched sort of truculent make-believe.

– "The Coming Campaign in Zululand," *Pall Mall Gazette*, 13 Feb. 1879

This chapter examines a crucial transition in British conceptions of imperial masculinity and the authority of imperial narrative. In discourse surrounding the Anglo-Zulu War, tropes of spatial and psychological engulfment and penetration articulated the fracturing of the dominant myth of martial masculinity; the recognition emerged in British culture that idealized understandings of British imperial heroism were, in fact, products of fantasy, while imperial representations of the war were not only highly questionable but also betrayed a range of British ideals such as stoicism, chivalry, and honesty. While imperial discourse had, on one hand, so usefully associated African peoples and spaces with the notion of threatening monstrosity – instability, irrationality, brutality – it was also beginning to acknowledge that savagery belonged to empire itself.

When the British invaded Zululand on 11 January 1879, Britons expected that the ensuing war would be a short one: Cetshwayo, the Zulu monarch, and his forces would be promptly suppressed, their army disbanded, and the indigenous threat to the British confederation of South Africa eliminated. Upon reaching the iconic landmark of Isandlwana, a few miles from the border of Natal, the central column of the three-pronged British invasion pitched camp but did not entrench; Lord Chelmsford, its commander, had concluded that native forces were no real threat to the colonial army. On 22 January, Chelmsford led half of his troops further into the country in search of the Zulu soldiers that scouts had spotted early that morning. Meanwhile, the main body of the Zulu army, in wait in the hills, attacked the unprepared camp in force. Startled, disorganized, and panicked, the military body at Isandlwana was almost completely annihilated in a humiliating defeat. Though the British forces ultimately overtook Cetshwayo in July/August of that year, they were also embarrassingly defeated outright during other clashes at Ntombe Drift on the Pongola River (12 March) and Hlobane Mountain (28 March), much to the mortification of the imperial metropole. The war would cost eight months and £5,000,000 pounds,[1] and would shatter national confidence.

After these early disasters, the task of bolstering the public image of British imperial manliness required no small effort. Indeed, questions about martial efficacy would become central for the British during this war. As Michael Lieven, John Laband, and Ian Knight have argued, war heroes were manufactured by the media for a news-hungry metropolitan public in order to support the ideals of empire.[2] Newspaper reports and letters also register, however, a tension between this investment in gallantry and a profound anxiety about entrapment, swarming, and penetration by African forces – both martial and environmental. Not only did these metaphors render African others monstrous in the interest of colonialism, but also the nature of the monstrosity – grotesque and engulfing – fabricated in the accounts of battles served to articulate the very vulnerabilities of the martial masculine ideals so vehemently upheld in Britain. Furthermore, confrontations with the emasculation signified by tropes of engulfment and penetration so recurrent in the soldierly correspondence post-Isandlwana in turn triggered embellished narratives of heroism *and* the enactment of phallic violence used to emphasize British conquest, as testimonies of British prowess emerging in letters, the metropolitan press, and through war trophies simultaneously evinced intense brutality. Consequently, depictions of this excessive violence exposed the notion of the gentleman soldier, so integral to the legitimacy of the imperial project in Africa, as myth.

Since the recuperation of British manhood in the Anglo-Zulu War depended on violence, the crisis facing British identity became twofold: martial masculinity was shaken by the Zulus thoroughly routing the redcoats on multiple occasions; furthermore, British soldiers' need to prove themselves men by acting like barbarians entailed a profound reconsideration of the efficacy of the chivalric ideals that had reified alongside the Victorian revival of interest in medieval knights. When this crisis in masculinity could not be discursively contained, the image of the gallant war hero fragmented in the public imagination, as did the stability of military and narrative authority. In turn, doubts about the imperial project began to fester, paving the way for normative models of British masculinity to be re-examined in the next decade. Here, however, British arrogance toward the Zulus transitioned into widespread paranoia in the ranks; thus male narrative authority began to fracture in this contact zone.

Prominent in British accounts of the Anglo-Zulu War is the figuration of threatening African elements – bodies and landscape – as fluid, threatening to surround, engulf, penetrate, and consume. Some insight into the broader implications of such tropes can be offered by Klaus Theweleit's analysis of fascist discourse in Germany between the First and Second World Wars and its obsession with the threat of the "Red Flood." Theweleit argues in *Male Fantasies* that fascist "soldier males" of this period were motivated in their aggression toward communists – and, more precisely, communist women – by a deep fear of the dissolution of the self and body. Bolshevist forces were widely represented as a red wave, a surging mass, an overpowering flow, and therefore – for all the reasons of the supposed permeability of women's bodies, transgressive in their leakiness and ready exchange of fluids, the long tradition of associating women with water in Western history, and the imagined outward streaming of women's sexual energies – were figured as feminine. Furthermore, Bolshevik women, while at once, and indeed *because* they were, attractive to the sexually inexperienced and thus powerless soldier male, were profoundly threatening as potentially castrating forces. Theweleit uses Freudian analysis of this fear, instigated by the primary glimpse of the vulva, to pinpoint what he argues is the real root of this male anxiety. Freud suggests, "The sight of Medusa's head makes the spectator stiff with terror, turns him to stone ... We have here once again the same origin from the castration complex and the same transformation of affect!" Woman is represented as "a being who frightens and repels because she is castrated."[3] Theweleit, however, disagrees: "Even those men who see the vagina as a 'Medusa's Head' aren't afraid of the vagina's castrated condition, but of its castrating potential ... What men who fear vaginas must really be afraid of is the vagina's ability to take the male member into itself (to devour it, to swallow it up)."[4] The similarity between the fear of dissolution Theweleit identifies and British terror of engulfment in Zululand in 1879 is striking; British fear of Zulu potency as "castrating potential" emerges in these accounts of engulfment and lays bare the terror of emasculation and identity rupture.

Porous Boundaries

South Africa was of strategic economic and military importance to Britain in the 1870s: the Cape route to India at this time was of high commercial value and was still materially the main freeway of trade, even though the Suez was operational;[5] the route would also be key for distributing troops to Asia and the South Pacific, should mobilization be required;[6] and, finally, the 1867 discovery of diamonds in Kimberley sparked new industrial interest in this region. Britain thus sought paramountcy in South Africa, which meant suppressing Boer power by controlling the coastlines and maintaining political and economic dominance over the Boer republics, as well as quelling any indigenous threats.[7] The discourse of protecting natives from the Boers fuelled arguments for firm governmental policing and a uniform "native policy." To achieve this, confederation was considered to be the cheapest course of action. The British had annexed Natal in 1844, and from 1875 to 1876, Colonial Secretary Lord Carnarvon attempted to unite the states in Southern Africa through settlements.[8] When this failed, Carnarvon seized the opportunity afforded through the Boer-Pedi wars in the Transvaal to annex that vulnerable and bankrupted republic in 1877, appointing Theophilus Shepstone, then the secretary of native affairs for Natal, to lead the take-over.[9] The aggressive Sir Bartle Frere, then appointed as high commissioner of native affairs and governor of the Cape Colony and ordered to execute Carnarvon's confederation plan, worked to bring all indigenous societies into the British sphere of control either through extending protectorates or through conquest.[10]

The most militantly organized African power was the Zulu nation, led by Cetshwayo. For Frere, the Zulus seemed the main obstacle to federation; his solution to the threat of Zulu military strength was complete subjugation. A strip of disputed territory had put the Transvaal Boers and the Zulus further at odds in the Utrecht district. Though Frere and Shepstone supported the Transvaal claims, an independent commission established in early 1878 by Sir Henry Bulwer, the lieutenant-governor of Natal, ruled in the Zulus' favour.[11] A surprised Frere, having hoped to use the findings (presented to him on 20 June 1878) to provoke the Zulus into open conflict, suppressed the boundary commission's verdict until he could find a way to justify British invasion of Zululand.[12] In the meantime, a number of minor boundary violations developed over the course of the year that enabled Frere openly to oppose Cetshwayo and to argue that the Zulus were preparing for war against the British.[13] Although Cetshwayo had been unaware of these infractions, in December Frere nevertheless issued a clearly impossible ultimatum: the complete disbandment of the standing Zulu army, which was integral to the Zulu way of life, and an extortionate fine as reparation for the border incursions – all to be satisfied within thirty days. When these conditions were not met, though Cetshwayo was bargaining for time and trying to collect funds to pay the fine, Lord Chelmsford, lieutenant-general of the British forces, headed 15,000 troops across the Zululand-Natal border in January 1879.[14]

This decision to attack the Zulus directly was rooted in a sense of the vulnerability of territorial boundaries, infractions against which the colonists could not tolerate. Chelmsford agreed entirely with Frere's analysis of the Zulu threat: "The peculiar nature of the Natal and Transvaal border, its great extent and the fewness of the troops to watch it, rendered to my mind any attempt to defend it directly almost impossible, ... The best chance of saving the two colonies from the consequences of such an inroad, was to invade Zululand ourselves."[15] Mr Brownlee, secretary for native affairs in the Cape Colony, was similarly attuned to spatial disruption: "At present the Zulus are a standing menace to us ... The peace of the tribes around us and in our midst rests on a most unstable foundation."[16] Vulnerable geographical boundary lines, then, were from the outset markers of imperial instability. For instance, given that this discourse underlying the Anglo-Zulu tension hinged on anxiety about penetration, it may not be surprising that the British frequently depicted the Zulu army as a phallic threat. As Shepstone wrote in a dispatch to Carnarvon in January 1878, "the question is, what is to be done with this pent up and still accumulating power ... Zululand is from some cause or another in a great state of excitement."[17] Frere had similar ideas, describing the "large, powerful, and growing" Zulu force as "a volcano," from which "an explosion" was impending.[18] The British preoccupation with imbrication of the Zulu tradition of "washing their spears" (or doing battle) with breaking celibacy did nothing to decrease their anxieties about penetration of colonial boundaries. The corollary of these concerns was that the British colony and martial forces were positioned as potentially feminized bodies facing this volcanic force.

Alongside the promulgation of these anxieties about penetration, the rhetoric of needing to set forth and discipline phallic barbarity served both to position the redcoats as civilized and to garner military momentum. In this vein, Brownlee wrote, "No treaty or obligation can be binding on such a perfidious race as the Zulus, ruled by a treacherous and bloodthirsty sovereign like Cetywayo. Our future safety, as well as the voice of humanity, demand[s] that the power of the Zulus be broken, and that the innocent blood which is daily shed upon our borders should cease to flow."[19] Associating the Zulus with encroaching bodily fluid, Brownlee raises the Theweleitian spectre of dangerous flow so destabilizing to the rigid martial body. Frere, meanwhile, described Cetshwayo as "an ignorant and bloodthirsty despot," a "savage with thirty or forty thousand armed men at his command, whose system of government and personal pleasure rest equally on bloodshed."[20] Sir Henry Bulwer, less warmongering but more paternalistic, insisted that the restrictions set on Cetshwayo were "for the better government of the Zulu people and for their great advantage."[21] Thus, a proposed project of "stopping the wolf's ravages,"[22] or punishing primitive violence, was, as with so many other imperial projects, a crucial justification for declaring war on the Zulu kingdom. Yet, within months, the redcoats themselves would be indulging in the very barbarity that they attributed to their African other. Thus it seemed that the British body was susceptible to imbibing the kind of "savagery" the empire had associated with the enemy. As the metropole came to recognize this, the public image of the heroic soldier would come under intense strain.

Engulfment and Emasculation

For all the discussion about the threat of "pent up" Zulu aggression, Britain was so certain of a quick victory that the invasion of Zululand was not considered a significant event in the metropole; only one newspaper, the *London Standard*, sent a correspondent – Charles Norris-Newman – to cover it.[23] As Rider Haggard put it, "our generals and soldiers entered on [this war] with the lightest hearts; notwithstanding the difficulties and scarcity of transport they even took with them their cricketing outfit into Zululand."[24] Further along the spectrum of domination, British soldiers, confident of a swift and complete victory, frequently couched their sense of superiority in phallic images of technological supremacy. For instance, Sackville Lane-Fox, a young soldier in the Native Natal Infantry, demonstrated such contemptuous cockiness when he wrote home just before the war: "There will be a howling fight as the Zulus always come out in great masses and charge and of course they will be shot down by the thousand, but after the first fight the fun will be over and the nasty work of hunting them in the bush will begin, as they will get such a lesson that they will not show their faces in the open … The soldiers here think they will shoot a thousand of them by Sunday."[25] Lane-Fox's vicious enthusiasm signals the deeply racist fantasies of colonial adventure propagated in post-1850s school-boy culture and exemplifies key tropes often used in soldierly correspondence during this war, such as animalizing Zulus, licensing British indulgence in primitive violence, and at the same time revelling in superior technology. Lane-Fox's imagination of a "howling fight" and "hunting them in the bush" not only likens Zulus to animals (indeed, the image of them emerging in "masses" reiterates common imperial representations of indigenous people as insects), but it also typifies the "civilized" soldier's indulgence in primal violence. These two aspects of the same fantasy are mutually enabling in colonial communications. Further, the notion of disciplining the Zulu – teaching them "a lesson" – reinforces colonial entitlement. Finally, the celebration of superior British technology and weaponry, buttressing the fantasy of phallic prowess, functions crucially in representations of Zulu men as subjugated animals, of punitive action, and of British colonial efficacy. While the British carried Gatling guns, rockets, revolvers, and Martini-Henry rifles – all designed for distant killing – Zulu weaponry was more basic.[26] Though Cetshwayo's soldiers did possess a large number of European guns, most of these were "obsolete military muskets" disposed of by European traders in the African markets.[27] The Zulu assegai was a short stabbing spear with an oblong, pointed blade, usually eighteen by two and a half inches, set into a shaft two and a half feet long. It was designed for close-quarter fighting and, contrary to the remote slaying enacted by most British weapons, rendered bloodshed immediate and primary. When this weapon proved more efficacious in close combat, British soldiers were forced to re-evaluate the terms on which their superiority was based. Nevertheless, even as the camp at Isandlwana was under siege, deep-seated arrogance lingered, as Lieutenant Henry Curling, one of the few survivors of this clash, admits: "When we turned out again about 12, the Zulus were only showing on the left of our camp. All the time we were idle in the camp, the Zulus were surrounding us with a huge circle several miles in circumference and hidden by hills from our sight. We none of us felt the least anxious as to the result for, although they came in immense numbers, we felt it impossible that they could break through."[28] Though this attitude of aggressive dominance did not change, the assumption of superiority shifted abruptly after Isandlwana, as the redcoats were forced to rethink their supposed invulnerability.

The delayed British recognition of the severity of their situation at Isandlwana was partly due to cockiness at all levels of command. Chelmsford's column had arrived at Isandlwana in the afternoon of 21 January, and although standard camp procedure was to laager the wagons and entrench the perimeter, Chelmsford, dismissing Zulu martial capacities, decided to forgo these precautions.[29] The following morning, when Zulu movement to the southeast was reported, Chelmsford took half of his troops out in search of them. Meanwhile, a force of roughly 20,000 Zulu soldiers waited unseen behind the undulating hills just a few miles to the north of the camp. Once Chelmsford's men had left the vicinity, the Zulus attacked in force in their traditional fighting formation of a charging bull. As survivor Lieutenant W.F.B. Cochrane described the encompassing manoeuvre, "The Zulu system of attack … is easily traceable, the main body being opposite the left centre of the camp; the horns thrown out to the left rear and right front."[30] A reserve force advanced behind the main body, supplementing the right or left horn of the attack as needed.[31] Cochrane's commander, Colonel Durnford, was so confident about breaking the attack that he took his division away from the encampment and into the field, thus further dividing the British forces and exposing those left at the base. Meanwhile, the Zulus had encircled the British, using the landscape to mask the extent of the charge, and, while occupying Durnford's force, attacked the camp by surprise in its exposed rear.[32]

The British repeatedly figured this attack as devastating engulfment; survivors' accounts, almost without exception, emphasize a sense of being mobbed, overwhelmed, and perforated. Resonating strongly with tropes of racialized swarming, this kind of imagery not only suggested that Britain's foes were profoundly other, but it also indicated the redcoats' emasculation, which further registers in the language of penetration. Commandant Browne described the advance as "a dense swarm."[33] Richard Stevens of the Natal Mounted Police echoed, "We saw the hill black with them coming on in swarms,"[34] while gunner Arthur Howard of the N/5 bemoaned, "The awful black devils watched the General out of camp, and then, as soon as his command had got clear away, they came down like bees out of a hive, and there was an awful slaughter."[35] In these accounts, the crowding is directly linked to race – blackness is treated as coterminous with swamping. Trooper Barker of the Natal Carbineers wrote, "The Zulus were advancing … I noticed, or rather heard, a rush from behind, and on looking round I saw the soldiers who were left in camp literally surrounded by Zulus, who had evidently come in from the rear … Zulus seemed to be behind, before, and on each side of us."[36] Barker's account emphasizes that the consequence of engulfment is rear penetration. These depictions of swarming othered the Zulus, likening them to insects or animals, and denying individuality by describing one great, shadowy, inhuman mass.[37] As becomes clear in the historical record, this engulfment and the panic it elicited constituted a crucial, major moment of rupture in British ideas of dominance and masculinity. In spite of the asymmetrical distribution of arms and technological power, forces understood as primitive humiliatingly exposed the vulnerability of British martial bodies – constructed so intently as bounded, impermeable, and dominant – in the colonial space. This particular defeat thus constituted an emasculation that would be replicated throughout the Anglo-Zulu War and would also irretrievably change Victorian understandings of imperial masculinity.

After the devastation of Isandlwana, letters giving accounts of subsequent battles echoed this panic about envelopment and its attendant emasculation. On 12 March, an impi (a Zulu corps) decimated a company of the 80th regiment that was camped on either side of the Pongola River at the Ntombe Drift. Seventy redcoats occupying the north side were attacked in the early morning fog while their thirty-six comrades on the opposite side attempted to provide cover for them to escape across the river, against which the Zulus had entrapped them. Only twelve made it across.[38] In the midst of the ensuing retreat to Luneberg, Josiah Sussens testified, soldiers were surrounded, "caught … [and] assegaied on every side."[39] Similarly, Major Tucker reported that "the Zulus … were around the wagons and on the top of them, and even inside with the cattle, almost instantly. So quickly did they come … The sight in the river, they tell me, was frightful – Zulus and white men all mixed up together, yelling, howling, and screeching."[40] Tucker was haunted by not only the sense of swarming but also the image of the unruly blending of the races "all mixed up together" in chaotic tumult. Such unruly mixing indicated that, beyond being penetrated, the British martial body was in the midst of dissolution, its constituent parts thrown into chaos. That this dissolution takes place in the river perhaps augmented the threat of engulfing flow that Theweleit identifies in martial history.

Ntombe was by no means the last allegorical castration the redcoats would encounter. Shortly afterwards, on 28 March, Colonel Buller led his forces to attack a Zulu fortification at Hlobane Mountain. After gaining substantial elevation and engaging in fire, the British realized the Zulu were closing in, cutting off their descent from the mountain, as a young volunteer named Mossop recounted: "A Zulu impi closed in behind [us]. We were trapped."[41] A dramatic account of this moment was printed in the *Natal Mercury*: "Colonel Buller … perceived that strong bodies of Zulus were climbing every available baboon path, with the intention of cutting us off … At the same time two large columns were seen approaching along the top of the mountain to the eastward, and another dense black mass of men, the main Zulu army[,] were observed coming on from the Southward."[42] The description of "baboon path[s]" both animalizes the Zulus and implicates the topography itself in this devastating attack. As for the Zulus themselves, as at Isandlwana, they are figured as a "dense black mass"; emphasis on the formation of "columns" suggests impending penetration. In a similar vein, the following day, at the Battle of Kambula, a correspondent from

Colonel Wood's column observed "immense black masses of Zulus" approaching the British camp,[43] echoing this phallic imagery.

Amidst all of this emphasis on surging forces, perhaps the best example of representing the Zulus as a phallic, all-encompassing rush comes from Sir Evelyn Wood's account of Hlobane: "Down the rugged mountain side streamed and tumbled a resistless surging torrent of black creatures, which constantly smitten with leaden hail, and checked by the difficulties of the descent, broke indeed, but like a huge on-coming wave, only to spread our encircling foam-like smaller bodies, which, gathering in volume, again swept on with renewed force down and round the track."[44] Wood dehumanizes the Zulus by comparing them to a rushing torrent or giant wave. This "naturalizing" of the "surging" forces also casts both the warriors and the African landscape as phallic spectacles hostile to the colonial agents. African nature itself would seem to be against the British in this description. Meanwhile, the redcoats are established as "bodies" subject to this "encircling": British boundaries and male impregnability are directly at risk, but, furthermore, the soldiers, because they are positioned as targets, garner sympathy by seeming to have no other choice than to fight desperately the faceless force that threatens to annihilate them – a situation that licenses lawless ferocity among the British troops.[45] Read through a Theweleitian lens, however, Wood also casts the Zulus as a monstrous force that is sexually threatening; the emasculating mass of Zulus – a "resistless surging torrent," a fluid "wave" – is frequently described with imagery that oscillates between a penetrating phallus and an engulfing vagina dentata.

Captain Edward Essex's private letter about Isandlwana suggests exactly this combination: the Zulu formation began as a "gradually thickening" line – a growing column – but soon, it "assum[ed] a circular form, appeared to be constantly fed from their left and was increasing in thickness in that direction."[46] Essex's account thus describes the enemy's advance as a kind of mouth closing in to consume, its inner curves spiked with assegais. As this body neared, it "formed a dense black semi-circle, threatening us on both flanks. Their line was constantly fed from the rear of its centre, which seemed to be inexhaustible. Affairs now looked rather serious as our little body appeared altogether insignificant compared with the enormous masses opposed to us."[47] The "enormous masses," "dense," "threatening," and "inexhaustible," that pushed toward the British flanks moved to swallow the "little body" whole: "I looked around and was horrified to see that the enemy had nearly surrounded us and was beginning to fire from the rear, coming up in that direction at a tremendous pace."[48] For Essex, sharp rear penetration is, not surprisingly, horrifying. But his observation also marks a crucial vacillation of metaphors: Essex's account, until this moment of invagination, has feminized the African army by associating it with fluidity, grotesqueness, and female anatomy; but he then describes the Zulus firing up into the British rear "at a tremendous pace," transforming once again into the piercing phallus. Chaos ensues, according to Lieutenant Horace Smith-Dorrien: "They came right into the camp, assegaing everybody right and left ... On looking round we saw that we were completely surrounded and the road to Rorke's Drift was cut off."[49] This sense of penetration manifested in a realization of lost prowess. Even the phallic rifle dropped in estimation: Lieutenant Newnham Davis referred in retrospect to his weapon as "a foolish thing" – during the chaos, "the [Zulu] man caught hold of it and pulled it out of my hand."[50] With the British military phallus disabled and its body punctured and emasculated, the perforation of individual bodies began, and the feminization of British soldiers intensified. Survivors described infantilization: fleeing Isandlwana, Lieutenant H.D. Davis confessed that when he attempted to stab an attacking Zulu with his bayonet, the fellow "got hold of the rifle, and pulled it out of my hand as if I had been a child."[51] Infantilization thus compounds feminization to refigure the British male body as unbounded, since babies – sites of uncontrolled leaking of all sorts – were also coded alongside women as having no firm borders. These violations of bodily boundaries were thus emasculating, humiliating, and destructive to British identity.

The historical fact that engulfment and penetration led to dismemberment is just one instantiation of this deflating destruction.[52] Stevens laments, "The Zulus were in the camp [at Isandlwana] ripping our men up, and also the tents and everything they came across, with their assegais. Never has such a disaster happened to the English army ... There will be an awful row at home about this."[53] Stevens's sense of violation is immediately followed by embarrassment – and he was right about the empire's humiliation. The metropolitan papers expressed "shame and indignation" at this "calamity almost unparalleled in our military annals,"[54] recognizing that "our reverse in South Africa inflicts a deep wound on our national pride."[55] British military leadership came under intense criticism as the nation acknowledged that "our troops were ... out-generalled."[56] A number of political cartoons, such as the one shown in figure 2, emerged to articulate martial emasculation at the level of command; here, Lord Chelmsford is depicted as a young boy who, playing soldier, got "himself into a nasty mess."[57] His "mother" (a feminized Disraeli) humours him by giving him more lives as if they were toys; this feminization of the prime minister, insofar as contempt

Figure 2. "The Mother's Pet" (*Fun*, 19 March 1879)

for the feminine is being deployed as a way to both articulate and enact humiliation, indicates that popular confidence in the government was ebbing considerably. Figure 3 depicts a later moment in the war, when, after the redcoats' other losses, the accomplished General Wolseley was brought in to offset the bungling and secure victory.[58] Here, he pushes the inept Chelmsford and Sir Bartle Frere in a pram. While the latter two are figured as infants, even Wolseley, as a nurse, is feminized. Once again, infantilization and feminization compound emasculation to disrupt martial identity.

If the image of martial masculinity was suffering at the level of government, it was also collapsing at the level of individual and collective martial forces in South Africa. In the aftermath of Isandlwana, the surviving British had to confront the dismemberment, which entailed violations of bodily boundaries and the transgressive flow of internal fluids, of their comrades who lay in pieces on the field. Returning

Figure 3. "The Double Perambulator" (*Fun*, 11 June 1879)

late on the night of 22 January, Chelmsford, fearful of attack while marching in the dark, pitched a quick camp among the slain, and then hustled his soldiers back to Rorke's Drift on the morning of the 23rd. Wagons, equipment, and bodies were left as they lay, and a recovery mission wasn't sent out until May. Archibald Forbes, possibly the most famous war correspondent of his time, reported on this return to Isandlwana in what became a very well known passage: "Some [of the bodies] were almost wholly dismembered, heaps of yellow clammy bones. I forebear to describe the faces, with their blackened features and beards bleached by rain and sun. Every man had been disembowelled. Some were scalped, and others subject to yet ghastlier mutilations."[59] The affective tenor of this grim depiction of devastation, focusing as it does on ruptured bodies – "bones," "beards," and "blackened features" (segments and pieces, not wholes) – is echoed in the personal accounts of Chelmsford's men. Private James

Cook wrote to his father, "The sight at the camp was horrible. Every white man that was killed or wounded was ripped up, and their bowels torn out; so that there was no chance of anyone being left alive on the field."[60] Also writing to his father, Sergeant W.E. Warren divulged, "You could not move a foot either way without treading on dead bodies. Oh, father, such a sight I never witnessed in my life before. I could not help crying to see how the poor fellows were massacred. They were first shot and then assegaied, the Zulus mutilated them and stuck them with the assegai all over the body."[61] These accounts mark an extremely important shift in attitude; the affect generated here hinges on the vulnerability of the adult male soldier who "could not help crying" and calls out for paternal support, as well as on the dissolved male bodies on the field.[62] No longer steadfast pillars of empire, the dead men lay prostrate, their organs and blood spilling out and seeping into the soil, becoming one with the traditionally feminized earth.[63] Neither were the surviving soldiers invincible; their open grief and tears rendered them boyishly vulnerable.

Thus justification for this war along with imperial self-positioning take on a strategy of anti-conquest – in this moment post-Isandlwana, British masculinity is stripped of its power, and colonial soldiers become "massacred," "mutilated" victims.[64] Private William Meredith positions the British army precisely in this way: "It was a pity to see about 800 white men lying on the field cut up to pieces and stripped naked. Even the little boys that we had in the band, they were hung up on hooks and opened like sheep. It was a pitiful sight."[65] Here, images of disemboweled, victimized boys associate violated innocence with attacks on empire. Likewise, Meredith's own candidness about the experience of trauma both augments the sense of suffering and asserts his own vulnerability. Second, the real focus of "pity" is the evisceration of white bodies. Affect hinges on racialized exposure, as in Patrick Farrell's description: "It was enough to make your blood run cold to see the white men cut open, worse than ever was done in the Indian Mutiny."[66] Farrell's direct gesture to the panic surrounding the Indian Uprising of 1857 implies a need for swift imperial response.[67] Such a dynamic, however, constituted repetition with a difference: while the brutality of imperial retribution in India worked to set a precedent for vengeance in Zululand, the offending indigenous resistance and its impact on British identity was framed differently. With respect to India, the British media were able to deflect focus on masculine martial vulnerability by couching the uprising as an attack on British domesticity, wherein vulnerable women and children were the victims of the violent Asiatic. As Jenny Sharpe puts it, that colonial crisis was "managed through the circulation of the violated bodies of English women as a sign for the violation of colonialism."[68] In Zululand, however, it was clear that the vulnerable victim was now, undeniably, the very pillar of imperial conquest, the British soldier – now emasculated by the powerful Zulu; this time, the empire had to acknowledge the fault lines in its martial foundations. What this means, in turn, is that the traditional understanding of British masculinity as formidable, agent, and powerful fractured; now, it was penetrated, ruptured, and dismembered manhood, rather than violated English womanhood, that stood as the sign of crisis in imperial authority.

Importantly, the imperative for retribution for this dismemberment is buttressed by sentiment registered in the sympathetic bodies of those whose "blood run[s] cold" with knowledge of loss. The *Natal Mercury* exemplified this strategy on 12 March 1879, in an article entitled "Honor to the Slain": "There is not a heart in the country that does not feel sore with constant contemplation of the distressful theme, nor a tongue that has not spent itself in discussing it. There has been a morbid fascination in the topic that has proved irresistible to all of us, and made sustained attention to other subjects a moral impossibility."[69] If affect was registered in sympathetic bodies, bodies that claim shared community through physical compassion,[70] then the ensuing emotional outpouring demanded reparation – in both senses of compensation and repair.

The Monstrous Landscape

The fears of engulfment and penetration by the Zulus and the subsequent colonial affect generated by loss and vulnerability required recourse and vengeance – through the subjugation not only of Zulu fighters but also of the landscape of Zululand that was both, in British representations, intertwined with African men and, as accounts of Isandlwana, Ntombe, and Hlobane demonstrate, functional in the problem of engulfment and emasculation. In other words, the emergent threat to the boundaries of British bodies also manifested in British understandings of the African landscape itself as simultaneously yonic and phallic – as monstrous. Figurations of the landscape, in turn, point to the specific modes by which imperial masculinity and authority are understood to be compromised (a theme discussed in chapters 2, 3, 5, and 6). If the landscape of Zululand was itself resistant, then, in the imperial rationale, once the war was formally over, the territory was subdued, subsumed into the narrative of progress. Yet, even as colonial writing about the war used the African landscape to register British domination, it implicitly acknowledged the land's centrality to indigenous resistance. For instance, toward the end of the conflict, once Ulundi was taken, an article in the *Natal Witness* argued that

> one is struck by the marked contrast between the appearance of the country at the present time and a few weeks ago. Not long since the neighbouring fertile lands were the scenes of battle, desolation, and other evils attending war, no matter where or how conducted. Now everything presents a peaceful aspect, and those who until very recently were anxious to meet the invading forces of the white man in battle, are now industriously engaged rebuilding their old kraals.[71]

Of course, the narrative of colonial prosperity is exceptionally transparent here: the *Natal Witness* associates indigenous resistance with "desolation" and "evils" and contrasts it with post-conquest colonial governance yielding "fertile lands," peace, and industry. But, importantly, this article also works to link the landscape with conflict itself; the country appearing "desolate" or "peaceful," as per the conditions of fighting, points to the landscape's significant role in the outcome of the battles. Not only this, but the undulating African topography immensely hampered British communication.[72] Curling complained in September 1878 that sizeable gaps in British intelligence about the land interfered with efficient movements: "There are no maps of the country at all. Those printed in England are entirely imaginary and are probably compiled from books of travel. Several times on the march to this place we found that the rivers marked on the map had not existed and we always had to send on the day before to find out whether water was certain to be found at the halting places."[73] British invaders had little objective knowledge of the space, and relied instead on imaginary constructions of the landscape. These flaws in British "knowledge" about Zululand underscore the limitations to imperial technologies of surveillance. In turn, the redcoats struggled in the most practical of matters: because there was no road network in Zululand, crossing rivers and passes was a huge problem for the invaders, especially with supplies and wagons (here, a flowing force literally threatened to carry imperial forces away), and the climate was daunting with its alternately hot and frigid conditions, frequent rain, and conditions for bacterial infection.[74] British mobility was thus severely limited. Meanwhile, the Zulus' knowledge of the land buttressed their resistance efforts; the very landscape was an asset to them – they knew its contours, mobilized readily, and took advantage of the topography in battle.

Consequently, colonial renditions of the war frequently conflated the Zulus, and the threat they posed, with the landscape. That their ability to hide in the countryside intensified the terror of their engulfing attacks was nowhere more evident than at the Battle of Rorke's Drift.[75] Harry Lugg, a trooper in the Natal Mounted Police, quoted his comrade in describing the approaching Zulus "as black as hell and thick as grass."[76] This simile worked to integrate the Zulus with the terrain, but Lugg's observation that "the place seemed alive with them" also presented the land, in turn, as invested with Zulu influence.[77] Similarly, Private Henry Hook of the 2/24th recalled that, in the middle of the night, "a war-dance ... roused them up again, and their excitement was so intense that the ground fairly seemed to shake."[78] The conflation of the Zulu threat with the land itself in turn meant that British masculinity was subject to destabilization through engulfment or penetration by the very ground the redcoats invaded.

Meanwhile, in the aftermath of Isandlwana, Lieutenant Q. McK. Logan of the 2/24th regiment sensed another kind of engulfment during the night Chelmsford's returning troops camped alongside their slain: "We could see the Zulu signal fires all around us, and I never expected to get out of Cetshwayo's territory alive, as we appeared from the position of the fires to be completely surrounded."[79] With the fires lit on the surrounding hills, visually the Zulus entirely encircled the company. Once again, however, metaphors for monstrosity suddenly invert as this sense of enclosure overlaps with a phallic presence. For the correspondent Norris-Newman, who accompanied Chelmsford's force at this time, British martial failure yielded a sign of monstrous indigenous dominance:

> We began to tumble over dead bodies lying in every direction, and in some places ... men were found lying thick, as though they had fought till every cartridge was gone, and had then been surrounded and assegaid. Within a few hundred yards of the top of the ridge ... the grotesque and large shadow of Isandhlwana reared up in front of us, and showing clearly against the sky in the evening light.[80]

At the very moment that Norris-Newman acknowledges the state of the now dissolved army, the towering African landmark, as a grotesque figure exceeding its own boundaries, "rear[s] up" in the face of British loss as a dominant presence signalling Zulu power. Thus, the traditional representation of the colonial landscape as passively awaiting conquest begins to change: here, the environment becomes agent and even aggressive – in both its vaginal and phallic renditions – impinging profoundly on understandings of British martial masculinity and its vulnerabilities. This shift in imperial perspective would register in the romances of H. Rider Haggard, which, as the following chapter explores, rework the established colonial relationship between the gendered landscape and imperial prowess in colonial discourse.

Such concerns about spatial transgressions during the war also manifested in panic about border invasion. After Isandlwana, the majority of white survivors struggled into Helpmekaar, Natal, where they, shaken and unequipped, for days fully expected an onslaught of Zulu warriors. Though history has shown that Cetshwayo had no desire to invade Natal, British colonists nevertheless awaited this event with terror. Major Francis Grenfell, a Welshman in the 60th Rifles in Chelmsford's column, confided, "We are working night and day at the defences of Natal. There is nothing to prevent an invasion."[81] Tom Turner, a civilian from Hereford, echoed this sense of exposure, writing from Pietermartizburg that danger "lies in our large border so unprotected, nearly all our men away in the country, and an extensive border lying quite open to the enemy."[82] Fearful as this prospect was, there was the additional concern that the martial success of the Zulus would precipitate a rising of native groups within the colonies:[83] "a small minority of whites, by the reputation of invincibility, hold their own against the overwhelming majorities of blacks. Now that Cetewayo has effectually destroyed that reputation the outlook before our colonists is gloomy in the extreme."[84] This looming threat of indigenous resistance materializing within the colonial zone, threatening to consume the colony, led some to believe that this war "has assumed dimensions which imperil the very existence of our South African Empire."[85] In other words, this humiliating martial defeat at Isandlwana significantly destabilized not only British martial masculinity but also imperial identity itself. Crucially, these fears of territorial penetration and engulfment buttressed the prevailing discourse of exposure, vulnerability, and dissolution. In order to recover itself, the empire needed a hero or two.

Manufacturing Heroes

With the effective martial strategies of the Zulu producing this level of fear and shock, the Victorian perception of the redcoats as far more efficacious than "a savage army like that of Zululand" shifted to the sobering realization that these African soldiers had fractured Victorian conceptions of manhood.[86] Since this recognition yielded an outpouring of grief channelled through the construction of the British soldier as innocent lad, national masculine identities needed to be rebuilt in order to reconcile national mourning with imperial identity. British print culture was fundamental to this reworking of manhood by producing images of heroism and providing reassurance that the army retained the capacity to do the work of empire.

Part of the reason the metropolitan media had such a strong hand in the representation of events in South Africa was that detailed reports from the front could be weeks or months in arriving at home; longer and less incomplete dispatches were transported via steamer while only the most basic of information arrived via official telegram.[87] Filling in the blanks, metropolitan publications frequently took poetic licence, depicting, for example, Commander Pulleine being "cool and collected" as he stoically rallied his men to defend the camp at Isandlwana.[88] Newspapers would often offer wildly unfounded narratives that resembled romantic exploits more than reports. A popular myth celebrated a young soldier, Melville, who, attempting to rescue regimental colours during Isandlwana, was overcome in pursuit, and "spent with loss of blood, ... with the colours wrapped around him ... sank down to die, happy in the soldierly conviction that honour was saved."[89] Martial devotion was glorified as the heroic Melville was said to be

> last seen cutting his way through over 100 natives, cutting them down like grass with his sword,[90] as he was determined to save the colors of the regiment ... After being mortally wounded in seven places he rescued the colors, which he had tied around him, and swam the river in time to lie down and die, knowing ... that he had saved the honor of his country and regiment. A more noble or glorious death, of course, no soldier could possibly die.[91]

Pulleine had indeed appointed Melville to carry the colours, but Melville had lost them while attempting to escape across the Mzinyathi (Buffalo) River and was killed on the opposite bank. It is thus difficult to miss the papers' wilful insistence on the predominance of traditional ideals of martial masculinity.

Contrary to this prevailing imperative of the stiff upper lip propagated by the papers, survivors' accounts of Isandlwana, perhaps unsurprisingly, demonstrate stark terror, disorganization, and confusion. J.F. Brickhill, an interpreter, escaped down Fugitive's Trail: "our stampede was composed of mules, with and without pack saddles, oxen, horses in all stages of equipment and fleeing men all strangely intermingled – man and beast, apparently all infected with the danger which surrounded us."[92] This chaos and panic present a very different narrative of conduct at Isandlwana than that which the newspapers invented before survivors' letters started to arrive at home.[93]

Perhaps the most sensationalized myth of stoicism during the Anglo-Zulu War is the dominant representation of the unlikely British victory at Rorke's Drift.[94] Though this Zulu raid on the British outpost amounted to pillaging on the heels of the victory at Isandlwana, the British media construed the event as an integral stand against the invasion of Natal.[95] The *Natal Mercury* asserted that the Zulus' "intention was to enter Natal and lay waste to the colony. The reserve made the attack on Rorke's Drift, and their repulse saved the colony."[96]

The idea that the British could still withstand military penetration was fundamental in reviving both national morale and images of British manliness. In fact, the notion of British fortification (when successful) in the face of Zulu onslaught was embellished throughout the war. Martial investment in this celebration of fixity can be understood in light of Theweleit's theorization of stiffening as resistance to emasculation. His suggestion that fascist impenetrability in the face of the red flood is a strategy by which "the man holds himself together as an entity, a body with fixed boundaries ... He defends himself with a kind of sustained erection of his whole body, of whole cities, of whole troop units."[97] In other words, fortification works to reaffirm male boundaries, to recuperate the phallus: "Our soldiers ... want to avoid swimming at all costs, no matter what the stream. They want to stand with both feet and every root firmly anchored in the soil. They want whatever floods may come to rebound against them."[98]

Theweleit's assessment is strikingly applicable to the "flood" at Rorke's Drift. The representation of fixity at Rorke's served to counter the panicked dissolution of the martial body at Isandlwana; newspapers lauded the stand at Rorke's as the quintessential example of British stalwart self-possession and duty. British print culture made heroes of Lieutenants Bromhead and Chard, whose alleged unflappability and presence of mind served to rally their men. Lugg's account in the *North Devon Herald* was suitably dramatic: when news of Isandlwana and the impending attack on Rorke's arrived at the outpost, the messenger supposedly said, "'You will all be murdered and cut to pieces,' and the only answer he received was, 'We will fight for it, and if we have to die we will die like Britishers.'"[99] Preparations, however, did not unfold quite like this. While this defence was indeed sustained against incredible odds, it was not, as the papers would have it, the result of stoicism and levelheadedness. The lieutenants' first panicked impulse was to begin packing up camp and mobilizing the wounded immediately for a trek back to the comparative safety of Helpmekaar – and this was after, as Hook testifies, "a note was received by Lieutenant Bromhead from the Column to say that the enemy was coming on, and that the post was

Figure 4. Monument at Isandlwana Battlefield. Robert Pack/Alamy Stock Photo.

to be held at all costs."[100] It was only when Commissioner Dalton convinced them that if they ran, all of them, including the invalided men, would be slaughtered in the open, that the lieutenants agreed to hunker down. When the attack came, resistance was a matter of desperate fighting, as Hook twice put it, "like rats in a hole."[101] Though the defenders at Rorke's had little other choice than to fight frantically for their lives, the victory would be lauded as a gallant forestalling of a Zulu invasion into Natal. As Lieven suggests, "the need for national reassurance ensured that Rorke's Drift would be presented in the newspapers as an epic of youthful heroism, and the military authorities and the government were happy to endorse that version of events."[102] No fewer than eleven Victoria Crosses were awarded to the soldiers at Rorke's. To this day, evidence of the sustained fantasy of fortification can be seen in the particularly Theweleitian example of phallus-recuperation in figure 4. As if to offset the symbolic prowess of the African landmark, this memorial to the battles at Isandlwana and Rorke's Drift asserts its own solidity – fittingly walled and fenced off from the surrounding sea of grass, which itself has been mowed near the obelisk.

These kinds of presentations of heroism lasted throughout the war. They also became increasingly nuanced and narrative. For instance, Forbes depicted a confrontation between opposing champions during a skirmish on the Mfolozi Drifts, near Ulundi, on 3 July, in which the British achieved the advantage.[103] Lieutenant William Beresford, Forbes's close friend, had become an iconic warrior around whom national visions of manhood coalesced. As Beresford, ahead of his comrades, chased after the retreating Zulus,

> the Zulu induna [leader], bringing up the rear of his fleeing detachment, turned on the lone man who had so outridden his followers. A big man, even for a Zulu, the ring round his head proved him a veteran. The muscles rippled on his glistening black shoulders as he compacted himself behind his huge flecked shield of cowhide, marking his distance for the thrust of the gleaming assegai held at arm's length over the great swart head of him. Bill steadied his horse a trifle, just as he was wont to do before the take off for a big fence; within striking distance he made him swerve a bit to the left – he had been heading straight for the Zulu, as if he meant to ride him down. The spear flashed out like the head of a cobra as it strikes; the sabre carried at "point one" clashed with it, and seemed to curl around it; the spear-head was struck aside, the horseman delivered "point two" with all the vigour of his arm, his strong seat, and the impetus of his galloping horse; and lo! in the twinkling of an eye, the sabre's point was through the shield, and half its length was buried in the Zulu's broad chest. The brave induna was a dead man before he dropped; the sword drawing out of his heart as he fell backward. His assegai stands now in the corner of Bill's mother's drawing room.[104]

The image of clashing male bodies here is central, although only the Zulu man's is objectified. His physical stature, rippling muscles, and "glistening black shoulders" render him an intimidating opponent. Crucially, being a commander, a veteran, and a clearly powerful man, he is represented as a worthy, "brave" adversary for the pursuing Englishman. Emphasis on the induna's qualifications is necessary for Beresford's pursuit to be understood as heroic and not as a simple act of butchery. The induna's virility, however, is kept markedly in the realm of the primitive; not only does his body occupy Forbes's main focus, but he is also aligned with the animalistic via his "cowhide" shield and his spear, flashing like a "cobra." By contrast, Beresford is not just a body but rather a character whom the passage constructs as familiar. He is immediately presented as a leader of men, courageously outriding his "followers." The informal appellation of "Bill" suggests a comradely relation available to the reader, as if Beresford were the hero of some boys' adventure fiction, while the reference to his habit of steadying his horse, "as he was wont to do before the take off for a big fence," further adds dimension to his character. Moreover, horsemanship entails notable connotations of class. Beresford thus becomes the familiar gentleman hero who hunts the animalized Zulu man.

The fencing/hunting/sporting trope both resonates with Victorian conceptions of masculinity and also figures penetration: the outcome of this clash is determined by whose force strikes home. From the imagery of the Zulu recoiling his muscular frame in order to "thrust" his "gleaming assegai" toward the Englishman, to that of the phallic cobra, and finally to the lieutenant's lunge of his sabre that, "with all the vigour of his arm, his strong seat, and the impetus of his galloping horse," pierces the induna's "broad chest," this passage is rife with connotations of libidinal struggle.[105] Thus, as if in response to the Zulus' rear infiltration of the British army at Isandlwana, Forbes's passage works to reassert that it is the British who do the penetrating.

After Beresford's victory, the passage closes with the striking observation that the induna's assegai was taken as a souvenir. The hunting imagery again has disturbing implications for Beresford's and Forbes's treatment of the induna: given that the Zulu warrior has been likened to wildlife here, the captured assegai functions quite clearly as a trophy, marking British subjugation of what is understood as primitive. Such invidious behaviour is completely in line with what John Hoberman identifies in the colonial Victorians as "the perverse impulse to treat killing as sport."[106] Hoberman suggests, "The most vicious aspect of the colonial world was the emergence of Negro-killing as a sportive exercise. 'Man-shooting is the finest sport of all,' said General Wolseley, who (like others) saw the Zulus as 'dangerous black game that made the hunt especially exhilarating.'"[107] With hunting so important for Victorian manhood, the assegai as memento acts as a physical representation of British virility,[108] while the idea that a material signifier of Zulu prowess sits in a British woman's drawing room is part of a fantasy of castration – a rejoinder to the emasculation the British had experienced at the hands of the Zulu.

Thus this brutal trope of hunting Zulus was deployed to re-establish English prowess. Norris-Newman, the war correspondent, celebrated British sniping skills at the Battle of Gingindlovu (2 April 1789), as he and a friend picked off Zulu men with their rifles from the top of a wagon: "Palmer (who is a crack shot, having hunted large game in the interior for years) brought several to the ground … After the battle … Palmer and I took and divided the trophies of war, including their native dress, arms, and accoutrements; and we keep them yet, as most prized and hardly-won trophies."[109] As John M. MacKenzie has argued, hunting, because it "required all the most virile attributes of the imperial male – courage, endurance, individualism, sportsmanship"[110] – was, for late Victorians, directly linked to masculine capacity. Meanwhile, trophy collections testify to prowess: material evidence was necessary for Norris-Newman, as for Beresford, to substantiate a theretofore beleaguered sense of martial abilities. However, while this evidence, whether in the form of objects taken from fallen warriors in the field or in testimonies lurking in letters home or in war reporting, was supposed to recover diminished British pride, it simultaneously exposed the horrendous brutality of the supposedly gallant agents of empire.

Panic and Brutality

This construction of heroism, however, was only so effective. Metropolitan anxiety about the redcoats' capacities, and particularly their physiques, led the press to suggest that British ranks in South Africa were filled "with a class of recruit who is altogether overmatched in point of age and physique by the savage soldiery he has to face. A raw, weedy boy, as are too many of our recruits nowadays, is individually no match for one of Cetewayo's Zulus."[111] Redcoats, in other words, were not manly enough. Augmenting this problem were accounts of British panic, trembling upper lips, and unmanly nervousness emerging in both imperial correspondence and the metropolitan press. Major Tucker, of Colonel Wood's column, wrote to his father on 19 March that his soldiers "were still very uneasy [since Ntombe] ... Off went a couple of rifles and all went into laager and fort; the nights are very dark and no doubt they fired off at imaginary Zulus ... These young soldiers are more bother than they are worth. A fellow nearly let off his rifle last night at a log of wood, but an officer happened to visit him at the moment he was challenging it for the third time and so saved an alarm."[112] Even as the war drew to a close and the redcoats gained the upper hand, the troops remained paranoid. Correspondent Melton Prior publicized this anxiety: during the march to Ulundi on 6 June, a false alarm sounded when officers imagined "a black mass approaching"; shots were loosed all over the laager, even wounding some redcoats. Prior attested, "A more disgraceful scene I have never witnessed."[113] Such embarrassment was far from unusual in this war. *Telegraph* correspondent Phil Robinson described another false alarm on 1 July as sparking "the direst disorder." This unmanly display exceeded confusion: soldiers refused, "until officers actually used physical force in the shape of kicking, to return to their posts outside ... Their steadiness in the face of the enemy has, on more than one occasion, shown signs of shortcoming."[114] Prior describes a scenario, similarly mortifying in its betrayal of the ideal of martial fortitude, that occurred on 3 July, the night before the charge on Ulundi. Imagining a Zulu charge, the troops on watch dashed to the laager: "Some clambered over the wagons, while others crawled underneath, in their mad endeavour and haste to get inside ... It was certainly much to be regretted, but still more so that two hundred men of a certain regiment, which shall be nameless, actually left their rifles in the trench in their haste to get into camp."[115] If the word "cowardice" is not mentioned in these accounts, it certainly is implied.

Despite these reports of paranoia in the ranks, some press continued to laud the bravery of the troops in the face of loss. The *Daily Telegraph* of London asserted:

> There is nothing except mournful glory in the behaviour of the officers and men who have fallen, however seriously the affair may reflect upon the military dispositions of their leaders ... So far from being a blot upon the British annals, the conduct of these men and officers in their desperate strait casts new lustre upon our arms. They were not conquered, but overwhelmed ... not only without shame, but with sorrowful pride and satisfaction ... At any cost, with whatever necessary strength, the reverse must be effaced, the savage victors chastised, conquered, and disarmed.[116]

Asserting the valour of the common soldier came at the price of acknowledging problems in martial leadership, which would have been nearly impossible not to do anyway. But this passage also illustrates a crucial shift in Victorian attitudes toward imperial masculinity during the war, even as it leads with the attempt to deny the "blot upon the British annuls" and the "shame" of defeat. Again the supplement emerges to buttress the fault lines in imperial masculinity: in supplementing these fissures in the dominant traditional model of masculinity with assertions that "glory," "pride," and "lustre" shone in British conduct, the *Daily Telegraph* worked to produce the fiction that traditional male ideals had endured despite the blunders and cowardice in the ranks and at the level of command. At the same time, this article illustrates a profound sense of loss, mourning, and sorrow: it gestures to the loss the nation had suffered – not just in terms of fallen soldiers, but also in terms of imperial dignity. Consequently, its author demanded a particular kind of retribution, a "chastis[ing]" of the "savage victors" in which the British would again emerge as the triumphant penetrators "at any cost." The *Morning Post*, meanwhile, foregoing the *Telegraph*'s ameliorative rhetoric, put the problem to the nation much more bluntly: "Our prestige has suffered a terrible blow, and must be regained at all hazards. It will rest with our troops to avenge the slain and to extinguish the Zulu power for ever."[117]

Thus, if the emasculation suffered at Isandlwana, Ntombe Drift, and Hlobane Mountain required a recuperation of British heroism, this process of recovery was in turn predicated on brutal violence as martial prowess was desperately asserted through conquest. Justifying this assertion of disciplinary power and military dignity, however, necessitated acknowledging the Zulus as worthy adversaries whose strength required severe force. In April, the *Westminster Review* released the following observation that at once epitomized British arrogance and racism and reiterated a need for conquest over the primitive:

> The terrible disaster in Zululand which has lately befallen our usually victorious troops has roused the whole nation to desire to know more of a people and a country perhaps hitherto too slightly regarded. We are so apt to consider a war with barbarous tribes on the frontiers of our remote colonies as a matter of small moment, and to look upon victory as certain, that the news of the massacre of eight hundred of our gallant troops ... by a horde of naked savages took everyone by surprise.[118]

While many British came to recognize Cetshwayo's military strategy and theoretical aptitudes, and Zulu skills and determination, such attributes were frequently represented in terms of animal qualities, such as ferocity and fearlessness, so as to maintain imperial hierarchies. The *Brecon County Times* published a letter by Sergeant W. Morley who had been at Isandlwana and who suggested the Zulus "were like lions and not afraid of death. As soon as one man fell another took his place ... The way our camp was taken could not be more cleverly taken by any of our Generals ... They came up like bees from behind the camp."[119] Morley represented the Zulus as cunning, relentless, replaceable, swarming, and indiscriminately destructive.[120] Though admiring their tactics, he nevertheless depicted a primitive and unstoppable force whose knowledge of the landscape gave them the advantage over the redcoats. With less reverence, a soldier who survived Hlobane wrote, "We had got to hate those Zulus ... something like the manner a man hates a snake, or a tiger, or a hungry wolf, knowing that if we did not destroy it we shall ourselves be destroyed."[121] Representations like this implied that conquering such animalistic warriors necessitated harsh methods of taming.

In order to justify such subjugation, imperial narratives needed to navigate the issue of unequal weaponry in the two armies. A correspondent for the *Natal Mercury* insisted, "The assegai in the hand of the Zulu is quite as efficacious as the breech-loader in the hand of the European, because the Zulu makes up by agility and quickness of movement for the differences in the weapons."[122] While recognizing Zulu prowess,[123] this assertion simultaneously elides the redcoats' huge technological advantage. Although the Zulu army did possess a quantity of rifles, the warriors were not fully trained in using them, nor did they possess numbers of arms comparable to those of the British forces. Furthermore, they didn't have the rockets, newer Martini-Henry rifles, or Gatling guns of the Europeans. The declaration that the two armies were equally matched with respect to weaponry thus worked to license the relentless violence in which the British indulged after their major defeats, when the tables finally turned at the battles of Kambula Ridge and Gingindlovu.

Britain's brutal triumph at Kambula was central to recovering martial identity; combatants' accounts emphasize the relationship between punitive violence and recuperation of Britain's prowess. This merciless battle was understood explicitly as an act of vengeance, as Lieutenant Alfred Blaine's narrative of "shoot[ing] them down as they retreated" made clear: "We all declared that now we would pay them out for the day before. 'Remember yesterday [the Battle of Hlobane],' we all shouted out, and I can assure you we did, and had our revenge."[124] For another soldier, Kambula rejoined Isandlwana; the redcoats were "fully resolved to avenge our comrades' lives that had been lost on the 22nd January, only too well known throughout the wide world."[125] As this description suggests, violence redressed a tattered national reputation as much as it avenged fallen men. Indeed, as Private Joseph Banks understood it, Kambula "wiped out effectually every other disaster that has happened."[126] And yet, that the violence of this battle was understood specifically as recuperating masculine prowess in turn gave rise to a new set of representational problems regarding British martial identity: it was not good press to emphasize the ruthlessness of British persecution of the Zulus, since such brutality undercut the image of the gentleman soldier. As Laband and Knight note of war correspondence, "since the required emphasis was on adventure, heroism, glory, and noble death, preferably selflessly offered up for a comrade, they habitually did not dwell on the horrors of the battlefield ... It was permissible to praise the bravery of a noble adversary like the Zulu, but not to write about the horrible mutilations inflicted on them by Martini-Henry bullets."[127] Thus, reports and letters home often worked to establish the British "strength" for which the *Daily Telegraph* called, without betraying the full reality of retribution that attended Kambula.

Nevertheless, a gross brutality emerges in narratives from the front. Captain D'Arcy wrote in a letter published in the *Eastern Star*, "We killed a little over 2300, and when once they retired all the horsemen in camp followed for eight miles, butchering the brutes all over the place. I told the men, 'No quarter, boys, and remember yesterday,' and we did knock them about, killing them all over the place ... We are all in high feather at having such a good fight with the Zulus."[128] Similarly, Private John Snook's testimony detailing ruthless killing following the Battle of Kambula was printed in the *North Devon Herald*: "About eight miles from camp, we found about 500 wounded, most of them mortally, and begging us for mercy's sake not to kill them; but they got no chance after what they had done to our comrades at Isandhlwana."[129] The same dehumanizing brutality infusing D'Arcy's and Snook's narratives appears in Commandant Schermbrucker's account of the pursuit that was printed in the *Natal Mercury*:

> They fairly ran like bucks; but I was after them like the whirlwind, and shooting incessantly into the thick column, which could not have been less than 5000 strong. They became exhausted, and shooting them down would have taken too much time; so we took the assegais from the dead men, and rushed among the living ones, stabbing them right and left, with fearful revenge for the misfortunes of the 28th inst. No quarter was given.[130]

In likening the warriors to routinely hunted animals, Schermbrucker denies the humanity of the men he slaughters. Further, as is typical in front-line representations of Zulus, Schermbrucker treats the men, whom he describes as a phallic "thick column" – a potentially penetrating threat that needed to be subdued – like one faceless mass. More crucially, however, in enacting this carnage, the British opt to kill with assegais instead of their longer-ranging guns, indulging in closer-range, physically engaging killing, drawing out the experience, rather than taking the option of shooting from a distance. In colonial discourse, this constitutes a regression. Indeed, Schermbrucker describes himself as a "whirlwind" – becoming an unpredictable, free-flowing force, moving closer to nature and the primitive. Thus, while imperial discourse pegged Zulus as barbaric and bloodthirsty, the British, by the end of the war, had come to embody the very stereotype that they had ostensibly set out to subjugate. Irretrievably, the myth of the gentleman soldier began to fracture.

This fracture began to widen with the metropole's outrage in response to narratives of Kambula and Gingindlovu, where the redcoats had wreaked similar carnage. Denial of these atrocities was the authorities' first line of defence. In Parliament, debates arose about reports on the cruelties at Gingindlovu: asked whether he was prepared to act in consequence of such reports, the secretary of state for the colonies, Sir Michael Hicks Beach, stated that he did not believe them, but, if indeed they were true, he would leave dealing with them to the military authorities.[131] He was not the only figure to try and wash his hands of responsibility. Colonel Wood, in command at Kambula, controverted the occurrence of the slaughter described by Snook. In response to this denial, the *Hereford Times* argued, "On these official contradictions of ruthless cruelties perpetuated in the open face of day, an additional slur is cast upon England. Europe is led to believe English officers untruthful as well as cruel."[132] But this was not just a matter of individualized unmanly character; it also concerned systematic withholding. The *Northern Echo* took issue not only with the redcoats' betrayal of the traditional image of British martial courage and heroism at Gingindlovu, but also with the military's efforts to discursively contain these failings:

> From the first terrible disaster at Isandula [Isandlwana] to the ignominious retreat from Ekowe we have hardly ever been told at once the whole truth about our losses, or about the slaughter inflicted upon the Zulus ... It would appear from the details now to hand of the Battle of Gingihlova that the first telegram was equally misleading. Instead of our forces being attacked by an overwhelming number of Zulus, the Zulus, only 5,000 strong, hurled themselves upon 7,000 British troops strongly entrenched and defended by artillery and Gatling guns ... Although the Zulus retreated, they did not fly, and their gallant pursuers "hung back whenever it seemed likely a stand would be made ..." No quarter was given to the Zulus. All the wounded were killed ... We are waging [this war] in flagrant violation of the laws of war.[133]

The *Echo* not only mocked the cowardice underpinning redcoat brutality as it described the "gallant pursuers" backing away from a confrontation when the exhausted retreating Zulus turned to meet them, it also attacked the very validity of martial narratives that sought to represent British masculinity and create imperial history.

Protests that shameful soldierly conduct dishonoured the nation amplified. The Peace Society condemned the war "as tending to corrupt the national conscience, to dishonour the national character, and to obstruct the spread of Christianity in the world,"[134] and called upon the nation to challenge its military's brutality: "Public opinion should demand that the bloody and disastrous war in South Africa should be brought to a speedy end ... It is a purely aggressive war ... It has occasioned the destruction ... of several thousands of Zulus, who were guilty of no offence but defending their own country against an unprovoked invasion."[135] Characterizing the war as "ignoble," the Peace Society emphasized that the costs of the war were not only in "blood, [and] in treasure," but also in "character"; because of redcoat conduct, "the reputation of England as a Christian nation before the face of the world" was at significant risk.[136] Other voices echoed this articulation of the disgrace Britain had brought on itself: the Aborigines' Protection Society vehemently objected to the invasion of Zululand, missionaries spoke publicly to denounce the war as "brutal and unjust," and the *Spectator* asserted that accounts of the burning of native villages were "to the disgrace of civilization."[137] Metropolitan recognition that the barbarity Britain had attributed to Cetshwayo and the Zulu nation was emerging in British soldiers, martial leaders, and government may be encapsulated in a satirical poem published in *Fun*, published on 8 October 1879, entitled "Evidently a Savage." Beginning with a description of "an uncivilized king" who "living so far from the West" could not "digest" that "No right *he* enjoyed / To remain un-annoyed / While retaining the right to molest," the poem's initial verses seem to be examining the Zulu king who, in British discourse, had been identified as primitive and aggressive. As the poem progresses, however, it becomes evident that, by this ruler who "thinks he possesses the right / To limit his neighbours in might," the speaker means British imperialism, embodied at various points in Frere, Chelmsford, and Wolseley, the latter of whom steps in after "the enemy routed and put him to shame": "the savage collected his band / And, having more thoughtfully planned / His subsequent moves / (As the consequence proves), / Effectively conquered the land." Notably, this British victory is not celebrated but rather is lamented as an act of savagery: "civilization stood dumb / And justice was hopeless and glum / When the savage made plain / His plans to maintain / His enemies under his thumb."[138] Through this war, *Fun* argued, Britain had been martially upstaged and had also betrayed the ideals of civilization and justice. With critical discourses such as this circulating in the metropolitan sphere, the image of the war hero would never be quite the same in the public imagination.

The Growth of Doubt: Implications for Traditional Models of Masculinity

This British brutality entailed a confrontation with the traditional ideals of chivalrous martial valour. That such barbaric violence came on the heels of humiliating defeats and pervasive cowardice meant that these attempts to recuperate martial prowess had very limited efficacy. As Rider Haggard, who had served as master and registrar of the High Court for the Transvaal during the war until tendering his resignation in May 1879, afterwards wrote, "The naked truths of such a business as the Transvaal surrender [which happened soon after the Anglo-Zulu War], or of the present condition of Zululand, are unpleasant reading for an Englishman, there is no doubt."[139] Having been relatively close to events, Haggard did not accept the contrived narrative of heroism – neither the idea that the British had behaved well nor that they had valiantly saved Natal from invasion:

> The details of the Zulu war are matters of melancholy history ... With the exception of the affair at Rorke's Drift, there is nothing to be proud of in connection with it, and a great deal to be ashamed of, more especially its final settlement ... Cetywayo was never thoroughly in earnest about the war. If he had been in earnest, if he had been determined to put out his full strength, he would certainly have swept Natal from end to end after his victory at Isandhlwana. There was no force to prevent his doing so: ... [he] was only anxious to defend his country.[140]

In sum, then, British martial conduct during this war had been shameful, inefficacious, and aggressive, and British desperation and brutality had marred the national image of chivalrous and stoic masculinity. Despite the bolstering efforts of institutional writing, the image of the colonial war hero changed significantly after the Anglo-Zulu War. Haggard remained among those unconvinced of colonial efficacy in Zululand, and suggested that the deterioration of these ideals were also transparent outside the metropole: "The lessons of our performances in the Zulu and Boer wars ... have not been lost upon [the Zulus], and they are beginning to think that the white man, instead of being the unconquerable demigod they thought him" – doubtless a British fantasy – "is somewhat of a humbug."[141] In deriding the British imperial agent as a fraud, Haggard articulates that traditional martial ideals were unfulfilled, and that both imperial and indigenous forces were beginning to recognize this. This portrayal of the "white man" as "humbug" is pursued, a few years later, in Haggard's first adventure romances, the success of which arose from, at least in part, a fantastic indulgence in the romantic idea of the "unconquerable [white] demi-god." Yet, while Haggard's romances ostensibly celebrated traditional masculine ideals, they simultaneously undercut them by illustrating, at the level of narrative, what the redcoats had already demonstrated: the failure of British men to live up to such impossible fictions. Even more disruptive than this failure of masculine prowess, however, was the evident inability of British discourse to contain such martial failings in Zululand, as they became visible to the metropole; because of the ways in which confrontations with the Zulu unfolded, and were represented, narratives of empire in Africa were failing to manifest as artifacts of manly achievement and embodiments of sound judgment, reliability, and assurance. For both the historical archive and Haggard's texts, imperial narratives themselves began to show that their own authority was starting to come apart at the seams.

Chapter Two

H. Rider Haggard's Inversions: Vulnerability and the Narrative Volatility of Imperial Romance

We declare proudly that "we always muddle through," but this, after all, is a boast that only fits the lips of the incompetent.

– Rider Haggard, *Days of My Life*

Across a range of genres, H. Rider Haggard, though irredeemably a proponent of empire, compiled a thorough critique of governmental policy in South Africa – with respect to both Zululand and also the Transvaal after the First Anglo-Boer War (1880–81). His non-fiction, frequently calling for a more consistent colonial policy for South Africa from the Home Office, often ridiculed governmental tendencies "to ignore or underrate dangers that are not immediately visible, and therefore never to be ready to meet them" – and he cited the Anglo-Zulu War as a prime example of this failure.[1] For Haggard, the British government, particularly in the colonial context, failed to live up to his martial masculine ideals: "patriotism, courage, ... patience in disaster, [and] fidelity to friends and a noble cause."[2] Meanwhile, his first commercially successful works of adventure fiction, *King Solomon's Mines* (1885) and *She: A History of Adventure* (1887), also irredeemably invested in the imperial project in Africa, indulged in fantasies of this kind of virile British manhood; in doing so, however, they ridiculed and critiqued dominant norms of martial masculinity – stoicism, valour, fortitude – and narratives from the front that, as recent events had shown, were neither realistic nor adequate for justifying imperial undertakings. Men had failed to live up to the myth of impenetrability; Haggard exploited this myth in order to undercut and then redirect imperial narrative.

The frame narratives of Haggard's most popular adventure romances render visible devastating flaws in their internal narrators. This revelation, in turn, highlights the works' portrayal of the African landscape as resistant, threatening, and penetrating both physically and emotionally – and thus positions British men as vulnerable and porous. Moreover, the works' investment in homoerotic dynamics challenges dominant masculinity, and, as Victorian romances, the novels necessitate significant narrative omissions – both of which destabilize the extant pillars of imperial legitimacy. The long critical tradition of taking Haggard's depictions of lively jaunts into unknown African territory at face value is beginning to change. What I am interested in here is unpacking how irony works in Haggard's texts – not to suggest that Haggard is critiquing the project of empire itself, but to illustrate that he is articulating that the dominant norms of imperial masculinity altogether constitute a fantasy, and, in light of recent history, a very limited one, that no longer serves the imperial project and no longer sustains imperial ideology. Haggard uses irony to show differences between conventional codes of masculine prowess and his own depictions of male behaviour in the imperial context. Through these differences, he critiques the bases of imperial masculine identity – that is, of narrative authority, impenetrability, fortitude, chivalry, and, most crucially, moral justifications of imperial subjugation.

"New Departure[s]"

Haggard's personal experiences informed his disillusionment with British martial accomplishments in South Africa. He had arrived in the Cape Colony in August 1875 to work as aide to Sir Henry Bulwer, a former neighbour of Haggard's father,[3] and lieutenant-governor of Natal during the Anglo-Zulu War. Haggard was present for the British annexation of the Transvaal in Pretoria on 12 April 1877 and actually raised the British flag after the declaration. While he became master and registrar of the High Court for the Transvaal in August 1877, serving under Justice Kotzé, in May 1879 he "broke all ties with the Government" and went in for ostrich farming,[4] remaining, however, quite politically opinionated. As we saw in the preceding chapter, Haggard saw nothing to be proud of with respect to the Anglo-Zulu War and expressed shame about Wolseley's settlement.[5] Compounding this sense of shame, the British government, in order to make peace with the Boers after the devastating British losses at Majuba Hill in 1881, agreed to return independence to the Transvaal, a move that Haggard protested in a letter to Sir Bartle Frere: "The natives are the real heirs to the soil, and should surely have some protection and consideration, some voice in the settlement of their fate. They outnumber the Boers by twenty-five to one ... Leading all these hundreds of thousands of men and women to believe that they were once and for ever the subjects of Her Majesty, safe from all violence and cruelty, and oppression, we have handed them over without a word of warning to the tender mercies of one, where natives are concerned, of the cruellest white races in the world."[6] Haggard offered a similar lamentation in his book *Cetywayo and His White Neighbours* (1882) – that the Transvaal was yielded to the Boers "under stress of defeat," that "the country was abandoned," and that "the vast majority who had remained faithful to the Crown, was handed to the cruel despotism of the minority who had rebelled against it."[7] In these disparagements of martial and governmental practice, Haggard began to confront British failure in manifesting chivalrous ideals and paternalism. Neglecting its role of righteous protector of the natives in the Transvaal, Britain undercut its identity: "Such an act of treachery to those to whom we were bound with double chains – by the strong ties of a common citizenship, and by those claims to England's protection from violence and wrong which have hitherto been wont to command it, even where there was no duty to fulfill, and no authority to vindicate – stands – I believe – without parallel on our records, and marks a new departure in our history."[8] Haggard thus articulated a "departure" from a fiction of martial standards long since held in the British imagination, but that had been revealed as fantasy by the wars in South Africa. This departure from chivalry was intensified by the breakdown of manly composure: "When it became known that peace had been declared as a corollary of our defeats … I saw strong men weeping like children, and heard English-born people crying aloud that they were 'b[lood]y Englishmen' no more. Soldiers were raging and cursing, and no one tried to stop them."[9] In affective terms, political capitulation on top of martial loss broke the stiff upper lip; the corollary of this rupture in the national identity of martial dominance and political steadiness was a rejection of what "Englishness" had become, and an infantilization of the nation's "strong men," now "weeping like children." British imperial identity had reached a turning point; British culture now had to reconcile itself to the failure of the impenetrable, fortified ideal, and begin to imagine what this would mean for the empire's future.

This turning point for the role of dominant masculinity in empire also had wider contexts of imperial endangerment. The Anglo-Boer War and its defeats came on the heels of the Anglo-Zulu War, which had yielded moral failure on top of martial bungling. Moreover, despite an upsurge of imperial feeling emerging in the 1870s, which was in part a strategic response to the long depression that began in 1873,[10] imperial control was beginning to slip globally. Colonial rebellions had begun to proliferate from the 1850s onward, with the 1850–53

Khoekhoe resistance in the Cape Colony, the 1857 Indian Uprising, the formation of the Irish Republican Brotherhood in 1858, the Morant Bay uprising in 1865, and the Egyptian National Movement coming to a head in 1881–82, all challenging notions of a stable global empire. Against this backdrop of instability, Haggard argued that similar kinds of violence would erupt in Zululand, endangering imperial incursions, since Wolseley's settlement terms had left the nation much aggrieved. Using imagery similar to the kind of phallic engulfment described by British soldiers in the Anglo-Zulu War, Haggard drew on established colonial rhetoric depicting the Zulus as a sexualized threat to the British colony.[11] He quoted Shepstone in describing Cetshwayo's army as a pent-up "engine" whose "forces have continued to accumulate and are daily accumulating without safety-valve or outlet."[12] Haggard harkened back to the remembrance of a threat of "some fifty thousand men, comprising the whole manhood of the nation ... continually on the boil."[13] Again, this imagery suggested the impending spilling over of fluids. Describing Cetshwayo's "clamouring regiments" as "Charybdis"[14] – the mythological whirlpool that threatens to suck in, surround, and swallow its victims – Haggard echoed the tropes of engulfment and swamping so prevalent in accounts of the Anglo-Zulu War, and, notably, Colonel Wood's account of "a resistless surging torrent of black creatures, which ... broke indeed, but like a huge on-coming wave."[15] With castration the implied threat here, Haggard suggested that the standard of manhood that had come to mark British martial performance, authority, and governmentability had become inadequate to meet these libidinally framed threats to empire.

Haggard wasn't alone in his concern about the efficacy of white imperial masculinity. Late nineteenth-century popular adventure fiction recognized that, from the male bodies that encountered, were tested by, and survived contact zones to the male-operated colonial administration system and the production of the imperial archive, and to the national technologies and institutions that depended upon and perpetuated male dominance, both narratives and practices surrounding imperial power hinged on representations of male prowess.[16] Frequently, adventure fiction from this period attempted to bolster dominant forms of imperial masculinity through depictions of heroism. Yet, by virtue of these insistent, valiant attempts – these claims about manliness that need to be made over and over again – it is also clear that the genre understood the weak points in imperial ideology. But while exuberant celebrations of manly prowess indicate prevalent, underlying insecurities, my focus here is on more direct forms of critique from within the ranks of empire's most enthusiastic proponents – those who believed in the virtues of imperial control and yet recognized the moral and ideological contradictions embodied in the traditional gendered agents of empire.

I argue that Haggard's first bestsellers, *King Solomon's Mines* and *She*, question the status of traditional martial masculinity and critique dominant presentations of male prowess in unprecedented ways. This is somewhat of a departure from long-standing arguments that Haggard's romances tended through various strategies to seek to recover, protect, recuperate, replicate, or glorify imperial masculinity through celebrating virility, muscularity, and patriarchal strength.[17] Indeed, criticism's somewhat entrenched understanding of the treatment of imperial masculinity in these works has continued to underpin recent scholarship that reads these novels in broader directions.[18] That the enduring legacy of *King Solomon's Mines* and *She* has in many ways hinged on popular attraction to white, heroic, imperialist masculinity helps to situate this critical trend.[19] I urge recognition, though, that Haggard's adventure romances destabilize narratives of imperial experience and exhibit the ideological tension existing within and between imperial texts and the fractured and conflicted nature of much popular fiction. As Robert Dixon puts it, the adventure romance is not "a unified text expressing a single point of view" but rather "a complex site of discursive boundaries."[20] Haggard's fictional works, far from simply acting out fantasies of empire or frankly championing British masculinity, playfully ridicule dominant models of British masculinity while simultaneously underscoring the limitations of imperial narrative authority. Both texts deploy a complex narrative structure with layers of editorial commentary that frame each story to demand critical scepticism of its narrator's representations of masculinity and rationalization of empire. Two editorial hands – the fictive "editor," who publishes the manuscript of the adventure, and the narrator, whose own editorial additions to his manuscript serve to create critical distance between the reader and the story itself – help to establish parody, irony, and occasional jocularity that deprecate masculinity and critique imperial prowess.[21] I also submit that the legibility of Haggard's critique of dominant forms of imperial masculinity requires recognition of the anxieties about bodily integrity circulating in the public sphere vis-à-vis representations of the Anglo-Zulu War. In other words, my attention to Haggard's narrative strategies is situated against the abiding impact of British understandings of historical events on his practice. Though ultimately invested in the imperial project and paternalism, Haggard confronts the vulnerability of imperial manhood as traditionally defined, implicitly suggesting that new terms of imperial identity, based less in a fortified than in an imperfect, critical, and therefore flexible masculinity, are needed to carry the project forward. At the same time, Haggard's works, particularly *She*, also question some of the key moral justifications of British imperial practice, coming to some very disruptive conclusions about the relationship between governance and desire.

I have argued that understandings of the male body as impenetrable, imperial narratives as solid, and British authority as legitimate operate as interdependently authorizing technologies of control; this chapter demonstrates that *King Solomon's Mines* and *She* use these parallel structures of authority to interrogate simultaneously the traditionally valourized masculine ideals of physical strength, chivalric command, and credible history. That is, Haggard's romances use their narrative frameworks to critique their own reliance on these forms of male prowess, and suggest that these linchpins of empire were no longer enough to sustain imperial ideology, because they were in fact different sides of the same fantasy. Recognizing auto-critique in Haggard's romances does not mean that he wasn't concerned with appropriating and subduing black labour, or wasn't ultimately invested in white male prowess – quite the contrary. It is precisely because he was interested in both of these issues that his texts, interested in naming the problem, are critical of the kind of white masculinity that had traditionally been lauded up to this point in the Victorian period, but that, after the outcomes of the Anglo-Zulu and Anglo-Boer wars, *and* the failure to discursively contain redcoat brutality, was no longer a viable fantasy. As Haggard's texts demonstrate, prominent formulas for heroism weren't enough to answer the contemporary military and ideological challenges of African resistance.

Central to Haggard's exploration of male vulnerability in the face of this resistance is the gendered African landscape that, rather than being solely a conquest, itself acts as an authority over British manhood, permeating its important masculine fortifications. It has been well established that Haggard's narratives, by feminizing and sexualizing the landscape, work to subjugate both colonial spaces and female power represented as embodied in the topography. But what I am interested in here is the relationship between what is nevertheless in many ways an active, threatening landscape and the fault lines in Victorian masculine ideology. These romances' complex treatment of the landscape as intoxicating, terrifying, unmanning, and agent suggests that some of the threats to which imperial male bodies are most vulnerable involve being constitutionally or emotionally swayed (so, affective fortifications are in danger), surrounded and overwhelmed, or enveloped and consumed. In such configurations of the landscape in relation to the heroes, the poles of subjectivity and objectivity (self and not self) can begin to slip, and the protagonists become passive and/or affected, losing their claim to "the well-formed mind" and their maintenance of their psychic boundaries – the "control, reserve, and discipline" that constituted Victorian imperial masculinity.[22] This occurs in both texts, but with particular potency in *She*.

Finally, critical distrust of the narrative and renditions of the male body as vulnerable and susceptible converge intensely on homoerotics in both adventure romances. Of course, because imperial expansion demanded repopulation and sexual reproduction, whether in the colonies themselves or as supplied by emigration from the metropole, the emphasis in Haggard on homosociality and homoerotic tensions undermines the conventional model of heterosexuality so fundamental to Victorian empire. But there is also more going on here: not only do undercurrents of homosexuality fundamentally threaten the myth of the hyper-masculine imperial man as impenetrable, they also threaten, by virtue of the narrative omissions they necessitate in the Victorian imperial context, the stability of narrative itself. Thus, through the self-sabotaging complexities of narrative frameworks, the ostensible heroes' subjection to African terrains, and the function of homoerotic indulgence, *King Solomon's Mines* and *She*, parodying the established idea of the quintessential British hero to undercut the notion of masculine credibility, capability, and impenetrability, suggest that dominant formulas of masculinity espoused within the traditional male adventure and romance novel not only leave Britain's narratives of imperialism deeply fissured but also profoundly disrupt British imperial legitimacy.

"Hard in Exercise": Norms of Colonial Masculinity in Adventure Fiction

Haggard's departure from the tradition of triumphant Christian British masculinity parodies the stoic, reliable, calm, and self-regulating figure that dominated the popular imagination at the end of the nineteenth century. In the popular adventure fiction of, for instance, Captain Marryat, R.M. Ballantyne, W.H.G. Kingston, Captain Mayne Reid, G.A. Henty, William Gordon Stables, and Thomas Hughes, ideals of muscular Christianity underpinned the construction of normative masculinity. Thomas Hughes's immensely popular *Tom Brown's School Days* (1857) in particular offered an emergent model of masculinity to which young boys of empire could aspire: Tom Brown "still had the traits of his raffish forebears, in terms of 'grit' and 'pluck.' But he now tried to combine the fighting spirit with the even older, more honourable ideal of the polite gentleman who based his very being in what the middle classes most admired: respect."[23] Tom, though an exemplar, comes from a larger culture of martial honour:

> The Browns are a fighting family. One may question their wisdom, or wit, or beauty, but about fight there is no question ... They are a square-headed and snake-necked generation, broad in the shoulder, deep in the chest, and thin in the flank ... No failures knock them up ... [They] are scattered over the whole empire on which the sun never sets, and whose general diffusion I take to be the chief cause of the empire's stability.[24]

This emerging imperial male ideal was strong, broad-shouldered, athletic, capable, quick-thinking, steady-nerved, Christian, bodily and culturally impenetrable, militarily adept, and British, of course, and was deeply structured on particular kinds of denigrating representations of indigenous men. Ballantyne's extremely influential adventure novel *The Coral Island* (1857), set in the South Pacific, contrasts the islanders – the "wild, blood-thirsty savages"[25] – with the heroic chivalry of Jack, the boys' leader, who asserts that the damsel Avatea "was a woman in distress, and that was enough to secure to her the aid of a Christian man."[26] In Ballantyne's sequel, *The Gorilla Hunters* (1875), the same group of boys, now men, travel to Africa, the supposedly ideal setting, as Ralph, the narrator, understands it, for the development of manhood: "I firmly believe that boys were intended to encounter all kinds of risks in order to prepare them to meet and grapple with the risks and dangers incident to a man's career with cool, cautious self possession ... founded on experimental knowledge of the character and powers of their own spirits and muscles."[27] The rational composure of white men in this work is juxtaposed with the emotional nervousness of their guide, Makarooroo: Ralph muses, "I never saw a man so deeply affected as was our poor guide, and when I looked at him I felt extremely anxious lest his state of mind should unfit him for acting with needful caution."[28] In Ballantyne's imagination, the African's nervousness, indicating failed manly development, contrasts with British composure.

Henty, too, set a number of novels in Africa, and, though published in the decade after Haggard's early imperial romances, they nevertheless indicate the prevailing didacticism concerning masculine ideality. In Henty's fiction the qualities of athleticism, capability, and Christianity help boys become men. His African adventures, *Dash for Khartoum* (1892), *By Sheer Pluck* (1897), and *With Kitchener in the Sudan* (1900), all feature the transition of young boys with absent mothers into military figures who resist the advances of African religious cultures and become successful, manly subjects in the process. In Henty's personal "Preface" to *Dash for Khartoum*, he advises, "My dear Lads … cowardice is of all vices the most contemptible," and reaffirms patrilineal stability by suggesting, as a remedy, "always go to your best friend, your father, and lay the case frankly and honestly before him."[29] In the text itself, physical prowess is also commendable: the young football players (or soldiers-in-training) at Cheltenham decide on a "strict training" regime of "getting up early and going for a three or four mile run every morning, taking another run in the afternoon, cutting off pudding and all that sort of thing"; they consider "it a mere waste of bone when a fellow doesn't put some flesh on him."[30] This disciplining of the male body within and beyond the text valourizes a capable body prepared for imperial war. Such regimentation pays off for Edgar, *Dash*'s hero, who rescues two "ladies" being robbed by "tramps." These derelicts are "no match for Edgar, who was in hard exercise, and in regular practice with the gloves, and whose blood was thoroughly up."[31] Afterwards, he refuses all thanks, insisting "it is a pleasure to punish such ruffians."[32] In *With Kitchener*, a lineage of independence is celebrated as Gregory discovers that his father refused to bend to his own father's wishes in exchange for financial support. Even more commendable, being "daring, full of resource, [and] quick to grasp any opportunity,"[33] he joined the army. Both works suggest that, for the self-reliant man, the military is a respectable opportunity to develop character and "attain an honourable position."[34] While Frank, *Pluck*'s hero, establishes his independence by joining an expedition to West Africa, the same qualities of heroism, adventurousness, and military acumen are acclaimed. Frank performs numerous valorous deeds, including courageously delivering a helpless girl from a mad dog. "Frank stood perfectly cool" as the animal charged, for which the boy is rewarded with praise: "That's bravely done, young master … and you have saved Missy's life, surely."[35] He furthermore employs his physical skill and stamina to rescue four of his fellow schoolmates pinned against an incoming tide, for which his worth is acknowledged:

> "I owe my life to you, Frank, I shall never forget it, old fellow."
>
> "It's been a close thing," Frank answered, "but you owe your life as much to your own coolness as to me, and above all Ruthven, don't let us forget that we both owe our lives to God."[36]

Humble *and* Christian, Frank goes on to prove his merit in the wilds of Africa, not only surviving captivity, but demonstrating his white male knowledge and military aptitude to the Ashanti and earning a necklace of gold nuggets from them for his resoluteness, courage, and honesty. This muscular Christian ideal, modelled to young boys for decades, dominated colonial adventure fiction, but came up against critique in Haggard's work.

Parodying Colonial Masculinity in *King Solomon's Mines*

These traditional examples of imperial manhood would seem to provide the discursive parameters within which masculinity is represented in *King Solomon's Mines*, and yet, a number of features of the romance signal that Haggard's treatment of colonial masculinity moves in a new direction. In addressing key components of imperial masculine identity (itself an ideological function of colonial fiction) – narrative authority, dominion over the landscape, and homosociality – Haggard's text makes a number of ironic inversions that mark out difference from these established norms in masculine imperial writing about Africa. As Linda Hutcheon has shown, parody is not always comic and can be both reverent and critical, as it often is in *King Solomon's Mines* when marking out "critical distance" between manhood as popularly conceived and manhood at the logical conclusion of those conceptions in the context of South Africa in 1881.[37] Hutcheon has also made clear that irony, in addition to demonstrating contrast between the parodied convention and the parodying text, "judges."[38] Crucially, in deploying irony to intervene and evaluate, *King Solomon's Mines* does not belong to the genre of parody, but rather employs parodic technique. In remaining firmly in the genre of adventure romance, Haggard's text directs its judgment back against its own genre, even as it celebrates it. The ironic inversions that *King Solomon's Mines* initiates are often enhanced through the adventure's frame narrative structure, which facilitates the reader's distance from and subsequent doubting of the text's internal narrator, Quatermain, who also destabilizes his own narrative authority. Furthermore, the narrative places unresolved limitations on white male efficacy that disrupt models of stoicism and fortitude. It is in this context that white male homoerotic desire emerges to parody homophilic imperatives of colonial adventure fiction to lay bare their ideological limitations and to present the white martial male body as potentially penetrable. Together, these narrative disruptions of imperial male constructions of power invite readers to confront dominant conceptions of British martial manhood as limited fantasies.

These parodied limitations of imperial manhood materialize in the narrative of Alan Quatermain, seasoned elephant-hunter, who writes the story from his hospital bed while recovering from an unrelated lion attack. As the text unfolds, a fictional editor asserts his presence, framing Quatermain's tale and at times contradicting the narrator's interpretations. In a nutshell, Quatermain agrees to guide Sir Henry Curtis and Captain Good into unfamiliar African territory in search of Curtis's estranged brother. Their clue is an ancient map (infamously resembling a woman's torso), with two mountains labelled "Sheba's breasts," and a deep yonic pit, marked as "mouth of treasure cave,"[39] that charts the path to King Solomon's treasure, of which Curtis's brother went in search. The three explorers procure an African guide, Umbopa, whose fine frame and stature endears him to the British men, and the band crosses the mountains into Kukuanaland, ruled by the evil usurper king, Twala. After rescuing the helpless damsel Foulata from execution, defeating Twala and his treacherous witch, Gagool, and restoring Umbopa (who, reinstating his birth name, Ignosi, turns out to be the rightful king) to the throne of Kukuanaland, the British men press on to the mines in search of treasure. The women (Foulata and Gagool) die; the men, barely escaping alive, subsequently stumble upon Curtis's brother in the desert, and then return, diamonds in pocket, to civilization. Reading these depictions of heroism as assertions of colonial gender hierarchies is certainly reasonable. For example, Curtis's reunion with his estranged brother can be read as a fantasy of "paterfamilial restoration."[40] On closer examination, however, the stability of this plot and its resolution is troubled by the subversive encoding of masculinity throughout the narrative.

The (de)consolidation of dominant heteronormative masculinity in this novel plays out on many fronts, including the ability to narrate reliably; the male body's subjugation to the active, feminized environment; and homoerotic tensions that lay bare the logical conclusion of imperial homophilic ideology. As I've discussed, the co-legitimizing pillars of imperialism in Africa – the impenetrable white male body, masculine authority, and colonial writing – are also mutually disruptive when one of these bastions fails to remain intact. This mutual destruction between narrative authority and male efficacy is precisely what happens in *King Solomon's Mines*. Crucially, the narrative itself is a product of the relationship between the authority to write and the maintenance of masculine prowess and credibility; Quatermain's authority comes from his righteous claim

> to tell the story in a plain, straightforward manner ... it only remains for me to offer my apologies for my blunt way of writing. I can only say in excuse for it that I am more accustomed to handle a rifle than a pen, and cannot make any pretence to the grand literary flights and flourishes which I see in novels ... I venture to hope that a true story, however strange it may be, does not require to be decked out in fine words.[41]

Asserting his masculinity through his facility with his "rifle," Quatermain positions himself as a man of practicality and survival – and cues the reader to recognize that he is the adult, tested, and fully realized version of imperial masculinity. Although it is his real-world experience of the "African wilds" that licenses his word, Quatermain positions his experience in contradistinction to any "grand literary flights and flourishes," stories "decked out in fine words," or even "handl[ing] ... a pen" at all. Indeed, the narrative requires the premise of a lion attack in order for Quatermain to pause in his adventuring to write. But though seeming to treat experience and writing as antithetical, Quatermain confirms their relationship by associating truth, or the legitimacy of experience, with plainness, even bluntness, as he bases his authority on what he claims is a simple and realistic style. This formal trait of plainness features in the aesthetic values of the fin-de-siècle adventure romance genre broadly, arguably a reaction to the domestic triple-decker novel associated with feminine writing, and "an antidote to the feminizing" realist text.[42]

Meanwhile, Haggard himself expressed dissatisfaction with the English market's penchant for "American" novels. He complained of the readership's taste for works whose "heroines are things of silk and cambric, who soliloquize and dissect their petty feelings ... Their men – well, they are emasculated specimens of an overwrought age, and with culture on their lips, and emptiness in their hearts, they dangle round the heroines till their three-volumed fate is accomplished."[43] Haggard's distaste highlights his association of a gendered writing style with national identity; for Haggard, the tastes of the British public were perhaps not manly enough. That the practice of writing itself was deeply connected to gendered authority is even more true with respect to the history of British representations of Africa: those who had been there, seen it, and survived it, simultaneously demonstrated hardiness, capability, and prowess; and their representations of that experience both embodied and perpetuated a two-pronged authority – that of the body, and that of the word.

Investing in the simple "truth" that Quatermain claims to reveal is not, however, Haggard's solution to the problem of a literary "atmosphere like that of the boudoir of a luxurious woman, faint and delicate, and suggesting the essence of white rose";[44] rather, his claim "to tell the story in a plain, straightforward manner" and his subsequent inability to do so underscores Quatermain's narrative inadequacy. Haggard celebrates "the swiftness, and strength, and directness of the great English writers of the past"[45] – but suggests, nevertheless, that these qualities belong to history. As Stephen Arata explains, fin-de-siècle "romance writers continually announce their inferiority to their predecessors. This is the best our shrunken age can produce, they say … [Robert Louis] Stevenson agrees. 'It is a small age, and I am of it.'"[46] Authority over "truth" was now dubious: after the British wars in South Africa, and particularly after the controversy surrounding the Battles of Kambula and Gingindlovu, questions about accuracy emerged, and the authority of front-line narratives was being challenged in the metropole.[47] Written in the aftermath of these discursive defects, *King Solomon's Mines* destabilizes the location of authority in masculine simplicity in at least three ways. First, the pointed discrepancies between the narration and the editorial comments question the validity of Quatermain's narrative. Second, Quatermain, despite claiming to deliver an undecorated narrative, can't help but romanticize the landscape as he himself falls into making those "grand literary flights and flourishes" – or, at least, bathetic attempts at them. Third, Quatermain's eroticization of male characters not only undercuts his claim of unfiltered representation but also parodies dominant codes of manliness in adventure fiction and imperial ideology more broadly. Same-sex desire both highlights the failure of internal regulation and imagines the male body as penetrable – both of which are problems for traditional masculine identity and its role in empire.

The editorial hand that frames Quatermain's rendition distances the critical reader from the narrator and encourages scrutiny of his reading practice, despite his promise to deliver "a true story." For instance, upon first spotting the yellow-haired Curtis, Quatermain describes him as looking like "an ancient Dane," and notes, "I found out afterwards that Sir Henry Curtis … was of Danish blood."[48] The editor, however, contradicts this interpretation: "Mr. Quatermain's ideas about ancient Danes seem to be rather confused; we have always understood that they were dark-haired people. Probably he was thinking of Saxons."[49] (Quatermain also later tells us that Good speaks Saxon.) This interest in ethnological traits resonates strikingly with the work of James Bonwick, Haggard's contemporary and prolific historian who wrote *Our Nationalities* (1880). Bonwick interprets the Danes as the "good" kind of conquerors, who confer benefits onto their colonies: "Their conquest and settlement of nearly every port in Ireland gave the country the blessing of foreign trade."[50] Bonwick also describes the Danes as noble: "One of the handsomest races in the world, ... they were the grandest race of conquerors, perhaps, known in history ... They knelt to no man."[51] Conversely, the Saxons, other conquerors, were "false, vain, capricious, selfish – the worst of all Teutons ... famous for cruelty."[52] These historical connotations of Dane and Saxon suggest that, while Quatermain interprets Curtis as the noble kind of conqueror, the editor implies that, despite what Quatermain thinks, Curtis and Good may in fact be associated with the wrong kind of conquest. Thus the text undermines both Curtis's heroic status and Quatermain's reliability.

This kind of inconsistency between the narrator and editor, however, is not singular; Quatermain makes frequent, obvious errors in reading and attribution. For example, Quatermain describes the battle between Ignosi's troops and Twala's by quoting a verse that he attributes to the *Ingoldsby Legends* (his favourite book, next to the *Old Testament*): "The stubborn spearsmen still made good / The dark impenetrable wood; / Each stepping where his comrade stood / The instant that he fell."[53] The passage, of course, is not from the popular *Ingoldsby Legends*, but from Sir Walter Scott's very well-read *Marmion*. It is unlikely that this is Haggard's misattribution; Scott's enduring popularity extended to the tastes of Haggard's editor, Andrew Lang.[54] Furthermore, this is an "error" that would have been legible to a reading public quite familiar with both texts. The significance of Quatermain's mistake lies in his inability to read tone; believing that his attempt to articulate the sublimity of battle drew on a whimsical, comic text that delighted its audiences with quaint tales and mirthful parody, Quatermain not only demonstrates ignorance but, in actually quoting *Marmion*, also raises the spectres of both English treachery in the colonial context and resistant native honour. This unsettles Quatermain's narrative as well as the honour of his nation.

Finally, another reason to doubt Quatermain is that, after promising discretion about Curtis's fraught history with his brother when Good suggests that "Mr. Quatermain will, I am sure, keep this history to himself" – Quatermain proudly announces, "I rather pride myself on my discretion"[55] – the narrator fully discloses the gist of the gossip to his entire readership. Whether Quatermain is completely unaware of his transgression or is speaking ironically here, he is, either way, not to be trusted.

In addition to these discrepancies, Quatermain is unable to stick to providing a "plain, straightforward" account when he is faced with narrating the African landscape. This deviation indicates Quatermain's self-contradiction while also illustrating his own oblivious subjection to the seductions of the space in which his manhood is ostensibly tested. In this process, his earlier attempt to root authority in the simplicity of "masculine" prose gets repeatedly undercut as he becomes increasingly fanciful, persuaded by this body. For instance, his highly subjective interpretation imposes libidinous desires onto the sunrise:

> The east began to blush like the cheek of a girl … the golden moon waxed wan, and her mountain ridges stood out clear against her sickly face like the bones of a dying man; then came spear upon spear of glorious light flashing far away across the boundless wilderness; piercing and firing the veils of mist, til the desert was draped in a tremulous golden glow, and it was day.[56]

Despite Quatermain's earlier intentions, fancy pervades this description. The language of penetration – the "spear[s] of glorious light … piercing … the veils" – is whimsical indeed, but, in its depiction of the landscape as both feminized and sexually active, it also prompts us to reconsider the relationship between these masculine British "agents" and what has been called the passive landscape in this adventure romance.[57] The passage above depicts various forms of activity in the feminized landscape. As the phallic spears of light shoot "far away across the boundless wilderness," the landscape is imbued with a specifically sexualized power. This power is penetrative and culminates "in a tremulous golden glow." This implication of sexual progression is strengthened as Quatermain's troop mounts the gigantic rock breasts and approaches the nipple-like formation to find "the flying rays of light from the setting sun … stained the snow blood red, and crowned the towering mass above us with a diadem of glory" (99). The breast-turned-phallus – "the towering mass above us" – dominates the comparatively insignificant men. They sit against the snow, which has been "stained … blood red" by "the flying rays of light" in the African sky. The landscape thus moves from a virginal to sexually active mode – and these men are subjected to this activity. Once they cross Sheba's breasts and descend into Kukuanaland, "The brook of which the banks were clothed with dense masses of gigantic species of maidenhair fern … babbled away merrily at our side, the soft air murmured through the leaves of the silver trees, doves cooed around … it was like Paradise. The magic of the place … seemed to charm us into silence."[58] As the troop moves down the map/body, closer to the "mouth of treasure cave," the landscape shifts from harsh desert to a lusher, softer, alluring realm. Undoubtedly feminized – we do not need to have examined

Buel's frontispiece discussed in the introduction to recognize the allusion to pubic hair in the "dense masses of gigantic species of maidenhair fern" – the space is also vocal, with the "brook … babbl[ing]," the "soft air murmer[ing]," and the "doves coo[ing]." This active voice of the landscape subjugates the men as it "charm[s them] into silence."[59] Not only does this vast body penetrate the men in this way, but the very depiction of this body intervenes in the traditional conceptualization of female sexuality as passive. Again, this depiction of the landscape as active and impactful is entirely in line with the shift in imperial perspective brought on by the events of Anglo-Zulu War: in accounts from the front that depicted the landscape and the Zulus – often conflated with it – as both phallic and vaginal, but in either case sexually charged. The landscape that concealed enemy warriors and resisted British epistemology is, here too, agent and vocal, and it subdues the protagonists who are themselves supposed to occupy that role.

In addition to romanticizing the landscape, Quatermain gets romantic in his descriptions of other men – namely, Curtis and Ignosi/Umbopa – as he eroticizes men's bodies throughout his narrative. In doing so, he not only disrupts heteronormative masculinity and troubles the biological imperative of white reproduction in the colonial context, but he also indicates that he may be leaving much of his narrative unspoken; readers are given hints rather than a plain account of his experience with other men. We first see both Quatermain's desire and its attendant aporia in his considerations of Sir Henry Curtis. Curtis has been read as a "masculine ideal," "the epitome of military masculinity," "the epitome of a British gentleman," and the "inheritor" in the system of patrimony.[60] While he may indeed be the culmination of various codes of masculine ideality, he is also – precisely because of this hyper-masculinity – the figure within whom the limitations of homophilic martial masculine culture are laid bare, specifically through the parodic mode of exaggeration. Curtis is the romance's focal point for homosocial desire and homoerotic spectacle. Quatermain, the mediating gazer, marks right away that Curtis "excited my curiosity"; he was "one of the biggest-chested and longest-armed men I ever saw … I never saw a finer man."[61] Hyperbolic in size and form, Curtis is both an object and fount of homosocial desire; he finds his match, his complementary other, in Umbopa, whom both he and Quatermain devour with their eyes:

> Sir Henry told me to ask him to stand up. Umbopa did so, at the same time slipping off the long military great-coat he wore, and revealing himself naked except for the moocha[62] round his centre and a necklace of lions'

claws. He certainly was a magnificent looking man; I never saw a finer native. Standing about six foot three high, he was broad in proportion, and very shapely. In that light, too, his skin looked scarcely more dark, except here and there where deep, black scars marked old assegai wounds.[63]

On the one hand, Umbopa meets Victorian ideals of martial manhood: he appears in a "military great-coat," wears a trophy ("lions' claws") attesting to his hunting capacity, and is tall, broad, and muscular. Moreover, survival is written on his body in the form of "old assegai wounds."

But if Umbopa aligns with dominant masculine identity, he is also subdued as he is marked as other. The narrative gaze sets him up to be inspected by the reader, but he is also forced to stand for Curtis' inspection. Quatermain's continued focus on the "magnificen[ce]," the "proportion," and the "shapel[iness]" of his body and the racialization of "his skin" compounds this objectification. Finally, this racialized martial body is sexualized: Umbopa "slip[s] off" his coat – this is the language of allure – while the "moocha" at once emphasizes his nakedness, his loins, and his otherness. Indeed, in the notable absence of women up to this point in the context of male-dominated colonial adventure, race becomes the primary marker of difference; Umbopa, as racial other – certainly sexualized here – begins to take the place of gendered other. And yet, his readily recognizable manliness marks this encounter as distinctly homoerotic. As Christopher Lane has argued, transracial homosexual drives had the potential to disrupt national unity with respect to the colonial project by troubling the complete subjugation of indigenous groups.[64] What interests me here, though, is the way in which masculine martial discipline meets its ideological limitation at the edge of the contact zone – the manliest sphere, where white women supposedly cannot survive. In this scene, male admiration for its ideal – the trained, muscular, disciplined body – tips over into steamy excess, into an erotic gaze. These homoerotic dynamics contradict extant mandates about the internal regulation of sexual energies;[65] thus the homophilic directives of imperial adventure are shown here to yield subversive homoerotic desire. This desire exudes from Quatermain's gaze upon the giant, muscular forms, and also arises between the two facing off, with Curtis's stare and body language positioning him as dominant:

Sir Henry walked up to him and looked into his proud, handsome face.

"They make a good pair, don't they?" said Good. "One as big as the other."

> "I like your looks, Mr. Umbopa, and I will take you as my servant," said Sir Henry in English.
>
> Umbopa evidently understood him, for he answered in Zulu, "It is well"; and then, with a glance at the white man's great stature and breadth, "we are men, thou and I."[66]

In this mirroring – or fantasy of idealized masculinity intersecting with desired otherness – in which Umbopa is "almost the same but not white,"[67] the men are positioned opposite one another, with an audience that acknowledges, "they make a good pair." The tableau is not unlike the staging of a marriage, especially considering the sexual tension already established alongside Curtis's approval of Umbopa's appearance and decision to "take" him as his "servant." Given the long history of gendered marital servitude in British culture, Curtis's statement is not out of place in a scene connoting betrothal. The ceremony is complete when Umbopa gives his agreement, "It is well," and then replaces the antiquated pronouncement of "man and wife" with "we are men, thou and I." This utterance, in this context, renders manhood contingent upon homosociality and homoerotic desire. What we see here evokes, but is different from, the kind of male society depicted in adventure fiction discussed above in which boys and men train together in colonial contexts but remain strictly disciplined and self-contained; idealization of male bodies is entailed but not openly indulged. This scene thus makes a parodic intervention in the codes of normative male behaviour: at the same time as it celebrates homophilia, it inverts the heteronormative ethos of fraternity by establishing direct sexual tension between these idealized male bodies. As Hutcheon has shown, parody can be both ridiculing *and* reverent or, as she puts it, can combine "respectful homage and ironically thumbed nose,"[68] and that is precisely what we see here. Certainly, homoerotics have long imbued hyper-masculine narratives, but here, simultaneously, they are *indulged* to the point where Haggard invokes sexual tension through the tableau and script of a marriage scene. Not only do these stressed homoerotics destabilize masculine norms, but they also mean that the possibility of the penetration of the white martial male body – Curtis – has to be confronted.

White homosexuality is thus activated through the sexualization of male African bodies. The introduction of Curtis to Umbopa constitutes a significant initiation of this energy, but is not where it ends; in fact, it ends with Curtis's confrontation with Twala – Umbopa turns out to be a conduit for homoerotic satisfaction, but is displaced by Curtis himself. Importantly though, the narrative's treatment of Umbopa lays the foundation for these dynamics. For instance, Umbopa's continued eroticization intersects importantly with his militancy so as to establish the phallic tension between the forces of the usurper king and the resistance. We see this explicitly when Umbopa reveals his phallic tattoo, which is also a sign of dominion:

> He slipped off the "moocha" or girdle around his middle, and stood naked before us ... He pointed to the mark of a great snake tattooed in blue round his middle, its tail disappearing in its open mouth just above where the thighs are set into the body.
>
> Infadoos looked, his eyes starting nearly out of his head, and then fell upon his knees.[69]

Increasingly eroticizing Umbopa, who again "slipped off" what is this time his last remaining article of clothing, the narrative suggests that this "snake" hidden under his moocha legitimates Umbopa's rule for male onlookers; men here are fixated with the sign of physical and symbolic maleness itself. Infadoos's kneeling in front of Umbopa is a gesture of submission to his king, but it is also strongly sexualized. These dynamics of ocular desire transcend the text as readers become drawn into this voyeurism, likewise becoming implicated in this fixation with sexualized prowess. Indeed, the persistent popularity of *King Solomon's Mines* speaks to an enduring cultural inclination towards this scene of desire. Thus the romance's narrative both articulates the disruptive power of homophilic reverence and is itself disruptive: "all the big and little boys who read it" become implicated in this erotic dynamic, and their own adherence to regulated, normative masculinity faces dislodging.[70]

As the sexualization of Umpoba demonstrates, African bodies are depicted as objects of imperial desire, but their sexualization displaces a white, racially homogeneous homosexuality. So again, in the absence of a gendered other in a sexual dynamic, racial others serve to provide erotic difference. In this dynamic, white bodies are also envisioned as objects of desire for African others. For instance, when Good is forced to carry on through half the novel without his trousers, to the continual delight of Kukuana individuals who admire "his beautiful white legs,"[71] he embodies one fantasy of the white male desired by his others. But the more obvious object of desire, Sir Henry Curtis, who comes to be "looked on throughout Kukuanaland as a supernatural being" – or, perhaps, the "demigod" that Haggard derided in *Cetywayo* – enters into a more complex sexual relationship with another racialized other, the usurper king.[72] As Curtis and Twala prepare for a duel to the death, they face each other while "the setting sun caught their stalwart frames and clothed them both in fire. They were a well-matched pair."[73] This scene, with both opponents bathed in what the narrative has established as the light of a libidinous African sky, recalls the earlier "nuptial" scene between Curtis and Umbopa, and its attendant sexual tension. Here, however, the dynamic progresses to a post-matrimonial climax as the two warriors engage: "The excitement grew intense; the regiment which was watching the encounter forgot its discipline, and, drawing near, shouted and groaned at every stroke."[74] The homosocial gaze intensifies as crowds of other men sacrifice order to satisfy their ocular desires and release tension. Quatermain fixates on Curtis, "his great arms twined around Twala's middle. To and fro they swung, hugging each other like bears, straining with all their mighty muscles for dear life and dearer honour. With a supreme effort Twala swung the Englishman clean off his feet, and down they came together, rolling over and over on the lime paving."[75] The careful overlay of sexual language in this passage allows for both an intense sexualization of the fight and a protective resistance to precisely this eroticization; discursively, the text has it both ways. When Curtis beheads the usurper king – that is, finishes him off – the corpse crashes to the ground, and, in his final exhaustion, "Sir Henry, overpowered by faintness and loss of blood, fell heavily across it."[76] Curtis, though victorious, is physically spent, having lost considerable bodily fluids in a sexualized struggle; he collapses, flaccid, over the body of his counterpart. In light of the available erotics established earlier in the fight scene, this climax is doubly coded. The idealized male form, then, paradoxically proves its strength by opening itself to the possibility of penetration, and in doing so looses firmness, rigidity, and regulation. The fantasy of racially dominant white martial masculinity is thus self-limiting. Also limited, however, is the fantasy of a stable, reliable, "plain" history of colonial conquest: because homosexuality cannot be openly narrated in popular Victorian narratives, some omissions are necessary – some things must be left unsaid; some loves dare not be named. In *King Solomon's Mines*, the homoerotic experience resists imperial narrativization and must defy the imperial imperative to catalogue, report, and fully know the contact zone and its history.

It may be a fine line between Haggard's conformity to the male erotics of the adventure genre and his ironic inversion of them, but his particularly sexualized depictions of the male form function as transgressive excess when considered alongside other parodies of dominant conceptions of manhood in the text. While racially homogeneous homosexuality may not be available to *King Solomon's Mines'* protagonists, other forms of affect are explored in order to disrupt normative, stoic masculinity. For instance, the three white men actually hold hands as they creep through the darkness of the eclipse, and veritably cuddle each other when confronted by eternal burial when trapped in the mines: "Laying my head against Sir Henry's broad shoulder, I burst into tears; and I think I heard Good gulping away on the other side ... Had we been two frightened children, and he our nurse, he could not have treated us more tenderly."[77] Notably, it is in this context of terrifying engulfment by the feminized landscape that these men are most in need of homosocial comforting. Again, the breaking of the stiff upper lip ruptures the imperial narrative that insists on a particular kind of homosocial masculinity; this dependency – infantilizing Quatermain and Good, feminizing Curtis – pushes beyond the boundaries of acceptable homophilia. Similarly, the chivalric ideal also comes under critique through Foulata's plea to Captain Good for protection. While Mawuena Kossi Logan reads this scene as earnest in its treatment of white gallantry,[78] I suggest that, in its overwrought focus on Good's paternalism, Foulata's supplication parodies the genre's formulaic preference for damsel rescue as a foundation of manhood. The key context here is that Good is notoriously receptive to female advances, and Quatermain is deeply suspicious of them. Foulata's plea to Good to save her from the phallic spearhead of Scragga, the king's son, sets up what is also a formulaic confrontation between the forces of "civilization" and "barbarity." When a melodramatic wail ("Oh, cruel; and I so young! What have I done that I should never again see the sun rise out of the night, or the stars ... Woe is me ... Oh, cruel, cruel!") receives no response from her captors, she appeals to Good, who is "of a susceptible nature" when it comes to women:

> With all a woman's quickness, the doomed girl interpreted what was passing in his mind, and with a sudden movement flung herself before him, and clasped his "beautiful white legs" with her hands.
>
> "Oh, white father from the stars, throw over me the mantle of thy protection; let me creep into the shadow of thy strength, that I may be saved."[79]

Invoking silly moments from earlier in the novel – namely Good's loss of his trousers and the absurd story that the Britons offer of coming from outer space, again assuming the dubious part of "demigod[s]" – the narrative does not allow Foulata's appeal to white strength to be read with earnestness. Instead it suggests that she leverages what is ultimately Good's weakness. In so doing, Quatermain's narrative distances the reader from the potential pathos of Foulata's misfortune and emphasizes Good's "susceptab[ility]" to Foulata's flattering depiction of the "strength" of his paternal "mantle of protection."

We have already seen how the masculine protection of feminine vulnerability has been deployed in adventure fiction to establish manhood – take Edgar's chivalrous rescue of the ladies from the tramps, Jack's determined liberation of Aveatea from indigenous oppression, or Frank's daring rescue of Missy from the mad dog, for example. But here, masculine identity's need for a damsel to protect is laid bare as Good, the rescuer, becomes the focus of the narrative's scrutiny. Quatermain, "being elderly and wise"[80] – deploying irony here to make fun of himself even as he undermines Good – uses his narrative position to critique Good's reading practice. In doing so, he undercuts Good's masculine identity of protective strength – an identity that Haggard himself saw destabilized after the retrocession of the Transvaal to the Boers, which, again, for Haggard, constituted "treachery" to both natives and settlers who had claim to "England's protection."[81] In Haggard's assessment, Britain had failed to uphold the identity of chivalrous protector. Indeed, even though Good steps in to save Foulata here – and his intervention is not of the heroic sort a reader might expect ("'All right, my hearty, I'll look after you,' sang out Good, in nervous Saxon. 'Come on, get up, there's a good girl'")[82] – he later fails to protect her from Gagool's knife. The target of parody here, then, is Good's attachment to an ideal – an ideal that is ultimately shown to be in practice quite limited.

This very refusal of *King Solomon's Mines'* narrative to conform to the aesthetic of masculine straightforwardness so typical of the boys' adventure fiction genre is what enables the romance to appropriate and undercut this formal trend. Quatermain's inability to deliver the story either truly or frankly, numerous fissures in the narrator's claims, and his repeated romanticization and eroticization directly undermine masculine imperial authority precisely because such authority itself hinges on the axes of the capable manly body and credible male writing. Because imperialism was so dependent on narratives about the nature of manhood, this problem of writing destabilizes justifications of imperialism. Without ignoring *King Solomon's Mines'* participation in discourses of racism and misogyny, we can acknowledge its historically specific critique of extant practices of imperial masculinity, and that it is a much more complex text than criticism has acknowledged. Furthermore, the narrative's ironic distance from the text presented potentially groups the work with modernist narratives emerging in the early twentieth century;[83] moreover, understanding Haggard's work through such a modernist framework offers a reconsideration of how to situate modernism itself.

Ultimately, though, within the context of the British imperial project in Africa, we need to reconsider more carefully, and with more precision, the basis, targets, and mechanisms of colonial anxieties in order to work out how they are actually operating. Haggard, in identifying the inadequacy of one of the ideological armatures of imperial discourse, generates a critique that implies the necessity for new imperial norms and more effective governmental tactics. In fact, it is in the very production of this critique that a new model of imperial masculinity materializes – one that is not simply flawed, but is also highly aware of its own imperfections and internal contradictions, one that begins to draw authority from this critical distance it creates through parody. Crucially, this generative potential arises in the gap between the masculine imperial identity being parodied and Haggard's version – unreliable, vulnerable, penetrable, transgressive – for, as Hutcheon puts it, parody inscribes both "continuity and change," which enables this "bitextual synthesis" to create "something new."[84] Thus, parody itself enables the emergence of a new imperial identity that aims to recognize its faults, permit omissions, and confront its own imperfections – and thereby contain them. In other words, an imperial narrative that encompassed its own limitations and shortcomings made a still greater claim to authority through its self-reflexivity, its omniscience, and its mode of permitting its own transgressions and failures through the solicitation of laughter. To ignore this is to fail to track how imperial fantasy performs its own symptomatic diagnosis and repair. Yet, this mode of imperial stabilization could not have it both ways; it could not enable such omissions and transgressions without losing its delicate rhetorical maintenance of the moral high ground. Haggard takes up this problem in *She*, which produces an ongoing critique of imperial culture that confronts the moral limitations of imperial logic.

IV. *She*'s Reflection: Confronting Moral Weakness

Much Haggardian criticism is aware that his texts are discursively volatile,[85] but this volatility tends to be downplayed by assertions regarding the conservative politics of the author or text. As with *King Solomon's Mines*, critical discussions of *She* tend to argue that the adventure romance works to rejuvenate or recuperate British masculinity, raising and then assuaging anxieties about imperial stability. In light, however, of the romance's complex destabilization of its own narrative through its heroes' fundamental limitations, its interrogation of imperial governance, and its critique of the efficacy of male writing, I suggest that the widely recognized sense of loss pervading this adventure romance articulates the degeneration of traditional chivalric identity, and that the inadequacy of these heroic ideals is in fact the target of Haggard's critique. In other words, *She* underscores the irredeemable flaws in contemporary conceptions of masculinity as confident, heroic, powerful, and so on, as central characters resonate with but do not conform to traditional exemplarity. One of many expressions of this divergence in *She*, as in *King Solomon's Mines*, is homosociality and homoerotic tensions between male characters – which reveal the ideological limitations of homophilic aspects of idealized masculine practice, figure the fortified male body as penetrable, and necessitate narrative omissions. The romance also, however, in figuring "She" as a quintessential imperial man, laces ostensibly heteronormative gender performance with homosexual desire – in turn, disrupting heteronormative desire itself. Another divergence from traditional ideals manifests in the heroes' passivity and vulnerability, accentuated through the agent, threatening, consuming landscape. Yet perhaps the romance's greatest disruption of British identity is its destruction of its narrator as the text's moral centre; Holly's rationalizing, his failure to remain impermeable to the temptations of empire, undercuts his narrative. While *She* is playful, ridiculous, and ultimately parodic, it nevertheless uses this failure to underscore the moral limitations of masculine imperial conquest that challenge dominant British identity.

The text's interest in narrating empire is readily apparent at the level of both narrative structure and plot. The rather wacky story is introduced by an anonymous editor who supposedly received the manuscript of the adventure from its narrator, Horace Holly. On a cold night at Cambridge University, Holly, a distinguished scholar, hears a pounding at his chambers and admits his friend, Vincey, who, at death's door, relates to him the bizarre story of his family ancestry. Over two thousand years previously, Vincey's Grecian ancestor, Kallikrates, and his beloved princess, Amenartas, encountered a terrible white queen in Africa, who fell in love with Kallikrates but killed him in a fit of jealous rage. Amenartas escaped to bear Kallikrates's child and foster the Vincey line. Holly, now nominated guardian of Vincey's young son, Leo, is left with Vincey's letter for the boy, to be opened on his twenty-fifth birthday. When this date arrives, Leo reads that the aforementioned terrible white queen is probably still alive, and he calls for vengeance. Consequently, Leo, Holly, and Job (Leo's unlikely nurse) head to Africa, where they and their hired servant, Mahomed, get shipwrecked by a squall. Finding themselves in the hands of the Amahagger, the cannibalistic subjects of the undead despot, Ayesha, or, She-who-must-be-obeyed, they are conveyed to her lair. In the process, Leo inadvertently marries a local, Ustane, and suffers a deep spear wound in a deadly fight with the Amahagger (who also kill Mahomed for dinner). Meanwhile, Ayesha recognizes in Leo the reincarnation of her beloved Kallikrates. Accordingly, she kills off Ustane, seduces Leo (both he and Holly are entirely defenceless against She's beauty and fall hopelessly in love with her), and commences plans to take over the world, starting with Britain. Fortunately for the metropole, when Ayesha attempts to guide Leo to everlasting life by first passing through a magical pillar of fire herself, her immortality is reversed, and she withers and dies. Job expires of shock, but Leo and Holly escape to Britain, and Holly sends his narration of the strange tale to the anonymous editor, who then publishes it, with appropriate footnotes.

This narrative frame thus underpins the romance's critique of three central facets of masculinity: heroic identity, imperialist venture, and narrative authority. The framing positions Leo as feminized in the neoclassical overtones of his description and renders him a predominantly useless character – a shadow of the kind of imperial hero typically revered in the adventure genre – and not a normative ideal, as he is often read.[86] Through Leo, dominant ideals of Victorian masculinity are parodied and rendered unattainable. Similarly, the text critiques the ideology of imperialism itself, and it does this through the representations of Ayesha. Though many critics have interpreted Ayesha as a feminine threat, others suggest that she is more predominantly a figure of empire. I argue that not only is her imperial status highly gendered while her embodiment of unbridled imperial masculinity represents a monstrous colonialism, but also that this gender inversion parallels other slippages in masculine identity positioning wherein feminized and racialized threats (in the forms of engulfing landscapes and desiring women) render the imperial men profoundly vulnerable as they become passive objects of desire in the colonial setting. Together, these representations suggest that imperial masculine identity is slippery and mutable, and subject to destabilization through different forms of engulfment and penetration. In turn, and most crucially, the status of Ayesha's immoral despotism, because of Holly's infatuation with her, serves to highlight his fallibility as narrator of empire. The frame narrative emphasizes that Holly's role departs from the tradition in triple-decker British literature of the narrative position of moral centre. He is instead a figure who, the editorial commentary suggests, makes deeply unreliable assertions and whose authority is profoundly undercut, which calls into question the historical legitimacy of the kind of travel/adventure narratives that *She* – "a history of adventure" – purports to be. Understanding Haggard's text as subversive of imperial narratives encourages scholarship to reconsider its approach to cultural roles, motivations, and subtexts of adventure fiction from this period; reading *She* as a critique of imperial identity and imperial authority sheds new light on complicated discourses among fin-de-siècle masculine coteries, instantiates the romance's complex engagement with empire, and, like *King Solomon's Mines*, exhibits early signs of an ironic narrative that would be more fully explored by modernism.

One angle of *She*'s critique of imperial identity manifests in its treatment of Leo, ostensibly the normative ideal. Our reading of Leo is informed by the fictional editor, who, after initially marking the man as a "glorified specimen of humanity,"[87] forms a very different opinion of him after reading Holly's manuscript of the adventure: "there appears to be nothing in the character of Leo Vincey which in the opinion of most people would have been likely to attract an intellect so powerful as that of Ayesha. He is not even, at any rate to my view, particularly interesting."[88] Meanwhile, retaining the romantic formula, the editor surmises that perhaps "Ayesha, seeing further than we can see, perceived the germ and smouldering spark of greatness that lay hid within her lover's soul ... [which,] watered by her wisdom, would bloom like a flower and flash out like a star, filling the world with fragrance and with light."[89] Floral imagery, however, is atypical for the figuration of a late nineteenth-century muscular hero (even if he is pretty), and feminizes this supposedly manly man. From here, the adventure uses Leo to explore the dubious status of imperial masculinity. If Haggard first invokes recognition of an ostensible imperial hero in the broad-chested blonde, he then highlights the character's irredeemable vacuousness. Leo's heroic ideality seems to be manifested in his imperial crusade, his dedication to resolving the mystery of his ancestry, and his physical desirability – but this desirability comes to overshadow any real substance in him. Indeed, women indiscriminately "insist on falling in love with him," this "statue of Apollo come to life," this "handsomest man in the University."[90] Continuing with the editor's initial admiration, Holly repeatedly signals Leo's physical prowess throughout the novel, frequently obsessing over his size and strength. Leo thus becomes an object of male fascination whose ongoing association with historical grandeur further romanticizes him. Fetishized in these ways, Leo becomes an abstraction – not a manifestation of ideals, but rather a sign of their very ideality.

If Leo signals the superficiality of normative ideals, they are nevertheless the ideals that *men* in the romance desire – consequently, the male bodies in this homoerotic dynamic are subject to fantasies of penetration. For one thing, the text's homosocial saturation is farcically conspicuous. From the overt fetishization of masculine grace, to the insistent primacy of Leo's patrilineal history (both his nameless dead mother and his female ancestor Amenartas play only brief biological roles), to the male-dominated university, an exclusively male society is actively, anxiously, maintained.[91] Holly's exaggerated jealousy over any heterogendered love concerning Leo is emphasized in his assertion, "I would have no woman to lord it over me about the child, and steal his affections from me ... I set to work to hunt up a suitable male attendant."[92] As Job becomes the atypical nurse in accordance with Holly's unusual whim, the narrative thus underscores an obsession with male relations that is indulged at the expense of women. But even when women do enter the equation (mostly to entrench further Leo's desirability and displace the desiring homosocial gaze onto women), Leo remains a passive object of desire as women fall in love with him. In all of these love plots, conventionally gendered power dynamics are reversed. Leo's ongoing passivity – being the slate on which Holly's adoration is inscribed, being saved from drowning by Holly's iron grip, getting rescued by Ustane, being stabbed by the Amahagger, getting carried across the African interior, being rescued from the brink of death by She, being ultimately compelled to embrace her – is one of his most prominent features. Thus, his character inverts the role of the traditional hero: rather than recuperating martial masculinity, Haggard uses the figure of Leo to undermine notions of heroism, to feminize and render passive and potentially penetrable the heretofore celebrated figure of imperialism. Feminized, objectified, and weakened, Leo is thus not the novel's figure of virile imperial masculinity; rather, imperial masculinity in its most aggressive form is embodied in She.

Ayesha has been interpreted variously as "a focus of desires and anxieties related to women's power": "the ultimate virginal site for exploration and discovery"; "an all-powerful mother"; "an odd blend of [angel and monster] – an angelically chaste woman with monstrous powers, a monstrously passionate woman with angelic charms"; "the quintessential New Woman"; "the ultimate in feminine 'evil'"; and as representing "the murderous female heart of Africa."[93] Thus, She is typically interpreted as antithetical to the patriarchal, masculine society to which Holly and Leo belong.[94] While other scholarship acknowledges that Ayesha is marked by empire,[95] I argue further that She's embodiment of imperial masculinity undermines the credibility of imperial narratives by bringing into focus the problematic mechanisms of imperial control – and the moral limits of imperial ideology that are more fully fleshed out through Ayesha's corrupting influence on Holly and his narrative. She's alignment with empire and her desire-driven governance crucially foreground Holly's parallel subjugation to his own lusts in the context of narrating imperial adventure. It is this fundamental limitation in Holly's narrative that forces considerable doubts about the legitimacy of imperial narratives of Africa.

Ayesha's connection to British imperialism is underscored by two related forms of desire, both of which also constitute a danger to British identity: unbridled desire and despotic governance. Ayesha's association with passion is twofold: She at once is the object of desire, to which male characters become subjected as they lose restraint and self-control, and is herself subject to desire. In turn, Ayesha's enslavement to desire is precisely what renders her unfit for government: her obsession with Kallikrates underpins her despotic methods of government. Importantly, there are key parallels between Ayesha's rule and British colonialism that force recognition of the relationship between imperial desire and brutal conquest, as I explore below. She embodies, in other words, British masculine power at its worst.[96]

Ayesha's signification as the logical conclusion of idealized imperial strength becomes clearer when read through Derrida's notion of *différance*. In the chain of signification, the trace of différance "relates no less to what is called the future than to what is called the past, and it constitutes what is called the present by this very relation to what it is not, to what it absolutely is not."[97] Thus, in terms of concepts or ideas, the determination of différance "no more allows the opposition between activity and passivity than that between cause and effect, or indetermination and determination"[98] – or the poles of extreme femininity and hyper-masculinity. Haggard's treatment of Ayesha exemplifies this dissolution of polarity: "all the conceptual oppositions that furrow Freudian thought relate each concept to the other like movements of a detour, within the economy of difference. The one is only the other deferred, the one differing from the other."[99] Différance suggests that the two identities of self and ostensible other are fundamentally linked: in the same way that Ayesha's eternal life bears traces of death and ghostliness, her extreme femininity, her "greater loveliness" than an "angel out of heaven,"[100] is not an autonomous concept but rather bears the trace of hyper-masculinity. Meanwhile, masculinity in the novel is simultaneously outlined by Ayesha's qualities – these supposedly polar depictions of femininity and masculinity are integrally linked. But if Ayesha's hyper-femininity and masculine imperial authority are mutually constitutive and thus mutually destabilizing, other polarized identity positions underpinning gender norms in this text are likewise blurred: other and self, passivity and activity, and sexed binaries of desire. Through this range of destabilizations, dominant norms of masculinity are challenged.

A pertinent example of such dissolution of polarized identities is the strong relationship between British identity and British representations of Africa. As Patrick Brantlinger argues, Africa typically functioned in the nineteenth century as a kind of darkened mirror of British imperialism itself. The representation of the African other was a kind of projection of undesirable, repressed qualities of white British subjectivity onto an external form. In this sense, representations of Africa in popular fiction frequently elicited a sense of uncanniness among readers. Conrad recognized this in his rendition of Kurtz as the embodiment of colonial exploitation and the logical conclusion – madness – of acknowledging the ethics and mechanics of the imperial project. Brantlinger suggests that when the Victorians "penetrated the heart of darkness, only to discover lust and depravity, cannibalism and devil worship, they always also discovered, as the central figure in the shadows, a Stanley, a Charles Stokes, a Kurtz – an astonished white face staring back."[101] Thus, if conceptions of Africa served as reflections of both heroism and "guilt and regression,"[102] then Ayesha, a white presence and gendered other dwelling in the heart of an African mountain, becomes part of this double world that is used to confront both the damning desire associated with imperial conquest and the consequences of imperial narratives. Ayesha, then, while at once reflecting a range of concerns within British society, also represents the discourse not just of imperialism, but specifically of traditional imperialist masculinity: She points to anxieties surrounding male behaviours, institutions, and identities through the distanced position of gendered other as concerns about masculine efficacy, eternality, and vulnerability become visible through male characters' boundless desire for her – or, their desire for the various forms of power that she embodies. Considering the palpability of the homoerotic overtones in *She* that threaten to tip the work into a racy tale of male love that nevertheless maintains a popular heteronormative appeal through the presence of the femme fatale, it is no wonder that Ayesha, the figure of anxiety about the nature of masculinity, is cast as a woman.[103]

The same framework of identity slippage that works to figure Ayesha as an embodiment of rampant imperial desire underpins the romance's troubling of the landscape's traditional role as passive, and as criticism typically understands it in Haggard's work. Though it nevertheless functions dominantly in *She*, as in *King Solomon's Mines*, as racial other, the landscape in this text slides into humanized activity in order to articulate the limitations of imperial masculine prowess in the colonial context. Just as Ayesha slips into an identity position seemingly polar to her ostensible performance of hyper-femininity, the African landscape in *She* threatens to engulf and penetrate British men, who, in the process, become passive and objectified. For instance, as the white adventurers approach the great rock marking the journey into She's domain, Holly observes that it "was shaped like a negro's head and face, whereon was stamped a most fiendish and terrifying expression ... There were the thick lips, the fat cheeks, and the squat nose standing out with startling clearness against the flaming background."[104] As we saw in imperial depictions of Zulu tactics during the Anglo-Zulu War, once again the African body is conflated with the African landscape as a kind of generalized threat. This construction of racial alterity expresses the uncanny – the landscape as radical other takes on a dehumanized yet recognizable form – and that which is rendered racially, geographically, and radically other powerfully impacts the subject, Holly. This imposing geological structure is "terrifying" and "startling"; Holly reads it as "an emblem of warning and defiance."[105] In this way, the traditionally passive and feminized landscape is rendered agent and threatening, stamping its impression upon the white men.

This threat to white male bodies intensifies as the environment takes on an increasingly active, feminized persona. As the troop approaches the east coast of Africa by sea, a squall that is figured as a vagina dentata threatens to engulf the adventurers. The storm is rendered mouth-like through its "awful shriekings," its "duller, deeper roar," and "the voice of the breakers."[106] Holly's description of the "torn bosom of the ocean" marks the sea as female, while "a little space of open-mouthed blackness" threatens consumption, as do the breakers, "smiting and gnashing together like the gleaming teeth of hell";[107] only by physically clinging together in desperate homosocial fortitude do the men survive being swallowed up by the sea. Similarly, the description of the treacherous chasm through which the party enters towards the Pillar of Life strongly resembles a vulva,[108] from which Holly and Leo are able to emerge only by clasping together to avoid falling into a giant yonic gulf.[109] Thus, as in the archive of British accounts from the war in Zululand, in adventure romance, too, we see the fantasy of male stiffening working hard to counter the threat of feminine engulfment that renders the male body so vulnerable, and challenges the tenets of heroic martial manhood.

But if one danger is that the integrity of men's bodily boundaries will be compromised by being consumed (and ultimately penetrated), the other danger is that their bodies, traditionally constructed as active and vigorous, will become passive and powerless. This threat, again appearing in the form of being physically overwhelmed, continues as Holly contemplates the sublimity of the African landscape: "To the right and left were wide stretches of lonely, death-breeding swamp, unbroken and unrelieved so far as the eye could reach ... To the West loomed the huge red ball of the sinking sun, now vanishing down the vapoury horizon, and filling the great heaven ... with flashes of flying gold and the lurid stain of blood."[110] The language of imposing vastness (the "wide stretches ... unbroken and unrelieved," the "loom[ing] sun," the "great heaven") and danger ("the death-breeding swamp," the "lurid stain of blood") asserts anti-conquest rhetoric,[111] but while such positioning garners readerly sympathy for the adventurers, it also signals the recognition of their comparative insignificance and their subjection to the landscape. Bodies risk being not only smothered by the imposing environment, but penetrated by it, as the "stain of blood" hints at the dissolution of bodily borders. Thus the violence underlying "that measureless desolation,"[112] though serving a dominant and worn-out trope about Africa's dangerous unfathomability, nevertheless articulates the precarious position of the British: the landscape, as feminized, racialized, radical other, renders the adventurers fatally passive in relation to its capacity to overwhelm and consume.[113] Crucially, this radical other's activity works to reposition subject and object: agency is subtly but powerfully transformed. Through this slippage, the British subjects become men to whom things happen – rather than saving themselves, external factors come to their rescue – subjects become objects, objects become subjects, and this in turn starts to blur the positions of self and other. In *She,* because each pole is no longer defined by agency or passivity as antithetical, the locations of subject and object begin to overlap. This is precisely what happens with respect to Ayesha's supposed position of colonial femininity and its relationship to imperial masculinity: She, while threatening imperial masculine identity, also embodies it.

While Africa becomes a darkened mirror of Britain, and the active landscape serves both to unman and dehumanize the British, women in the romance take on a different subject position by acting as reflections of repressed male anxieties about competency, stability, and heteronormativity. Consequently, not only do men's anxieties become visible, but, at times, women become agent while men become objectified. In his letter to his son, Vincey Sr's potential credulity, a characteristic traditionally associated with childhood, not manhood, is cast onto a female subject: "you will choose to investigate what, if it is true, must be the greatest mystery in the world, or to put it by as an idle fable, originating in the first place in a woman's disordered brain. I do not believe it is a fable."[114] Vincey thus asserts his belief in Amenartas's tale, but, rather than risking gullibility, sets the responsibility for fallaciousness on his ancestress's shoulders. Women in the text continue to reflect male anxieties about powerlessness; the Amahagger woman's sexual forwardness in kissing Job (to his terror) parallels Ustane's desire for Leo and foreshadows Ayesha's fixation on "our hero." English men thus become the objects of scrutiny or desire: the Amahagger women "examined us with curiosity, but without excitement. Leo's tall, athletic form and clear-cut Grecian face, however, evidently excited their attention, and when he politely lifted his hat to them, and showed his curling yellow hair, there was a murmur of admiration. Nor did it stop there."[115] In this way, Holly projects his own fascination with Leo's idealized form onto the Amahagger women; their interest stands in for his own desire. Thus, Holly's narration complicates heterosexual desire by lacing it with homoerotic tenor; heteronormative gender performance and sexuality – both foundational pillars of imperial conquest – are interrupted by deviations from masculine norms.

If, however, this projection enables all sorts of homosocial manoeuvres, from the preservation of masculine dignity to the erotic gaze, then the novel also demonstrates, by virtue of its resilient silliness, its own awareness of the ridiculousness of the prominent male insistence on pride and its attendant refusal to take women seriously. For instance, Holly, for the very reason of his self-proclaimed misogyny, becomes an object of ridicule. As he approaches She-who-must-be-obeyed with inward trepidation, he refuses the enforced custom of slithering in subservience and instead "marched in boldly after Billali,"[116] his native guide, who himself obeys She's mandate. But the result is not quite what Holly intended: "it was more or less of a failure ... It is so absurd to advance into the presence of savage royalty after the fashion of an Irishman driving a pig to market, for that is what we looked like, and the idea nearly made me burst out laughing then and there."[117] Though reasserting a racialized hierarchy through this comparison, Haggard also satirizes British masculine dignity. Similarly, in an earlier conversation between these two characters, when Billali explains to Holly, "In this country the women do what they please. We worship them, and give them their way, because without them, the world could not go on; they are the source of life," Holly replies, "'Ah,' ... the matter never having struck me quite in that light before."[118] A joke is made at Holly's expense, as he, in consciously refusing to respect women, misses this obvious biological principle. Because of this running pattern of Holly's biases inviting mockery, his projection of masculine anxieties onto female figures is likewise rendered ridiculous. Reading Ayesha's character alongside this critical tone illuminates that the imperial masculine qualities associated with her are problematic and subject to critique. Under Ayesha's despotism, rule by force is represented as monstrous; as *She* explores the use of absolute power as extended by British imperial practice though the distanced, othered figure of She, who is neither eternal nor invulnerable, it critiques the moral relativism here attending imperial rule.

In many ways, Ayesha herself reflects the dominant image of British imperialist masculine extremes back to the readership: she rules with an iron fist and her word is law; she is an enterprising scientist whose proficiency surpasses what is known in the rest of the world; and she takes what she wants without question. Ayesha does not embody the characteristics of passivity, gentleness, comfort, and patience that have been traditionally associated with women. Rather, her rulership is forceful, impulsive, and unforgiving: "sometimes when [the Amahagger] vex me I could blast them for very sport, and to see the rest turn white."[119] This invocation of "sport" gestures back to Leo's and Holly's earlier enthusiasm for shooting, and further orients Ayesha as masculine. Ayesha also occupies the world's foremost position of technological prowess. She sustains her great age because she has "solved one of the great secrets of the world."[120] She is able to see beyond the immediate through her "font-like vessel" not by "magic," as Holly cries out (here occupying the traditional position of colonial subject bewildered by superior technology), but via her science.[121] The same is true of her abilities to "blast" and to heal. She has even bred a race of servants, mute and deaf, to attend to her needs: "it hath taken many centuries, and much trouble; but at last I succeeded. Once I succeeded before, but the race was too ugly, so I did away with it."[122] If Ayesha, as Holly suggests, is a terrifying creature, then her breeding technology and casual genocide is monstrous. Since breeding technology – one of the most celebrated achievements of English science – is associated with the draconian Ayesha, it is also here associated with immorality.[123] Finally, if Ayesha succumbs to her own whims with respect to governing and scientific pursuit, she also, in true despot fashion, allows her desires to drive her decisions, including murdering Ustane, her rival. Thus, She, in her knowledge, power, and desire, embodies British imperial masculinity: "her proud, ambitious spirit ... would, I had little doubt, assume absolute rule over the British dominions, and probably over the whole earth, and though I was sure that she would speedily make ours the most glorious and prosperous empire that the world has ever seen, it would be at the cost of a terrible sacrifice of life."[124] It is the confrontation with this truth, and the pairing of glory and prosperity with killing, that renders Holly at once so terrified yet desirous of She, and that positions the British Empire and its agents as despotic. Indeed, his own narrative collapses under his desire for her and what she represents.

While Ayesha is an unrestrainedly desiring figure, she also raises the spectre of uncontrollable desire in men; indeed, Holly's inability to put reason before passion is precisely what renders him an unreliable narrator. Although in numerous critical interpretations, Holly is frequently conflated with Haggard,[125] Holly as narrator is actually, through his own ethical failings, narrative inadequacies, and editorial reflections on his own writing, distanced from the reader and rendered an object of scrutiny. His manly resolve is eventually undermined, and he becomes subject to his lusts, just as Ayesha is – and in fact her subservience to passion proves to be the very reason that "this beauty, with all its loveliness and purity, was *evil*."[126] As Ayesha admits, "passion leads me by the hand – evil have I done … and from age to age evil shall I do."[127] Meanwhile, the narrative pointedly extends this struggle between desire and restraint to men generally when Holly suggests, "I would give my mortal soul to marry her … and so, indeed, would any other man, or all the race of men rolled into one."[128] Since this struggle is projected onto the idea of woman as external object, She also signifies the male confrontation with the failure to overcome physical temptation.

This problem of passion trumping morality foregrounds the trap into which Leo later falls as he kisses Ayesha over Ustane's corpse immediately after She murders her. Ayesha's excuse, "If I have sinned it is for love of thee; let my sin, therefore, be put away and forgotten,"[129] uses her end to justify her means – which is the same very simple but misguided logic that underlay British violence in Zululand and rested on the discourse of civilization/savagery as justification. And in *She*, it is the native Ustane who gets wiped out in the fray, a sacrifice that both parallels historical circumstances and plays into Leo's fetishization and passivity. Further, like Leo, our narrator also becomes complicit in She's justifications. Though initially condemning Leo's and Ayesha's wrongs, pronouncing, "those who sell themselves into a like dominion, paying down the price of their honour, and, throwing their soul into the balance to sink the scale to the level of their lusts, can hope for no deliverance here or hereafter,"[130] Holly ultimately forgives Ayesha's violence: "No doubt she was a wicked person, and no doubt she had murdered Ustane when she stood in her path, but then she was very faithful, and by a law of nature man is apt to think but lightly of a woman's crimes, especially if that woman is very beautiful, and the crime is committed for the love of him."[131] Holly's narrative thus pointedly reveals the moral fallacy here, tracing it out as he overtly buys into it. His ethics continue to slip as he considers Leo's luck in attracting

> such awful beauty ... such divine devotion, such wisdom and command over the secrets of nature, and the place and power that they must win ... it is not wonderful, that though Leo was plunged in bitter shame and grief ... he was not ready to entertain the idea of running away from his extraordinary fortune.
>
> My own opinion is that he would have been mad if he had done so.[132]

In this discussion of man's temptations, pleasing notions of "divine devotion," "wisdom and command," and "power" are, in the context of empire, fundamentally intertwined with "bitter shame and grief," and "awful[ness]"; in order to access all the temptations that She offers, he must accept that they come at the high price of morality. From Holly's perspective, this sacrifice is the only sane choice; in this way, the narrative concertedly emphasizes that Holly's ethics are deteriorating. This shift can be tracked temporally; in editing his own narrative, Holly footnotes, or revises, his description of Ayesha as "a mysterious creature of evil tendencies": "After some consideration of this statement, I am bound to confess that I am not quite satisfied of its truth. It is perfectly true that Ayesha committed a murder, but I shrewdly suspect that were we endowed with the same absolute power, and if we had the same tremendous interest at stake, we should be very apt to do likewise under parallel circumstances."[133] Holly's initial impression of "evil" points to the transformation he undergoes – his morals decay as he succumbs to desire and bends his principles in order to authorize immoral actions through legitimizing the pursuit of lust. Passion in turn subdues and unmans both men: "We could no more have left her, than a moth can leave the light that destroys it."[134] The slope is slippery: first yielding to temptation, then justifying moral lassitude, and then finally moving to permit murder, Holly's ethical dissolution illustrates one of the central problematics plaguing imperial Britain. In addition to withering as the text's supposed moral centre, Holly also demonstrates further the alignment of his inner self with the desiring, dominating, despotic She; their fallible morals become entirely commensurable.[135]

This understanding of Ayesha as othered masculine self rather than othered woman has implications beyond the rethinking of textual anxieties surrounding the New Woman, female authority, and female power; it critiques male behaviour and, more specifically, male writing. The scene of She's demise illustrates this precisely, demonstrating both her transformation into a relic of writing and the men's rather "unmanly" reactions:

> "Oh, *look! – look! – look!*" shrieked Job, in a shrill falsetto of terror, his eyes nearly dropping out of his head, and foam upon his lips. "*Look! – look! – look!* she's shrivelling up! she's turning into a monkey!" and down he fell upon the floor, foaming and gnashing in a fit.
>
> True enough – I faint even as I write it in the living presence of that terrible recollection – she *was* shrivelling up; the golden snake that had encircled her gracious form slipped over her hips and fell upon the ground; smaller and smaller she grew; her skin changed colour, and in place of the perfect whiteness of its lustre it turned dirty brown and yellow, like an old piece of withered parchment. She felt at her bald head: the delicate hand was nothing but a claw now, a human talon like that of a badly preserved Egyptian mummy, and then she shrieked – ah, she shrieked! – she rolled upon the floor and shrieked![136]

What remains is "hideous little monkey frame, covered with crinkled yellow parchment."[137] Here, She becomes aligned with writing itself as her white skin "turn[s] dirty brown and yellow, like an old piece of withered parchment." The "delicate hand" – that traditional signifier of careful script – regresses, becoming a clumsy, inarticulate "claw … a human talon." And if Ayesha represents the dark side of a male imperialist frame, this final scene means that, rather than submitting to the inscription of male writing,[138] She, in her shrivelling, effectively embodies the demise of male writing itself. Indeed, Ayesha's prowess withers, or rather "shrivel[s]"; the "golden snake" encircling her hips, echoing the phallic snake tattoo signifying Ignosi's right to rule, here "slipped … and fell upon the ground," suggesting impotence as she grows "smaller and smaller." She's withering also replicates the failure of heroes to live up to masculine ideals of fortitude even as they confront this truth about the limitations of masculine writing. Holly confesses, "I faint even as I write it," and that he and Leo, "overcome with the extremity of horror … too, fell on the sandy floor of that dread place, and swooned away."[139] Leo's hair turns white from the shock, while Job, frothing in hysterics and collapsing from "shattered" nerves,[140] is certainly no nearer to idealized manly stoicism. Indeed, up to this climactic moment, the text has left a trail of examples of failed male prowess; both central male "heroes" frequently indulge in high-pitched exclamations of panic. From when Holly loses Leo in the squall, to Holly's awakening from a nightmare, to Mahomed's slaughter, and, finally, to Ayesha's final torments, feminizing shrieks abound, encoding male vulnerability.

Such vulnerabilities also appear in the form of sexual threats to the male body. Holly's first encounter with the Amahagger men – against whom the British pitch their own strength – is mediated by "the flash of cold steel, and a great spear was held firmly against my throat, and behind it other spears gleamed cruelly."[141] Sexual dynamics are further stressed when Job "ejaculate[s]" at the Amahagger's arrival, and Holly notes that all are "tall and strongly built ... and nude, save for a leopard-skin tied round the middle."[142] The Amahagger's fixation on Mahomed (which is later revealed to be rooted in their desire to "eat" him) suggests predation as "a shadowy form with an uplifted spear" approaches Mahomed: "The man advanced, and the tall shadowy form bent forward. 'Yes, yes,' said the other, and chuckled in a somewhat blood-curdling tone."[143] Amahagger men are again rendered rapacious, with white fears of personal vulnerability partially displaced onto Mahomed, who, as racialized other, serves as contrast to white martial bodies in the absence of a gendered other, when he is forced towards the cooking fire by "the resources of barbarism behind him, in the shape of a huge Amahagger with a proportionately huge spear."[144] As we have seen, the colonial administration, in its trepidation of indigenous power in South Africa, often imagined the threat in terms of "pent up" sexual excitement – and the association of "washing spears" (i.e., battle) with breaking celibacy served as a focalization for the administration's fear of penetration.[145] In *She*, the Amahagger's "proportionately huge spear" carries these historical connotations of desire, invasion, and emasculation; formulaically, white prowess has to prove itself against "savage" sexual aggression, and Mahomed himself is disposable. Thus, when Job notes that he has his gun, "but Mr. Leo has only got his hunting-knife, though that is big enough, surely,"[146] the stage gets set for a racio-phallic confrontation.

The physical struggle between these phallic weapons, involving a few heroes against many natives, is readily analogous to narratives of colonial wars and makes clear the limitations of white prowess. Importantly, the white men don't win here – they, once again, get overwhelmed. Holly depicts Leo "in the centre of a surging mass of struggling men"; the Grecian ideal becomes a phallus himself: "Up above them towered his beautiful pale face crowned with its bright curls (for

Leo is six foot two high)" – Holly pauses in his relation of the action to give us Leo's height –

> and I saw that he was fighting with a desperate abandonment and energy that was at once splendid and hideous to behold. He drove his knife through one man – they were so close to him and mixed up with him that they could not get at him to kill him with their big spears ... It was more than man could do to hold his own for long against so many and at last he came crashing down upon the rock floor, falling as an oak falls.[147]

Because the oak was an established metaphor for British identity, this passage is particularly charged, especially in light of the recent failure of the British soldier "to hold his own for so long against so many" in the materially and culturally significant battles of Isandlwana, Ntombe, and Hlobane in the Anglo-Zulu war. As Captain Essex put it as the Zulu army in the formation of the encompassing *impondo zenkomo* (beast's horns) approached the British camp at Isandlwana, "our little body appeared altogether insignificant compared with the enormous masses opposed to us."[148] And like Leo, the Redcoats, when the combat commenced at Isandlwana, were fighting with bayonets rather than bullets – a contest of stabbing prowess was thus similarly foregrounded. In this context, Leo's crashing fall, while at once bound up with the sexualized innuendoes of penetration, simultaneously works as a metaphor for the loss of illusions of insurmountable strength, and readily suggests the cyclical rise and fall of empires, which, as criticism has established and Ayesha's deterioration – implicating imperial fortitude and narrative – suggests, is one of the romance's central preoccupations.

Ayesha's death throes are not the text's only signal of the inadequacy of the male pen: a number of minor narrative discrepancies, in which the role of the editorial hand is central, undermine Holly's narrative authority. One of these is the problem of the protagonists' names. While the editor asserts that he changed them for reasons of privacy, Holly records that Ayesha's reflection on the heroes' names suggests an integral tie between their meaning and the signifiers themselves: "Leo! ... why, that is 'lion' in the Latin tongue. The old man hath named happily for once"[149] and "'Holly' is a prickly tree."[150] The editor's assertion, meanwhile, renders truth elusive: these semantic connections indicate that either the editor did not change the names or Ayesha did not actually say these things. Another discrepancy appears in the supposed failure of Holly, an intelligent Oxbridge professor, to recognize what is very clear to the reader – that the Amahagger, stoking the cooking fires and fondling Mahomed, intend to eat the unfortunate guide. Holly's ethnographic footnote about the Amahagger's cannibalistic methodology suggests the scene may have been primarily a point of interest to him as a scholar.[151] But most importantly, Holly's description of She's last moments directly undercuts his own credibility: "I never saw anything like it; nobody ever saw anything like the frightful age that was graven on that fearful countenance … and let all men pray to God they never may, *if they wish to keep their reason.*"[152] In other words, the shocking events that instigated Job's fatal fit and that aged Leo twenty years were so traumatic as to deprive onlookers of their senses. Holly indicates here that his own ability to reason – and his failure to provide an ethically sound analysis of the adventure supports this – has been lost before he even sat down to write this narrative. Thus, the very narrative of the romance undercuts its own legitimacy, suggesting that everything asserted in this tale of male survival needs to be questioned because the male pen, far from being recuperated, has been profoundly undermined.

Vulnerability

Haggard's adventure romances undercut all at once the efficacy of the muscular male body, male history, and their attendant imperial authority. In playing up the queerness of their adventuresome protagonists, these works inverted the model of heterosexual reproductive labour that the rhetoric of colonialism demanded, presented a model of the martial male body as penetrable, and indicated the intractable presence of narrative lacunae. This critique of imperial writing from Haggard's early adventure romances also resonated within a larger literary debate about the efficacy and sustainability of traditional models of what was understood to be masculine writing. While Andrew Lang, working to "counteract modern ennui,"[153] applauded romance as a genre of escapism at the same time as claiming that romance texts were powerful because they related experience in plain, "real" language, Haggard's works suggest that experience could not be captured in the sort of writing that Lang championed. In highlighting the instability of frame narration and "history" more broadly, these texts not only disrupt dominant representations (of Africa, of colonialism, of male identity, of history) within fictional literature, in which the use of imagination is foregrounded by the nature of the genre, but they also impinge upon the ways in which travel literature, as well as the eyewitness accounts, testimonials, and reports from colonial outposts are read, understood, and questioned. These narrators' pointed shortcomings also indicate the emergence of the development of a readership's ironic distance from the text that characterized many modernist texts. Subverting the reliability of imperial narrations and accounts, *King Solomon's Mines* and *She* suggest instead that in the face of desire for the African body – whether it is sexual desire or desire for recognition of power – British manhood collapses, becoming vulnerable to the fissures in its own construction of self. The traditional model of masculinity was losing relevance in the face of fast-paced global changes, effective colonial resistance, and confrontations with the events of imperial war that contradicted myths of martial chivalry; the fictions of imperial manhood were becoming unsustainable, even as Haggard's texts worked to diagnose, contain, and repair fantasies of imperial identity.

These narrative structures predict severe moral consequences for the British male, national, and literary body without critical re-evaluations of traditional modes of constructing masculinity, producing knowledge, and establishing authority. As part 2 of this book demonstrates, retaining the fiction of traditional conceptions of masculinity had severe consequences for the British military, national, and literary body. The following two chapters, bridging historiography and popular fiction, explore the violent ramifications of miscalculations about heroism, the limitations of imperial historiography, and the generic panic that attended the fall of Khartoum. While chapter 3 establishes how representations of imperial inefficacy manifest in General Gordon's Khartoum journals and contemporary war reporting, chapter 4, examining Richard Marsh's *The Beetle*, shows how panic about martial failure emerges in the sphere of popular Gothic fiction. Part 1 has shown that both war correspondence and adventure romance became intertwined in a way that not only transcended and expanded each root genre but also fostered emergent strategies of representing gender, race, and narrative that had a lasting impact on the representation of colonial relations in Africa. Likewise, part 2 illuminates key formal and discursive links between siege journals, newspaper reporting, and imperial Gothic fiction that indicate the profound degree to which the terrifying consequences of failed martial prowess permeated imperial culture.

PART II

Gothic Penetrations

Chapter Three

Transgression and Loss: General Gordon and Gothic Imagination

The worst news which came from Zululand, the news which told of the surprise, defeat, and slaughter of our brave troops there, did not approach in gravity to the momentous character of the tidings that reached England yesterday.

– *York Herald*, 7 Feb. 1885

Part 1 of this book argued that imperial disasters (both military and moral) in Zululand brought into relief the vulnerability of martial masculinity, governmental control, and narrative integrity. Cultural anxieties about the destabilization of these keystones of imperial legitimacy manifested in Haggard's adventure romances, yielding new treatments of the frame narrator and damning critiques of these foundational technologies of authority. Following this disruption of imperial masculine ideals emerged increasing disfigurement, through Gothic modes, of both the fantasies of the impenetrable heroic martial body and the stable imperial narrative. In part 2, I outline the progression of these critiques across institutional writing and popular fiction. As with literature emerging from South African contexts, discourse between texts confronting imperial loss in northeast Africa transcended genre to inform both new generic developments and mechanisms of critiquing the codependent relationships between the male body, masculine authority, and narrative itself.

Through this process of generic evolution, institutional literature surrounding British military disaster in Sudan points to the specific modes by which dominant conceptions of martial masculinity continue to rupture in the body of Victorian empire writing as fin-de-siècle power peaked. This chapter examines British narratives of the loss in 1885 of Khartoum, a British outpost, to Sudanese forces. It considers General Charles Gordon's account from inside the fort and the flurry of reporting in the metropole to illuminate how the ruptures of conceptions of martial masculinity and narrative authority that emerged during the Anglo-Zulu War widened with higher stakes, increased critique, and greater devastation with respect to these modes of imperial ideology. In the public archive of this historical moment, both martial masculinity and imperial narrative are destabilized as Gordon's record of the siege underscores the inadequacies of heroism, embodies significant problems of narrating empire, and articulates disruptions to imperial epistemology that occur through temporal chaos. Crucially, Gordon had extremely limited knowledge about events beyond Khartoum; the metropolitan press had an equally deficient understanding of what had transpired in Sudan. The emergence of such limitations in both sets of texts underscores the inadequacy of rationalist discourse in entrenching imperial authority, but for the newspapers, this inadequacy meant that the generic parameters shifted, as fiction and fantasy infiltrated imperial reporting to undermine empire's claim to sense and reason. Thus, imperial discourse began to unravel itself.

On 26 January 1885, after a year-long siege, Sudanese forces led by Muhammad Ahmad al-Mahdi invaded Khartoum to wrest power from Gordon. The stoic figure of Gordon himself, along with the daring mission he had undertaken, had attracted a strong interest in the British Isles. As the *Daily News* (London) put it, "The picture of this solitary man, making his way a thousand miles beyond the reach of civilized troops, to the aid of garrisons beleaguered by innumerable hosts of half-civilized Arabs, deeply impressed the popular imagination."[1] Britain, having sent a rescue mission half a year after Gordon's departure, was rocked by the news of Khartoum's defeat, for "everyone was expecting daily to hear, not of the fall of the capital of the Soudan, but the successful joining of hands between General Gordon and Sir Charles Wilson, and the collapse of the Arab movement."[2] The nation was utterly devastated at the loss of its valiant hero, isolated in the east and seemingly abandoned by a government that had contributed too little, far too late. In countering this imperial failure and "bitter humiliation" of their now considerable tactical disadvantage with affirmations of Gordon's competence,[3] various metropolitan papers highlight a cultural fixation on the outpost's temporal resilience. For the *Manchester Courier*, Gordon's "energy and … vigorous measures" had enabled Khartoum to "h[o]ld out in [a] protracted manner."[4] The *Western Mail* (Cardiff) celebrated Gordon's ability to "hold at bay possibly from 10,000 to 20,000 of the Sudanese … for the greater part of a year."[5] The *Manchester Guardian* consoled its readers with the assertion that Gordon had "stemmed for a whole year the forces of destruction which but for him would long since have swept down the river."[6] As these examples signal, in this imperial context, temporal markers of British fixity emerged as key modes of evaluating power, national identity, and martial masculinity. Indeed, temporally defined masteries such as sustained boundaries, the speed of information, and martial deployment were indispensable technologies of imperial power. As in Zululand, however, supposedly primitive forces' superior control over these modes of power amounted to a severe blow to imperial identity.

Within a few years of the imperial disasters in Southern Africa, the dubiousness of imperial heroism once again came into the public eye as events in Sudan unfolded. In fact, some of the key players from the Anglo-Zulu War made notable reappearances in the Khartoum crisis. Colonel Buller and General H. Steward had fought in Zululand and served on the Nile Expedition.[7] Moreover, General Wolseley was once again sent in to rectify the situation in Africa, in this case heading the unsuccessful rescue mission. The evolution of the stakes for imperial masculinity was not lost on the press: "It will take all Lord Wolseley's skill as well as all his luck to extricate his army and the British Government from the predicament in which they are placed. The task before him in South Africa when he effected the capture of King Cetewayo was merely child's play in comparison with the difficulties in his way against the Mahdi of the Soudan."[8] Thus, imperial masculinity was again tested, and was again confronted with failure. As chapter 4 will demonstrate, this failure in masculine efficacy was rendered in the popular sphere as much in terms of narrative deficiency as stunted manhood – and these failures, suggests Richard Marsh's imperial Gothic novel, were intensely alarming since it was British imagination itself that was brought under scrutiny.

The fall of Khartoum, meanwhile, exemplifies the intersection of perceived decline in governmental and military efficacy, since both institutions played key roles in Britain's epic failure to hold the post. This chapter considers two sets of texts surrounding this event, to demonstrate British recognition that the empire's control over spatial and temporal technologies was disintegrating, and to sketch out the attendant limitations of failed imperial epistemology. First, I examine Gordon's published journals, which were written under siege, because they illustrate this event's destabilization of imperial ideology. Gordon's journals articulate increasing doubts about heroism that characterized responses to the Anglo-Zulu War and Haggard's adventure romances, the intractable problem of rationally narrating empire, and the tenuous hold that imperial agents had over spatial movements and technologies that impinged on imperial temporal command. In short, the journals reflect the proliferating instability of masculinity, authority, and narrative in British imperial culture. I then examine representations in metropolitan newspapers and magazines of the fall of Khartoum during the two-day interval in February 1885 in which news of the disaster had reached Britain but nothing was yet known of the fate of Gordon himself. Since the historical role of the British press in memorializing Gordon, criticizing governmental policy, and influencing public thought during this period of social agitation has been thoroughly acknowledged in scholarship on Gordon, my exploration here focuses on this imperial loss's contribution to the blurring of generic boundaries between institutional media and popular fiction. In situating my reading of metropolitan newspapers' articulation of imperial loss between the previous chapter's examination of Haggard's critique of dominant idealizations of imperial masculinity in his romances, and the following chapter's engagement with Richard Marsh's depiction of the perverse desire fundamentally underpinning imperial narrative, I aim both to emphasize the complexity of Victorian Britain's orientation toward empire and to underscore the potential of discursively uncontainable events in the contact zone to subvert boundaries of genre, destabilize narrative, and thereby fracture the tenets of imperial ideology. Here, in the metropole's confrontation with its inability to locate physically its imperial hero, Gordon, after the fall of Khartoum, these subversions manifest in the appearance of Gothic elements as the imperial centre attempts – and fails – to work through social uncertainty and anxiety, not just in the literary sphere, but also in texts that ostensibly rationally narrate empire.

Loss and Vexation: A Strategic Predicament

Although Britain's connection with Khartoum was somewhat tangential, it was not one that Parliament could break easily. The empire's central interest in the region was protecting the Suez Canal, which had come under British control in 1875 after Britain, under Prime Minister Benjamin Disraeli, bought up the majority of the shares in the canal from the Khedive (viceroy), Ismail.[9] Linking the Mediterranean to the Red Sea, the Suez facilitated the shortest trade route between Britain and India, Ceylon, British Burma, China, Australia, and New Zealand. As the German Chancellor Otto von Bismarck so famously put it, "Egypt is of the utmost importance to England on account of the Suez Canal, the shortest line of communication between the eastern and western halves of the Empire. That is like the spinal cord which connects the backbone with the brain."[10] Although Egypt, through whose territory the canal passed, was officially a vassal state of the Ottoman Empire, the canal was, in practice, controlled by Britain, as it constituted an imperial lifeline.[11] By the late 1870s, Britain had begun to assert financial management and impose reforms in Egypt, which heavily impacted the fellahin (agricultural workers), landlords, and Egyptian army.[12] When Ismail, finally responding to his military's protests, opposed the European governments, he was swiftly deposed by the Ottoman Sultan. In 1881, led by Colonel Ahmad Arabi, the Egyptian people and army rose up against the new Anglo-French-backed Khedive, Tewfik (Ismail's eldest son), protesting heavy taxes, corporeal punishment, cuts to the military, and separate legal systems for Egyptians and resident Europeans.[13] Anti-European riots erupt throughout Egypt, and Arabi explicitly threatened to destroy the canal in order to defend Egypt.[14] The British government, though keen to avoid occupying Egypt or investing in it as a protectorate, was committed to preserving the imperial trade route. William Gladstone's government intervened, sending General Wolseley and 20,000 troops to take the canal towns and pursue Arabi into the interior. Wolseley bombed Alexandria in August 1882, seized Ismailia, and destroyed Arabi's forces in the particularly ruthless Battle of Tel-el-Kebir in September. Although the British effectively occupied Egypt, their aim was to re-establish the khedivate, ensure that no other power would dominate Egypt, and then back away.[15] Such a manoeuvre, however, proved incredibly difficult.

Gladstone failed at first to recognize that protecting the Suez involved confronting newly arisen conflict in Sudan. As General Gordon would later write in his Khartoum journal, "[Sudan] is joined to Egypt, and to my idea it would be difficult to divorce the two."[16] Since 1821, Sudan had been under the administration of Ottoman-controlled Egypt, which had established an Egyptian contingent stationed in the capital city of Khartoum. In 1881, a fakir named Muhammad Ahmad had declared himself the Mahdi ("guided one"; the spiritual leader of Islam), proclaimed a holy war, and led armed resistance to the Ottoman-Egyptian colonization of Sudan. Resentment from imperial conquest sixty years previously, along with hardship inflicted by high taxes and resistance to the economic disruption resulting from the suppression of the slave trade, had yielded a population ready to revolt. By the end of 1883, the Mahdists had gained secure footholds in southern and western Sudan.[17] Gladstone's government was unwilling to engage with what it saw as Egypt's expensive problem, and rendered the Mahdi the Khedive's responsibility. Under Tewfik's direction, Hicks Pasha's expedition of 10,000 Egyptian soldiers embarked on a campaign in Sudan to overcome this uprising[18] When the Mahdists decimated these troops at

Sheikan on 5 November 1883, the British government, alarmed at what seemed a martial threat to the Suez, concentrated its forces in Egypt.[19] Mahdist forces, meanwhile, continued to grow in Sudan, and began to close in around Khartoum.

This was an awkward situation for the British government, which, effectively governing Egypt, was responsible for the Egyptian soldiers, as well as the British consul and *Times* correspondent, Frank Power, trapped in Khartoum. Sending Gordon to the Sudanese capital was an improvised, desperate attempt at a solution. Gladstone's government settled on appointing Gordon in part because of his expertise in the region: he had been employed by the Egyptian Khedive as governor-general of Equatoria in 1873, and of Sudan in 1877–79.[20] The subject of some historical debate, his vague orders were to assess the situation, report to the cabinet, and evacuate Khartoum.[21] Gordon, however, after arriving in the Sudanese capital on 18 February 1884 with his second officer, Colonel J.D.H. Stewart, decided that a full evacuation was not an option: it would take considerable time,[22] and the northern Sudanese tribes occupying the escape route of the Nile could meanwhile join the Mahdi. Further, withdrawing from Khartoum without a cooperative replacement government would effectively end British influence in Sudan. Gordon, armed with a firman from the Egyptian Khedive appointing him governor-general of Sudan, instead focused on fortifying the city, with the idea that the Sudanese rebellion could be pacified.[23]

Gordon woefully underestimated the Mahdi's strength. The siege of the city began on 13 March. Gordon, as the image of a dominant white defender facing the Mahdist masses in the desert, came to occupy a central place in the sentiments of the British public – a place reinforced by an emotive telegraph he had sent to the *Daily Telegraph* (London) detailing his hopes for Sudan and requesting the prayers of Britons.[24] In turn, the public criticism toward Gladstone mounted as the prime minister refused to send troops to support Khartoum and/or rescue Gordon, both because of the expense and Gordon's disobedience with respect to his orders to evacuate Khartoum.[25] Eventually, in August 1884, Gladstone's government succumbed to widespread public pressure to order preparations for the Nile Expedition – a rescue mission consisting of almost 10,000 troops from across the Commonwealth, and seemingly representing the empire uniting to rescue the embodiment of imperial martial masculinity.[26] The expedition was headed by the same "rescuer" who responded to the colonial debacle in Southern Africa – Wolseley. Finally departing Cairo on 25 September, the relief troops made excruciatingly slow progress due to the Nile's cataracts,[27] transporting copious gear as well as adequate food and water for thousands of men and camels, and various organizational challenges: it would be almost four months before the expedition reached Metemmeh, still a hundred miles north of Khartoum.[28] When the British forces finally glimpsed Khartoum on 28 January 1885, they were just two days too late to rescue their general and outpost, which had endured a 317-day siege. Gordon was killed when the Mahdists penetrated the fortress, but, despite the propagandistic reconstructions of his last moments in the Victorian media, the actual circumstances of his death remain elusive.[29]

In the metropole, Gordon's demise prompted a nationwide sense of betrayal, sadness, and anxiety about the fate of civilization. In the larger scheme of empire, the failure to reclaim Khartoum or rescue Gordon was actually of little material consequence: Whitehall had overestimated the Mahdi's interest in invading Egypt and taking the Suez,[30] and for Britain, Sudan was a mere appendage to Egypt. Yet the defeat deeply wounded national pride and imperial identity. Gladstone was roundly condemned for declining to act and was often blamed for Gordon's death. Gordon himself, with his reputation for a stiff upper lip, stoicism, and resolution, signified as an archetypal masculine figure of empire. The *Daily News* propagated precisely this image of him: "What he has done is unequalled in modern history, and will make him famous for all time. Like a hero of antiquity riding out to fight giants and dragons, he bravely went to meet unknown dangers."[31] This allusion to St George suggests a legacy of Christian martial nobility, and is entirely characteristic of the profusion of "uncritical hero worship" that responded to the crisis in Sudan.[32] This discourse surrounding Gordon, hinging as it did on ideas of gallantry, most palpably emphasized sacrifice and loss. While we might expect the metropole to have celebrated Gordon's sacrifice, since his apparent selflessness was considered noble, the idea that Gordon gave his life for the empire did not actually manifest as a positive outcome. The public was devastated at the loss of their hero, angry about the government's imperial policy, and nervous about the consequences of Gordon's death; for the metropole, Gordon's killing indicated that the British Empire, having reached perhaps too great proportions, was in mortal danger of colonial backlash. The *Daily News* brooded, "The fall of Khartoum may have a serious and a far-extending effect on the whole of our dealings with Oriental races,"[33] while the *Leeds Mercury* suggested that "the ascendancy of Europe and the civilization of the West in the face of the armed revolt of the fanaticism of the East"[34] was at risk. The stakes of Khartoum's loss, as the metropole understood them, were epic.

Two significant responses to this context of mourning heroism emerged in Victorian culture. On the one hand, this devastating blow to empire was appropriated as an impetus for reasserting and consolidating imperial authority, as Gordon's call to "smash up the Mahdi" was frequently invoked as a galvanizing notion.[35] As Egmont Hake, editor of the Khartoum journals, suggests, "His journals are his last words to the world ... Englishmen who value England's honour may well read them with a heavy heart – with eyes dimmed by tears ... His journals tell us ... what is best for the Soudan ... The Mahdi's power must be smashed."[36] Importantly, this pattern of loss and retribution surrounding events in Sudan was similar to the formula deployed during the Anglo-Zulu War, in which the national mourning occasioned by the unfathomed deaths of young British soldiers at Isandlwana worked to leverage imperial fantasies of reprisal – fantasies that, in the end, came at the expense of the identity of the gentleman soldier. In 1885, the empire again attempted to use the failure of its own masculine boundaries to fortify itself and re-establish a firm martial stance. This time, however, that fantasy of reprisal would remain unfulfilled, at least for the next thirteen years; the empire was denied the immediate gratification of retribution it sought in restoring the image of martial fortification.

On the other hand, metropolitan culture realized that such staples of British identity as the intact soldier's body, the stability of imperial narratives, and the efficacy of military technology were being transgressed. Though used for imperial propaganda and, to a degree, for sanctifying Gordon, the Khartoum journals simultaneously and subversively played a complex role in activating metropolitan anxieties, unhinging traditional concepts of masculine authority, and, certainly, debunking Gordon's sainthood. While at once a national rallying point, the fall of Khartoum also became a focus of doubt – not only with respect to the capacity of Gladstone's government but also the limitations of imperial power and the bounded imperial body in its various manifestations: the individual male body, militarily fortified territory, and the larger imperial network of operations, communications, and ideology. Similarly, once news of the loss of Khartoum reached London, the newspapers began to exhibit symptoms of imperial insecurity, which operated both at the level of discourse and of genre. As the final section of this chapter demonstrates, the papers exposed the limitations of imperial technologies of authority through their attempts to supplement various absences, and they destabilized the ostensibly rational logic of reporting empire by resorting to the extra-rational in order to process imperial loss. These relationships between pervasive uncertainty, collapsing authority, and generic transgressions anticipate the concerns of fin-de-siècle Gothic fiction, as Marsh's *The Beetle* exemplifies, hinging as it does on the problem of epistemological limitations. While failures of the supplement and the Gothic turn emerging in the papers illustrate the fragility of technologies of authority from within the metropole, Gordon's journals demonstrate the profound instability of imperial ideology from the margins of empire. Gordon's own unstable writings – which subvert dominant conceptions of heroism, notions of historical mastery, idealizations of fortified territory, and ideas about the efficacy of imperial technology – implicitly challenge imperial authority.

Transgressions at the Margins of Empire: Gordon's Khartoum Journals

The diaries that Gordon kept were smuggled out of Khartoum over a number of months via steamers along the Nile. The last (Book 6) was conveyed on 15 December 1884, to Metemmeh, where it was later given to Sir Charles Wilson, who was heading the advance expedition.[37] Published on 25 June 1885, the Khartoum journals immediately became best-sellers.[38] Circulating widely, both due to publicity efforts and because Gordon intended them for the Victorian public, the text's illumination of imperial problems reached a broad readership.

The Khartoum journals' Conservative editor, Hake, exploited the public's investment in Gordon to consolidate a particular image of masculine heroism.[39] In his introduction, Hake casts Gordon as benevolent, noble, and chivalrous,[40] but also as a kind of penetrator, able to enter alien territories then lead, direct, and take control over indigenous systems. Investing Gordon's text itself with moral authority, Hake prescribes the journals as mandatory reading for the working classes: "they cannot occupy their leisure time better than in reading them, and, indeed, in learning them by heart."[41] Hake goes on to leverage Gordon's demise in his sketch of true patriarchy: "from his death we may learn at least how fit he was to teach us while he lived, how fit to hold his country's honour in his hand ... Let us mark well ... what his journals say for him now that he is dead."[42] In short, Gordon's journals were co-opted as imperial propaganda that, in order to buttress Gordon's critique of Gladstone's Liberal government, presented Gordon as insightful, authoritative, and fearless.[43] In this context, national mourning served as a platform to eulogize the qualities that Gordon ostensibly embodied and thereby reinstate a unifying imperial identity defined by chivalrous masculinity.

Yet those invested in Gordon's association with imperial honour were unable to project a full recuperation of manhood; Gordon's narrative points to a range of means by which the traditional concept of the unshakeable, solid, and ultimately fortified imperial man was unhinged. Thus, while Khartoum's fall was deployed to rally the nation, the disaster – and more significantly its representation – remained predominantly a focal point of doubt. Crucially, these apprehensions about imperial efficacy were not limited to the capacity of Gladstone's particular government; they also centred on the broader limitations of imperial power and the bounded imperial organism in its various manifestations: the individual male body; militarily fortified territory; and the larger imperial network of operations, technology, communications. In four key ways, Gordon's journals accentuate the failures of these manifestations of empire to entrench ideology: Gordon directly critiques the discourse of heroism; the narrative's unruly form challenges the notion of the contained, simple, objective, and therefore knowable history; Gordon's account complicates the image of the fort as an impermeable, carefully regulated space (in fact its boundaries were quite fluid and porous); and, finally, the diary emphasizes the utter lack of temporal mastery the imperial forces held over extant information technology.

Gordon situates his discussion of heroism alongside the defence of Khartoum; both topics hinged on impenetrability. Doubting the authenticity of traditional forms of masculinity, Gordon acknowledges both fear in his defensive position and the urge to suppress it: "a man should never be [frightened]. For my part I am always frightened … I do not believe a bit in the calm, unmoved man. I think it is only that he does not show it outwardly. Thence I conclude no commander of forces ought to live closely in relation with his subordinates, who watch him like lynxes."[44] While Gordon insists that it is crucial to hide fear from the "lynxes," his "subordinates" in Khartoum, he challenges "the world's view" that real men are never afraid. His disbelief in "the calm, unmoved man" suggests that the stiff upper lip is merely an ideal. Despite attempting "not [to] show it outwardly" at Khartoum, Gordon is very clear with the British readership about being fearful, going on to admit, for instance, that "any loud noise, in this clear air, makes me jump (i.e., be, for a moment, afraid)."[45] For Gordon, then, heroism was a myth: "I cannot say I think we are over great heroes (the fact is, that, if one analyses human glory, it is composed of nine-tenths twaddle)."[46] He even suggested that one "can find no chivalry" in Britain.[47] More caustic still was Gordon's critique of the army's manly virtue, or lack thereof, while mainstream discourse persistently reaffirmed British prowess in the face of the Sudan crisis. Reporting on the relief expedition's progress with camel riding, Jack Cameron, the war correspondent for the *Standard* (London), asserted that British soldiers of the Desert Column (one branch of the expedition) had become "extremely expert in the management of their animals … No body of Arabs in the Orient could ride or manoeuvre camels with so much skill as can now our English soldiers, and even the camels themselves seem changed in nature, and are developing qualities hitherto not credited to them."[48] For Cameron, English orderliness extended even to camels. The *Daily News* also portrayed the relief mission as embodying "the pluck, the endurance, and the perfect discipline of the British troops."[49] Gordon, meanwhile, offers a contrasting, scathing sketch that disputes the dominant notion of the army's stoicism, physical resilience, reliable eye-witnessing, and, of course, dignity. Imagining the imperial forces struggling across Sudan on camels, Gordon, was characteristically irreverent: "as they mount they will go over the other side and swear ... [They will have] aches and pains in every part of the body (I should be inclined to put them on ambulance saddles, one on each side: awkward if they meet a baggage caravan)."[50] Using slapstick to undercut the image of the masterful adventuring soldier, Gordon depicts a woeful lack of skill as aspiring riders climb onto the camel only to topple over the other side. He contradicts impressions of stoicism as he suggests these soldiers are not tough enough to face all of the physical discomforts of the desert: far from impervious to pain, they succumb, ridiculous spectacles, riding in "ambulance saddles" – colliding in them, even. Finally, this sketch constitutes the antithesis of stoicism in both its subjects *and* Gordon's inability to accept that he needed to be rescued.[51]

Gordon is graver, however, when imagining the Sudanese landscape's very real threat to British bodies. Echoing tropes rampant in accounts of the Anglo-Zulu War, Gordon imagines the desert engulfing the military body. Downplaying the martial prowess of the Ansar ("followers of the Prophet"), Gordon argues that, in Hicks Pasha's notorious defeat, the country was the true enemy – with cumbersome artillery, Hicks's troops were delayed from reaching water, and then, in the unforgiving climate, were overcome by enemy forces. Into the journal page opposite this rumination, Gordon pasted a passage from Herodotus detailing Cambyses's ill-fated expedition into Ethiopia. Herodotus notes that a genuine account of Cambyses's demise did not exist, but "the report was that heaps of sand covered them over and they disappeared." Gordon annotates this passage: "Hicks' army disappeared. This expedition was made into these lands."[52] Such envelopment signals castration, as Gordon dwells on martial impotence when facing African forces. Furthermore, the layered significance of Herodotus's and Gordon's suggestions that these armies "disappeared" emphasizes the inadequacies of the history of empire and therefore deficiencies in imperial power. Thus, while those publicizing Gordon's journals attempted to use them to celebrate heroism, the journals themselves resist this celebration.

If the content of Gordon's prose consciously reflects on the question of identity and challenges dominant trends in the constitution of masculinity, the form of the text itself defies the idea that knowledge of empire can be accessed through a reliably ordered, objective, and disciplined narrative; Gordon's journals were considerably unruly. Although the documents were intended for government examination prior to their release into the public sphere, they do not present as reports; Gordon's control over his accounts of events and his own arguments is profoundly questionable. Frequently vacillating between addressees (typically identified only as "you"), he repeatedly obsesses over the same ideas, though constantly breaks off from a train of thought to pursue random topics in a variety of directions. Hake recognized the need to impose some kind of editorial order on the journals, again and again interjecting to interpret Gordon for the readership. After one of Gordon's recurrent ravings about the British government's effective desertion of Khartoum, Hake demonstrates the need to mitigate Gordon's mania in a footnote: "Whenever General Gordon deals with this subject, he shows how thoroughly angry he is, and his anger increases as he proceeds. Hence the frequent reiterations of his resolve not to leave. – Ed."[53] Only pages later, when Gordon, reflecting on the murder of his two white associates, Stewart and Power, to whom he had given permission to make a dash for the next British outpost down the Nile in order to advocate for reinforcements,[54] writes, "I dare not, with my views, say their death is an evil," Hake jumps in and "translates" this potentially inflammatory rumination: "there should be no misconstruction placed on these words ... He merely meant, 'I dare not say that two brave, just, upright men are not happier in the future life than in the present one.' – Ed."[55] Hake's repeated interjections indicate that the Khartoum journals required mediation in order to force a fit with imperial ideology.

Gordon himself recognized the unruliness of his writing; he wrote on the covers of nearly every book constituting the journals that they would need to be "pruned down" before publication, and indeed they did sprout wildly in different directions.[56] This chaotic narrative structure is entirely in line with Fergus Nicoll's characterization of the journals as constituting "a mind unravelling, with Gordon's imaginary exchanges going well beyond satire into the realms of paranoia and delusion."[57] Gordon's narrative disorder is congruous with his reputation among his contemporaries who doubted his mental grounding. Described by turns as a "fanatic of the Puritan type," a "half-cracked fatalist," and downright "mad" by various members of Parliament, Gordon was understood in many circles to be, at the very least, eccentric.[58] While the narrative unruliness of his journals reflects the looseness of the grasp that he and consequently his readers could have had on events in Sudan, even the journals' physicality challenged the notion of discipline: they consisted of a mass of scrap paper and cardboard rather than conventionally bound pages. Gordon's journals were not tidy, cogent, or linear; neither materially nor structurally did they reflect the manly virtues of solidity, regularity, and firm demarcation. Rather, the narrative and physical instability of the journals embodies the instability of heroic masculinity that Gordon critiqued directly.

Much like the composition and materiality of the Khartoum journals, the fort itself, as Gordon represented it, was loose and unbounded. At Khartoum, failures of masculine imperialism registered largely in terms of a lack of spatial and temporal mastery. Transgressions of spatial boundaries surrounding the fort and British failure to regulate the exchange of information across these lines became central nodes of anxiety for Gordon. We might understand how these inabilities to regulate the environment impacted Western senses of identity and prowess through Laura Otis's examination of the intertwined metaphors of membranes and imperial counter-invasion. Otis argues that, during the peak years of the European empires, when developments in science and medicine within these cultures intensified, the "membrane model" was used to define "self" and "not self," with the notion of the intact boundary serving as a mark of individual and social health.[59] Within this framework, identity is based on resistance to external forces; penetration of the membrane amounts to "an unmanning."[60] Thus, when Khartoum fell, metropolitan conceptions of imperial health faced a re-evaluation of imperial identity.

And yet Gordon's journals relate that, even before the Ansar succeeded in overtaking the outpost, the material conditions of bodily movement across the borders of Khartoum during the siege complicated the "self" and "not self" dichotomy that, as Otis demonstrates, had come to underpin British social organization. Khartoum had been hemmed in by the Ansar, who cut the telegraph between Khartoum and Berber (and thus Cairo), on 10 March, effectively cutting off all communication except the odd tidbit smuggled to and from Berber – 192 miles north of Khartoum – and later Dongola, by messengers and spies.[61] This meant that, throughout most of the siege, the exchange of information was extremely sketchy: the post was frequently intercepted by Mahdist agents, though Sudanese runners were sometimes able to get messages through enemy lines to Gordon's contacts beyond the Mahdi's forces. Nevertheless, the material conditions of Khartoum did not conform to the European analogy between the healthy cell, healthy body, and healthy society. As Gordon's Khartoum journals make clear, pro-Mahdist Sudanese inhabited the city as a matter of course, including men who preached in favour of the Mahdi.[62] Gordon even gave written permission for departure to those who wanted to join the Mahdi.[63] Additionally, Mahdist soldiers, escaped slaves and captives, and messengers from either side – and with them letters, intelligence, and rumours – constituted a fluid exchange in and out of the city.[64] This lack of regulation was potentially threatening, as in the case of enemy spies – and, indeed, the false rumour emerging later in London that Khartoum had fallen due to internal treachery highlights British obsessions with infiltration. This movement across the fort's boundaries, however, was also largely beneficial – soldiers defecting from the Mahdi usually brought their arms with them, and could offer manpower. Male slaves who came in were also entered into the army. Gordon usually derides the incoming people, but occasionally he celebrates their arrival – especially when taking note of visibly capable male bodies.[65] Still more valuable to Gordon was the intelligence that newcomers could offer. In some ways their information was crucial – they often gave reports of the Ansar's movements, the status of other cities, and the fate of British steamers – and in other ways the details they offered constituted only wild rumour. Either way, these outsiders were Gordon's main source of information. He does not often repress "how very vicious one feels towards Her Majesty's Intelligence Department for not giving us any news"[66] – that is, for refusing to use spies to deliver information across the Mahdist lines. British intelligence in fact did use spies, just ineffectively. Thus if Khartoum's membrane was quite permeable, even while under siege, Gordon was actually highly dependent on this exchange of bodies for the survival of the imperial outpost – and this dependence was entirely outside imperial control. That Gordon's journals demonstrate so clearly that his post was not self-contained troubles not only the idea of the internally ordered, bounded British body but also the role of imperial narrative in perpetuating this myth.

On top of this daily cross-current of bodies, Khartoum's geographical boundary lines themselves were also distinctly fluid: with the Blue and White Nile comprising three quarters of its borders,[67] Khartoum was physically surrounded by a flowing mass (figure 5).

Theweleit's discussion in *Male Fantasies* of how Western discourse has conceived threats to the male militant body in terms of fluidity and flow, discussed in chapter 1 in the context of Southern Africa, is also relevant to the Siege of Khartoum. Through this theoretical lens, the water surrounding Khartoum is symbolically dangerous, since the rivers themselves constituted the quite literally fluid membrane of the fort.

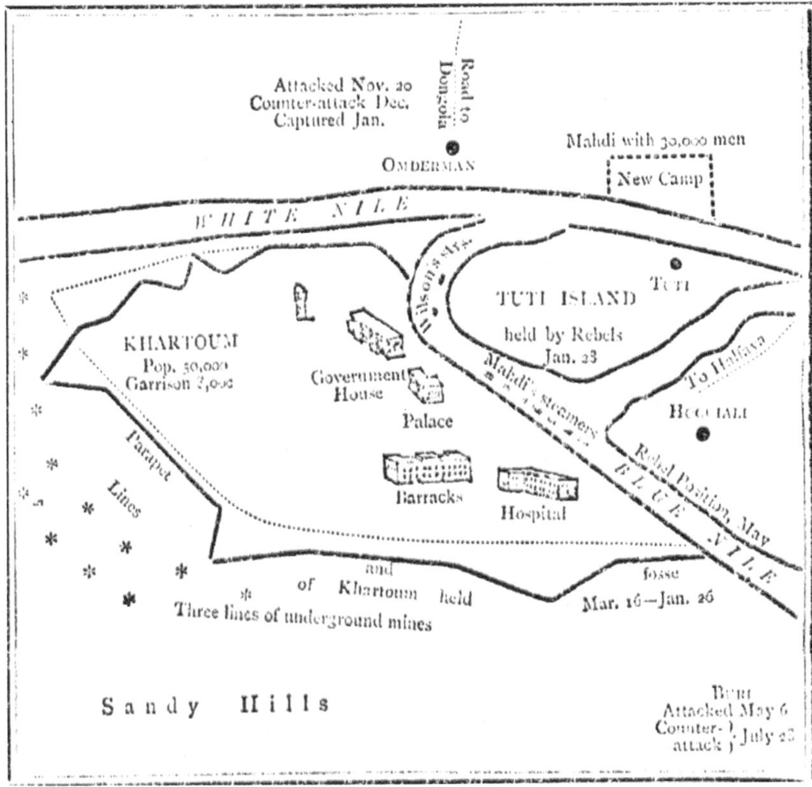

Figure 5: Khartoum under siege (*Pall Mall Gazette*, 6 Feb. 1885, 8)

These waters also constituted a battleground; Mahdist attacks on the forts and on Khartoum's steamers frequently came from across the Nile (and, later, the relief expedition would encounter rebel forces lining the banks of the Nile and pelting British ships with heavy fire).[68] The fort's aqueous boundary line resonates with the deep fear Theweleit identifies among soldier males: forces that threatened the body's boundaries with dissolution are pervasively conceptualized as fluid. Gordon instantiates this trend in describing the growth of enemy forces as a "gathering of waters."[69] The historical pattern of menace/counteraction that Theweleit illuminates manifests at Khartoum as the threat of engulfment by the Mahdists besieging the fort – the castrating potential of the volatile force that sought to penetrate the capital – is countered by the establishment of fixity: the post is held "together as an entity, a body with fixed boundaries"; the soldier "defends himself with a kind of sustained erection of his whole body, of whole cities, of whole troop units."[70] Gordon recognized the menace associated with the enveloping waters: his short note "we have painted the steamers up; they are whited sepulchres"[71] epitomizes the convergence of Theweleit's layered metaphor of death/water/flow that endangers firm boundaries. In fact, pragmatically, the Nile River ended up being the means by which the defence of Khartoum became considerably disadvantaged: when Stewart and Power raced back down the Nile, their steamer caught on a rock and partially sank. It was devastating enough to morale that Stewart's party was lured ashore and then killed by Sudanese supposedly friendly to the British, but more strategically crushing was the fact that Gordon had sent with Stewart dispatches, Stewart's log, other letters, and worst of all, the cypher keys. These fell into the Mahdi's possession, and he gained invaluable intelligence about British movements, supplies, and strategy, not to mention the ability to decode any captured British letters. In a sense, this dash down the Nile was the beginning of the end. Ultimately, both the destabilizing aspects of the fluidity of Khartoum's boundaries and the eventual penetration of the fort upended the notion of the solid, bounded martial body so integral to imperial identity, and devastated the imperial fantasy of fortification.

If the lack of regulation of bodies across space was mostly theoretically problematic, the inability of Britons on either side of Khartoum's walls to manipulate the movement of information within a controlled timeframe was disastrous at a practical level and devastating for morale. Gordon's final word in his journal is to complain to Whitehall, "You send me no information, though you have lots of money."[72] Gordon's incidental acquisition of a September newspaper in November of 1884 was the last intelligence he was to receive, and he was desperate for information as the Mahdi, with time on his side, starved out the capital. This constraint of British military prowess, specifically in terms of temporal control, profoundly impacted metropolitan affective experience. In *War at a Distance*, Mary Favret analyses the relationship between the temporal structure of wartime and the limits of epistemological stability, arguing that, particularly during the late eighteenth and early nineteenth centuries, wartime and the arrival of news from abroad crucially developed modern understandings of time. These periods established time as an organizing principle, and units of time as valid forms of experience. More precisely, the regularity of news delivery, whatever the content, worked to stabilize and consolidate the nation in the face of the uncertainty and disorder of war. In other words, whatever violence was happening at the limits of empire, the metropole retained a rhythm that worked to contain instability: "This instrument of timekeeping [i.e., newspapers] rather performs an artful conversion of existential uncertainty into predictable pattern: noise into meter."[73] Gordon's journals demonstrate that his lack of news excluded him from this metre. His entry from 5 November illustrates the extent of the delays in intelligence that undermine the image of imperial mastery. Kitchener had sent some letters to Gordon (the general found them useless) wrapped in newspapers from 15 September. By chance, these papers found their way to Gordon: "they are like gold … we have had no news since 24th February, 1884! These papers gave us far more information than any of your letters."[74] These papers proved to be one of the few sources of intelligence Gordon would receive. Gordon was thus stuck in what Favret calls the "meantime" – that is, waiting for news and experiencing all of the "undifferentiated intensity" that attends the instability of the missed beat in the rhythm of anticipated information.[75] Favret identifies another epistemological gap experienced with news reception – the distance between the event itself and the reporting of it – and argues that this gap manifested as an absence of security: "living 'in the meantime' of war means living in constant anticipation and dread; simultaneously … it means living belatedly. Caught out of alignment with chronology, feeling itself would become intense, and intensely unmoored."[76] Gordon's journals express precisely this sense of powerlessness. On 13 December 1884, just days before he smuggled the last instalment of his diaries out of Khartoum, and while waiting for the Nile Expedition to relieve the town, Gordon admitted, "certainly this day-after-day delay has a most disheartening effect on every one. Today is the 276th day of our anxiety."[77] Not only this, but the journals record that Gordon's experience of time was also falling out of metre: on 12 November, he reflected on that day's battle between his steamers and the Ansar, writing that "I have lived *years* in these last hours!"[78] Upon publication, these journals made public the limits of Gordon's control and the shortcomings of the martial network. They also underscored that the delay in news meant a gaping hole in Gordon's knowledge, and, in turn, a wrench in the imperial machine: the role of surveillance and knowledge production in the establishment of imperial power in this important case was defunct. In the absence of useful information, Gordon supplements his reports with copious descriptions of the daily happenings within Khartoum and, in so doing, underscores the vastness of what empire, in its margins, could not know.[79]

Gordon's journals, though deployed by their editor to leverage the loss of a hero and rouse the nation to adhere to the identity Gordon was said to embody, nevertheless register in powerful ways these four modes by which martial masculinity dissolves in colonial Africa. In turn, the metropolitan readership would need to grapple with the journals' implications of deficient heroism, narrative instability, the mythological status of the bounded imperial body, and existential uncertainty. Perhaps most salient for Britain, however, was the issue of not knowing – not knowing exactly how Khartoum ultimately fell; if, and eventually how, Gordon had died; or how to tell either the history or the future of empire without the tool of surveillance. This crisis of representation, especially evident in the institution of the public press, played a key role in a cultural turn to the imperial Gothic when affect visibly superseded objective report.

A Crisis of Representation: Gothic Pressings

While Gordon was in a position of ignorance in Khartoum, the same kind of affective disruption – the missed beats in the rhythm of modern time – manifested in the metropolitan intelligence offices and the public sphere. The empire received almost no information from Gordon during the siege, and collective anxieties ran high, particularly during the interval between when Britain learned on 5 February that Khartoum had fallen just days before relief arrived, and the devastating confirmation on 7 February that Gordon had fallen with it. These minimal scraps of information were received by telegram, included no report, and had respectively taken nine and eleven days to reach London. Faced with this informational void, the metropolitan press struggled to narrate the incomprehensible to the nation. The British news press, as an institution, traditionally authorized empire by laying claim to authenticity in its reporting, producing knowledge of the foreign, and mapping out distant spaces.[80] Yet these tactics proved inadequate in this particular case of reporting loss. I argue that the press, unable to obtain reliable information from Sudan, took a subtle but unmistakably Gothic turn as it attempted to achieve representational legitimacy by filling the gaps in its knowledge. As it sought to represent the loss of Khartoum, the press drew on Gothic iterations of the sensational and the fantastic – thereby undercutting the narrative stability that it sought to inculcate, and further undermining the efficacy of narrative itself. While political affiliations often influenced discussions of the imperial disaster, representations of loss and transgression in the metropolitan press in this case are remarkably cohesive, partially because of the scant information available, and partially because of the widespread cultural investments in particular versions of imperial identity.

The Gothic, that "great liberator of feeling,"[81] is a slippery genre whose expressions often resist definition, although we readily recognize many of its conventions: oppressive yet wild settings, struggles for power, cloistered men, forms of live burial, doubleness, guilt and shame, the unspeakable, the monstrous, and the supernatural.[82] We also recognize its association with moments of cultural anxiety about the problem of knowing and producing reality. When realist narratives have proved insufficient for describing troublesome affective elements of the real, literary expressions have drawn on Gothic elements in order to imagine the state of things when reality itself resists comprehension. What this means, though, within the structure of imperial logic is that the very attempt to introduce the extra-rational as a way to patch gaps in narratives of imperial surveillance becomes a mechanism by which rational metropolitan authority is undermined.

While the Gothic is not categorically coherent across history, geography, and literary forms, nevertheless many of the characteristics that distinguish the genre appear in the archive of the British press between 5 and 7 February 1885 as it reckoned with Khartoum.[83] Certainly Khartoum's recent history lent itself thematically to Gothic exploration: it offered a deeply religious hero sequestered in what would effectively be his tomb (surrounded by the looming Mahdist monster, Gordon, eventually doomed, indeed faced a kind of live burial), and in this isolation there was in effect a doubling of the hero (the sequestered physical man, and the myth, sustained by his reputation in metropolitan circles); it offered a wild, unforgiving landscape and a walled fortress (settings of a long struggle for dominance); and, when the fort finally fell, history offered the empire the oppressive shame with which the Gothic is so often rife. However, the conventions deployed that most directly impacted traditional conceptions of masculinity were uncertainty and limitations on the power of language, the monstrous, the destruction of the subject and its borders, and isolation.[84] In tracing the relationship between the emergence of these tropes in the papers, the dissolution of the martial male body (collective and individual), and the instability of writing as an imperially buttressing institution, my aim is to lay the foundation for how Gothic elements emerge to undercut imperial legitimacy through the masculine imperial figure across rationalist and, as we'll see in chapter 4, fictive genres.

During the period of deep public anxiety between 5 and 7 February, Gordon and the imperial chivalry that he symbolized became focal points of epistemological imperatives while Britain awaited news of whether Gordon had been killed in battle, taken prisoner, or was holed up in Khartoum's citadel with a few loyal soldiers, still fighting. The metropolitan press faced the linked problems of how to discern truth in the absence of crucial information and how to respond to their readers' hunger for news and their need for reassurance. Generally speaking, the papers attempted to meet these challenges in two divergent ways. One impulse yielded extensive catalogues of the military situation through maps, chronologies, and repetitive narration. As was evident in publications during the Anglo-Zulu War, the logic of the supplement manifests in the archive of empire – thus these catalogues simultaneously undid the effects they attempted to achieve. The other impulse was to turn to the supernatural to supplement what was missing from the real. The public's desperation for information underscored the conditions of isolation, the epistemological crevasse, and the imperial failure to produce knowledge that underlay the metropole's relation to the siege. These contexts set the conditions for the emergence of Gothic elements that themselves highlight the role of fantasy in the maintenance of imperial legitimacy.

In the absence of knowledge about Gordon's fate and the particulars of Khartoum's fall, detailed chronologies of the mission, from Gordon's departure from England up to the latest telegram from Cairo, were poured onto the pages of metropolitan newspapers. But since chronologies could only satiate so much hunger for information, there also appeared sketch after sketch of Khartoum's topography, the surrounding war zone, and histories of governmental decisions, military movements, and Gordon himself.[85] Some papers profiled the Mahdi, trying to pin down the troublesome figure.[86] Once this reservoir ran dry, papers resorted to demographics;[87] statistical information about Khartoum; notes about the rainy season and the town's commerce; maps of its major buildings;[88] measurements of its river frontage; and rundowns on local agriculture, manufacturing, average temperatures;[89] the town's founding and population;[90] its architecture; its patterns of flooding; and its dusty summers.[91] The *Pall Mall Gazette* even offered rather picturesque sketches of Khartoum on the Nile, complete with sailboats (figure 6).[92] Of course, none of this information could stand in for what the nation was really in need of knowing.

Quickly running out of information about Sudan, the papers resorted to reporting on the reception of the news in Britain. These reports served to fill the pages, but they also attempted to articulate the sense of loss and anxiety that constituted social feeling at this time, for "rarely ha[d] any news caused such a sensation in the Metropolis."[93] Across the board, newspapers' assessment of national feeling focused almost exclusively on "excitement" and "sensation";[94] because the papers could not adequately articulate the mourning and agitation experienced in the

River View of Khartoum.

Figure 6 River view of Khartoum (*Pall Mall Gazette*, 6 Feb. 1885, 4)

metropole, what they produced was predictably repetitive and reductive. This inherently insufficient attempt to represent the affect arising from imperial loss, in turn, rendered that which could not be expressed still more elusive.

Yet, because so simplified, this national response was also represented as united – fortified, even – amidst loss.[95] Papers depicted "people congregated round the principal newspaper office eagerly reading the telegram announcing the news";[96] Britons "gathered in the streets and perused the broadsheets by the light of shops and gaslamps. The opinion of all classes appeared to favour active operations against the Mahdi in order to recover Khartoum."[97] Readers were offered the image of British people huddling together to share feeling; by imagining "a deep, horizontal comradeship,"[98] the nation redefined itself during its moment of loss, and in turn fortified itself by reiterating the constitution of its members. Stoicism and unity were privileged: "This is a national calamity and must be met by a national resolve. Such will be the feeling of the vast majority to whatever political party they may belong."[99] Such heavy-handed templates for respectable reactions were undergirded by more subtle expressions of national solidarity. For instance, the fantasy that the captive Gordon would be returned "to the arms of his country" implied a national body united in the desire to welcome home its embodiment of masculine heroism.[100] Bolstering this idea of a stable, stoic imperial core was doubtless preferable to dwelling on the empire's mistakes, failures, and omissions.

These journalistic manoeuvres, however, supplemented more than shaken identity and epistemological limitations; they also sought to reaffirm the righteousness of Gordon's mission. To this end, domestic papers printed continental expressions of sympathy for Britain as a nation, such as, for instance, the idea that "all Europe must sympathise with the English nation, cruelly betrayed by fortune in an enterprise wherein she represented Western civilization in the face of African barbarism,"[101] or that "the disastrous intelligence excites universal regret."[102] Imagining such external affect reiterated the moral legitimacy of Britain's intervention in Sudan and confirmed collective affect in response to calamity; simultaneously, it distracted readers from the lack of news from Sudan.

Imperial reputation, however, was still at stake. While, on the one hand, these reflections of mourning were nationally consolidating, on the other, less sympathetic international reactions produced indignation – and thus consolidation from another angle. The *Glasgow Herald* noted French papers relishing British defeat and incompetence: "The *France*, the *Paris*, and the *Intransigeant* exult over English misfortunes, and remark with satisfaction that further disasters probably await us, for our army, observes the *France*, is an army of mercenaries and our officers utterly incapable."[103] The *Vienna Allgemaine* meanwhile asserted that Gladstone's "blunder[ing]" policy had "lowered England's reputation throughout the world,"[104] and the *Tageblatt* in Berlin agreed: "The English never knew where the enemy stood. Their intelligence was miserable; even their spies were the Mahdi's agents."[105] Thus it was clear to Britain that its response to the catastrophe would impact national repute: "England is now placed upon her trial … Every Continental nation will watch with eager curiosity the line of action which we may adopt … Any sign of weakness on our part will be quickly observed, and the least symptom of a want of nerve or resolution will be hailed as proof that the greatness of our Empire is at last upon the wane."[106] The press thus suggested that the disaster at Khartoum meant that the very empire was at stake. "Prompt and vigorous measures" were widely urged.[107] This claim, while outlining a key moment in which Britain would redefine itself, also served to draw readers away from the gaping epistemological hole constituted by the loss in Sudan. In fact, all of these machinations of identity construction – crucial as they were to imperial consolidation – were also used to distract Britons from the fact that the press was operating on an utter dearth of factual information about how Khartoum fell and what had happened to Gordon – facts that, when recognized, would undercut the empire's assumption of epistemological mastery.

Tellingly, there was also a general silence on the fate of the defenders and civilians of Khartoum. A few papers reported, in one sentence, "rumours that two thousand persons were massacred at Khartoum."[108] No attempts were made to process the massacre; the press had no details, and the slaughter was beyond description.[109] The *Birmingham*

Daily Post acknowledged that the remaining Egyptian garrison in Khartoum had "probably been massacred to a man" but simultaneously downplayed the deceased's humanity, describing the soldiers as "unfortunate instruments of a fallen tyranny."[110] This inability or reluctance to describe or comprehend such violence once again points to imperial failure to confront the real consequences of empire.

All of this obsessive knowledge production and imagination of national community nevertheless ventured to contain events that flouted comprehension, and to create order and stability in the face of chaos. Predictably, this was not particularly effective in mitigating metropolitan angst: "Among the general public intense anxiety as to General Gordon's fate outweighs every other consideration. The absence of any definite news regarding him only increases a feeling of despair."[111] This oft-reprinted example of the attempt to express the social agitation surrounding this event resonates with Kelly Hurley's suggestion that the "Gothic in particular has been theorized as an instrumental genre, reemerging cyclically, at periods of cultural stress, to negotiate the anxieties that accompany social and epistemological transformations and crises."[112] In other words, when the newspapers' efforts to organize imperial events failed either to articulate or assuage the sense of loss and anxiety permeating the metropole, the press's other strategy attempted to work through loss by using Gothic representational strategies. In the face of an information vacuum immediately after the report of Khartoum's fall reached London, Gothic tropes of uncertainty, linguistic inadequacy, treachery, monstrosity, and isolation began to proliferate through the press. The following exploration of how these tropes manifested demonstrates that as each of these fantastic elements invaded the rationalist discourse of the news, this imperial institution became less and less stable.

Unable to hide the epistemological gap that their inadequate supplementary material underscored, the press emphasized and even sensationalized the notion that "Gordon's fate … is at present a mystery."[113] This prevailing uncertainty paved the way for fantastic conjectures; in the absence of dependable intelligence with which to write this history, press writers turned to fantasy. Because "the wildest rumours" and "conflicting" reports were rampant throughout London,[114] only speculations on Gordon's fate could be given – and they were: "Rumours vary immensely … It was said, for instance, that the rebels had only gained possession of the outworks, and that Gordon was still holding the citadel," working "to hold his own against the rebel attacks."[115] Appealing as this was, other fantasies emerged: "Another report says that General Gordon is now in the hands of the Mahdi, and yet another adds that he is now wearing the Mahdi's uniform."[116] One paper was sadly optimistic, suggesting that "unless Gordon was killed at the head of his men resisting the attack before Khartoum fell, he will probably before long be able to exercise a very useful influence in the councils of the Mahdi."[117] Meanwhile, the Irish press, writing from a comparative distance from the frenzied hub, perhaps most clearly recognized the empire's epistemological limitations.[118] As a Dublin paper put it, "The most ominous circumstance of the whole muddle and bungle is, perhaps, that neither in London nor in Cairo will the whole grave truth be known."[119] Thus the role of the imaginary in institutional processing of the loss of martial identity, imperial territory, and narrative itself began to develop in a marked way. What the public could not know was that by the time speculations about Gordon's fate appeared, along with the calls for action outlined above, Gordon was already dead. When his death was confirmed late in the evening on 7 February, calls for his rescue promptly ended. What remained, however, was the textual husk of patriotic affect; the news of Gordon's death would mark the futility of hopeful "rumours" of his survival, and the newspaper archive would remain to haunt the empire with its powerlessness to restore him and the martial masculinity he signified.

Just as the troubling uncertainty of what had passed in the contact zone fuelled the fantastic suppositions in the metropole, the inadequacy of language in describing the full horror of the event underlay and informed much of the initial response to the report of the fall. A correspondent stationed with the expeditionary forces wrote to the *Daily Chronicle* (London), "No tongue or pen can adequately describe … the effect produced in all hearts by the fatal announcement."[120] Another journalist confessed, "I cannot adequately describe the sensation which has been made in London by the fall of Khartoum, and at the uncertain fate of General Gordon."[121] So, when rationalist discourse failed to communicate meaningfully the affective consequences of imperial loss, the press drew on Gothic imagery that tended to gesture to the supernatural and evilness.[122] Ideas of darkness also prevailed: the *Northern Echo* (Darlington) complained that a "darkness … shrouds the fate of the hero," while the *Bristol Mercury* admitted, "No fresh light of any importance has yet been thrown upon the fall of Khartoum, and the fate of Gordon is still shrouded in doubt," and even Dublin's *Freeman's Journal* suggested that a "black omen is under our eyes."[123] In conjunction with darkness, the papers deployed other Gothic conventions such as sacrifice, spectacle, oppressive surroundings, and evil spirits: for the *Morning Post* (London), the loss of Khartoum constituted "one of the darkest pages of English history, for … a British envoy and plenipotentiary was allowed to be sacrificed to the Mahdi"; for the *Ipswich Journal*, the situation was a "sickening spectacle," and for the *Freeman's Journal*, "the Soudan maze is becoming every hour more entangled, and the British position ... inextricable," and thus confined.[124] The *Bristol Mercury* even implied that evil had entered the nation itself when the paper criticized the government's detractors who "seized upon the national calamity with ghoul-like enjoyment, in the hope of making party capital out of it."[125] The word "ghoul" appeared in English in the late eighteenth century and was derived from the Arabic "ġūl," meaning "a desert demon believed to rob graves and devour corpses."[126] Thus, linguistically as well as figuratively, the menace of the desert infiltrated the metropole. The papers, at a loss for realist language, had resorted to describing the consequences of empire by reaching for the fantastic.

Close on the heels of this fanciful imagery emerged various fabrications of events in Khartoum. The British metropolis invented a story of betrayal – that a disloyal Egyptian soldier had opened the gates to the enemy. This was total fiction, but almost universally declared.[127] Pragmatically, the treachery fantasy let the government off the hook somewhat: because betrayal could have happened at any time, it was ostensibly unrelated to the delay in the relief expedition. Importantly, though, invention supplied detail where knowledge could provide none; the *Preston Chronicle* suggested that "on the night of the 25th ult., Farag Pasha and other Egyptian leaders entered into secret negotiations with the Mahdi and got all the Egyptian troops on one side of the city, and that whilst one sent boats another opened the landway."[128] In reality, Mahdist incursion into the fort occurred when the receding Nile exposed a crucial weakness in the fortification. A previous flood from the White Nile had filled in a trench on the southwestern side of the fort, levelling a defensive mound and taking out the landmines Gordon had planted. This flow and ebb had yielded a stretch of passable land leading right up to the fort. With diversions deployed elsewhere, 40,000 Ansar were able to penetrate the forces in this location.[129] Khartoum's defences quickly collapsed from there. The material fact of the very landscape – in this case, the flowing waters of the Nile – neutralizing Khartoum's defence not only echoes Gordon's depiction of the Nile as menacing and Theweleit's assessment of the threat of flowing monstrosity to the martial male, but also resonates with the earlier imperial experience of Zululand's topography contributing to martial loss and penetration; once again, Africa itself seemed to engulf the British invader. What the fiction of human treachery ultimately provided, however, was confirmation "that Gordon's pluck, gallantry, energy, and determination had not failed, but that the place had been opened to the besieging force."[130] In other words, British imperial masculinity remained intact, and was merely cheated. There were, of course, other inventions. Gloomy conspiracy theories enhanced the notion that trickery was afoot: "Very alarming rumours prevail in the West-End clubs as to the fate of Gordon, who, it is stated, was killed some two months ago, when it is alleged Khartoum fell."[131] The *Morning Post* printed a theory that Gordon's assurances that Khartoum was "all right," smuggled out in late December, were the Mahdi's forgeries – trickery designed to lure in the rescue mission.[132] Thus, recognizing that the papers handled uncertainty by imagining treachery in order to protect the fictions of imperial competence and Mahdist duplicity underscores not only the presence but also the central function of the fantastic in serving imperial narratives across genres.

The actual circumstances of Gordon's death were not demystified in Western scholarship, let alone the British public, until 1982, when Douglas Johnson, after examining Sudanese accounts from Arabic archives, published his findings of what probably happened to Gordon: he was shot by mistake while being taken prisoner, while the Mahdi, for obvious strategic reasons, had wanted the Englishman captured alive. As far as Victorian Britain was concerned, however, Gordon was killed by an undifferentiated shadowy body – and that is exactly how the Ansar were depicted in the press: as a radical other seeking to engulf the British masculine body.

One way the press othered the Mahdists was the classic pseudo-anthropological turn that sought first to treat the enemy as an object of study and then to relegate them to a previous era.[133] For instance, the *Daily News* reported that, before Egypt colonized Sudan, a battleground at Halifyeh was "seat of a native Soudani dynasty."[134] Its neighbour, Shendy, was also described as "the decayed capital of a Soudani dynasty; and the descendants of the Kings of Shendy have transmitted from father to son their legacy of undying hatred towards the rule of the Egyptians."[135] The *Hampshire Telegraph and Sussex Chronicle* went further than this in historicizing Sudanese resistance and divorcing it from British-Egyptian imperial interests in suggesting that "dynastic feeling as well as religious enthusiasm must be taken into account in formulating a complete explanation of the Soudan rebellion."[136] The press thus not only situated the enemy in the ancient world,[137] it also insisted that their implied prejudices were antiquated and out of touch with modern contexts. Predominantly, however, the press's imperative to identify the unknown opponent as other manifested in its depiction of the enemy as monstrous and sexually threatening. Consider how *Berrow's Worcester Journal* depicts Gordon's resistance in sexual terms: "Two days before Sir Charles Wilson's arrival the place which England's envoy for nearly twelve months held in England's name, defending her honour against a fierce foe that swarmed on every side, was surrendered by Egyptian treachery."[138] Here, Gordon and the defence of Khartoum are explicitly associated with England, while Khartoum itself, although it had become a kind of metonym for Gordon, is explicitly feminized. England is thus both the masculine defender of feminine honour and the feminine subject whose honour is being defended. Thus, in "defending her honour," England faced the trial of maintaining its own chastity against a "fierce foe that swarmed on every side." This defence amounted, of course, to a trial of England's martial efficacy in facing a sexually aggressive, grotesque body. The fact that multiple papers referred to Wolseley's imagined rescue of Gordon and Khartoum as "consummation"[139] suggests the underlying sexual investments of rescue, penetration, and invasion – except, rather than rescued by British heroism, the imperial outpost was defiled by the engulfing monster.

In sketching out this grotesque threat to Khartoum and British forces, the press referred almost exclusively to the Mahdi's followers as the "hordes."[140] With Khartoum fallen, the rescuing British expeditionary forces suddenly became, in metropolitan eyes, incredibly vulnerable to these "surging hosts of the Mahdi's followers."[141] Imagery of swarming Arab masses threatening Wolseley's men appeared in the news, echoing representations of Zulus engulfing the redcoats during the Anglo-Zulu War. The *Belfast News-Letter* and the *Freeman's Journal* both printed a vision of this plague: "The hot season will be upon our troops in about three weeks. The Muhdi's fanatical hordes, flushed with success, will be able to swarm around the British posts, and the wavering and friendly tribes are likely now to become open enemies."[142] Here, "flushed with success" suggests that the anticipated surge of assault would be driven by the excitement of having penetrated Khartoum. The *Northern Echo* was less subtle in making a similar point about the Sudanese being sexually threatening: "The little army of England is all but surrounded by the hordes of the Mahdi. Those hordes will be aroused and stimulated by the news of the capture of a hero long deemed invincible."[143] Evidently, the sexual connotations of engulfment and penetration suffusing accounts of the Anglo-Zulu War were also potent here in the depiction of an "aroused and stimulated" martial enemy. Some papers feared Sudanese assaults on the British "to their rear"[144] and "mysterious rear movement of the strong force of Arabs";[145] the expression of concerns about unexpected penetration was becoming less and less delicate.

If configuring African resistance as a sexual threat picked up on imperial discourse about the Zulus, so did the erasure of Sudanese humanity in favour of abstractions and descriptions of environmental elements. The press represented the Sudanese as "the tide of insurrection,"[146] a "raging sea of rebellion,"[147] and a "floodtide of Arab fanaticism"[148] threatening to break on the frontiers of civilization. This uprising of course would also mean the expansion of a still relatively unknown, threatening entity. As in Southern Africa, these depictions imagine the colonial other as a flowing, fluid entity; the Ansar are no exception to Theweleit's theory of how threats to masculine bodies are historically conceived as watery engulfment. Just as the redcoats in Zululand sought to stiffen against the "resistless surging torrent of black creatures,"[149] the metropole imagined its avatar as a rigid, immoveable pillar in the face of the flowing threat. The *Morning Post*, for instance, insisted, "Khartoum has fallen, but not through any weakness or diminution of the indomitable energy of the great man who for many months past has stood behind its walls like a rock against which the angry waves of Arab fanaticism dashed themselves in vain."[150] In addition to watery forces, the Mahdists are reduced to "fanaticism," "insurrection," or "rebellion" – abstract forces that exist primarily as elements oppositional to the empire. Thus when the *Standard* wrote, "This country has become engaged in a duel with the savage fanaticism of the Desert,"[151] it not only denied the humanity of Britain's opponents, it also solidified for the metropole that, once again, they faced a war on an idea, an indiscrete entity part of the territory itself, a radical other. The Mahdist forces are thus conceived as a monstrous, fluid, sexually driven, grotesque body, exceeding its own origins as the uprising spread, and threatening to encompass and consume the discrete, bounded, imperial martial body – and, by penetrating Khartoum, sending Wolseley's forces running in retreat, and beheading Gordon's punctured body, it effectively did so.

Lastly, the trope of isolation circulating in British culture instrumentally heightened the psychological tension surrounding this historical moment by buttressing the nation's fixation on Gordon's engulfment by monstrous forces. In addition, it served to mythologize him, offering the metropole the fantasy of the hero it needed – the hero who was more than man could be, because the reality of Gordon's fallibility fell short of quenching the nation's need for a representative figure of prowess. Thus, depictions of Gordon's isolation tended to manifest in two, often intertwined, ways. The *Daily Telegraph*'s imagery of a "ring of iron clos[ing] upon him"[152] characterizes the first – that is, emphasis on Gordon being utterly alone in a world of African others, whose grotesqueness threatened to consume him. The second drew on the supernatural to mythologize Gordon as an outlier, a messianic figure, with special qualities and a higher calling that set him on a pedestal of masculine martial holiness.[153] Gordon's physical isolation in many ways gave a powerful charge to the aura of messianism surrounding him; the threat of the "iron ring" both emphasized his singularity and inspired affect in the papers: "Gordon was all alone"[154] – that is, without white companions – "cut off from the outer world."[155] For "fac[ing] alone the fanaticism of the Soudan," he was esteemed: "Alone in his solitary citadel, surrounded by a sea of foes, he has battled with the forces of barbarism."[156] This Gothic imagery of Gordon's body swallowed by the monstrous threat enhanced the mythology, even hagiography, surrounding him. Long biographies of Gordon appeared in the media, emphasizing his stoicism, stunning career, insight, and religious devotion. One publication proposed that Gordon "was inspired";[157] another suggested that his "noble character and … sense of the divinity of duty" underlay his "semi-sacred reputation";[158] yet another described his governing powers during the siege as "mysteries."[159] Gordon's Christian stoicism was also emphasized: "[his] strong faith shines ever before his eyes like a pillar of fire in a dark and desolate wilderness."[160] This rendition of Gordon as otherworldly saint offered the metropole the pleasing narrative that morality was on the side of empire.

If metropolitan reverence of Gordon set him apart from his fellow humans, so did the power of prophecy and other magical powers often attributed to him. Gordon was supposed to have held a "conviction" that he would be "caught at Khartoum" and "forebodings … of [a] long premeditated treachery."[161] He was also thought to hold other mystic powers: the *Liverpool Mercury* assured its readers that, "if General Gordon is alive, we may rely on his magic personality to keep himself safe,"[162] while the *Morning Post* suggested that Gordon had "powers which his foes may well have regarded as supernatural."[163] But if the papers associated Gordon with the supernatural while he was alive, they also, in a sense, rendered him a ghost. The press's narratives of Gordon's life and service had the tone of obituaries – and they were certainly read as such after 7 February. Meanwhile, the widespread printing of his last telegraph invoked his disembodied voice, summoning it from the liminal space between fact and uncertainty. In the metropolitan experience, the figure of Gordon was already hovering in the threshold between death and life. These mechanisms of memorial, combined with the lack of closure surrounding his death and his missing body, positioned Gordon as a persistent spectre in the British imagination – a sphere which, as we've seen, played a central role in recording this particular historical moment.

Turning to Imagination

Metropolitan print culture illustrates that, because of the inherent limitations in imperial technology, surveillance, and knowledge production, the role of the imaginary and fantastical was central in generating the narrative required to meet the affective needs of the nation. Anxieties surrounding martial masculinity and military prowess were articulated, negotiated, and amplified through Gothic conventions that worked outside ostensibly rational institutional logic because the purportedly objective accounts of the fall of Khartoum inadequately represented the event's consequences for the empire and national identity. The press thus drew on the literary sphere to articulate this historical moment. Some papers compared the fall of Khartoum to dramatic productions. The *Liverpool Post* lamented, "Never has destiny contrived a more mournfully perfect tragedy. On all hands dangers and dilemmas appear."[164] The *Dundee Courier and Argus* used Shakespearean tragedy to voice national loss: "'The pity of it, Iago, the pity of it,' was the sad and dazed expression of the Moor of Venice to his lieutenant, as that viper poured the poison of detraction and lies into his leader's ear. To hear of the fall of Khartoum and capture or death of Gordon … is indeed pitiful."[165] The paper's choice to reference a Shakespearean tragedy rather than one of his history plays, which generally formulate martial masculinity as penetrating and feature heroic endings, is telling. Quoting *Othello*, which during the nineteenth century tended to be performed as melodrama with the title character in blackface, instead emphasizes the self-inflicted death of a heroic body that is compromised through its blackness, but that, beyond the theatre, is underneath always white. Understanding the loss of Gordon through the lens of *Othello*, then, enabled the *Courier* to imagine its disadvantaged hero betrayed, but in such a way that the ostensible durability of whiteness would outlast the tragedy. This Scottish paper continued to emphasize "the theatrical like character of the situation":

> Just as General Gordon and Sir Chas. Wilson are "coming to touch," the Mahdi rushes in, carries the heroic defender of Khartoum into captivity, and receives the astonished Sir Charles Wilson with a volley of musketry. Nothing so complete, so startling, so sudden, and so embarrassing has ever been witnessed out of a novel or of the stage of transpontine drama … It only needed the capture of Sir Charles Wilson, the officers, and special correspondents … to complete the climax.[166]

Once again, in this sexualized dynamic of power, Gordon/Khartoum plays the part of damsel waiting for the rescuing "touch" of imperial reinforcements. It is this feminizing of the hero, not simply the routing of his gallant British rescuer, that is "so startling" and "so embarrassing" to imperial masculinity that it cannot quite be understood as real – hence the "theatrical like character of the situation." The *Standard* even suggested that these theatrics were still in progress: "The curtain is about to rise for the fifth act of the Egyptian drama; at its close shall we witness the apotheosis of the Mahdi, or shall we see this new John of Leyden ascend the funereal pyre, and bury himself beneath the ruins of his burning palace?"[167] Whether the reference to Leiden draws primarily on the historical death of the prophet and Anabaptist rebel against the Holy Roman Empire or to Giacomo Meyerbeer's 1849 opera, *Le Prophète*, this writer turned to the repository of yore to imagine a grim – and politically theatrical – death for the Mahdi because the real conditions of the historical moment could not fulfill this imperial need.

Other papers compared the siege to a segment in an epic: "The whole story of the defence of Khartoum reads like a romance borrowed from the pages of some chronicler of the age of chivalry."[168] The "hero of antiquity" was associated with epic literature from a time long past: "The entire civilized world … has for months past watched with interest the Homerian epic, whose hero was Gordon. What a powerful mind, what an unwavering energy must have been … in this mysterious man who did such incredible deeds!"[169] To articulate the kind of heroism the nation needed Gordon to embody, the press had to look to the ancient past and the epic fiction of an antique author. The turn to the fanciful here indicates the inadequacy of the real; Britain, across forms of writing, had to imagine and reimagine ways of articulating both masculine ideality no longer attainable and the troubling implications the attendant imperial loss had for national identity.

Thus, when the emergence of Gothic representation in the papers usurped the deployment of empirical knowledge, troubled the press's role in providing objective accounts, blurred expectations across literary genres, and relied on the Gothic to buttress imperial authority, metropolitan anxieties about boundary violation, governmental failure, and technological limitations remained acute and unresolved. Neither could the government or military offer a resolution, despite widespread calls for a full-scale invasion of Sudan. The nation recognized its reputation was at stake: the *Daily News* queried, "Can the British army retire now without making England the laughing stock of the world?"[170] Other papers urged, "We cannot 'scuttle' ... Weak as this Government is, it will not further humiliate the country; it will continue to advance towards Khartoum."[171] Beyond the great embarrassment the loss entailed, Britain also envisioned material backlash: "A flight would mean a confession to the Eastern world that we were beaten, and it would mean war and mutiny from one end of Asia to the other."[172] The panicked calls to reinforce garrisons across the empire, particularly in India, testify to the metropolitan conviction that "there would be real and terrible danger, not to our soldiers only, or to Egypt, but to the British Empire, if we were now tamely to turn our backs upon Khartoum and scuttle out of the Soudan as fast as possible."[173] In fact, so sure were most papers that British imperial forces would retake Khartoum that they reported that preparations for war were already under way.[174] Britain's decision, however, was not to execute "prompt and vigorous measures," but rather to retreat. British forces in Sudan were in no shape for a sustained attack on the Mahdi, and Wolseley recalled them. Then, in April, the Penjdeh incident[175] distracted Britain from its humiliation in Sudan, and the empire turned to protecting its jewel, India, from Russian ambitions. This was a particularly anticlimactic turn of events, considering the national hype about smashing the Mahdi. Wolseley's retreat cost Britain "honour"; the nation was left with a prevailing sense of penetration and the dissolution of its imperial boundaries. Imperial revenge would have to wait until the "reconquest" of Sudan in 1898. Finally, Britain's doubts about the efficacy of martial masculinity could only have been amplified when Gordon's voice emerged from beyond the grave via his Khartoum journals, published in June 1885. This text went to work destabilizing the discourse of heroism, narrative order, spatial integrity, and the coherence of martial machinery.

The inability of institutional writing or history itself to resolve these accumulating national anxieties is not surprising when we consider the notable increase in the late 1880s and 1890s of imperial Gothic fiction, a genre that tends to be preoccupied with decline, degeneration, decay, and invasion.[176] The following chapter explores how imperial Gothic fiction drew on the profoundly unsettling epistemological limitations that Gordon's Khartoum journals and the metropolitan press brought to light and highlights the role of imagination in knowledge production and representation by considering in depth one of the most widely read representatives of the genre. In Richard Marsh's *The Beetle*, penetrations in Northeast Africa remain a ghostly lingering presence, and, echoing this historical archive, are figured as sexual trauma. The Gothic novel, hinging on paranoia about invasion from the East, employs the tropes of penetration and dissolution not only to articulate empire's inability to surveil the foreign other but also to terrify by imagining subjugated manhood, refusing to offer resolution, and destabilizing national literary identity. In effect, *The Beetle* engages the failures of imperial technologies and authority rendered so evident in Gordon's journals and in the metropolitan newspapers in order to invite an interrogation of history, fantasy, and desire itself.

Chapter Four

Marsh's Perforations: Desire, Imperial Decay, and the Narrative Instability of *The Beetle*

Egypt still lies open to the attacks of its enemies ... Our policy ... may be briefly described as the reconquest of the Soudan. The Khalifa and his fanatical followers are as much as ever a standing menace to the peace and good government of Egypt.

– *Western Mail*, 6 Feb. 1897

With the absence of resolution following the crisis in Sudan, Northeast Africa remained a disquieting presence in the British imagination.[1] Gordon's death and the loss of Khartoum remained open wounds in the metropole, signals of imperial instability. As John Tosh puts it, "no imperial event at this time occasioned more alarm or soul-searching" than this predicament.[2] That Gordon's death was never explicated, his remains never recovered, only added to national uncertainty; that the so-called reconquest of Sudan was deferred until 1898 meant that Britain's dishonour went unavenged. Victorian Britain's broader relationship with the region, however, entailed anxieties about cultural resistance, imperial economy, and social and physical health, along with this martial vulnerability. Egypt, becoming "more than ever a focal point for imperialist anxieties and passions," came to symbolize "the mystifyingly obdurate power of what we might call geopolitical otherness."[3] Egypt, with a history of complex civilization that Britain recognized, functioned as a locus for African resistance to imperial rule. Indeed, African nationalism often focalized around Egypt as an alternative motherland.[4] Meanwhile, British preoccupations with Egypt were also economic – by 1897, the Suez Canal, still crucial for resource extraction and trade, also signified political vulnerability.[5] Finally, the association of contact zones like Egypt and Sudan with venereal disease (supposedly transmitted back to the metropole by returning soldiers) offered yet another Eastern threat. In this particular manifestation of paranoia, Africa signified explicitly as a menace to the martial male body.

Drawing on these contexts, this chapter explores how popular fiction deepened the ruptures widened by institutional representations of martial loss, governmental failure, and epistemological limitations in the wake of the fall of Khartoum. We have seen how H. Rider Haggard's critique of the adventure romance genre underscored the complex relationship between the writing and the unwriting of imperial fantasy; this narrative tension would reappear and even intensify in subsequent imperial fiction. In many ways, *King Solomon's Mines* and *She* carved out the discursive space necessary for later writers to explore further the instability of imperial fantasy and its attendant fantasies of colonial masculinity. Perhaps the most important successor to Haggard's narrative strategy of auto-critique is Richard Marsh's *The Beetle* (1897). While *The Beetle* is most frequently read in relation to Bram Stoker's *Dracula,* it echoes Haggard's suspicion of narratives of empire in Africa. Haggard's and Marsh's works explore similar threats of foreign invasion from imagined African others, anxiety surrounding gender and heteronormativity, and confrontations with alternative knowledges. All three texts are preoccupied with bodily destruction, cannibalism, and masculine physicality. They also share similar strategies of critiquing imperial writing, likewise interrogating the relationships between authority, the impermeable male body, governance, and narrative. In exploiting this interplay, both authors manage to execute their arguments using motifs that tapped into timely and popular fears, imaginations, and desires.[6] While Haggard explores the Anglo-Zulu War's disruptive effect on imperial masculinity and the imperial narrative, Marsh tackles the legacy of the fall of Khartoum and the ongoing Mahdist uprising in Sudan, still very much a concern for Britain in 1897. As Ailise Bulfin has recently demonstrated, loss in Sudan was a central context for Marsh as he composed *The Beetle*: not only did he begin writing it the same year that Kitchener launched the Sudan campaign (1895), but the death of Gordon was still very much a spectre in the Victorian imagination. Bulfin makes the point that *Punch* magazine's 1896 cartoon depicting the ghost of Gordon appearing to a militant John Bull in the desert and warning him to "Remember!" the imperial disaster at Khartoum suggests that public political discourse was also using the Gothic to signify resistance to empire.[7] More specifically still, W.C. Harris and Dawn Vernooy have convincingly shown that *The Beetle* implicitly links the invading monster to Britain's history with Egypt and Sudan by referencing Wadi Halfa and Dongola – both important sites for British deployment of troops in the highly topical attempt to subdue Sudan.[8] But where

Harris and Vernooy argue that Marsh's text expresses "a wish to overcome a recalcitrant Orient,"[9] I aim to demonstrate that, like Haggard's work, *The Beetle*, discursively complex, disrupts imperial deployments of power as it processes the cultural fallout from Khartoum. Crucially for this process of disruption, *The Beetle* follows *King Solomon's Mines* and *She* insofar as it is framed by an editorial force, and it uses this frame narrative to demand critical readings of authoritative claims and to highlight imperial decay and problems of governance.

An eccentric piece of late-Victorian Gothic fiction, *The Beetle* exhibits the theme of decline and loss so typical of texts of this period. Resonating with prevalent popular concerns about the British economic and cultural stake in Egypt and the consequences of the disaster at Khartoum for imperial and metropolitan manhood, Marsh's work explores the effects of invasion of the body, understood both as physical entity and as narrating, history-making authority. *The Beetle* interrogates the boundaries of both bodies and narratives, ultimately linking these forms through the "erotics of reading,"[10] and, in doing so, it critiques justifications of patriarchal governance and imperial legitimacy, which ultimately become leaky, grotesque, and profoundly unstable. In this way, the novel hyperbolizes the consequences, for British identity, of martial and governmental failures with respect to Sudan in the 1880s. The four-part narrative begins with the perspective of Robert Holt, an unemployed clerk, who, emaciated and exhausted, crawls into a mysterious house in search of shelter. Inside, he is hypnotized, assaulted, and possessed by the Lord of the Beetle, a bi-gendered, shape-shifting priest(ess) in the cult of Isis. He is then sent on a mission across London to steal a packet of letters from celebrity parliamentarian Paul Lessingham, written by the latter's fiancée, Marjorie Lindon, which the Beetle then uses to draw both her and Sydney Atherton, her confidant and would-be lover, into its schemes. Sydney's narrative conveys his supposed devotion to Marjorie, his fiery competition with Paul, and key aspects of the Beetle's plan for vengeance. Marjorie's story then takes over to recount her dedication to Paul, her encounter with the near-dead Holt, and the events leading up to her capture by the Beetle. Detective Champnell's narrative follows, accounting for Sydney and Paul's truce in order to rescue Marjorie, the newly formed band's chase after the Beetle and its victim, her ultimate (if incomplete) rescue, and the culmination of various narrative threads.

One way to read the search for Marjorie is as a quest that galvanizes male bonds and establishes the efficacy of the British network of communication, patriarchal social networks, technology, railways, transportation, the telegraph, and so on. This, of course, would reaffirm and recuperate British imperial prowess in the wake of losing so badly in Sudan. This reading would also complement an understanding of Paul Lessingham as a broken man rebuilt, having overcome his fear of his Eastern adversary and being sparked into action by the threat of losing his prized fiancée.[11] Seemingly affirming this transformation, Champnell observes Paul's arousal into activity: "he was getting a firmer hold of the strength which had all but escaped him … he was becoming more and more of a man."[12] Such a narrative of recuperation, however, is ultimately unfulfilled: not only is resolution absent, but, upon closer examination of the dynamics between characters, genders, and narration, the idea of noble male lines of defence is profoundly troubled. Critics tend, to varying degrees, to recognize the gender-disrupting work this novel enacts but frequently read *The Beetle* as participating in, rather than challenging, an extant imperialist patriarchal ideology.[13]

While recognizing that the novel's problematic construction of the East is crucial for understanding the terms by which *The Beetle* engages the Egyptian Question and its impact on British manhood, I also want to suggest that the novel's rendition of the East is more complex than many critics have allowed; while activating numerous stereotypes about the Orient and articulating various forms of threat, Marsh's text simultaneously highlights these fears in order to draw readers' attention to his real target: British conduct. In underlining the relationship between character, body, and narrative to destabilize male authority, *The Beetle* pulls apart traditional narratives of British manliness and governmental policy. Such norms frequently celebrated men's bodies as being bounded, solid, and impermeable. As Elizabeth Grosz points out, traditionally it is

> woman's corporeality [that] is inscribed as a mode of seepage … The metamorphics of uncontrollability, the ambivalence between desperate, fatal attraction and strong revulsion, the deep seated fear of absorption, the association of femininity with contagion and disorder, the undecidability of the limits of the female body … its powers of cynical seduction and allure are all common themes in literary and cultural representations of women.[14]

But we saw in the archive surrounding the downfall of Khartoum that the British martial outpost was highly permeable, disordered, engulfed, subjugated, and the object of the Mahdi's desire – and this permeability was coming to the fore in cultural perceptions of imperial masculinity. Thus, while men's bodies have tended to be defined in contradistinction to the inscription Grosz articulates, *The Beetle*, emerging from the context of imperial loss, inverts this ontology, representing men's bodies and/or narratives – their credibility – as leaky, unstable, and subject to various forms of penetration.

Penetration

As I have suggested, *The Beetle* lends itself to comparison with Haggard's work. It similarly parodies codes of masculinity in the wake of imperial vulnerability, provoking both anxiety and humour simultaneously.[15] But, if likewise teasing, this text also draws its reader into a particular fantasy of male subjugation, albeit a darker one. The archetypal invaders, the Beetle and Ayesha, share some strong and obvious similarities: both possess magic of sorts; both are sexually aggressive, ostensibly female but transcending boundaries of gender, monstrous, the object of both fascination and repulsion, and driven by their desires; and both hold men in subjugation via the power of either gazing or being gazed upon. But the foreign threat is progressive; in Marsh's work, it actually succeeds in entering the metropole, penetrating not just narratives instantiated from travel abroad, but those materializing from within the metropolis. Indeed, set not in the colonial sphere but in the core of England's capital, *The Beetle* presents readily recognizable spaces: the plush carpet of the Beetle's lair is compared to the turf of Richmond Park; the Beetle's directions take Holt eastwards across the capital through Walham Green, Lillie Road, Brompton, Fulham Road, Sloane Street, Lowndes Square, and so on; and when Marjorie is captured, she is "borne through the heart of civilized London."[16] Thus, Marsh brings the impacts of imperial projects in Egypt and Sudan on British masculinity directly to the home front. He moves beyond the narratives about and from contact zones to suggest that the national body of writing – imagination itself – has been compromised by dark desire. As in *She*, that which is understood as other is shown to emerge from within – except Marsh takes this revelation to a new level of disconcertion by illustrating the complex relationship between fantasies about the penetration of masculinity and writing, itself understood as a phallic extension of male prowess.

In this Gothic text, masculinity crumbles, the male body dissolves, and ultimately narrative, as the vehicle of constructing male authority, disintegrates – all of which is refracted through the presence of the monster, the Beetle, the Eastern threat. It is a figure of hostile penetration: it hypnotizes and mesmerizes, and its cult of Isis deploys rape, mutilation, and burning to yield the disintegration of the English body.

The threat of hypnosis was particularly unsettling, for it signified a penetration of both psychic boundaries and physical autonomy.[17] The Beetle, as a figure of gender ambiguity, also resists categorization and, like Britain's historical East African others, is epistemologically defiant, though in Marsh's fiction such slipperiness manifests itself in physical modes. Holt reflects that, upon first seeing this "someone," "I could not at once decide if it was a man or a woman. Indeed at first I doubted if it was anything human. But … it was impossible such a creature could be feminine … His age I could not guess … The cranium, and indeed, the whole skull, was so small as to be disagreeably suggestive of something animal."[18]

Foreshadowing the Beetle's subsequent transmogrification, this passage uses zoological language in an unsuccessful attempt to offer an identifying description of the creature. As in the accounts that follow, the Beetle resists narrative confinement and avoids being pinned down as an object of study – indeed, it literally bursts out of the bucket under which Sydney attempts to pin it.[19] Holt later reconsiders the Beetle's gender: "I wondered if I could by any possibility have blundered, and mistaken a woman for a man; some ghoulish example of her sex, who had so yielded to her depraved instincts as to have become nothing but a ghastly reminiscence of womanhood."[20] Holt's inability to classify the creature according to dominant categories of gender and their attendant normative imperatives sparks revulsion and contempt. Sydney is likewise unable to place the Beetle in terms of age, race, class, caste, or nationality.[21] The creature's ability to transmogrify and mesmerize constitutes competition from an alternative knowledge system, while its characterization of both Holt and Lessingham as thieves provides a counter-narrative to those of the white British men in this novel.[22] Its voice, likened to a "rusty saw" – an object that coarsely divides things in to two – comments on Holt's "white skin" as it entices him to stand by its bedside, objectifying Holt's race even as it interrogates his sexuality.[23] And, certainly, it embodies direct sexual threat, emasculates as it mesmerizes, and haunts those it has penetrated. Just one example of this appears in Sydney's lab: "There was a sound of droning … the fashion of [Paul's] countenance began to change, – it was pitiable to witness. I rushed to him. 'Lessingham! – don't be a fool – play the man!'"[24] The Beetle, then, is a lingering presence that threatens to overthrow masculine composure. As Julian Wolfreys puts it, "Marsh's beetle-human hybrid provides a powerfully exemplary grotesque embodiment of late Victorian anxieties."[25] But where Wolfreys suggests that its "body is grotesque because it is unstable, excessive, ambiguously traced by so many fragments of identity,"[26] I argue that the Beetle's grotesqueness emphasizes that maleness and male authority, traditionally associated with fortification and solidity, itself undergoes permeation, lysis, and dissolution. This dissolution becomes evident when we consider the text's treatment of its masculine narrators and figures.

Subjugation

Male degradation features almost immediately in the text through the figure of Robert Holt. The novel's most overtly emasculated man, Holt experiences a range of penetrations: he is homeless because unemployed,[27] and therefore has no "fortress" beyond his own body; he is mesmerized and surveilled by the Beetle; and ultimately his narrative is unstable. In approaching what turns out to be the Beetle's lair in search of shelter, he encounters an entrapment that destroys his remaining autonomy. As Jennifer McCollum suggests, the house is presented with "vagina-like imagery": "When [Holt] sticks his arm through the hole [of the window] he finds that 'it was warm in there!'"[28] But while Holt starts out as the penetrator of the space, once he is inside, the sexual metaphor flips, and he becomes engulfed by "panic" at "the presence … [of] something evil."[29] In an attempt to resist this dark presence, Holt becomes rigid and frozen, "stricken by a sudden paralysis,"[30] much like Theweleit's Freikorps officers terrified of feminized flow. Nevertheless, he is emasculated: Holt admits, "I made an effort to better play the man. I knew that, at the moment, I played the cur."[31] His bodily control fails, as he is overpowered and "constrained": "I could not control a limb; my limbs were as if they were not mine."[32] Holt's incapacity becomes more entrenched as he renders himself sexually dominated by the creature:

> On a sudden I felt something on my boot, and, with the sense of shrinking, horror, nausea, rendering me momentarily more helpless, I realized that the creature was beginning to ascend my legs, to climb my body … It mounted me, apparently, with as much ease as if I had been horizontal …
>
> Higher and higher! It had gained my loins. It was moving toward the pit of my stomach. The helplessness with which I suffered its invasion was not the least part of my agony … I had not a muscle at my command.[33]

A spatial logic underpins both Holt's terror and the generation of readerly horror: with deliberate slowness, the creature begins at Holt's extremity, and then creeps toward his face, threatening increasingly vulnerable sexual appendages and internal organs along the way. In other words, the creature moves from Holt's periphery to his core, paralleling the novel's invasion narrative as well as the slow paralysis of Gordon's defences at Khartoum. Holt's subjugation is absolute and rendered in overtly sexual terms as he is emasculated by the creature mounting him and "embrac[ing]" his lips with its phallic "myriad legs."[34] Holt's experience of subjugation presages Lessingham's description of being captured and sexually assaulted in "that horrible den" in Cairo, where he is "emasculated" and rendered "incapable of offering even the faintest resistance."[35] Such loss of autonomy is humiliating – as Holt reflects, "such passivity was worse than undignified, it was galling"[36] – but it also challenges masculine imperatives of activity and impenetrability, rendering dominant models of masculinity fallible. Furthermore, a larger, and by now familiar, pattern emerges in the way male vulnerability is figured in fin-de-siècle culture. Set against the established context of Holt's eastward movement and penetration into the space of the colonial other, the depiction of fixity and penetration in this passage takes on a larger significance as it comments on broader implications for Britain's masculine identity. Using martial language such as "invasion" to represent rape, and emphasizing his inability to "command" his body, Holt's narrative resonates with the 1885 Sudanese threat to Britain's martial avatar at Khartoum, where the initially penetrating British martial body attempted to hold a boundary line, but with similarly horrific slowness, was paralysed and overcome. Thus, almost from the outset, *The Beetle* channels affect associated with the penetration of dominant models of masculinity through Gothic horror, while it represents the site of such penetration as not only the martial, but also the metropolitan, body, which now becomes entirely subject to the power of the feminized Eastern other.

That this feminized other, with its indefinable sexual aggression, is ultimately unreadable to the penetrated Holt increases the threat to his masculine prowess insofar as he can not quite name it. When "the man in the bed" bids Holt "Undress!", "A look came on his face, as I stood naked in front of him, which, if it was meant for a smile, was a satyr's smile, and which filled me with a sensation of shuddering repulsion."[37] Here, "satyr" signals lasciviousness, male-on-male rape, and the blurring of lines demarcating species – the union of two orders come together in one monstrous body. Holt's inability to classify or read this monster, especially in terms of gender, undercuts his powers of discernment and his ability to narrate. In fact, as Holt admits to being suspicious of tricks being played on his "abnormally strained imagination,"[38] these physical and mental weaknesses render his narrative authority unstable.

The full ramifications of subjugation for the male body and authorship are evident in Holt's increasing leakiness. Returning from his burglary mission, Holt's body becomes pervious:

> I was in a terrible sweat, – yet tremulous as with cold; covered with mud; bruised, and cut, and bleeding, – as piteous an object as you would care to see. Every limb in my body ached; every muscle was exhausted; mentally and physically I was done; had I not been held up willy nilly, by the spell which was upon me, I should have sunk down, then and there, in a hopeless, helpless, hapless, heap.[39]

His body, assaulted and possessed by the Beetle, becomes grotesque. While concepts of the male body as bounded were fundamental to British masculine identity at this time, fluid exchange with Holt's environment through sweat, blood, and mud renders his body porous and open, as opposed to bounded and closed.[40] Here, the male, not the female, body becomes grotesque.[41] The very form of this passage reflects the absence of boundaries; the sentences run on, ramble, and are held together by semi-colons as closure is continually deferred. Further, the alliteration in the final sentence doubly prolongs the closure, not only through repetition, but also through the use of soft sounds. The fricatives "h" and "s" defy both the boundary of the sentence and of the body; these last four words together produce a panting sound, as the breath quickly moves in and out of the body, circulating convulsively. Thus this passage, both thematically and formally, dismantles the construction of the male body and male narrative as bounded, and therefore authoritative.

Meanwhile, surveillance is the crucial vehicle of Holt's penetration. As in Khartoum, technologies of information in *The Beetle* signify as an Eastern advantage rather than as an imperial possession; surveillance again belongs to the other. Holt reflects that, leading up to his invasion, "I had the horrible persuasion that, though unseeing, I was seen; that my every movement was being watched."[42] The creature's eyes "held me enchained, helpless, spell-bound. I felt that they could do with me as they would; and they did."[43] The erotics of looking are overtly intertwined with power here, as this scene foreshadows Paul's description of his captor in the den: "while she talked, she kept her eyes fixed on my face. Those eyes of hers! … They robbed me of my consciousness, of my power of volition, of my capacity to think, – they made me wax in her hands."[44] This visual penetration disables both men. Physically powerless, they also lose control over language, which, as Minna Vuohelainen argues, undermines the validity of their narratives and suggests weakness in the British psyche and identity.[45] Paul confesses, "I do not think that after she touched my wrist I uttered a word,"[46] just as Holt becomes incapable of speaking his own story: "[the words] came from me, not in response to my will power, but in response to his ... What he willed that I should say, I said."[47] This loss of power over his own narrative devastates Holt's prowess: "For the time I was no longer a man; my manhood was merged in his."[48] Even worse, as we find at the end of the novel, Holt himself did not in fact write "his" narrative; rather, it has been compiled second-hand through Marjorie's and Sydney's memories. This cobbled-together history, on reflection, becomes extremely unstable. Shortcomings in masculinity are thus explicitly connected with narrative deficiency.

Unreliability

Atherton, on the other hand, since "the sensitive something which is found in the hypnotic subject happens, in me, to be wholly absent,"[49] resists the Beetle's mesmerism and thereby seems to affirm his own manliness.[50] Furthermore, because of his stature, attractiveness, breeding, and status, he appears to occupy the role of traditional hero.[51] These qualities, however, are brought to the fore only to show how even the novel's most traditional model of masculinity is also subject to "foreign" invasion as his narrative opens itself up to critique.

First, though, Atherton gets dislodged from the position of patriarch in a number of ways. He becomes Marjorie's object of humour as she relentlessly ridicules him, emasculating and infantilizing him. He also proves himself to be unreasonable, moody, impulsive, and morally flawed. A gentleman scientist, he excitedly "plan[s] legalized murder – on the biggest scale it had ever been planned," and there are certain obvious problems with his ethics:

> If weapons of precision, which may be relied upon to slay, are preservers of the peace – and the man is a fool who says they are not! – then I was within reach of the finest preserver of the peace imagination had ever yet conceived.
>
> What a sublime thought to think that in the hollow of your own hand lies the death of nations, – and it was almost in mine.[52]

His imperial ambitions tie him directly to an expansionist, belligerent stance of which the Aborigines' Protection Society (founded in 1837) would have been quite critical; Sydney plans destructive experiments in "one of the forests of South America, where there is plenty of animal life, but no human."[53] Dismissing both the presence of indigenous humanity and the value of animal life, Sydney reveals the morals of his military research projects to be profoundly misdirected.[54] As Anna Maria Jones aptly puts it, "Of all people, Sydney Atherton seems ill-suited to hold 'the life and death of nations' in his ham-fisted hands."[55] Failing to uphold the masculine ideals of control, restraint, and honour, Atherton becomes a threat to, rather than a figure of, British identity.

He also fails as a sound writer of history; Atherton's accounts are frequently discrepant. For instance, his descriptions of Lessingham's physique are inconsistent, he is evasive about his reasons for letting Holt escape after robbing Lessingham (provoking Champnell to remark, "at certain seasons, Atherton is a queer fish, – but that sounds very queer indeed"),[56] and he withholds the fact that, after a night of drinking with Percy Woodville,[57] he is probably quite drunk (as his behaviour also indicates) when the Beetle appears at his laboratory in the middle of the night. His drunkenness and potential omissions render his account rather dubious. In Atherton's words, "My own senses reeled"; "whether or not I had been the victim of an ocular delusion I could not be sure."[58] Thus, if the ostensible standard of British manliness is feminized, infantilized, vacillating, and profoundly unreliable, then the standard British ideal when it confronts imperial challenge in Africa, as General Gordon articulated very directly in his Khartoum journals, is very much in trouble.

Sydney's questionable status intensifies when he admits to the Beetle that its attempts to con him would not work, since "I'm a bit in that line myself, you know."[59] This admission begins to align Atherton's practices with those of the creature. Harris and Vernooy also read Atherton as a counterpart to the Beetle, but, in their reading, Sydney presents as an asset to Britain.[60] Indeed, in terms of his position as a scientist and technological producer, his role is very much bound up with militant imperial imperatives and national prowess. But Atherton, with his gendered shortcomings, ends up destabilizing British masculine identity through his embodiment of the disruptive qualities belonging to the very other to which he is ostensibly opposed. In other words, Atherton becomes associated with the East and its attendant threats through his very desire for knowledge. The text intensifies this association: while Sydney's inventions are, on one hand, products of Western science and technology, textual references to his work suggest otherwise. The chapter entitled "Atherton's Magic Vapour" connotes sorcery, Atherton's laboratory is a "wizard's cave," and he boasts to the Beetle, "You may suppose yourself to be something of a magician, but it happens, unfortunately for you, that I can do a bit in that line myself ... My stronghold ... contains magic enough to make a show of a hundred thousand such as you."[61] It is Atherton's very interest in "magic" that draws him to the Beetle's mysterious powers: "If the thing had been a trick, then what was it? Was it something new in scientific marvels? Could he give me as much instruction in the qualities of unknown forces as I could him?"[62]

Recognizing that the Beetle's abilities exceed his own epistemology, Atherton reaches for his own national canon, paraphrasing Shakespeare as he muses, "There is more in heaven and earth than is dreamed of in our philosophy."[63] In *Hamlet*, whether Hamlet says "our," as in the quarto edition, or "your," as in the folio, the "philosophy" in question is the "new learning" of Protestant education, a form of worship presented as masculine in contradistinction to the feminized Catholic doctrines. Horatio, to whom Hamlet is speaking, figures as the stoic, impregnable, Protestant manly man. When Hamlet says there are truths beyond our/your philosophy, he figures himself as outside of this virile identity, defying the parameters of the dominant masculine ideology.[64] Thus, when Sydney paraphrases Hamlet, he resonates with this rejection of the dominant humanism, othering himself and aligning himself with the effeminate supernatural in his desire for knowledge. In turn, in associating himself with the damned Hamlet, Atherton effectively damns himself. While Hamlet, damned as he is, is not sexually predatory, the Beetle is. And so, of course, is Sydney. Atherton, as we know, also seems to have extraordinary sexual powers. As Marjorie relates, "I have heard it said that he possesses the hypnotic power to an unusual degree, and that, if he chose to exercise it, he might become a danger to society."[65] Her seemingly lighthearted teasing, set alongside Atherton's other disruptive qualities and the very real danger to humanity he poses through his "pleasant little fancy ... for slaughtering my fellows,"[66] renders this "hypnotic power" akin to the Beetle's. Lastly, as the Beetle compares itself to Atherton, it remarks, "Those who hate are kin."[67] Sydney is a menace who is subtly, like the Beetle, associated with the East; threats traditionally associated with the foreign now emerge from within male British bodies, from within the metropole itself.

Indeterminacy

Paul Lessingham, too, represents infiltration of the foreign into the domestic male body. Similarly to Holt, Lessingham starts out an emasculated figure. His story of penetration emerges as he relates his capture and subjugation in Cairo by the Children of Isis, which rendered him a "fibreless, emasculated creature."[68] Significantly, by the novel's close, he has not recovered fully, and it is implied that he never will. However, while he is a penetrated figure, Paul simultaneously figures as a sign of indeterminacy.

Descriptions of Lessingham are vague. For Holt he is "a fine specimen of manhood."[69] The Beetle says only that "he is good to look at" – "He is straight, – straight as the mast of a ship, – he is tall, – his skin is white; he is strong," – giving an idea of manly qualities rather than a physical image of Paul.[70] Atherton gives different accounts altogether, emphasizing Paul's slenderness. But while Lessingham's body resists being confirmed, the same is true of his character; his backstory is heterological. The Beetle describes him as "all treachery," "false," and "hard as the granite rock, – cold as the snows of Ararat. In him there is none of life's warm blood."[71] Importantly, the Beetle's story and Paul's are discrepant; Lessingham maintains he was imprisoned and violated, while the Beetle rages, "he has taken [her] to his bosom" only to "steal from her like a thief in the night."[72] Holt notices in the Beetle's reflections "a note of tenderness, – a note of which I had not deemed him capable," suggesting a backstory challenging to Paul's account. Meanwhile, for Marjorie, Paul is "stronger, greater, better even than his words."[73] But then, for Sydney, Paul is an empty person: "If you were to sink a shaft from the crown of his head to the soles of his feet, you would find inside him nothing but the dry bones of parties and politics."[74] Sydney's description typifies the insubstantiality of both Paul's character and body; he is secretive, reticent, and very keen on hiding his past from Marjorie.[75] No interiority for Paul is ever offered – glimpses of his internal state are provided only through the lenses of other characters. And, what these characters seem to know of him is only what "all the world knows";[76] a public veneer obfuscates the hidden, insubstantial private. His presence is iconic rather than material; he is "the god of [Holt's] political idolatry," while the phrase "the Great Paul Lessingham" is loosed repeatedly and inherently signals inadequacy.[77] But most importantly, like the Beetle, Paul is unclassifiable and resists really being known.

His dominant characteristic is eloquence – his own means of enchanting.[78] Even Atherton is won over by Lessingham's speech in Parliament; yet his rhetoric and performance, rather than its content, prove compelling. The same is true for Marjorie when she first encounters Paul's prose: "The speaker's words showed such knowledge, charity, and sympathy that they went straight to my heart." His words are thus the means of her enchantment, "the first stirring of [her] pulses."[79] Lessingham thus functions as a mesmerizer of the citizenry and is thereby positioned alongside two other magicians in this text, Atherton and the

Beetle. Lessingham becomes even less substantial as the novel refuses the readership direct interiority. In this way, Marsh argues that the authenticity of narrative and narrative forms are limited by instabilities and contradictions highlighted by the foreign threat but instantiated within British male narratives themselves.

Such narrative instability is reflected in Paul's bodily discomposure. The Beetle's earlier prediction of the violent dissolution of Paul's body ("he shall be ground between the upper and the nether stones in the towers of anguish, and all that is left of him be cast on the accursed stream of the bitter waters") unfolds disconcertingly, from the internal ruptures of the parliamentarian's "local lesion" to the crumbling that Champnell witnesses: "I was conscious of his pallid cheeks, the twitched muscles of his mouth, the feverish glitter of his eyes … The mental strain which he had been recently undergoing was proving too much for his physical strength."[80] Importantly, his physical weakness is linked to his debilitated narrative prowess as his mental fortitude also threatens to give way. However, if these gendered bodies are shown to be unstable and grotesque, the novel further argues that narratives emerging from these bodies are also frighteningly unstable.

Grotesque Narrative

Part of a broad preoccupation with truth, the late-Victorian interest in hermeneutic method and close reading is instantiated in this novel in at least three ways. First, *The Beetle* engages with the problematic, so fundamental in detective fiction, of using information to track down truth. Second, it asks readers themselves to be critical of narrative, not to imbibe it passively. Third, it cultivates criticality in the readership by forcing evaluation of characters' discernment. Importantly, the representation and enactment of this struggle to identify and relate truth emerge in a cultural moment confronting the pivotal denial of historical certainty with respect to imperial disaster in Sudan, and, more specifically, how Britain's hero, subjugated by Mahdist forces, fell at Khartoum. As chapter 3 argued, this failure to achieve epistemological mastery profoundly disempowered imperial narrative and the martial men responsible for contributing to it. Accordingly, what we see in Marsh is the unravelling of the narrative authority of men in positions of power as they attempt to produce knowledge about the other. While, as we have seen, Marsh's characters' reading practices and their accounts are decidedly fallible, it may be Paul's story of his capture in Egypt, framed by Champnell, that most destabilizes narrative.

Paul's story about his captivity in Egypt at the hands of the Priestess of Isis is not a cleanly enclosed, complete, or contained story; he rambles, interrupts himself with metanarrative reflections, and refers back to the present moment, disrupting boundaries of time and locations of the present. These incisions into his narrative are frequent: "You will smile, – I should smile, perhaps, were I the listener instead of you"; "You must forgive me if I seem to stumble in the telling"; "I do not, of course, pretend to give you the exact text of her words, but they were to that effect"; "I have hesitated, and still do hesitate, to assert where, precisely, fiction ended and fact began"; and so on.[81] Not only does he keep disrupting the flow of events in his tale, but he also undermines its truth value – in other words, his own methods of narration make it leaky, uncertain, and unbounded.

And while he is able to offer what I am arguing is a narrative in grotesque form, his mode of expression has been yet further compromised. Paul's trauma manifests itself in the inability to recognize written language, to produce it, and to speak: "I suffered from a species of aphasia."[82] When he tells his story to Champnell, he can't utter the name of his tormentor – and this reflects his impotence: "You see for yourself, Mr. Champnell, what a miserable weakling, when this subject is broached, I still remain. I cannot utter the words [Holt] uttered, I cannot even write them down."[83] Significantly, this unravelling of narrative prowess hinges directly on the sexual subjugation of the corporeal: "The most dreadful part of it was that I was wholly incapable of offering even the faintest resistance to her caresses. I lay there like a log. She did with me as she would, and in dumb agony I endured."[84] In Paul's case, the British subject's penetration is a consequence of Eastern desire. Fundamentally, though, in Marsh's text, desire – for the exotic, to be desired by the exotic, and for possession of qualities traditionally associated with the East – simultaneously underlies the British imagination.

The problematic of using imagination to construct knowledge of the East is central in this work – and that's where Champnell comes in. Since he's a detective, "it falls on him to draw together the various strands, to decipher the clues and provide a sense of closure, though … as it turns out, this can hardly be said to happen,"[85] for Champnell's narrative is ultimately inconclusive. Because Champnell fails in this role, his analysis of this case suggests that writing is not, in fact, a concretizing power. Its ostensible function is to record and nail down events, but it cannot contain the disruption the Beetle instigates. Champnell's narrative fails to capture history, and it does not contribute to a stable reality; in other words, this encounter with empire refuses to be contained. Thus, while Thomas Richards argues that the imperial archive – the obsessive control of knowledge and the accumulation of data – was used to build empire, *The Beetle*, I suggest, demonstrates some considerable limitations to the solidification of knowledge through "authoritative" male writing. Indeed, Champnell's narrative, instead of providing satisfaction, explanation, and demarcation of boundaries, in fact does quite the opposite.

Champnell's narrative serves two major functions. First, in its representation of masculinity, it critiques fin-de-siècle romantic and militaristic male prowess. Second, in manifesting narrative inadequacies, it illustrates leakiness and instability, profound contradictions concerning protection and boundary fortification, and the grotesqueness of fantasy and erotic experience. In providing a relatively removed perspective, Champnell's narrative parodies the forms of masculinity in which both Atherton and Lessingham attempt to indulge. Champnell considers the premise that violence makes Paul a man once more; when Lessingham "shook Sydney as if he had been a rat, – then flung him from him headlong on to the floor," Champnell reflects, "Never had I seen a man so transformed by rage. Lessingham seemed to have positively increased in stature."[86] Even Sydney rewards him for this:

> By God, Lessingham, there's more in you than I thought. After all, you are a man. There's some holding power in those wrists of yours – they've nearly broken my neck. When this business is finished, I should like to put on the gloves with you, and fight it out. You're clean wasted upon politics. – Damn it, man, give me your hand![87]

This episode activates and presents one model of masculinity – the lover sparked into violent action at a threat to the object of his interest – while at the same time, through physical dominance, forging or repairing fraternal ties. Ultimately, though, this model proves inadequate. Paul's recovery is incomplete for, soon after this boost of energy, we find "this Leader of Men, whose predominate characteristic in the House of Commons was immobility, was rapidly approximating the condition of a hysterical woman. The mental strain which he had been recently undergoing was proving too much for his physical strength."[88] Paul's failure as a man is coded through his likeness to stereotypical portrayals of feminine irrationality. But also, Sydney's characteristically unpredictable reaction to Paul's attack on him parodies masculine competition in which yielding to the stronger victor supersedes all other considerations. Indeed, Sydney continues to render himself ridiculous through his excessive penchant for violence: "I stood cooling my heels on the doorstep, wondering if I should fight the cabman, or get him to fight me, just to pass the time away, – for he says he can box, and he looks it."[89] Violence and competition are presented as consequences of boredom and frustration rather than as necessary or noble.

As the search for Marjorie proceeds, Champnell's narrative ridicules this competitiveness, which in some ways is more about male honour and devotions than about Marjorie. For instance, Atherton and Lessingham are both dramatically indignant at the prospect of Marjorie's death, but Champnell's treatment of their lamentations undercuts the possibility of pathos by contrasting their expostulations with drier, more subdued descriptions, and by illustrating the competitiveness underlying their expressions of grief. For instance, Paul establishes his devotion to Marjorie by threatening Sydney: "If hurt has befallen Marjorie Lindon you shall account for it to me with your life's blood." Sydney, who we know is vacillating in his affections, then counters by bidding his own dedication: "Let it be so … If hurt has come to Marjorie, God knows that I am willing enough that death should come to me." Enter Champnell to frame their antics: "While they wrangled, I continued to search."[90] The narrative thus presents the two lovers continuing to quarrel over which of them is more dedicated to the maiden, while the detective focuses on her actual rescue. Subsequently, when Marjorie's discarded garments are found, both lovers jump the gun in assuming her death and professing to avenge it. Snatching at a tress of snipped hair, Paul exclaims,

> "This points to murder, – foul, cruel, causeless murder. As I live, I will devote my all, – money, time, reputation! – to gaining vengeance on the wretch who did this dead."
>
> Atherton chimed in.
>
> "To that I say, Amen!" He lifted his hand. "God is my witness!"[91]

Champnell's use of "chimed in" matches the register of neither Sydney's nor Paul's vows of retribution; instead, through its contrasting tone, it invites the readership to understand the lovers' declarations as melodramatic. Further, this undermining of Sydney and Paul frames these men as being too eager to accept that Marjorie is dead, leaping to establish their own valour. In effect, Champnell's account renders them buffoons rather than fearsome avengers of Marjorie's kidnapping.

If Champnell's narrative undercuts models of masculinity in *The Beetle*, it also undermines its own authority: it demands critical reading practice by unravelling itself and indicating its own profound instability. Problems with Champnell's narrative go beyond his inability to wrap up the story with a clean suture, and his failure to provide a complete archive of the events related; contradictions in his story invite the reader not to read passively. For instance, he writes that an English boy was brought to authorities in Egypt in "a state of indescribable mutilation."[92] This relation continues the theme of dissolution; his body, but also his mind, had been rent, for he died "without having given utterance to one single coherent word."[93] However, Champnell's statement comes on the heels of his other note that the boy had screamed, "They're burning them! they're burning them! Devils! Devils!,"[94] which is at least intelligible. Subsequently, Champnell insists, "Paul Lessingham ... has ceased to be a haunted man."[95] Well, not quite: "None the less he continues to have what seems to be a constitutional disrelish for the subject of beetles, nor can he himself be induced to speak of them ... there are still moments in which he harks back, with something like physical shrinking to that awful nightmare of the past."[96] Thus Paul, despite Champnell's assessment, is still very much "haunted" by the Eastern monster. Once again, as with *Punch*'s 1896 depiction of how Gordon's death in Sudan still haunted the metropole, the Gothic emerges in popular culture to express the disruption to British identity of African resistance to imperial imperatives.

As the novel draws to its conclusion, more narrative problems emerge, not least significantly the perforations in the notion of authenticity. Only in the last chapter do we learn that "Paul Lessingham" is a front name.[97] Because this is not disclosed at the start, it forces readers to rethink what they have been asked to believe all along. Furthermore, we learn that Marjorie's narrative was written during a period of madness – "she was for something like three years under medical supervision as a lunatic," and then her "restoration ... was a matter of years."[98] This absence of soundness of mind undoubtedly colours the reliability of her rendition. Even Champnell cannot offer a particularly reliable account, as it is "several years since I bore my part in the events which I have rapidly sketched."[99] As for Holt's narrative, it is a composition of information related to Atherton (who, we can only assume, has been asked to provide an account at the same time Champnell and Marjorie have set theirs down – that is, many years after the fact) and Marjorie (who, as we know, has to work back across the divide of madness to recount what Holt had divulged to her).[100] Further, the choice to present Holt's narrative as first person belies that aesthetic values have trumped transparency, which would have favoured presenting information as it was gathered – this is another strike against the objectivity seemingly claimed by this genre of multi-voiced narration. In these ways, Champnell's narrative seems to cannibalize not only itself but also the authority of the text as a whole.

But perhaps the most significant discrepancy evident in Champnell's prose is his simultaneous loathing for the foreign entity assaulting Marjorie and his fantasizing about her fate. In dialogue with a larger collective imagination, the novel ostensibly depicts Eastern desires as predatory, focusing on the burning of white women and the emasculation of white men via their subjugation and consequent impotence in failing to protect white women. Accordingly, the narratives within the novel use violence against women in order to solidify the vilification of the other. This process hinges on both the objectification of women's bodies – that is, as things that experience pain and assault – and an eroticization of torture via the circuitous route of the lusty foreigner. These violent erotics are expressed both in idea and in form, as Champnell's reverie illustrates. When Paul queries, "What must this wretch have done to her? How my darling must have suffered," Champnell muses, "That was a theme on which I myself scarcely ventured to allow my thoughts to rest."[101] But he does:

> The notion of a gently-nurtured girl being at the mercy of that fiend incarnate, possessed ... of all the paraphernalia of horror and dread, was one which caused me tangible shrinkings of the body. Whence had come those shrieks and yells, of which the writer of the report spoke, which had caused the Arab's fellow-passengers to think that murder was being done? What unimaginable agony had caused them? What speechless torture? And the "wailing noise," which had induced the prosaic, inundated London cabman to get twice off his box to see what was the matter, what anguish had been provocative of that? The helpless girl who had already endured so much, endured, perhaps, that to which death would have been preferred! – shut up in that rattling jolting box on wheels, alone with that diabolical Asiatic, with the enormous bundle, which was but the lurking place of nameless terrors, – what might she not, while being borne through the heart of civilized London, have been made to suffer? What had she not been made to suffer to have kept up that "wailing noise"?[102]

No new information is given here – the details were conveyed in the reports received; Champnell lingers here for emphasis.[103] The idea of suffering is reiterated through references to "horror," "dread," "torture," "agony," "endured," "anguish," and so on, and is emphasized through sensory language such as "shrieks," "yells," and "wailing," and kinetic signifiers like "rattling," "jolting," and "tangible shrinkings of the body." This impact on the body is significant; Champnell physically feels the effects of the assault he's conceiving, and the implication is that, due to this process of reading sensational language, a parallel dynamic between the reader and the text occurs. This impact is specific: Champnell's rendition emphasizes penetration, not only in terms of resonances throughout his body. In addition to the phallic connotations of the "enormous bundle, which was but the lurking place of nameless terrors," the idea that "the helpless girl" suffers as she is "borne through the heart of civilized London" suggests an ultimate invasion of the nation, a transgression augmented by Britain's powerlessness to protect its "own flesh and blood."[104] Importantly, the conditions enabling this violation are created by the Beetle's disruptions. While its own gender is ambiguous, the creature also hijacks Marjorie's gender presentation and dresses her in menswear, thus using her forced performance of masculinity to avert suspicion of sexual assault. Because both bodies are at once male and female, both sexes become subjugated. At the same time, masculinity itself gets perforated: if the Beetle and Marjorie can perform passable masculinity, then not only have women permeated maleness, but also maleness is uprooted from essential ontological categorization.

Alongside this penetration of the ideally invulnerable body emerges the penetration of the ideally invulnerable mind. While Sydney, physically intact, resists mesmerism, Holt and Paul intimate that their defencelessness against it is rooted in physical weakness. Champnell, the rational private detective, would seem to possess the most impenetrable faculties; so why does he let his imagination run away with him? The storytellers emphatically reject certainty: Lessingham admits he is never sure if he imagined his story, while Atherton confesses, "Were I upon oath, … I should leave the paper blank."[105] As Roger Luckhurst suggests, these "ellipses" intensify the trepidation associated with the monstrosity of the Beetle.[106] Nevertheless, the most horrific elements emerge when the narrators draw on their own imaginations in attempts to produce knowledge. Champnell's imaginative exploration of horrors within the "jolting box" is a case in point: the violent fantasies presented in this novel emerge from these male characters and from the circulation of their narratives. Indeed, this presentation is the very function *The Beetle* itself, as cultural artifact, fulfills. Crucially, as this passage illustrates, the central focus of violence is not Marjorie herself as an individual, but English women in general. Champnell thinks of her not as *that* gently-nurtured girl, but as "*a* gently-nurtured girl" – she stands in for all white women of a certain class and nationality. Similarly, the victim in Paul's story is a random "young and lovely Englishwoman" – a generic female body that suffers – while the women in the youth's story are just nameless "members of a decent English family."[107] Finally, we learn explicitly that the offending cult seeks out "white Christian women, with a special preference, if they could get them, to young English women."[108] For Champnell, Marjorie is an abstraction, and the notion of her suffering is rooted in a larger titillating fantasy that produces a sensual reaction: "The blood in my veins tingled at the thought."[109] Yet this fantasy that Marsh's text offers is equally about male subjugation: in various ways, their mental, physical, and narrative powers are penetrated and rendered grotesque.

The Auto-Grotesque

Marsh's Gothic novel enacts how popular literature and its circulation perform, through textual representation, the very stereotypes of Eastern desires they construct: literature depicting these desires itself enacts them. Writing thus becomes a profoundly destabilizing force because it reveals this desire and tracks the process of masculinity's disruption. If the Beetle commits violence directly, and Paul and Champnell enact it conceptually, then writers – other masters of rhetoric – similarly do violence by conjuring visions of women as primarily objects of abuse and sacrifice. In this way, women's individual identities are sacrificed in literature to the production and circulation of fantasy: they become reduced to beings that suffer. This process highlights the dependence of sexual energies on literature that activates fantasies about the East. Thus, British writing that betrays anxiety about penetration from the East in actuality demonstrates a kind of self-penetration, being from the start a body of leaky holes continuously circulating and recirculating different forms of violent fantasy.

Champnell's narrative is unstable because of factual insufficiencies, and it is grotesque insofar as it transcends the ostensible boundary between text and reader via the "erotics of reading," and the use of prose to elicit bodily excitement. If "the act of reading is itself erotic, especially when reading takes the form of critical apprehension – with apprehension being understood in all three of its senses at once: anxiety, perception, seizure,"[110] then the transcendence of boundaries happens on numerous levels through erotic acts: information gathering and fantasy production within the novel (which registers as sensual experience), the process of reading popular fiction for pleasure, and various acts of critical reading. Because of this transcendence, the narratives within the novel continuously expand, leak out, shift according to interpretation and apprehension, and resonate in different bodies in diverse ways; narrative becomes inherently grotesque and refuses to be contained within a stable body.[111]

Writing is thus represented in *The Beetle* as profoundly unstable. It is limited, as Holt asserts: "Pen cannot describe the concentrated frenzy of hatred with which the speaker dwelt upon the name, – it was demonic."[112] It betrays fissures, as he further observes: "In [Lessingham's] bearing there was a would-be defiance. He might not have been aware of it, but the repetitions of the threats were, in themselves, confessions of weakness."[113] And it traces the circulation of unacknowledged desires: while penetration ostensibly comes from the East, Marsh's text shows that narrative and the imaginative body of literature was always already grotesque, dependent on circulations and influences, and threatening to leak out of the body at any time. This destabilizes national literary identity even further: just as Paul's and Champnell's fantasies of penetration are products of their own imaginations, the fantasy of various forms of penetration emerges from within the national literary body.

Ultimately, the Beetle's function as a maddening, destabilizing force operates as a metaphor for the inability to distinguish reality from imagination. In this, and in its disconcerting repulsiveness, the Beetle parallels the instabilities of writing, speaking, and weaving narrative. This is precisely why the confrontation with the creature brings on the dissolution of manhood – because manliness and masculine prowess are understood in terms of the ability to write, make, and normalize reality. As a result, the male body here is penetrated beyond repair: Holt literally wastes away; Paul never recovers properly; Sydney, continuing with his fratricidal experiments, carries on as an example of non-ideal masculinity; and Champnell's narrative fails to perform its generic function of tying up the history and providing closure and understanding.

The dissolution of narrative certainty, so evident in Marsh's text, is thus arguably the condition of historical narrative itself – especially history derived from the complex archive of colonial violence. As chapter 3 argued, the problem of uncertainty with respect to executing and narrating the imperial project created affective turmoil in the metropole and forced Britain to confront the limitations of its imperial prowess as the nation came up against epistemological incompetence, which in turn destabilized British imperial identity. Marsh's *The Beetle* explores the cascading consequences of these destabilizing limitations through the lens of the Gothic. Part 2 of this book has thus demonstrated how war writing and popular fiction both confronted epistemological uncertainty by drawing on each other's generic elements to reflect imperial Britain's waning martial identity. We have seen how institutional writing turned to the fantastic to represent military failure, loss of masculine prowess, and dwindling narrative capacity. Fiction, in turn, confronted these deficiencies laid bare by Gordon's Khartoum journals and the metropolitan press, and dramatized the destabilization of gender and narrative. Otherness, suggests Marsh, has become more elusive, more threatening to imperial identity, and more abstract. In part 3, otherness becomes even more uncontainable, more indefinable. Chapter 5 moves from the realm of literature to consider institutional writing generated by British colonial agents in Sierra Leone at the fin de siècle. The events considered became the source material for a host of cultural materials (from late nineteenth- and early to mid-twentieth-century fiction, to comics, to children's books, to film, to video games), but for my purposes I want to consider how the archive in question not only resonates with Haggard, Marsh, and the archives concerning the Anglo-Zulu War and the loss of Khartoum, but also divulges fears about imperial masculine fortitude, authorship, and ideology in order to help us to comprehend the stakes of a particularly complex and disturbing intercultural encounter. If, as Grosz argues, "bodily fluids attest to the permeability of the body, its necessary dependence on an outside, its liability to collapse into this outside (this is what death implies), to the perilous divisions between the body's inside and its outside,"[114] then, just as Marsh's text emphasizes this bodily permeability in order to unhook the fabrication of narrative solidity, the archive surrounding the historical events explored next enacts the dissolution of narratives of governmentability.

PART III

Modernist Dissolutions

Chapter Five

Bodily Disintegrations: Forensic Exposure and the Human Leopard Society in Sierra Leone

That it exercises a weird and potent influence is undoubted; for, within the last seven or eight years, among those arrested and, in many cases, hanged for murders committed in its cause, are educated Christian clerks, traders, head men and chiefs of towns, and also catechists and missionaries!

– D. Burrows, "The Human Leopard Society of Sierra Leone"

Chapter 4 demonstrated how metropolitan popular fiction deployed a penetrating "foreign" threat to figure the monstrousness of British imperial desire; chapter 5 now looks again to the colonies to consider how confrontations with the foreign similarly disrupted the deployment of white male imperial power and undermined the authority of imperial ideology. Part 1 of this book outlined discursive links between war writing and adventure romances as understandings of martial masculine prowess ruptured in the face of sexualized African prowess, yielding a visibly vulnerable imperial narrative. Part 2 demonstrated the intensification of this destabilization across memoir, war reporting, and popular Gothic fiction, all of which depicted penetrated imperial manhood, identity, and historiography. These literary works articulate, at different historical moments, widely circulating concerns about the vulnerability, penetration, and invasion of male bodies, narrative, and authority itself. Part 3 moves to West Africa, pairing a colonial archive that excavates the foundations of imperial writing with Conrad's *Heart of Darkness*, which similarly confronts the impossibility of narrating colonialism in Africa within the framework of British national identity. In the archives of late nineteenth-century Sierra Leone, all the same tropes of engulfment, penetration, and dissolution emerging in the imperial discourses heretofore examined reappear to demonstrate the utter collapse of masculine authority. This chapter thus traces the historical deterioration of traditional models of British masculine prowess – particularly epistemological, martial, and institutional control over colonial subjects and geographical space, the notion of a cohesive and disciplined military body, and the security of writing – in one colonial zone. My exploration of the tensions surrounding the construction of the Sierra Leone colony and surrounding protectorate aims to illuminate the ways in which this contact zone fundamentally transformed empire, systemically, by being leaky, disordered, permeable, unstable, and threatening.

In the final decades of the nineteenth century, the colonial institution in Sierra Leone found itself organizationally overwhelmed by the violence of a particularly elusive indigenous secret society known as the Human Leopards. This fraternity conducted premeditated murders and sacrificial rites involving cannibalism and fetish making, notoriously terrorizing native communities, and donning leopard skins and iron claws to sustain their reputation as shape-shifters.[1] The Leopards met, killed, and ate in secret while living double lives as members of the community. Membership was often coerced through the consumption, unbeknownst to the consumer, of human flesh hidden within the larger meal, much like the myth of British press gangs sneaking shillings into men's toasting steins. The choice was then to join the society or die. New fellows were usually required to provide a relative for sacrifice. One or two members would then attack the intended victim in the guise and style of a leopard. The body would afterward be cooked and distributed among the fraternity for consumption, while fat from the kidneys would be used to lubricate a charm called *borfimah*,[2] thought to bring power, wealth, immunity, and protection from the British government to its bearer.[3]

Motivations of Human Leopards were a source of debate for curious ethnographers, whose suggestions on this front included virility, rejuvenation, materialism, vengeance, and colonial resistance. This chapter, however, does not aim to unlock the secrets of the Leopard Society, or evaluate the morality of their activities. As Michael Jackson rightly suggests, ethnographic investigations of the society often focus on sensational aspects, which can produce "essentialistic notions that by reducing the cults to the status of savage otherness deny the violent *situation* in which those who voice such opinions conspire, and deny the indigenous person recognition as a subject and maker of his own history."[4] The history and shifting economic contexts of the Leopard Society require a separate, focused, detailed, and comprehensive study – a lens that does not take as its central subject white masculinity and that explores the functions of the society in its own right.

My concern is primarily with British discomfort with the Leopard killings – with colonial incapacity to control them, administrative inability to capture their meaning in the records of empire, and the imperial confrontation with what these limitations meant for martial masculinity. Having said that, it must be recognized that this particular archive is both under-researched and embedded in a politically asymmetrical history, and that scholarship on historical indigenous African resistance to British colonialism greatly needs to be expanded. My aim in this chapter is to treat sensitively and respectfully a history that deserves careful unpacking to foster nuanced understanding in my readership; accordingly, in working to offer a sense of the fine texture of these largely unfamiliar colonial sources, my treatment of this archive involves both thorough detailing and some narrativizing, in hopes that this chapter will help lay the critical groundwork for scholarship to understand more meaningfully the dynamics of this fraught situation. Ultimately, while the history of the Human Leopard Society ultimately refuses to be contained, a consideration of the anxieties registered in the Sierra Leone colonial archive nevertheless illuminates some crucial limitations of imperial power and the unravelling of the efficacy of martial masculinity.

Indeed, aside from the obvious problems of murder and terror, this fraternity posed a challenge for colonial order and control: the murders continued, and the colonial government was powerless to stop them. A report by W.A. Noel Davies, assistant district commissioner, about similar murders by the Human Alligator Society in the nearby Shaingay District points to this visible instability: "The natives are beginning to think that the Government has no power over these people as they have seen them brought before the Circuit Court on several occasions and they have always succeeded in being acquitted."[5] The government was profoundly unable to surveil these indigenous subjects; the Leopard Men, with their double lives, nocturnal operations, knowledge of the shrouding hinterland, baffling crime scenes, secret signs and handshakes – not to mention their supposed ability to mutate and dissolve into the night[6] – disrupted colonialism's fundamental idea that empire could produce knowledge about, and thereby fix and contain, the indigenous subject. Colonial efficacy was thoroughly routed during this period, and, by 1912, so too would be British imperial virtue, authority, and legitimacy.

The empire did, of course, try to classify this indigenous other, and its attempts were highly invested in Britain's understanding of itself as civilized in relation to predictably horrific renditions of Human Leopard violence. The gory and phantasmatic elements of these accounts also distracted readers from recognizing Britain's historical disruption of indigenous socio-economic contexts. Most Britons at the fin de siècle received sensationalized accounts of Human Leopard crimes through the newspapers. Though rumours of were-leopards had reached Britain by the early 1880s at least, it was toward the end of this decade that reports of murder and cannibalism took on a more graphic tenor: "One woman was caught by the cannibals ... A portion of her leg was found by the roadside, and this was all that was seen of her after the capture ... The cannibals are really a band of natives who prowl about the country feeding on the bodies of other natives whom they capture and kill."[7] The killings were declared to be rooted in the "undoubtedly inherited ... horrid appetite" of the cult whose origin was "gruesome, though at the same time interesting": "It is the story of a fiendish revenge instituted by one tribe as a punishment for the treachery of another, and a strong illustration of native superstition and fear of the powers wielded by the fetish."[8] Into the 1890s, the shock value was increasingly leveraged as headlines emphasizing horror, cannibalism, and terror were deployed.[9] These articles seized on the visceral brutality of Human Leopard attacks, which generally took the form of ambush followed by dismemberment: "The leopard men then mutilate the body in a dreadful manner, taking away certain portions, and leaving the horrible spectacle on the roadside ... The last body found was that of a man. The head had been opened, and the brains taken out, the right hand and left foot cut off, and the heart also taken away."[10] In this heavy-handed way, violence, mutilation, and dismemberment were sensationalized as fear and terror were commercialized in print culture, causing a stir of titillation in the metropole directed toward Sierra Leone. Crucially, this information was divorced from important material circumstances in West Africa in order to heighten entertainment and elide British participation in the Human Leopard history.

This sensationalism of the 1890s anticipates the lingering preoccupation with and distortion of the Leopard Society and Africa at large into the twentieth century. This enduring fascination emerges in numerous fictional texts conceptualizing the Human Leopards as well as in a number of men's magazines in the 1950s and 1960s.[11] Additionally, Western museums began collecting Human Leopard paraphernalia and art depicting the society from the turn of the century onward.[12] That this historical archive has manifested in Western popular culture throughout the twentieth century suggests not only that understanding Britain's representation of the Leopard Men illuminates patterns in the West's ongoing representation of Africa, but also that the legacy of the West's fraught fascination, at the very least, speaks to the persistence of global imperial structures. In what follows, I examine the anxieties activated in this colonial archive in order to trace shifts in constructions of bodily, spatial, and textual authority – these concepts, once hinging so intensely on firmness, are ultimately undermined – and demonstrate their dissolution of imperial identity.

The Leopard Society arose out of very specific socio-economic contexts. Throughout the nineteenth century, British colonists had been actively regulating against the Atlantic slave trade and advocating "legitimate trade," based on agriculture, in the region. These policies shifted local economies in crucial ways. First, agricultural production (palm nuts, in this region) relied on the labour of productive bodies: indigenous chiefs acquired labourers by raiding weaker neighbouring groups in a system of domestic slavery.[13] Slave-harvested crops were then sold to European traders, and the cash they procured supported raiding parties. Second, British prohibition of domestic slave-trading and raiding meant that chiefs, instead of garnering wealth from neighbouring groups, turned to taxing and enforcing labour levies on their own people, which fomented discontent and encouraged revolving chieftaincies.[14] Power, influence, and economic advantage thus were subject to new and rapid changes. The use of *borfimah* to gain power arose from this context, as did the spike in accusations of supposed Human Leopards – when an individual was found guilty of being a member of this society, his property was taken from him and his family by the residing chiefs.

Though T.J. Alldridge, an agent for the Randall and Fisher trade company, district commissioner for Sherbro (after 1894), and a prolific writer about Sierra Leone, estimates that this secret society began some time around 1860,[15] it was in the 1880s that Human Leopard attacks became apparent to the British administration in Freetown. Villagers were being terrorized, so indigenous courts employed medicine men to hunt out members lurking within the community, and then frequently sentenced alleged members of the society to be burned.[16] Colonial records indicate that British administrators were aware of these executions,[17] but their reaction had nowhere near the intensity of the alarm raised in the early 1890s, when the local chiefs, again alarmed by repeated Leopard attacks on villagers, sent for an alternate authority from the interior – the Tongo Players. These "witch men," as the administration described them, who had appeared almost a decade previously for the same reasons, claimed to divine through ritual dance which members of a community were secretly Human Leopards. They then set to "pulling" (or discovering) and burning alleged shape-shifters in large numbers. Furthermore, the second time around, colonial agents – both African

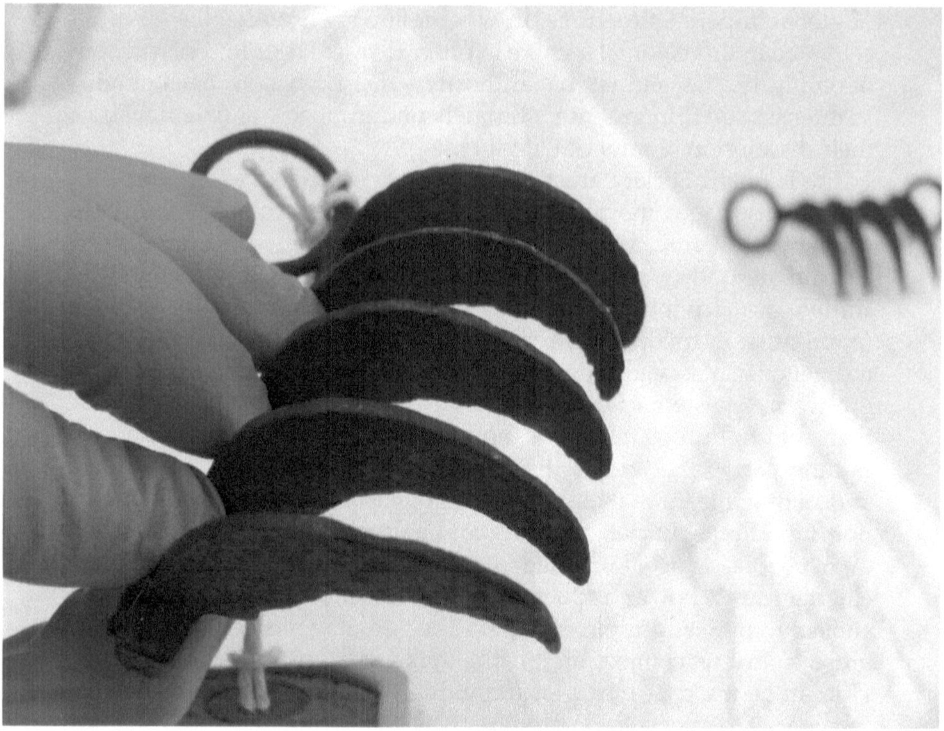

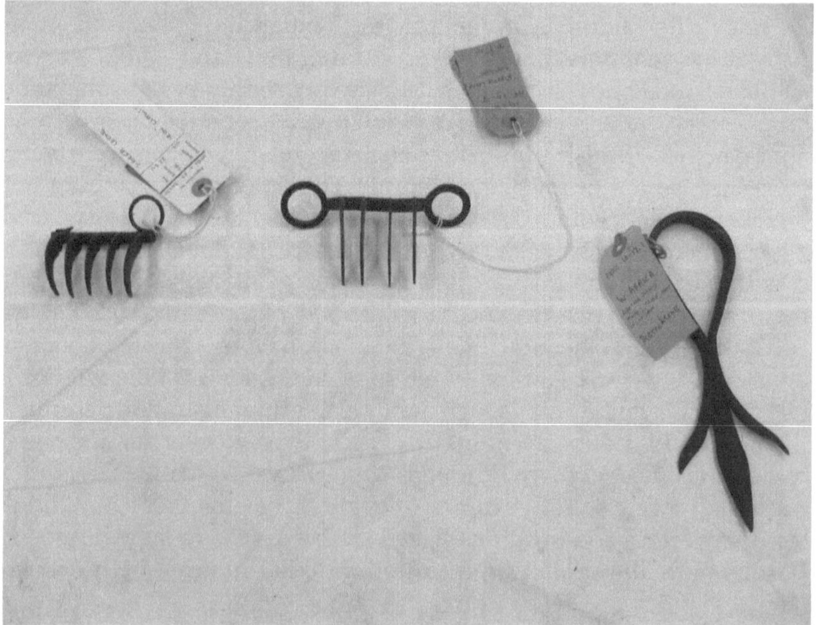

Figures 7 and 8. Human Leopard weapons. Photos by the author.

constables and white officers – became implicated in the brutality. It was this climax of events – and the attendant challenge to British authority and liberatory discourse that focalized around Tongo judgment – that finally demanded a higher degree of imperial attention. From this moment, Leopard violence in Sierra Leone remained a visible problem into the second decade of the twentieth century.[18]

The imperial confrontation with Human Leopard and Tongo murders comprised evidence of British disorder in four central ways. For one thing, the violence disrupted the trade and economy of the imperial machine. For another, the murders, eviscerations, and cannibalism fostered visceral discomfort and prompted an anxious colonial focus on maintaining physical boundaries – bodily and territorial. Again, this resonates with Theweleit's analysis of martial fears of flow and attendant forms of stiffening. Third, the society challenged local and national institutions responsible for imperial order by proving the British legal apparatus remarkably ineffectual in containing indigenous violence. Finally, the Human Leopard and Tongo world views, which followed the logic of *borfimah*, transmogrification, divination, and secret knowledge, directly opposed and evaded Western rational knowledge systems. These disruptions were problematic on various levels because of the co-authorizing – and thus mutually destructive – relationships between the efficacy of the white male body, authority, and narrative. Not only was it impossible for the administration to assert order in the surrounding districts, but it was also difficult to convey order in the reports. In this colonial archive, this "site of knowledge production,"[19] the British government came to acknowledge the limitations of writing and thus of the imperial project. Administrative narratives demonstrate that the colonial space refused to be contained; at the same time, they also became the very means by which the "disorder" associated with the Human Leopards and Tongo Players migrated from the contact zone toward the question of "Britishness," and the means by which the ideal of imperial law ultimately eroded. Colonial reporting, similar to the cannibalizing effects of the narratives of *King Solomon's Mines*, *She*, and *The Beetle*, becomes at once the evidence, agent, and embodiment of that disintegration.

The collection of materials that illustrates this disintegration comprises widely circulating texts, including fin-de-siècle British and African newspaper reports about the Human Leopards, ethnographical studies, and colonial ordinances, as well as private materials – confidential dispatches, investigative reports, and legislative council meetings. Reading these texts together helps to illuminate the ways in which colonial and martial anxieties resonate in multiple spheres and develop across generic dialogues. Because these archives are both "sites of the imaginary *and* institutions that fashioned histories as they concealed, revealed, and reproduced the power of the state," we need to attend to their enactment of fantasy as they struggle to govern.[20] While recognizing the force of dominant narratives, we can nevertheless examine moments of uncertainty, contradiction, emphasis, and failures in technologies of imperial rule in order to better understand the state's deepest weaknesses.

These weaknesses, in Sierra Leone, ultimately took the form of hypocrisy and ideological limitations: while the metropole sensationalized the Leopard killings, the more prominent terror was perpetrated by the Tongo Players – with, as the archive demonstrates, the tacit approval of the colonial state. Since, however, this truth was both less interesting and less appealing to metropolitan Britain, the circulation of these events was limited largely to colonial dispatches and confidential reports. In some ways, the central colonial crisis here was not the subversive activity of the Human Leopards but rather the question of white involvement with the Tongo persecution of alleged Human Leopards and execution of local laws or "country customs" – which took the form of beating people and burning them alive – and their attendant challenges to British authority. In short, these archives demonstrate that the Colonial Office recognized that their agents were complicit in the Tongo Players' mass murders of West African villagers; the precarious scaffold of imperial legitimacy collapsed. This is not, however, the story that was told to the public.

"A Very Complicated and Unsavoury Matter": Disruption and the Loss of Control

Popular attempts to narrate Human Leopard and Tongo activities exemplify the prevailing imperial trope of Western civility paternalistically ordering a savage space. Since, though, British "rights" to govern rested largely on perceived improvements in agricultural production, trade, martial prowess, and masculine exemplarity, not to mention many other familiar litmus tests of civility,[21] Human Leopard violence deeply undermined this narrative on a multitude of fronts, including its disruption of trade. In February 1892, Sub-Agent Thomas Buckley of the trading company Messrs. Fisher and Randall complained to the acting colonial secretary that, when an employee had visited the village of Bogo, "the place where the Country people have burned to death" and where cannibalism "notoriously prevailed," he found that "the Country through which he passed was full of Palm nuts but not a soul was seen during the journey." That is, no one was out harvesting the crop. Buckley laments, "The spot where the burnings have taken place was a sickening sight, there being a heap of white Ashes and remains of human bodies, sufficient evidences of quite a number of Executions." Nevertheless his central concern is production: "Our agent experienced much difficulty in prevailing on his men to accompany and guide him, so great was the terror they felt." The sub-agent implores the acting colonial secretary "to put an end to a state of affairs, which being within a few miles of Bonthe and easily accessible is a crying disgrace to our nation and to humanity itself."[22]

Buckley's humanitarian concerns articulate the threat of this violence to British identity, but they are underpinned by the disruption of economic networks. Two years later, District Commissioner Alldridge similarly meditated, "Were these diabolical customs eradicated entirely from the neighbourhood it would probably be the means of an increased population between Bambaiya and Bogo, which in its turn, with confidence restored amongst the farming people, might be expected to produce very beneficial results."[23] Visceral though it was, Leopard violence and its impact on indigenous people were perceived through an imperial lens and were situated in terms of their lasting repercussions for imperial commerce. That "this Society has created a general insecurity of life and limb, and caused stagnation of trade in the Imperri District"[24] were understood as equally problematic – the coordinating conjunction here does not favour one or the other of these clauses; these concerns are shared in one breath. In response to Leopard interference with trade, the administration established an ordinance in 1895 that rendered criminal the possession of a leopard skin, a two pronged knife, or *borfimah*. Nevertheless, surveillance of these possessions, let alone the secret society itself, proved extremely difficult.

Imperial culture did, of course, try to fathom the fraternity: ethnographers and the metropolitan press, seemingly equally fascinated by fetishes and cannibalism, attempted to document the Human Leopards and thereby contain them within imperial epistemology. American researcher Richard Strong attempted to break down the myth of shape-shifting associated with the Leopard Society through rational description of how "the members dress themselves more or less in leopard skins and either paint their bodies with annatto dye or rub yellow clay upon them," as well as of their killing methods: "They are armed with sharp iron hooks in the form of leopard's claws and teeth, and also carry short spears ... In some instances leopard fur is placed around the iron claws, bits of which may adhere to the clothing of the victim or to his wounds."[25] Strong thus worked to neutralize the society's cachet by explaining its methods, focusing on how members imitated leopards and invalidating the notion of transmogrification. Similarly, Alldridge attempted to expound the significance of their charms: after the victim had been killed, "the body was then opened, and some of the internal parts were removed for the purpose of obtaining the fat, which was considered necessary to preserve the magical powers of the Borfimor."[26] While this rationale sought to resolve Western bafflement, Alldridge further soothed his readers with the notion that the perplexing violence had been eliminated by imperial power: "Happily the persistent and effective measures adopted by the government have been so successful that I quite believe the Human Leopard Society is now simply a matter of history."[27] Cheerfully optimistic, Alldridge was wrong when he wrote this in 1901; the Human Leopards were glaringly active until the Leopard Trials in 1912–13 and even further into the twentieth century.[28] Another puzzle for ethnographers was the society's motivation for killing. The intrepid explorer Mary Kingsley discussed "murder societies" in her *Travels in West Africa* (1897), noting, "the last entered member has to provide, for the entertainment of the other members, the body of a relative of his own, and sacrificial cannibalism is always breaking out, or perhaps I should say being discovered, by the white authorities in the Niger Delta."[29] Kingsley's distinction between existence and discovery points to important limitations to British epistemological prowess, and suggests ongoing indigenous resistance to it. Despite her own direct experience in West Africa, Kingsley goes on to quote from newspaper reports to foreground the importance of fetish worship, demonstrating the co-legitimizing relationships between different kinds of circulating print culture. Also trying to understand the logic of Leopard killings, Sir William Brandford Griffith, presiding at a circuit court for Human Leopard trials, "formed the opinion that when they devoured the human flesh the idea uppermost in their minds was that they were increasing their virile powers."[30] For Griffith, as for others, this explanation made sense because it accounted for very real physical power struggles, which were central on imperial radars. Robert Gordon Berry, writing for the *Proceedings of the Royal Irish Academy* in 1912, similarly suggested that the cult's ritualistic killing brought wealth and influence, conferring "supremacy over the white man, in the white man not being able to find out what was being done, and that the eating of human flesh would give power over the white man."[31] Whether or not these assessments are accurate, Human Leopard motivation, for Griffith and Berry, came down to male potency, whether in terms of social, economic, or defensive power; questions of black virility seem to be foremost in British probing – after all, prowess was a language imperial figures could understand.[32] Yet, this power struggle was understood as being not only about economy and strength but also about epistemological defiance. In other words, the problem was (and this goes back to Kingsley's point) that there was a secret that could be and was hidden from the administration. The evasion of surveillance was as much a source of power as the *borfimah* itself – and the administration knew it.

As for British newspapers, their attempts to epistemologically master the Leopard Society depicted indigenous violence as profoundly other, sensationalizing the murders and thereby essentializing them. In so doing, these news reports removed the British Empire from the scene of colonial violence as material contexts were effaced while the gory, sometimes "sexy," details were dramatized: "A native of the Imperi country … was stabbed first in the back of the neck with sharp knives, and gashes were then scored down his back which, to an unskilled eye, might suggest their having been caused BY A LEOPARD'S CLAWS."[33] Emphasizing gore, drama, and otherness, this article goes on to relate the rescue of "a slave girl who had been tied to a tree and was about to be killed. She was brought into the mission at Bonthe and supplied by the nuns with civilized dress. Considerable amusement was caused by the difficulty in inducing her to wear the garments."[34] As this particular article shifts from attempted murder to focus on a subjugated woman rescued by Christians, strangely becoming a pseudo-comical conversion tale, it attempts to tick numerous entertainment boxes at once as it caters to imperial voyeurism.[35] These attempts to control the unknown subject through epistemological mastery thus further marginalized it by constructing titillating entertainment.

Cataloguing also functioned to counter perceptions of imperial epistemological impotence (an ongoing problem), although often its expressions were much more banal. For instance, administrators tended to gather copious and frequently pointless information about the colony and events and objects therein. Thomas Richards has rightly argued that the British Empire was crafted with paper and that unqualified imperial agents compensated for lack of knowledge by providing reports that were exhaustive but whose material usefulness was ultimately questionable.[36] A representative example of this pervasive impulse is Acting Civil Commandant S.M. Bennett's attempt to record in copious detail all of the property that was allegedly stolen by villagers accusing others of being Human Leopards.[37] This overly thorough documentation registers a desire to assert control through information gathering, despite being unable to suppress the violence.

In this interest of countering perceptions of British impotence, news reports often positioned colonial figures as rescuers. In one account, an elderly woman "disturbed a number of Leopard men" in the process of attacking a young woman. After the Leopard Men "bolted for their lives ... the poor girl who was found insensible was taken by Captain Soden's men to Bonthe for medical treatment." Aside from the ability of the elderly woman to frighten off a group of virile Leopard Men, this account is typical in its evocation of the myth of the white saviour: "The frontier police [a section of which Soden commanded] were becoming a powerful force and showing themselves very energetic in suppressing these cannibal outrages. Captain Soden with a force of police was scouring the Bargroo district in search of the Leopard men."[38] While the article depicted an "energetic," "powerful force" coming to the rescue and "scouring" the area for the culprits, in reality, the historical record shows that the colonial military struggled immensely, with little result, in their efforts to contain the Human Leopards.

The metropole did, at first, try to applaud colonial efforts. In the mid-1890s, when the first British-run trials of Leopard Men were beginning to be publicized, the papers rejoiced that the elusive society was "gradually being laid before the world by the energy and perspicacity of the Prosecuting Counsel."[39] This claim resonated with readers' desires for the relief that the empire was finally beginning to know its elusive foe. Yet, despite growing Western knowledge of Leopard violence, the phenomenon continued to defy British control: "Such a stern, swift meting out of punishment seemed likely to put a stop to the horrid deeds of blood committed by the society ... But the whole colony was roused into excitement by the news of another of these murders in the Emperi country."[40] Thus the Leopards proved an elusive, persistent force. As a result of continued indigenous evasion of imperial surveillance, the newspapers became increasingly critical of British capabilities. The *Sheffield Evening Telegraph* remarked, "Although several men have been hanged for these murders the authorities still believe they have not stamped out the practice,"[41] while the *Bristol Mercury* noted, "The English authorities hanged a dozen 'Leopards,' but our Frenchman [i.e., the correspondent] is doubtful whether the society is stamped out."[42] The *London Daily News* suggested, "The 'Human Leopards,' in spite of the recent trial, are still busy ... the crime of murder still continues frequent ... the Government have failed to put a stop to the 'custom.'"[43] As metropolitan confidence waned, the *Pall Mall Gazette* took the administration to task: "That such a state of things should exist in a small colony like Sierra Leone, which has been a British possession for close upon one hundred years, is little short of a national disgrace, and it is high time the authorities of Sierra Leone were brought to book."[44] This was far from the last criticism of Britain's capacity to "civilize" this colony that pinpointed the relationship between this capacity and national identity; amidst metropolitan titillation regarding the Leopard murders, public pressure was on the colonial government to prove its capacity to regulate the natives.

A significant factor in public discomfort with this regulatory failure was the perceived infiltration of civilization by Human Leopards. One such case held a special valence in the British imagination: in 1895, a man named Jowe, a supposedly Christian schoolteacher in Sierra Leone, was found to be a Human Leopard and was convicted of murder and cannibalism. He was publicly executed along with two other men, but his role as a colonial intermediary caused particular alarm as reports of his "extraordinary" conviction flared up in the papers.[45] One newspaper refused to accept Jowe's affiliation with colonial regulation: "The statement that Jowe … is an ex-Sunday school teacher is quite incorrect. He is a member of the lowest and most superstitious tribe, and cannot even speak English."[46] This denial of Jowe's infiltration of colonial institutions is invested in the narrative of efficacious imperial culture taking root in a thorough, beneficial, humanitarian mode. The notion that the reformed, "civilized" native was actually only deploying a colonial guise for his own purposes, thereby dislodging the culture that sought to dominate, threatened the empire's ability to know and represent "the native" as well as its own narrative of imperial power. Meanwhile, Jowe's liminal position also inspired numerous fabrications about the details of his particular case, such as John Cameron Grant's flagrantly racist novel, *The Ethiopian* (1900). The newspapers were no better. Some even asserted that Human Leopards, disguising themselves in the trappings of civilization, raised boys like cattle to satisfy "a hideously genuine appetite for fresh human flesh":

> Young boys are brought from the dark interior, kept in pens, fattened … and finally killed and baked. To these Thyestean feasts come not only the savage chiefs of the interior, but also, it is whispered, black merchants from the coast. Men who appear at their places of business in English territory in broadcloth and tall hats, who ape the manners of their white masters, are said to disappear annually into the interior where, we are told, they might be seen, in naked savagery, taking part in the banquets on plump boys in which they delight.[47]

This exceedingly sensationalist and entirely unsupported depiction exemplifies an investment in maintaining long-standing divisions between primitivity and civilization: the "interior" is "dark" and "savage"; the coast is associated with "English" clothing, industry, "manners," and even "master[y]." But there is an equal investment in rooting out the other *within* – the cannibal in Western clothing who only "apes" Englishness. The sensationalism of this passage is amplified by this process of discovery as secret violence "is whispered" about, as "we are told" about double lives, and as these Janus-faced citizens "might be seen" – or imagined – by readers. While capitalizing on the entertainment value of the murders, this article nevertheless typifies a distinct uneasiness about the invisibility of the transgressions that continued to occur.[48]

Lack of British control even started to manifest in colonial representations of the murders as an outbreak or contagion – an unmanageable, invisible foe. At a legislative meeting in 1912, Governor Sir Edward Marsh Merewether opined, "Nobody knows how far this state of things may go, and unless drastic steps are taken it may spread to Freetown."[49] Merewether's warning emphasizes the unpredictability of the violence, its potential to "spread," and its lethal consequences. Insofar as the Leopard murders are depicted as a contagion, the administration registers not only a struggle for containment, but also the risk of spatial disorder.

In addition to the epistemological and physical resistance of the Human Leopard Society, the administration ended up facing a further indigenous threat to colonial order. This problem arose in full force in the early 1890s. Because the Leopard cult was terrorizing villages, and the colonial administration was effectively useless in preventing the murders, local chiefs at this point sent for an authority from the interior: the Tongo Players, who arrived in the Imperri district to persecute alleged Leopard cult members. As news of the subsequent mass burnings of supposed Human Leopards reached the British administration, the Colonial Office in London struggled to get a grip on the circumstances in the region. Mr Bramston identified "a double process of extermination … *Firstly* by the Human Leopards … *Secondly* by the Tongo men, (i.e. the witch men of the tribes) who are supposed to be gifted with supernatural intelligence and to be able to tell at sight who is a Human Leopard." Bramston repudiated any "supernatural intelligence" by ascribing economic motivations and arbitrary selection to this violence: "a Tongo man, if he desires to obtain the land of some unfortunate native, promptly denounces him as a Human Leopard, gets him burnt, and takes his property."[50] The distracting emphasis on such material considerations, however, suppressed the empire's own role in factors underlying the violence. Further emphasis on shocking brutality and ostensibly alien phallic displays of power worked similarly to obfuscate imperial responsibility. For instance, Mr Brett, the acting Queen's advocate, represented this grisly Tongo judgment in sexualized terms:

> Tongohs ... [hold] a fetish dance or orgie, the principal man carrying about with him a large horn ... which towards the end of the Entertainment he proceeds to point at some of the surrounding villagers and at length calls out that he has discovered the guilty man and pronounces him to be a Human Leopard. Thereupon the poor wretch so chosen is set upon by the Chiefs and their satellites, beaten to death and his body burnt. Some times it happens that the man is not quite dead when the burning commences ... After this the chiefs proceed to the dead man's house, [and] take possession of everything belonging to him.[51]

In Brett's passage, Britain and its agents are positioned as disassociated from this violence; described as savage, inhumane, and mercenary, Tongo Play is depicted as isolated from the contexts of colonial invasion and rendered alien through the unfamiliar objects used along with the opacity of the judgment. This othered violence is deeply sexualized: "orgie" conveys debauchery, revelry, and libidinal tenors, while the phallic overtones of the "large horn" (an image central in British representations of the Tongo Play) signify the power to condemn. Other imperial accounts of Tongo Play emphasize that the moment of "discovery" is immediately followed by beating the accused with the similarly phallic Tongo cane. In depictions of Human Leopard attacks, too, images of rape are similarly invoked: Alldridge told the Royal Geographic Society that "some person in the guise of a leopard ... rushed upon the unfortunate and unsuspecting victim from behind";[52] the *Sierra Leone Weekly News* suggested, "The selected offering is pounced upon from behind and a sharp three-pronged fork is thrust into the back of the neck";[53] the *Hampshire Telegraph* stressed that the victim "was attacked suddenly from behind";[54] and, in the above excerpt from the *Sheffield Daily Telegraph*, "outrages" connotes sexual assault.[55] But colonial discomfort surrounding these sexualized power dynamics arises not because this violence is alien, but because it is familiar – and contesting. The representations of both the Tongo Play and the Leopard attacks as exercises in carnal dominance resonate with British practices and understandings of hunting. As John M. MacKenzie has argued, hunting out wild animals, especially dangerous ones and especially in colonial spheres, widely symbolized white mastery. Repeated references to the Tongo horn evoke the trophies collected, sold, and displayed in Victorian imperial culture: "The collection of horns and skins represent[ed] in their very inutility western man's dominance of the world. Horns perfectly symbolised the war of males for sexual conquest."[56] In Tongo Play, however, the horn is deployed by African authorities. Thus this judgment scene is profoundly *unheimlich*: while the phallic horn would be readily recognized as an indication of hunting prowess and zoological knowledge, here, a similar item is employed in a very different kind of hunt by an ostensibly very different master.[57] Once again, because hunting functions as "sexual sublimation,"[58] and the dominance belongs not to the white hunter but to African authority, Tongo Play caused intense perturbation within the colonial record. Thus when the Colonial Office euphemized the multi-faceted violence in the protectorate in the early 1890s as "a very complicated and unsavoury matter,"[59] it was, first, an understatement, and second, in contradistinction to expressions of wider cultural fascination with the attacks.

In addition to these challenges to trade, epistemology, efficacy, and authority, the underlying ideologies of the Human Leopards and Tongo Players were disruptive because they contradicted Britain's worldview. For Brett, the threat of an alternative knowledge system came close on the heels of violence. Deriding indigenous knowledge, he deplored what he called "the extraordinary ignorance and superstition of the Aborigines."[60] The British found indigenous beliefs about the Leopard Society and Tongo Players unnerving in part because they challenged Western conceptions of the body's solidity. David Pratten explains, "While European thought considers shape-shifting an interior process of altered consciousness, the peoples of the Guinea Coast perceive it as a change in objective reality and hence describe it as an exterior event."[61] Physical boundaries and the "division between humans and animals" were understood differently in West Africa, where they were "regarded as permeable," than they were in Europe, where they held "incontestable validity."[62] Jackson explains the resistant orientation of this alternative worldview toward Western governance: "Shape-shifting is a form of witchcraft. It suggests faculties outside the domain of secular activity and control. It conjures up images of the dark, trackless forests beyond human clearings and settlements – the domain of animality, the antithesis of social order."[63] Thus, the idea of transmogrification was itself particularly disconcerting because it defied Western rationality and scientifically determined, stable boundaries of the body, as well as colonial governance. Perhaps most problematic, though, was not that this worldview differed from European rationality, but that it actually began to infiltrate British logic. Writing to Lord Knutsford at the Colonial Office, Governor Sir James Shaw Hay earnestly disavowed the possibility of shape-shifting: "the natives hold that the culprits 'transformed' (or more correctly, dis-guised) as leopards pounce upon their victims."[64] Hay's need to emphasize disguise over transformation exhibits the logic of the supplement so prominent in other imperial narratives respecting Africa that this book has explored. Two months later, Brett speculated on the beliefs of Chief Gbannah Bunjay, who allegedly joined in summoning the Tongo, but was then identified by them as a Human Leopard and killed. Brett surmised, "He may or may not have believed in their powers. But, I should say the latter was the case; since had he in reality been a Cannibal he would scarcely have voluntarily run the risk of discovery."[65] Brett's circular reasoning betrays his uncertainty: Brett premises his assumption of Bunjay's disbelief in Tongo divination on the idea that the chief was a cannibal, which in turn presupposes Tongo accuracy. Thus Brett's own attempt to make sense of these events is markedly unstable,[66] a mental irregularity that is, in itself, a real problem for colonialism: "regression" of white men and their attraction to native practices were poignant fears of the upper administration. That the lower classes that tended to supply colonial positions were thought more susceptible to regression intensified this fear. Though the colonial administration widely deployed the myth of indigenous simplicity and superstition, some colonial agents yielded to native methods of trial, which provoked administrative alarm. From the level of individual white officers to that of administration and legislation, the disintegration of "civility" visibly manifests in this colonial archive – in representations of the colony itself, in regulatory failures, and narrative collapse. In fin-de-siècle Sierra Leone, colonial writing, instead of establishing British authority, both tracks and enacts the disintegration of imperial legitimacy.

Vulnerable Territory; Unstable Legitimacy

If the colonial administration was anxious about the efficacy of imperial writing and its perceived ability to govern, it was equally concerned with territorial boundaries and the threat of African "disorder" penetrating and disrupting what was understood as a masculine space. Critics of British imperial literature have identified a long-standing traditional construction of colonial geography as a female conquest,[67] but, in this archive, this representational economy changes: for the colonial administration, Sierra Leone was a conquest in which British identity was highly invested, but its territory also became conflated with the male-dominated colonial outpost and imperial body. The colony, as a masculine frontier subsumed within British identity, became a site of porousness, vulnerability, and disintegration of some of the most fundamental aspects of British imperial masculine identity: resilience, solidity, virtue, and civility. Importantly, the rendering of this colonial landscape through the metaphor of the male body and its attendant vulnerabilities impinges on the related structures of authority and writing. The relationship between British physical prowess, duty, and heroism in the supposedly ruthless contact zone, the ability to narrate that experience, and imperial legitimacy itself again emerges in this archive: when bodily and territorial boundaries destabilize, epistemological mastery and imperial authority also ultimately weaken. This process informed cyclical crises in masculinity that had upward consequences as the problem migrated from colonial instance to imperial conundrum: as with confrontations with Zululand's engulfing yet penetrating environment, Haggard's agent landscapes and passive men, Khartoum's leaky boundaries, and Marsh's depiction of grotesque narrative, empire in this case would need to reassess its reliance on a bounded, permanent, and virile masculinized national body. These wide-ranging concerns about masculine prowess were thus laid bare in colonial representations of the territory in question as masculine. Inevitably, contradictions and fissures emerge within these archival conversations; consequently, these particular records become not only a medium of fabricating imperial masculinity, but also the undoing of traditional British masculine prowess.

When the colonial archive imposed this gendered corporeal logic onto the Sierra Leone colony and surrounding protectorate, imperial vulnerabilities regarding cultural infiltration and economic stagnation were exposed. The administration was invested in demarcating ordered territory from unruly wilderness so that imperial culture could take root and trade could expand. In 1891 Governor Hay exemplified both this imperative and the resulting tendency to represent the colony as a body that required firm regulation: "just outside British jurisdiction, trade had fallen to a very low ebb indeed and the revenue of the Colony had declined … His Excellency recognizing that the back-bone of the settlement is its commerce … has put an end to those petty wars, which for so many years, paralysed trade in the Sherbro district."[68] Hay's personification of the colony conveys the centrality of trade – the colony's "back-bone" – to its function. But this understanding of the colony as body also suggested that, while indigenous conflict prevented the flourishing of trade that sustained the settlement, the notion of "paralys[is]" connotes systemic problems for the larger imperial body of which the colony was a part.

While trade constituted sustenance for the imperial body, it required careful control so that disorder – often figured as infection – in adjoining districts did not foment chaos within the protectorate. Having established this corporeal framework, writers of the archive worked to demarcate the colony's physical boundaries and maintain the pervasive cultural fantasy of the impermeable male body. This discourse of health/infection emerges in discussions of the Imperri country, where cannibalism and Tongo Players were most visible. Because of its proximity to Freetown, Imperri was a primary source of trade and cultural contact: entangled with the Bargroo, Jong, and Mamaligi rivers, the district was strategically important for collection and distribution. Consequently, order here was crucial for economic productivity, while disorder was understood as a kind of bodily infection, as Brett articulated: "this slip of country should be kept free of all internal derangement ... The inclusion of the Imperreh Country within our active jurisdiction would swell the Customs Revenue at Bonthe ... [and] do away with what at present is a festering sore upon our immediate borders, and an evil, the growth of which may tend to depopulate the country."[69] Brett's metaphor of bodily infection used to describe the effect of Human Leopard and Tongo activities on the colonial space intersected with imperatives for ordered space. For Brett, indigenous violence, that "festering sore," infected the membrane of the British colony, threatening to "grow" inward, and to interfere with vital supplies. In turn, this infection caused "internal derangement" and disrupted the empire's access to the sustenance of trade. The colonial territory was thus seen as vulnerable to a cultural invasion figured as bodily penetration.

The idea of protecting and regulating the colonial space – "restoring tranquility" by expanding the frontier – became a popular one.[70] Applying a similar rhetoric of moral authority and regulation to the issue of territorial access, Governor Hay leveraged the threat of cannibalism to justify territorial expansion.[71] In his dispatch, Hay demarcated spheres of order and chaos in suggesting that the frontier police, positioned along the frontier road, were to protect those within the jurisdiction, but not beyond.[72] For Hay, the colony was a moral space, while Imperri was a site of "inhumane practices" and "horrible crimes."[73] The boundary between such spheres was supposedly maintained by capable male bodies: "Constables were quartered along the Frontier to protect the people from the slave raids that had unhappily so long spoilt the country and prevented the cultivation of the farms."[74] These soldiers' bodies were figured as the gendered skin, the protective masculine frontier, of the colony. Crucially, British order and prowess depended on the impenetrability of this boundary.[75] When that boundary line failed, the instability of British control was undeniable; for, though the constitution of borders as stabilizing forces aimed to stave off threats to the administration's security, attendant ideas of territorial and bodily safety were directly undermined through Human Leopard and Tongo activity, both as pervasive, resistant indigenous violence *and* as cannibalism that threatened to dissolve firm boundaries between self and other through the physical incorporation of the other into the self. Thus, while the proposed solution was to expand colonial jurisdiction so as to control indigenous violence, what happened in the end was that colonial expansion only took within its borders the unruly elements; this masculinized space was ultimately penetrated by them.

If both the landscape and the imperial network are rendered through metaphors of male bodies, these bodies prove to be grotesque ones – bodies that, as we have seen throughout the literature explored in this study, become contiguous, leaky, and permeable. This state of affairs led to the dissolution of the bounded male body as it was understood – whether that body represented the colonial military, writing and authority, or national identity – and yielded a new recognition of male vulnerability. Indeed, the figuration of the landscape surrounding Sierra Leone as male – both passive in its ostensible insentience and active in its resistance, mutability, and porousness – paved the way for understandings both of maleness and of the colonial space to shift from bounded, impermeable, and firm, to nebulous, indefinite, and grotesque. As with the Anglo-Zulu War and the Siege of Khartoum, imperial narratives perceived the African landscape as aiding and abetting indigenous physical threats. For the colonists in Sierra Leone, the surrounding geography seemed to host and support the Leopard Society. A member of the West African Medical Staff, D. Burrows, suggested that membership flourished because "numerous rivers and mangrove creeks with their dark, noisome, and intricate passages, afford excellent facilities for the meeting of the 'lodges,' and an equally rapid means of dispersal to the members, in their swift canoes, after the terrible and mysterious rites have been performed."[76] These watery boundaries of Imperri, here so closely allied with Leopard secrecy and transgression, themselves resisted demarcation. The mangroves, with their twisted roots and dense, tangled thickets, rendered the shore indeterminate. This landscape, slippery, inaccessible, and unsurveillable to the West, seemed perfectly to enable ritual, cannibalism, and the dispersal of flesh. Burrows assigned a similar role to the foliage: "At the appointed hour, when it is quite dark, a strange flute-like whistling, like that of the Pipes of Pan, … is heard in the bush which comes right up to the outermost houses of the town or village."[77] This reference to Pan associated the Leopard Men with the non-human, hybrid body, the terror, and the lusty sexuality of the fantastic other. The desiring monster was located in the encroaching forest, threatening the human, the civilized, with its "strange," "dark," concealed spatial transgression. Grotesque and boundless, the landscape was not just physically but also psychically transgressive. Griffith confessed, "there is something about the Sierra Leone bush, and about the bush villages as well, which makes one's flesh creep … The bush seemed to me pervaded with something supernatural, a spirit which was striving to bridge the animal and human. Some of the weird spirit of their surroundings has, I think, entered into the people."[78] For Griffith, the landscape's grotesqueness threatened the human body's stability. Psychically transgressive, the bush, and the unknown threats it concealed, operated on Griffith's affective register. Furthermore, the unaccountable – "the weird spirit" – the opaque, resistant mystery, the "animal" in the African wilderness, seemingly "supernatural[ly]" transgressed human boundaries. Once again, the phantasmagoric angle of the Leopard problem overshadowed the socio-economic contexts of the increased violence in which Britain played an important role, but it also indicated the susceptibility of imperial sensibilities to the inexplicable psychic hold of the grotesque landscape.

Of course, the very spatial proximity of Human Leopard murders and rituals to the colony was further disconcerting for the colonial administration and the metropole because it undermined British efficacy and national identity. The rise of cannibalism alongside British-controlled establishments directly threatened imperial control and constituted intrusion – a situation incompatible with traditional versions of British identity. As Mr Garrett, the trade manager of Sherbro, put it, "I … came out with the determination to root [cannibalism] out, as I felt it a disgrace to my self as Head of the District that Cannibalism should be raging in a spot within active jurisdiction and not more than 15 miles in a line from Bonthe the Head Quarters."[79] Echoing this implication that Victorian imperial institutions should be better able to curb such violence, Mary Kingsley remonstrated, "these things are … acknowledged to have taken place in a colony like Sierra Leone, which has had unequalled opportunities of becoming christianized for more than one hundred years."[80] That a murder society could not only exist but also flout colonial authority undercut the civilizing narrative, imperial efficacy, and British national identity. The landscape's physical role in this resistance complicated boundaries between British and other; as both an extension of the colony and as grotesque, monstrous, and transgressive form, the landscape threatened to penetrate the settlement with the mysteries it shrouded. Thus the masculinized space of the colony came to represent a profoundly infiltrated colonial body *and* an internal menace that threatened to dissolve colonial identity itself.

Nevertheless, the landscape was not the only grotesque body; the Frontier Police force was also, in a sense, an indeterminate entity that disrupted structures of colonial order. On the ground, British colonists were not the immediately visible authority; moderately indirect rule meant that the imperial force imbibed African bodies into its ranks – African men occupied that liminal space between foreign and native influence.[81] This permeability of colonial authority troubled British representations of the Frontier Police as a stabilizing force for empire, for, as Henry Richard Fox Bourne, the secretary of the Aborigines' Protection Society, recognized from afar, "there are manifest dangers in the creation of an army, however small, and however well disciplined the men composing it, of which a main recommendation is that its divers components are acquainted with languages and localities unknown to the European officers placed over them."[82] Shared indigenous knowledge, combined with a degree of power, potentially subverted British authority. In the particular case of Sierra Leone, colonial military presence itself challenged imperial ideologies of control, and, by yielding to indigenous methods of justice, became complicit in what the administration understood as chaos. Disruptive events were desperately but inadequately tracked by colonial agents; the records betray an absence of structure in the colonial military body that British imperialism so championed, as well as disorder in the process of reporting itself.

In March 1892, Acting Colonial Secretary Quayle Jones recognized a devastating problem with the deployment of governmental power in Sierra Leone. Communications in the chain of command had failed miserably, resulting in perceived colonial complicity in the burning of villagers in the Imperri district. Writing to Lord Knutsford at the Colonial Office in London, Quayle Jones reported that the Sierra Leone government had recently learned of a suppressed report from Sub-Inspector Sawyer, a West African Frontier Police officer, who, on rounds in Imperri back in November 1891, had encountered a chief held in stocks at the village of Bogo:

> Chief Basshie of this village … is a very aged man. [H]e assured me that he would soon be killed by one Neppoh [the Tongo leader] who has ordered him to be placed in stock, for being found out to be a cannibal, but that I should pity his condition and save his life.
>
> This being their country custom I ask no more question [*sic*].[83]

Sawyer had been reluctant to become involved in indigenous affairs because military policy was non-interference beyond the colony's borders. What Sawyer had not realized was that, by that point in time, Bogo had been absorbed into British jurisdiction. Since he believed himself unauthorized to act, he continued up the river, leaving Bashie in stocks. His seemingly brusque disregard for Bashie's pleas starkly contrasts with his establishment of pathos for the elderly man locked up on public display, but it is precisely in this contrast that affect is discharged. In suspending resolution of Bashie's condition – Sawyer visually creates an ellipsis by starting a new paragraph – and responding with ostensible indifference that is directly dictated by colonial instruction, the sub-inspector's report highlights an absence of empathy in military policy.

He repeats, with increased intensity, this mixing of sterile facts with harrowing descriptions: "From Bogoe we started at 4 p.m. About 250 yards off this village is found a terrible sight, or 'the torment of Hell,' – Human bodies were seen blazing and tormenting in a large flame on this side of the road, these (I am informed) are those engaged in cannibalism. Proceeded on, we arrived at the village Gangarmah, at 5.15 p.m. Remained here for the night." That Sawyer is able to offer only times and measurements – the most basic of facts – in response to witnessing this brutality speaks to a constraint surrounding written representation of the violence. Nowhere does he use the first person to narrate his experience; his report notes that a terrible sight "is found," and human bodies "were seen." This rhetorical distancing with the passive voice points to the requirements of colonial inspection; licensed to do nothing else, he "proceeded on."

Sawyer finished his inspections in the other villages and returned down river: "From [Manoh Bargroo] we started at 12 midnight, and reached Bagoe at 4:15 A.M. Chief Basshie whom I left in stock (I am informed) has been burnt to death. Left Bagoe for Bendoo at 8 A.M. and arrived at 4.40 p.m." Again, Sawyer's pattern of parenthesizing poignant details with detached observation emerges to critique, with restraint, his liminal position of limited observation without any real power or authority. His repetition of "I am informed" signals both his inability to act and the instabilities of his knowledge: distancing himself from these executions through an unspecified mediator who informs him, he establishes his own involvement as passive and limited to reporting. Sawyer also compromises the finality of his own report by preserving uncertainty about the victims' guilt. His second iteration of "I am informed" echoes the first instance where Sawyer refuses to confirm that those executed were cannibals, and thus casts similar doubt on Bashie's Leopardism. Thus his report itself can offer only partial intelligence. Further, in his postscript, Sawyer adds, "I beg respectfully to suggest that these stations be reinforced as early as possible and Sub Officers who could read and write be placed in charge of each of the above Stations. The roads and Bridges throughout the District are all clean and in good order." This first sentence carefully hints at the colonial administration's failure to fulfill its self-appointed role of protecting villagers, while the second bluntly demonstrates the limits of Sawyer's agency. Thus what seemed to the Colonial Office a callous response was, rather, a subtle protest from a constrained position. Although the secretariats would blame Sawyer's inaction on inadequate transparency around jurisdiction, Sawyer's report demonstrates that the central issue was instead a larger problem of colonial powerlessness.

Sawyer submitted his report to the acting inspector general, Captain Lendy, who, for reasons that puzzled the administration, suppressed this document. His superior, Major Moore, upon discovering the truth, continued the cover-up and further contravened colonial organizational structures.[84] This mismanagement posed difficulty for the overseeing Colonial Office in London, which recoiled from taking any definitive action. In fact, in the minutes for Quayle Jones's dispatch, the secretariats remain noncommittal, opting to "await further infor[mation] before expressing any opinion" and to "express general approval of the steps he has taken."[85] The administration faced a number of questions: Who was to be held responsible for Sawyer's inaction? Who was to be held responsible for suppressing the report? What were the consequences of villagers perceiving British inaction when confronted with Tongo Play and executions? What did this suggest about order within British ranks?

In April 1892, Captain Lendy was held to account for suppressing Sawyer's report. His explanation was that he wished to avoid judgment on the Frontier Police. The Colonial Office secretariat's earnest comment that "it is astonishing that Capt. Lendy should have allowed a feeling of 'esprit de corps' to carry him so far, and that Major Moore should support him,"[86] hints at the underlying threat of the racially mixed body – and at the potential for fraternal bonds to render that body transgressive and ungoverned. The secretariat went on to urge "that the Constabulary officers must be made aware [/] *warned* that it is their duty to report fully to the Governor, whether they think that the matters to be reported may reflect on the Frontier Police or not, and that neglect to perform such a duty will entail serious consequences."[87] The secretariat thus read loyalty across race and rank as a threat, for such interracial bonding and attendant omissions clearly endangered the structure of national loyalties. The military body was supposed to be a well-oiled machine – disciplined and hierarchical – not an unruly system compromised by transgressive affect that contravened protocol.[88] But the fact that racial mixing was essential to the operations of empire only furthered the risk that imperialism would be the undoing of the order so foundational to Britain's national identity. In the coming years, the rhetoric employed by the administration in order to cope with this perceived emergent "esprit de corps" was ultimately forced to shift so that understandings of Britain's identity and the race of the "British" subject expanded, absorbing the other so as to rework fictions of a cohesive body.

The other important ideology underpinning the secretariat's mandate of disclosure understood writing and documenting as manifestations of "duty," as moral imperatives that impinged on national authority; what was written, or not, would directly impact imperial legitimacy. The secretariat's next thought recognizes this relationship: "It ought to be impressed on every police officer from the highest to the lowest that their attitude must never be one of indifference: that the Queen views with abhorrence all such customs ... Every officer in such regions should know it and have views of this kind on his lips."[89] In other words, emphasis on national policies of humanitarian orientations both underpinned and authorized colonialism. To be effective on both counts, this identity required uniformity; for the police to operate as British representatives, that militant body required cohesive ideology.[90] This very insistence, however, that the moral features of Britishness needed to be enforced among the colonial military body underscores the ideological deviations occurring at the frontier.

As concerning as Sawyer's lack of interference in Bashie's execution or the other burnings was, colonial governance slid further into disrepute when later that same April, the Sierra Leone administration discovered that the constabulary were either taking part or complicit in the Tongo burnings. The government ordered an inquest – held surreptitiously – and commissioned a Mr Huggins to "enquire into the truth of certain charges, made against the Frontier Police, of having taken an active part in or connived at the practice."[91] Huggins interviewed twenty-three witnesses and presented their translated statements to Governor Fleming,[92] who summarized these findings in his dispatch: "there can be little doubt, that the Police have taken part in the practices alluded to, but under what circumstances and to what extent I cannot as yet say."[93] The secretariat, in response to Fleming's report, deflected responsibility from the colonial administration by othering the Frontier Police while acknowledging their participation in the violence: "the men of the force are drawn from uncivilized tribes, with whom similar practices are common, and would therefore see nothing unusual or revolting in what was done. It can hardly be expected that the … traditions of their life time should be immediately eradicated by their being turned into policemen."[94] Thus one member of the secretariat explained the constables' non-compliance with British orders – though the clarity and directness of those orders were matters of dispute – by essentializing them as primitive natives, even while they constituted the imperial force. The secretariat, however, could not have it both ways: even according to the argument of this member, either the chain of colonial command had faltered, or the colonial force was, at its core, unstable and unpredictable.

While the Colonial Office in London could try to explain away Frontier Police participation in Tongo Play in this manner, it was harder to reconcile the problem of white involvement and supervision. Governor Fleming downplays Sawyer's responsibility: "Whatever may have been his fault or want of discretion in not releasing the old man from the stocks and thus indirectly having caused his death, I cannot think that he was nearly so much to blame as some of his superior officers."[95] There was good reason for this supposition. Two British officers, Captain Soden and Inspector Campbell, were directly implicated in the Tongo burnings;[96] Imperri chiefs had contacted both men and had conveyed their intentions of deploying Tongo Players to discover and burn Human Leopards. Governor Fleming reflected that "it seems strange that no communication was made to the Government by Inspector Soden of the letters which the Chiefs addressed to him when they asked permission to employ the Tongo men."[97] Fleming thus highlighted Soden's silence and pleaded ignorance for his own part as he acknowledged "the evidence tends to prove that either Captain Campbell or Inspector Soden or both of them did not, to put it in its mildest form, do what they should have done to discountenance or prevent what they knew to be contrary to repeated instructions from the Government of this Colony."[98] Culpability and "the conduct of the government officials" thus became the central question for the Colonial Office.[99]

We may be sceptical, though, of the genuine concern of the Colonial Office for getting to the root of matters: although anxiety surrounding the possibility of white men "regressing" is piqued in this archive, the impulse to deny it dominates.[100] In the draft minutes, the secretariat favours the idea that the white officers were largely ignorant of the Tongo Play, and thus generally did not need to be held responsible. The inquest itself, however, suggests intense anxiety about white involvement. Inquiries were made about whether the deponent witnessed any of the following occurrences:[101] 1) white men participating in Tongo Play (whether dancing, beating, or burning); 2) white men seeing alleged Human Leopards in stocks; 3) white men giving Neppoh, the head Tongo Player, money; 4) white men announcing support for Tongo Play or for the idea that Human Leopards should be burnt; 5) or constables (who were generally West African) participating in Tongo Play (whether dancing, beating, or burning). Thus the inquest's central concern was white responsibility and complicity. Metropolitan and imperial fears about different forms of "regression" were pervasive. Whether these anxieties took the form of the post-Darwinian unease regarding physical devolution of the British body, the social apprehension about dandyism and decadence,[102] or the notion that British citizens abroad would fall into the temptations and indulgences associated with the primitive, threats of British civility disintegrating occupied the forefront of the imperial imagination. The administration had begun to appreciate that what they had on their hands was what would in a decade be recognized as a Kurtz situation. As the government worked to discover which white men were involved with the burnings and to what degree, to identify the particular fractures in the ranked structure of the military responsible for these transgressions, and to contain this problem, the inquest became not only a manifestation of the anxieties concerning regression but also a means of generating further iterations of them.

The administration's general agreement on the inquest findings was that Frontier Police constables certainly enabled the mass burnings. Further, though never formally recognized by the Colonial Office, the records indicate that Campbell and Soden were both complicit in the Tongo burnings. William Stonewall Jackson, who delivered a letter from the chiefs to Inspector Campbell, "asking whether the leopard people were to be burnt or not," testified that he told Campbell that the chiefs believed "the Government has allowed them to play the Tongo" and that they were preparing to immolate thirty people. Instead of immediately denouncing this course of action, "Captain Campbell himself told me that he had no time to give me an answer and that I must go back."[103] Campbell knew that, without a firm denial of permission, the burnings would go ahead. He was not, however, the only white man participating in this violence, as another witness's account suggests. Buarké Gpangobah was accused of cannibalism through the Tongo Play; he was tied and put in stocks but, before being burnt, was able to pay a sufficient amount to procure his release. The fortunate man testified, "I was under the barré the whole of the fifteen days in stock. I saw a white man at Bogo. He came and looked at us in the barré at Bogo

Figure 9. Tongo Players. CO 267/401 18.04.1893 Conf. 24, NA.

but he asked us nothing."[104] There are also multiple statements that at least one British man was on cordial terms with Neppoh, the Tongo leader. Margay, another witness, related, "I saw a white man come to Bogo … Nepoh was at Bogo when this white man came. He had caught many persons and burnt them" – which means that the human remains and ash would easily have been seen by this man – "Neppoh dressed himself in the same way as when he dresses when he plays the Tongo and himself and all his boys came to the white man. The white man filled a tumbler full of rum and gave it to Neppoh and he drank it. The white man asked Neppoh to 'play' for him. Neppoh did so with all his boys."[105] Such a request would, of course, have been tantamount to encouragement and legitimation. Yet the situation grew still more complex. Gombee, another witness, testified, "I saw a white man come to Bogo … he made Neppoh and his boys dress in their Tongo dress … He looked through a small box standing on legs and put a black cloth over his head and 'so' drew them."[106] The photograph Gombee described later surfaced and was included in a subsequent dispatch.[107]

It was discovered eight months later that the photographer was Mr Garrett, the trade manager of the district. The Colonial Office was relieved that it was not a military officer who had given this tacit approval of the Tongo Play, but nevertheless was in favour of "further reprimand" of Garrett.[108] The administration was perturbed by its lack of control over its agents' problematic actions, that Garrett's desire to catalogue the other overwhelmed the imperative to discourage violent judgment of indigenous men, and that a white official was drawn to Tongo brutality.

The inquest also revealed – and other records support this – that, in the summer of 1891, the Imperri chiefs met with Inspector Soden at a factory owned by the French West African Company in Mohbondoh in order to follow up on a letter written to the governor asking for permission to employ Tongo Players for discovering Human Leopards.[109] Soden had not reported the full details of the outcome of this conference. Huggins took the testimony of Agent Kittell, who had interpreted at this meeting and translated the governor's written response to the chiefs:

> The Governor said ... that about the Tongo affairs he has nothing to do with the Tongo nor would he give them any advice respecting it. If the human-leopards caught persons the chiefs must have their towns properly cleaned and the bush cut down. The people should go in numbers and not singly so that they could protect themselves against the human leopards. If the human leopards continued to catch people he would hold the chiefs of the Imperri country responsible.[110]

If the governor's disavowal of responsibility here left room for the chiefs to call upon the Tongo Players, his threat of holding them responsible for Leopard murders further incentivized them to do so. The governor's strategic disengagement damned British efficacy, but it also illuminates the administration's understanding that the real problem here was an unruly landscape. The British rationale held that order could be attained by ensuring the "towns [were] properly cleaned and the bush cut down." Again relying on the idea that security could be established through clearly defined borders and boundaries – a panacea that on many levels failed to be effective, in part because borderlines become so uncontrollably blurred in this context – the governor's letter entirely dodged the issue of Tongo Play and remained firmly invested in the fantasy of demarcated zones of control.

In reply to this translated letter, "the Chiefs and their followers abused Captain Soden in the Mendi and Sherbro languages saying that he did not wish to make the country good. They said the country is theirs so they would see that the Tongo is played and whatever happens they don't care."[111] Soden's response to this was "[']I have told them what the Governor has written and I have nothing more to say. ['] Then Captain Soden got up and went off in a boat in the direction of Bonthe."[112] Soden did nothing to prevent the burnings, knowing that the chiefs intended to go ahead as announced. The Colonial Office, meanwhile, asserted, "Capt. Soden appears to have refused all sanction, and the Chiefs are said to have declared that they could play Tongo in spite of him," and the complicit white officials suffered few consequences.[113] Even while conducting the inquest, Huggins deflected blame from white colonial structures, assuring the governor that, even if orders had been properly communicated to the Frontier Police, the constables would have behaved in the same way.

Huggins's assertion, however, came at the expense of the fantasy of a cohesive military body:

> These men of the Frontier Police … belong to uncivilized tribes in [the colony's] vicinity, and retain without doubt their superstitious notions. [They] have been enlisted in the Frontier Police as it was thought they had better fighting qualities than the ordinary "Creole" of Sierra Leone. Even if it had not always been the practice … to issue both verbal and written instructions … not to interfere in any way with the people or their native Customs,[114] I feel sure that men like BONAR and FAHBANDEH would see nothing wrong in dancing the TONGO or watching human leopards burn.[115]

Thus Huggins, like Campbell, Griffiths, and Soden, also legitimated Tongo divination by presuming the guilt of the people burned, even while deriding the "natives" of "uncivilized tribes" for retaining the same "superstitious notions." And, like the member of the colonial secretariat who essentialized men of the Frontier Police, Huggins tried but failed to have it both ways: this military body he described, employed for its "fighting qualities," was, almost by definition, a mixed and uncontrollable body. In fact, the Frontier Police did not comprise solely West African men but also men from the interior who had migrated to the coast and were "absorbed" into the force.[116] The Frontier Police could not be both an effective colonial disciplinary institution and a scapegoat for when white colonial order broke down.

While Huggins and the Colonial Office were quick to excuse white officers, others were more reluctant. Colonel Ellis, one of a handful of men reviewing the inquest,[117] argued that if the police at Bogo knew that Tongo Play was prohibited in Imperri, "they should be punished, and if they did not know it, the officer or officers whose duty it was to make these facts known to them should be called to account."[118] Ellis thus highlighted organizational deficiency and called for stricter regulation of the martial body.[119] He also underscored problems with white conduct: "it also appears that a European officer [Garrett] *acted* in such wise as to lead the people to believe that the Tongo Play was sanctioned … He is largely responsible for the loss of human life that followed."[120] Ellis also pointed out, "a European officer did see persons confined in the stocks and took no steps to release them, and this merits further enquiry."[121] He later suggested that Huggins was "a very useful Officer to employ when the Government wanted a matter to be hushed up, and everybody concerned to be whitewashed. We had evidence of that in the manner in which Mr. Huggins conducted the Imperi enquiry when no one was ever punished for the terrible atrocities that had there been committed."[122] Ellis thus saw white complicity for what it was. Similarly, Sam Lewis, another inquest reviewer and a lawyer in the colony, condemned Soden's inaction following the Imperri chiefs' request for the Tongo Play: "no Letter or Minute of inspector Soden is found advising his transmission to the Inspector General in Freetown of the two letters of the chiefs. It is important to know what he did say in so transmitting them; because a silence on his part appears to me as significant as, and as tantamount to, an approval, or to no disapproval of the employment of the TONGO men for discovering alleged cannibals."[123] Concluding that Soden connived in the Tongo practice, Lewis also censured Captain Campbell's inaction, arguing that Jackson's testimony demonstrated that a colonial authority had given some level of permission for Tongo Play and indicated "a positive direction and approval by Captain Campbell" of this violence.[124] Campbell, then, was clearly implicated in the murders. Lewis argued that white officers had colluded in the mass killings of villagers: Soden had responded with silence when the chiefs insisted on Tongo Play;[125] Jackson's testimony implied some prior discussion between Campbell and the chiefs regarding burning Human Leopards; and Campbell, though he passed through Bogo during the period of Tongo Play and mass burnings, did absolutely nothing. Lewis cited, in addition, the absence of a white commandant when Parker, the interpreter, delivered his hotly contested message that the British were supporting the Tongo.[126] As he summed up, "The awful character of the foul secret murders with which cannibalism was credited, and the failure of reaching the offenders by legal means appear to have unfortunately influenced the Officers implicated, to connive at an unlawful practice which promised discovery and a way of stamping out the crime."[127] Although it failed to contain the Human Leopard Society and the Tongo Players, this archive, unsurprisingly marked "Confidential," tracks and illuminates the dissolution of colonial order and the ostensible moral grounding used to justify the imperial project.

Despite Ellis's and Lewis's demand for follow-up regarding British conduct, the colonial administration minimized white culpability. The secretariat favoured agreement with Mr Bayldon Walker, the acting Queen's advocate, who denied Soden's and Campbell's guilt, downplayed the significance of Garrett's photographing Tongo Players, and set the blame on the African men involved – Parker, Bonar, and Fahbandeh.[128] The secretariat also agreed with Dr Ross, the Freetown surgeon and reviewer who dismissed indigenous testimonies that fingered white men by insisting that the statements "of the uneducated and half civilized Aborigines of the Colony ... are to be received with caution as they do not understand the exact nature of an oath or the sacredness of speaking the Truth especially when they have a purpose to serve." This standard imperial strategy for marginalizing indigenous (especially non-Christian) testimonies served a history more favourable to empire. Ross went on to blame Bonar and Fahbandeh's involvement on "a misapprehension of their responsibilities and duties," suggesting that they were "influenced by their Native superstitions" rather than by colonial mismanagement or complicity.[129] The Colonial Office, meanwhile, avoided Lewis's astute reading altogether, affirmed the "correctness" of its officers' behaviours, and denied the major faults in the colonial structure. Nevertheless, while both branches of government ignored the visible moral decay in the chain of white command, the Colonial Office was still forced to acknowledge that imperial men had weakly handled both the Human Leopard attacks and the Tongo Play: "the hideous horror of the burnings and human leopards and cannibalism ... could not be allowed to exist on British soil; they have been handled by the British Officials in a gingerly sort of way as though the country was a sphere of influence in which our right to exercise authority was doubtful."[130] Colonial officers, in other words, had not been the decisive, strong, and determined figures that imperial narrative of masculinity and national identity demanded; rather, they behaved "gingerly," dithered, and backed away from "exercis[ing] authority." This short passage also clinches a number of the key problems that this historical case exposes: the violence in the contact zone that disavows

British control and runs contrary to forms of violence sanctioned by the empire; the inefficacy of the military in maintaining the illusion of imperial order; and the dubiousness of solid boundaries of influence. And, far from being reconciled in the accounts and reports about these challenges, this colonial archive reveals that these issues remained crucial points of weakness for the imperial project.

Fissures in the Archive

In this colonial archive, writing becomes both a mechanism and limitation of imperial power. There is no question that, by setting laws and legitimating colonial actions, the written word signalled British presence and deployed imperial power. For instance, Governor Hay wrote in 1890, "Having heard … that fifteen persons have been burnt in the Imperreh … I have deemed it my duty to write to the Chiefs requesting them to stop this cruel mode of punishment *at once* and have threatened to hold them responsible should any more cases be reported to me."[131] As with Hay's text, writing disciplined through instruction, but also by surveillance – hence the copious, almost compulsive recording and cataloguing within colonial spaces. But as a disciplining agent, the written word hit a wall in its attempt to contain Human Leopard murders and attendant persecutions. In 1890, Hay's confidence in the colonial pen abounds; after sending Brett to Bonthe to order alleged Human Leopards released and their plundered goods returned, Hay triumphed in the immediate result: "it will be noted by [Brett's] Report No. 38, that he has … in accordance with my instructions, seriously warned the chiefs as to their future conduct, and he does not think there will be a recurrence of such conduct."[132] While Hay – reinforced by the text of Report No. 38 – suggests that his "instructions" were force enough to elicit obedience, records show that, within a year, persecutions of alleged Human Leopards had resurfaced more violently and still more visibly.

The challenge of surveilling and documenting Human Leopard activities surpassed colonial capacities. As Hay confessed, "it is always difficult to procure sufficient evidence to ensure a conviction for murder against the accused in a Court of Law as the society is a secret one, and I am informed that most prosecutions have hitherto been abortive on this account."[133] Admitting inefficacy, Hay appealed to Knutsford: "I would be pleased to be favoured with your Lordship's views on this subject which is one with which it is most difficult to deal."[134] This tension surrounding the efficacy of writing reveals deep uncertainties about masculine prowess and control. In Knutsford's response to Hay, his hesitancy concerning this difficult subject manifests in his very writing: "~~In cases like the present~~ It appears to me that where, as in the present case, the offending chiefs are beyond the sphere ~~of~~ in which your government exercises active jurisdiction, your best course will be to use ~~your~~ such influence as you may possess, to induce these Chiefs to execute persons, ~~convicted~~ guilty of cannibalism, in a more humane manner."[135] Knutsford began and then scratched his wording, unsure of how to characterize these events or how to advise Hay. His replacement of "your [influence]" with "such influence as you may possess" demonstrates his realization that Hay may not have had much influence at all. Moreover, Knutsford's minute betrays indecision regarding the use of "convicted" or "guilty," suggesting a discomfort around the idea of demonstrable guilt: for Knutsford, it was not enough to say that those burned were convicted; he had to insist that they were indeed *guilty*. Once again, the presumption of guilt is based upon Tongo divination, which directly contravenes the imperial world view and religious orientation. Finally, his vague advice is to encourage chiefs beyond imperial jurisdiction to advocate for executions to be conducted "in a more humane manner."[136] Knutsford thus dodged addressing the disruptive challenges the Tongo Players posed, not to mention the entire issue of how to contain the Human Leopard Society. In these ways, writing leaves traces of uncertainty, tracks disrupted logic, and betrays a lack of control. Thus, while in many ways empire *is* built through the construction of colonial archives, imperial writing is also the undoing of "legitimate" empire: here, in Sierra Leone, the efficacy of writing the empire and the effectiveness of deploying power through writing both enter crisis in the act of producing textuality itself.

This question of manly writing – form, style, and penmanship – underlying British culture has already appeared in some of the popular fiction discussed previously in this study. Quatermain in Haggard's *King Solomon's Mines* states his refusal to populate his tale with "grand literary flights and flourishes" – though, of course, his narrative is replete with these.[137] Basing his story's authority in his "blunt way of writing," his "plain, straightforward manner," and his resistance to tales "decked out in fine words,"[138] Quatermain suggests that the desirable qualities of manliness are manifest in his writing itself. Similarly, narrative inefficacy is linked to dissolved masculinity across Marsh's *The Beetle*. For instance, Robert Holt, penetrated in body and mind, is unable to produce his own narrative; Paul Lessingham, a haunted man, yields only a narrative riddled with holes; and even the hapless Percy Woodville is described as "a champion hasher" specifically because his writing is like "hieroglyphics."[139] Thus, the effectiveness of writing registers masculine competencies.

If, in Victorian society at large, exemplary writing itself was understood to embody desirable qualities in the British man, this was especially true in the colonies. For instance, after the first known set of Human Leopard burnings in the summer of 1890, Hay wrote, "Mr Brett seems to have dealt with this matter" – that is, reporting on the burnings – "with much acumen and good judgment, and his reports are clear and well written."[140] Mr Meade responded from the Colonial Office, expressing "entire approval of your action in this matter, and of the manner in which Mr. Brett carried out the mission entrusted to him. He appears to have dealt with the case with much acumen and good judgment, and his reports are clear and well written."[141] This repetition of phrases – a mode in fact very typical of notes throughout this correspondence – signifies language's limitations in achieving nuanced expression; instead, a kind of shorthand based on previous text is employed as a way to convey only a very basic idea. For both Meade and Hay, "acumen and good judgment" depend primarily on "clear and well written" reports. Meanwhile, colonial efficacy is profoundly limited because no matter how "well written" the reports, events in and near the colonial space resist encapsulation through writing; no narrative was able to capture anything resembling a full story about Human Leopardism or Tongo Play. Further, writing itself, despite representations to the contrary, was deeply inefficacious in altering violent indigenous practice. But the limitations of colonial writing also entailed further breakdown of the dominant concept of impenetrable masculinity, not only because the men writing the colonial narrative failed to perform surveillance and knowledge transmission, but also because the colony itself was figured *as* male – and this gendered conception was used to justify the protection of trade and industry. Indeed, justification of imperial involvement, intervention in human rights discourse, and economic imperatives are all activated through the use of the male body as metaphor for the larger colonial beast. This means that, in the writing of the colony as male, both spatial and literary vulnerabilities underlying masculine associations function to destabilize the concept of impenetrable masculinity.

On a more material level, the structures constituting the system of recording, reporting, and distributing information are revealed as highly unstable. The above miscommunication between the Sierra Leone government and Frontier Police about jurisdiction and Leopard persecutions is a prime example.[142] Just as in Khartoum, botched imperial communication constituted larger failings impinging on imperial order. And if the bungled deployment of written information destabilized imperial prowess, so too did inadequate documentation.

Governor Fleming recognized the gaps underlying acts of recording, narrating, and creating archives as he evaluated reports about Tongo burnings: "There remain some points which are not cleared up as well as they might be, while evidence such as that taken must no doubt be scanned with a careful eye and not too eagerly digested as containing nothing but the truth."[143] Fleming's scepticism, acknowledging the limitations of colonial reporting, deployed the developing metaphor of the body to suggest that language the eye discerns and ideas the body imbibes are themselves potential threats to organizational stability. Again, the metaphor of the body was used to signal vulnerability and, in this case, threats to authority.

Fleming had good cause to question the information supplied from the inquest. These records were so inadequate that the Colonial Office in London could not even agree as to whether the Leopard Society even existed. One secretariat member asserted, "I disbelieve the cannibalism and believe that this was only a pretext by the Chiefs for plundering their victims [and] that the alleged cannibal murders were done by the Tongo men."[144] Inadequate surveillance power thus undercut authoritative imperial history. The relationship between writing and power, the male body, the colonial body, and national identity meant that because, in Sierra Leone, writing was a fraught, unstable, and porous mechanism, it could not effectively substantiate imperial rule. Thus, like the body of empire writing itself, these other spheres of masculinity, geographical space, and subjectivity also became grotesque, mutable, and unbound. Moreover, if this colonial archive is heteroglossic, divergent, and internally inconsistent, so too was the question of identity in the liminal zone of the frontier – a question that had particular implications for conceptions of British identity at large.

Implications for British Identity

Through the process of writing, imperial understandings of British masculinity mutated from a definite, bounded, internally regulated, and beneficent authority to a nebulous, porous, and, as we have just seen, oppressive yet weak entity in Sierra Leone. Gender identity constructions also shifted: this archive figured the Sierra Leonean landscape as male rather than as the traditionally passive female body. The emergent metaphoric relationship between the male body and colonial geography intervened in this long-standing tradition: now, a colonized space – an extension of national geography – was associated with a new idea of maleness, one that was both inherently passive (as landscape) and agent (as environment – threatening, dynamic, communicable).

The newly recognized porousness of this masculine territory meant that it was both vulnerable to external elements *and* contained those disruptive elements within its own borders; the colonial outpost itself was both the target and the threat.

The impact of these elusive, threatening elements on colonial identity extended also to the disruption of foundational social and legal codes. Human Leopard activity pushed British idealism beyond the limits of its own dogma: faced with an uncontrollable, uncontainable threat that destabilized the imposed colonial order, imperial agents resorted to rulings that contradicted British ideals of exemplarity. Having in 1890 lamented the indigenous system's lack of "supreme authority,"[145] the administration was, by the early twentieth century, resorting to suspending standard legal rights. Even in 1910, there was "some reason to suppose [Leopard violence was] on the increase."[146] The colonial government was growing desperate in the struggle to "to stamp out this evil," for "ordinary means have been comparatively unsuccessful."[147] In 1912, the attorney general claimed that "this is a very serious state of affairs and one that has to be dealt with in a drastic manner," putting forth a bill giving district commissioners "power to arrest any person, whose arrest and detention he may consider advisable in the interests of justice."[148] Further, the governor would have the power, in the absence of adequate evidence to convict, to deport the accused. Recognizing the ethical problems with such measures, he reiterated, "The power seems drastic, but the circumstances of these murders are so exceptional, that drastic powers are required."[149] Governor Merewether justified the implementation of this and other extreme measures – including the retrospective ruling that membership in what was vaguely written up as an "unlawful society" was illegal and punishable,[150] the proposal that special tribunals formed for trying alleged Human Leopards would consist of three British judges, and an alteration to the law of evidence[151] – by comparison to other colonial decisions: "If special powers were given to deal with such cases in another Colony, I see no reason why special powers should not be given in this Colony."[152] Recognizing his departure from constitutional British law, Merewether had to establish that the legal alterations proposed in Sierra Leone had an imperial precedent in order to preserve the narrative of moral righteousness. While the rhetoric deployed by proponents of these unconstitutional measures appealed to ideas of necessity, lawfulness, and precedence, such claims were contested by honourable members of the legislative committee, of which Mr Shorunkeh-Sawyerr, a lawyer, was the most vociferous. Respecting the proposal to make Human Leopard membership retrospectively illegal, Shorunkeh-Sawyerr protested that it lacked precedent and "it is not a principle of English law."[153] He also pointed out that "men were not unfrequently entrapped into membership of these Societies, and that membership was not a matter of volition."[154] These arguments ultimately did sway the committee's majority. As for the proposed changes to trials, the extant circuit courts, consisting of one colonial judge and two or three indigenous chiefs, would be replaced by a special tribunal consisting of one judge and two lay non-native assessors.[155] Shorunkeh-Sawyerr argued that this proposal was un-English: "I was in England in 1883 when Mr. Burke and Mr. Cavendish were murdered. The horror and indignation excited by such a crime did not lead [to] the British Parliament passing a law by which Fenians and others were to be tried not by a tribunal consisting only of legally qualified men."[156] Shorunkeh-Sawyerr's point here was that Merewether made an unfair distinction between instituting oppressive laws in the metropole and in the colonies, and he suggested that the suspension of constitutional rights in Sierra Leone violated British legal standards. He applied this approach to his protest of the proposed alteration to the law of evidence, which "places an accused at a greater disadvantage ... If it has not been done in England or Ireland, why should it be done here?"[157] J.H. Thomas summarized the central problems with the bill succinctly: "Power is given to Kings and Emperors to govern their subjects and deal with them righteously and also to punish those who act wickedly. I object to the Bill because it provides for suspected persons being tried without jury or assessors; this I consider is unfair and unjust."[158] In the end, the bill passed, despite these objections. Governor Merewether, contravening British investments in justice, dismissed these arguments: "It is impossible to compare what is done in England with what is done in West Africa ... I agree with the view that it is better tha[t] ten guilty persons should escape than one innocent man should suffer, but in this matter we do not want any of the guilty to escape. Members of this society are not only murderers but cannibals ... We ought not to waste any sentiment on them."[159] Merewether's justification is problematic for a number of reasons – it hierarchizes rights to due process on the basis of geography, presumes the guilt of the accused, refuses to acknowledge their humanity, and conflates justice with sentiment – but what is crucial for this study is that, confronted with a force whose logic transgressed the Western rationale, the British in Sierra Leone chose to fold English principles and slipped into what they had long conceived of as the trap of regression; British morality itself weakened, caved, and became grotesque.

Thus, the fantasy of the solid, invulnerable, impermeable male body was exploded by the crises with which Human Leopard and Tongo violence confronted imperial constructions of authority and legitimacy. The role of writing in undermining imperial legitimacy and British moral ideology is, again, fundamental: this archive constitutes a regulatory fantasy that ultimately fails – it exposes the complicity of white British men in atrocities that the West repeatedly characterized as peculiar to African cultures. Though both colonial writing and print circulation worked to efface the socio-economic components of history – the material motivations and parameters surrounding Human Leopardism and Tongo Play – and emphasize the phantasmatic elements of accounts of Africa, such as ritual murder, superstition, and shape-shifting, these texts also make visible their particular investments in the legitimation of racism, governmental brutality, and military prowess. As, however, this colonial archive fails to create a seamless or even viable history of British morality, it exposes the fissures in governmentability, discipline, and regulation. These archives thus make visible the dissolution of the bases of British identity; as masculine efficacy, male authority, the legitimacy of governmental rule, and state policy became grotesque, mutable, and arbitrary, fantasies about personal, social, cultural, and moral boundaries ended up crumbling away.

Chapter Six

Expanding Darkness: Narrative Complicity

One writes only half the book; the other is with the reader.
– Joseph Conrad, letter to Graham Cunningham, 5 Aug. 1897

In the colonial archive of fin-de-siècle Sierra Leone, we saw that British confrontations with indigenous resistance profoundly disrupted masculine imperial power. Colonial writing that traced epistemological frustrations, colonial inefficacy, white male vulnerability, fissures in the order of command, and colonial complicity in unsanctioned violence, was in these ways destructive to notions of legitimate imperial authority. Moving back to the realm of fiction, this chapter explores how Conrad's *Heart of Darkness*, read against the rest of the texts studied here, explores the same kind of epistemological uncertainty, unruly geography, and white "regression" depicted in Sierra Leone and exposes the ideological limitations of empire; I argue that imperial narrative cannot fulfill the imperial imperative of mapping, cataloguing, and knowing within the framework of imperial identity. Where narrative of empire intersects with these imperatives, both objectives cannot be fulfilled, since, as we saw in chapter 5, the epistemological compulsion to write the conditions and the history of empire necessitates the destruction of the myth of imperial gallantry, rationalism, and stoicism. In other words, pursuing one central mode of imperial power explodes the other. This problem emerges in and through the novella's narrative itself, which, as an agent and product of empire, both articulates imperial anxieties about its own instability and acts *as* the engulfing, grotesque threat by which it purports to be unsettled. The monstrosity in *Heart of Darkness* is not Africa, not even imperial violence and exploitation, but rather the seduction of the ideology that works to dissolve touchstones of identity, blur moral boundaries, and consume critical autonomy. This means of course that Conrad's text, like the others in this study, is fundamentally about Europe, and not about Africa. As we have seen, these masculine imperial narratives do not reveal nearly so much about Africa as they do about masculine imperial vulnerabilities. If we accept Chinua Achebe's point that "travellers with closed minds can tell us little except about themselves,"[1] then that *Heart of Darkness* takes as its primary subject imperial modes should not surprise us. As with other imperial narratives in this study, what interests me about Conrad's novella is how the text itself cannibalizes the imperial pillars of martial masculinity and narrative legitimacy, thereby undermining its own authority to represent Africa. As we will see, in *Heart of Darkness* narrative becomes a dangerous flowing entity that consumes imperial agents, narrators, and readers, seductively expanding to disrupt ideas of moral grounding and identity. That the same tropes of engulfment, penetration, and dissolution appearing in adventure romance, imperial Gothic, and colonial archives again emerge here, in more fully articulated forms, to proclaim masculine vulnerability and the disruption of identity underscores how both narrative content and form function to highlight ideological instability at this particular historical moment.

There are particular reasons to read *Heart of Darkness* against the archive of fin-de-siècle Sierra Leone. While geographically these settings are quite disparate, British approaches to each region are remarkably resonant.[2] In both cases, the African wilderness is consistently described as threatening, unknowable, and monstrous, and while this may be said of numerous British representations of Africa, *Heart of Darkness*, because of its canonical status, usefully illustrates the pervasiveness, depth, and enduring fascination of these kinds of ideas about Africa as suffocating and transgressive, along with attendant notions of British vulnerability and gender identity. Its narrative is also similarly troubled by, and then accepting of, white complicity with violence in the colonial sphere. In both cases, what begins as discomfiture toward brutality yields to the seductive appeal of silence; succumbing to the obfuscation of colonial realities irretrievably compromises both imperial epistemological drives and masculine integrity. Finally, both the Sierra Leone archive and *Heart of Darkness* articulate their own embedment in streams of imperial capital, and it is this very embedment that clinches their demonstration that empire's seduction comes at the cost of critical autonomy. Ultimately, *Heart of Darkness*, following Haggard, Marsh, and the mediations of a range of imperial failures, provides a microcosmic example of the process of the disintegration in British culture of imperial narratives of masculinity and masculine narratives of empire: demonstrations of vulnerability, fears of penetration, and recognitions of dissolution articulate the text's confrontation with the hollowness of masculine imperial identity. In the fin-de-siècle archive of Sierra Leone, we saw the historical disintegration of imperial masculine boundaries, authority, narrative, and identity emerge on the ground, so to speak; in *Heart of Darkness* we see these disintegrations manifest in British mainstream culture as fictional narrative acknowledges the corrosion of masculine pillars of imperial identity, and as British readers imbibe the devastating migration of imperial failure. Problems with traditional modes of white masculine authority were becoming more visible.

Reading *Heart of Darkness*

My argument that *Heart of Darkness* deploys its own narrative as an example of monstrous and engulfing imperial ideology in some ways straddles the somewhat binary critical history of the novel. Historically, the question of racism in Conrad's text has both proved divisive and profoundly informed subsequent critical inquiry. Achebe has famously – and accurately – charged Conrad's text with relegating Africa and African people to a backdrop for European self-examination.[3] While other scholars have also recognized that in *Heart of Darkness*, "Africa becomes an environment where irrational behaviour is the norm"; that, in many ways, the novel's main preoccupation is the problem of white regression;[4] and that, as Jim Holstun aptly puts it, "Conrad changed Africa from a human ecology under colonial stress into a site for metaphysical reflection and absurdist excess, creating in the process a highly influential idiom of racist but obliquely anti-imperial narration."[5] Yet some critics have jumped to defend Conrad by denying the racism in his representation of Africa.[6] Mongia Padmini's point that such Conradian criticism has avoided crediting Achebe's argument by insisting on the novel's complexity remains an important one, and indeed criticism must acknowledge the consequences of Conrad's egregious representations of Africa.[7] Padmini is right to argue that Cedric Watts, a would-be rescuer of Conrad from the charge of racism, misses that Conrad's critique of European greed does not neutralize Achebe's point that *Heart of Darkness* nevertheless still offers denigrating and reductive representations of Africans.[8]

In a similar vein, criticism has also sought to answer the question of whether the novel ultimately supports or critiques British imperialism. While Hunt Hawkins has argued that the novel's commentary concerns Belgian ruthlessness, and is not about British imperialism at all,[9] others have pointed out that Britain's relationship with the conditions of imperial exploitation in Congo is clear in the text: Ian Watt has identified numerous British models for Kurtz, including Emin Pasha, Edmund Musgrave Barttelot, Henry Morton Stanley, and Charles Stokes; Patrick Brantlinger has added to this list Captain Sidney Langford Hinde; D.C.R.A. Goonetilleke has linked Kurtz's disciple with Britain; and Maya Jassanoff's biography of Conrad has also demonstrated Britain's well-known economic involvement in the products coming out of Congo, including ivory and rubber.[10] Acknowledging this relationship between *Heart of Darkness* and British imperialism, William Atkinson, premising his argument on the novel's publication in the imperialistic *Blackwood's* magazine, suggests that, because the novel entered pro-imperial discourse, it reinforces imperial assumptions.[11] If my arguments in this study have proved persuasive, though, it should be clear by now that such a conclusion cannot be taken for granted, since a significant number of imperial narratives have proved to be self-cannibalizing. For Atkinson, Marlow's claim to invest in the value of efficiency – I will return later to how the idea of efficiency functions in the novel as a hollow signifier, an engulfing seduction – and his observations about "real work" ultimately equate to an argument in the novella that "good imperialists are British and bad imperialists are not."[12] Atkinson's ultimately reductive assessment of the novella ignores the problem of British complicity that other critics have underscored, and the problem of narrative complicity that I unpack below.

Moving away from the central binaries of racism/anti-racism and pro-imperialism/anti-imperialism, more recent criticism has focused on the novel's interest in ideology and the elusiveness of epistemic truth. Andrew Michael Roberts has investigated the novella's preoccupation with epistemological certainty, exploring Conrad's focus on "the problematic nature of questions of what we can know, how we can know it, and what degree of certainty is possible."[13] Katherine Isobel Baxter, suggesting that the modernist movement recognized ideology as ideology, argues that *Heart of Darkness*, in its obsession with indeterminacy, questioned the ability of language to communicate truth.[14] Her point that the frame narrator's repetition of – and thus surrendering to – Marlow's language constitutes the reader's "entrapment in the novella's systemic darkness"[15] is an important one, but, in my view, this systemic darkness is not constituted primarily by indeterminacy but, crucially, by the limits of ideology articulated through this complicity. Similarly exploring the novel's engagement with ideology, Nidesh Lawtoo suggests that *Heart of Darkness* presents the consequences of "psychic or affective mimesis, a form of behavioural imitation whose primary characteristic consists in generating a psychological confusion between self and other(s) which, in turn, deprives subjects of their full rational presence to selfhood."[16] For Lawtoo, the problem of subjection to ideology originates in primal human impulses responding affectively to "the rhythm of a 'martial noise,'" and joining in for the "joy of killing."[17] But in my reading, this problem goes beyond "mimetic phenomena: somnambulism, compassion, enthusiasm, emotional contagion, hypnosis, depersonalization, and suggestion"[18] – symptoms generally involving a suppressed state of awareness, a lack of critical cognizance of complicity. As I have been arguing with respect to other narratives of empire in this study, the narrative of *Heart of Darkness* not only recognizes the horrors of colonialism, but also articulates, via its own participation in the process of yielding to the seductive desires associated with capital, power, and dominance, the horror of capitulating to it. Thus *Heart of Darkness* emerges from a genealogy of imperial self-condemnation. Furthermore, in Conrad, as in these other texts, the consequence of such seduction is figured as engulfment, penetration, and ultimately dissolution of extant identity; this figuration of the consuming monster indicates just how devastating to British identity such desire and complicity are. In other words, these texts are not simply criticizing imperial behaviour; they are arguing, through their own moral failure, that imperial domination is ultimately destroying the foundations of national identity. Like Haggard and Marsh, Conrad is not interested in "readjust[ing] … Europe's distorted image of Africa" (an objective it did not achieve in any case);[19] rather, his text's warped representation of Africa becomes itself part of the apparatus that discredits imperial ideology and exposes its epistemological limitations.

Generally, though, criticism has recognized that Marlow is firmly embedded in imperialism, as is the frame narrator, as is the reader. As we will see, the very immersion of these narratives in empire figures imperial ideology as a destabilizing, transgressive monster oozing across the boundaries of reason, morality, and, identity. If not as strong a proponent as Frere, Haggard, Gordon, Marsh, or Hay, Conrad nevertheless worked for empire, as does Marlow. He, and his narrative, with all of its racist portrayals, its marginalization of Africa, *and* its criticisms of exploitation, are complicit in the imperial project. Articulating Marlow's complicity, J.M. Rawa points out the captain's fixation on Africa as the biggest "blank space" – the greatest conquest – and argues that Marlow's childhood "interaction with the map reveals his desire to capture an Africa that is apprehended as mysterious yet acquiescent and projects an image of Africa as a wild zone ripe for Western penetration and intervention."[20] While, however, for Rawa, Marlow's imperial hunger "may comprise his critique of imperialism,"[21] I aim to show that it is through Marlow's, the frame narrator's, and potentially the reader's engulfment in this ideology that such a critique operates. As in accounts from the Anglo-Zulu War, Haggard's romances, Gordon's journals, the war reporting about Khartoum, Marsh's imperial Gothic, and the Sierra Leone colonial archive, there is in *Heart of Darkness* an entity that, at once fascinating, terrifying, and desirable – territory, a body, wealth – threatens to consume the imperial forces. For Marlow, this monstrosity is at one level figured through the African landscape, grotesque and immense, threatening vulnerable masculine physicality. As Brantlinger has shown, "the African wilderness serves as a mirror, in whose darkness Conrad/Marlow sees a death-pale self-image."[22] Similarly to Haggard, Conrad combines the dark consuming drives of empire with the object of desire. In turn, that object is invested with the engulfing appetites of empire that threaten to dissolve masculine identity. But this monstrosity also manifests in the figure of Kurtz, whose "pulsating streams of light" ultimately penetrate Marlow's criticality, and consume him. The rest of this chapter explicates this process, arguing that this novel's narrative, at the level of content and form, works to excavate the moral foundations of imperial masculine identity and enfold not just its narrators but also its reader into a grotesque ideology that dissolves critical autonomy by inviting complicity with the imperatives of imperial desire.

Failure and Vulnerability: Bodies, Spaces, Texts

I have been arguing that in late nineteenth-century imperial literature, the legitimacy of authentic imperial narrative depended on the physical integrity and psychic regulation of the adventuring masculine agents who delivered it. Conrad's text is no exception. *Heart of Darkness* situates the failure of narrative legitimacy within failures of white masculine prowess, bringing the kinds of epistemological failures (and their implications for masculine authority and identity) that we saw in chapter 5, as indigenous resistance evaded the imperial technology of surveillance, into the realm of fiction. In this novella, the ideal of "the powerful, knowing, speaking male subject"[23] is not fulfilled. Marlow articulates imperial employment's fundamental role in informing identity; for instance, "the work" offers him "a chance to come out a bit – to find out what I could do" – it is "the chance to find yourself."[24] Yet from the text's beginning, imperial masculinity is woefully inadequate – and for Marlow, this appears to be more troubling than the consequences of empire for indigenous people. In what can be read as nostalgia for exemplars,[25] Marlow suggests that the Roman invaders of Britain "were men enough to face the darkness."[26] This glance to the past for models of heroism echoes a general longing for examples of knight errant figures, but it also associates heroism with the brutality that characterized the Roman invasion of Britain. For readers attuned to the violence of this history, Marlow's reflection evokes distrust of hyper-masculine dominance. Nevertheless, for Marlow, manliness is defined by imperial invasion: he contrives a standard of masculinity, gesturing by implication to the modern colonialists who are found wanting in a comparison to their predecessors: "*They* were men." The efficacy of fin-de-siècle white men is then explicitly pitted against "the immensity" of Africa when Marlow later ponders from the interior, "What were we who had strayed in here? Could we handle that big dumb thing, or would it handle us?"[27] As it turns out, the imperialists get "handle[d]" because they are, on balance, incapable. Fresleven, the captain whom Marlow replaces, dies because he fails to retain manly composure during an argument about chickens, and his own impulsive violence provokes a counter-attack for which he is unprepared.[28] Marlow's sixteen-stone companion on the trek to the Central Station is "rather too fleshy" – too undisciplined[29] – to make it in Africa, and has "the exasperating habit of fainting on the hot hillsides" – how unmanly – prompting Marlow to ask him "what he meant by coming there at all."[30] In other words, a man of his weak constitution does not belong in the challenging colonial sphere. Meanwhile, the station manager's single talent is his resilience to tropical diseases – he "had no learning, and no intelligence ... He originated nothing."[31] Then there's the manager's corpulent – again, read "intemperate" – uncle who leads the "Eldorado Exploring Expedition," which comprises men who are "reckless without hardihood, greedy without audacity, and cruel without courage; there was not an atom of foresight or of serious intention in the whole batch of them."[32] And of course, the "faithless pilgrims"[33] – Europeans idolizing ivory – don't know how to handle themselves, or their Winchester rifles, in the bush. When attacked on the river, they "fired from the hip with their eyes shut" – so, ineffectively – and counterproductively caused "a deuce of a lot of smoke,"[34] impeding both the steering of the steamer and the crew's vantage. Fully every example of white manhood is found wanting.

Importantly, imperialism itself has directly produced these shortcomings; these failures in masculinity stem directly from imperial greed and/or dominance. Fresleven "had been a couple of years already out there engaged in the noble cause, you know, and he probably felt the need at last of asserting his self-respect in some way,"[35] which led straight to his demise. Marlow's phrasing suggests, first, that "the noble cause, you know" is anything but noble, and second, that Fresleven had failed to assert his masculine importance. Indeed, the irony in Marlow's comment that when he discovers Fresleven's remains much later, "the supernatural being had not been touched at all,"[36] highlights the agent's frailty despite white assumption of indigenous reverence. Meanwhile, the sixteen-stoner whose corpulence and fainting remain his sole defining features came to Africa only "to make money, of course."[37] His ignobility underpins the failure of his masculinity. As for the Eldorado Expedition, "To tear treasure out of the bowels of the land was their desire, with no more moral purpose at the back of it than there is in burglars breaking into a safe."[38] The pilgrims carry the "taint of imbecile rapacity," while Marlow ventures to Africa for "all the glories of exploration."[39] He himself is irretrievably embedded in the imperial project insofar as he is materially involved in exploitative operations, and Rawa's example of Marlow's obsession with the map highlights the captain's role in imperial domination at the level of knowing and cataloguing. Thus, in *Heart of Darkness*, imperial men fail to achieve the identities to which empire is supposed to give them access; indeed, their imperial desires render them vulnerable to their own moral failings.

The novella's exploration of failed manhood includes Marlow himself, who as a relator of adventure fails to achieve the respect of his fellows, who don't take him seriously. The frame narrator, having already communicated Marlow's "propensity to spin yarns," reflects, "We knew we were fated, before the ebb began to run, to hear about one of Marlow's inconclusive experiences."[40] Marlow shares "the weakness of many tellers of tales who seem so often unaware of what their audience would best like to hear";[41] indeed, it seems the listeners actually suffer through his story – one of them sighs in a "beastly way," and someone interrupts his story to suggest that Marlow's emotive obsession with Kurtz is "absurd."[42] These responses hardly give credence to Marlow's storytelling. Within the novella's framework, Marlow's narrative of adventure in Africa is not venerated in the way that imperial adventure romance traditionally was – that genre itself was dying out, along with the ideal of fortified, capable, gallant, imperial masculinity; the imperial men in *Heart of Darkness* are weak, hollow, greedy, incompetent, and, in Marlow's case, oblivious to their own insignificance. Marlow's failures in manliness surpass the muted ridicule of his coterie. He physically does not match up to the robust ideal of traditional manliness, where the body is often understood as an artifact of manly survival – indeed, a fever almost buried Marlow.[43] No, Marlow (not unlike Kurtz) is mostly a voice, and when we do get a glimpse of him, his face is "worn, hollow, with downward folds and dropped eyelids."[44] In terms of coolness under pressure, Marlow admits to his own "nervousness" and lack of better sense as he describes impulsively flinging his shoes overboard in a panic.[45] His lack of traditional manliness is also reflected in his lack of confidence in his language; contrary even to claiming to tell a "plain tale," Marlow often pronounces that his story is impossible to convey – an issue numerous critics have explored. F.R. Leavis famously found the narrative too obscuring, too insistent that the tale was "'inscrutable,' 'inconceivable,' 'unspeakable,'"[46] which had the effect of muting the narrative's meaning. This is a criticism of Conrad, but it pertains to Marlow's narration, which, vague, rambling, non-linear, and constantly interrupted so that he can posit philosophical questions, does not adhere to the linguistic requirements of manliness that Andrew Dowling has identified.[47] Further, these narrative qualities also suggest that his very interpretive faculties are dubious, as Benita Parry shows: "His confusion about the substance of his narration, his misrecognitions, the discrepancies between what he shows and what he sees, his positing of certainties which prove to be dubious, these are the fiction's means of exhibiting that his endeavour to devise an ethical basis for imperialism is destined to fail."[48] There are also times at which Marlow does not even claim to be honest. So the problem of epistemological uncertainty features prominently, albeit somewhat differently, in *Heart of Darkness* and in the archive of fin-de-siècle Sierra Leone. When the indigenous violence of Human Leopardism and Tongo Play evaded British surveillance and control, colonial agents, faced with the limits of their prowess and capacities for regulation – and desperate to reassert both – became complicit with forms of violence incompatible with British masculine imperial identity. In Conrad, the devastating consequences of this kind of epistemological and then resulting moral failure – and we have seen it in the Anglo-Zulu War, the fall of Khartoum, and in Sierra Leone – for white imperial manhood become explicit: the failure to assert prowess through knowledge and narration is written on weak, empty bodies falling far short of traditional ideals of manliness. Conrad, through representations of male bodies and desires, renders imperial identity morally bereft and ideologically hollow.

If in both the archive of Sierra Leone and *Heart of Darkness*, white men in Africa are consistently unmanly and susceptible to ignoble desires, the British are also, in both cases, vulnerable to the collapse of territorial partitions – and such threats to these barriers are once again figured in fiction, as in the archive, as flowing, consuming, monstrous entities. *Heart of Darkness* refuses to imagine London as quarantined from colonial oppression. The buffering space between the metropole and the sins of empire collapses as the narrator emphasizes the material and figurative connection between London, Brussels, and Congo; though the novella's initial setting is the Thames, the "old river … [led] to the uttermost ends of the earth" – that is, to peripheralized colonial zones – carrying "the germs of empires."[49] But this flow is not unidirectional; white crimes in Africa impact Europe. In the archive of Sierra Leone, this registers as pervasive British compromising of Western logic – assumptions of the guilt of alleged Human Leopards manifested across the board, in governmental administration in the colony and in the Colonial Office in London – in order to justify white complicity in indigenous violence. And of course, such assumptions of guilt were based on subversive indigenous rationale, which had seeped into imperial ideology. In *Heart of Darkness*, Marlow registers the synchronous relationship between empire and colony through an imagined reversal of events as he reflects on abandoned villages in Congo, thinking that if Britain's others, "armed with all kinds of fearful weapons suddenly took to travelling on the road between Deal and Gravesend, catching the yokels right and left to carry heavy loads for them, I fancy every farm and cottage thereabouts would get empty very soon."[50] Here, Conrad not only activates what Stephen Arata argues is a metropolitan fear of reverse colonization (which foregrounds the material and ethical relations between imperial centre and colony),[51] he also invokes the problems of aggression and oppression undergirding the narrative of civilization and development. As in Marsh's fiction and the Sierra Leone administration's confidential history, Britain in *Heart of Darkness* becomes tainted – the threat to metropolitan identity that is projected onto an African other (in Marsh it was the desiring, lusty metropolitan imagination, in the case of Sierra Leone it was the collapse of moral order, and in Conrad it is greedy brutality) is shown to have been always already at home.

If the metaphor of water as passageway illustrates the dangerous collapse of the buffer between island nation and globe, between Europe and Africa, and constitutes a threat to imperial integrity, light figures as the civilizing mission, becoming dangerously seductive to imperial agents, in order emphasize "the noble cause's" speciousness and imperialism's moral instability. As Parry has demonstrated, "white and light … come to signify evil, confusion, and lies" in *Heart of Darkness*.[52] Marlow describes civilization as "light … like a running blaze on a plain, like a flash of lightening in the clouds,"[53] but light here is not wholesome. That the darkness-penetrating Romans "were no colonists," only *seems* to imply a differentiation between the ancient invading civilization and modern Britons:

> They were conquerors, and for that you want only brute force – nothing to boast of, when you have it, since your strength is just an accident arising from the weakness of others. They grabbed what they could get for the sake of what was to be got. It was just robbery with violence, aggravated murder on a great scale, and men going at it blind – as is very proper for those who tackle a darkness.[54]

This depiction of conquest strongly resembles Marlow's condemning description of Belgian exploitation in Congo, though I am also making the case that the text recognizes Britain's direct implication in Belgian brutality. Marlow's claim, though, that what he's talking about here *isn't* colonialism is important: the text sets up a false differentiation as Marlow posits that "what redeems [the conquest of the earth] is the idea only … an unselfish belief in the idea – something you can set up, and bow down before, and offer a sacrifice to."[55] Because this "idea" is "something you can set up" – that is, contrived – the "unselfish belief" becomes an uncritical devotion, a seductive notion that the old "noble cause, you know," can obfuscate base desire. Marlow recognizes, in other words, that "the idea" is a legitimating function of colonialism. Furthermore, and contrary to Joanna Smith,[56] I suggest that *Heart of Darkness* ultimately rejects the premise that "the idea" is redemptive. As Holstun wryly puts it, "When Kurtz sacrificed his victims and mounted their decorative heads at his compound, was he being aggravated and selfish or idealistic and selfless?"[57] The narrative critiques such devotion to an idea, Brantlinger demonstrates, on many levels: "If the 'natives' in their darkness set up Kurtz as an idol, the Europeans worship ivory, money, power, reputation. Kurtz joins the 'natives' in their 'unspeakable rites,' worshipping his own unrestrained power and lust. Marlow himself assumes the pose of an idol."[58] In this context, Marlow's participation in this dynamic highlights his own capitulation to this imperial imperative.[59] Thus the current of light associated with civilization and Kurtz is seductive but hypocritical, flashy but lacking moral basis. At the same time, darkness, which is so predominantly associated with Africa both in the novella and in British culture more broadly at this time,[60] also presides over the imperial centre as the "brooding gloom" hovers over London.[61] If London is "the monstrous town," Brussels is "the sepulchral city," and connotes death – and hollowness – even in its whiteness.[62] Currents of water and light, then, as they are deployed in this text, collapse boundaries between spaces as tangled imperial sins come home to destabilize metropolitan identity.

If the text renders imperial identity vulnerable via its figuration of the encroaching repercussions of imperial sin, it further renders masculine bodies deficient via their permeability in the contact zone. Picking up on the same problems of the unruly, obscuring wilderness and mysterious, encroaching bush that deeply perturbed colonial agents in Sierra Leone, Conrad figures Africa – Britain's other and thus reflection – as a baffling enormity threatening to engulf white men and lay bare their powerlessness. In other words, both the archive and Conrad use the same mode to articulate white vulnerability. On the one hand, Rawa is certainly right in suggesting that *Heart of Darkness* "depicts … [the West's] penetration" of Congo,[63] but, on the other, it is equally true that the narrative presents European prowess as subdued by Congo's monstrous environment. From the moment Marlow arrives on the coast and moves up "the mouth of the big river,"[64] the landscape is figured as a yonic force that consumes the more vulnerable human bodies. At the central station, the Eldorado Expedition "went into a patient wilderness, that closed upon it as the sea closes over a diver."[65] This allusion to fluidity picks up on imperialist narrative's figuration of threat as flowing force. As Marlow's crew moves along the river's fluid body further into Congo, the forest threatens to engulf them as well: "To the left of us there was the long uninterrupted shoal, and to the right a high steep bank heavily overgrown with bushes. Above the bush the trees stood in serried ranks" – as though the forest expressed its own version of martial prowess – "the twigs overhung the current thickly, and from distance to distance a large limb of some tree projected rigidly over the stream."[66] The environment not only densely encloses the steamer, but it also seems to warn of a resistant force only just kept at bay.[67] That the engulfing landscape is personified encodes the struggle for power in a sexual dynamic of invasion: "the mist itself … scream[s],"[68] the wilderness has a "face,"[69] and as the ship approaches Kurtz, Marlow notices that shallow patches of grasses could be "seen just under the water, exactly as a man's backbone is seen running down the middle of his back under the skin."[70] Smith also notes a sexual dynamic, pointing out that Marlow describes "the jungle's absorption of Kurtz as sexual cannibalism: 'it had taken him, loved him, embraced him, got into his veins, consumed his flesh.'"[71] This power struggle is registered in terms of bodily integrity. Similarly, this unruly wilderness's grotesque body – fluid, borderless, threatening – relentlessly defies Marlow's desire to map it, to know it: "We called … all along the formless coast bordered by dangerous surf, as if Nature herself had tried to ward off intruders; in and out of rivers, streams of death in life, whose banks were rotting into mud, whose waters, thickened into slime, invaded the contorted mangroves that seemed to writhe at us in the extremity of an impotent despair."[72] The landscape's perimeter is undefinable: the "formless coast" blends with rivers whose menacing currents Marlow calls "streams of death in life." Their muddy banks are liminal zones, neither water nor soil, on which the "contorted mangroves" establish themselves, and which, as we saw in the archive of colonial Sierra Leone, "with their dark, noisome, and intricate passages,"[73] further obfuscate the boundary between solid land and flowing water to resist mapping. In *Heart of Darkness*, the forest's grotesqueness is augmented through the particular libidinal codes that are used to render it: Marlow observes from the steamer "deep in the tangled gloom, naked breasts, arms, legs, glaring eyes – the bush was swarming with human limbs in movement, glistening, of bronze colour."[74] These body parts never constitute a whole human; the humanity within the forest is reduced to constituent bodily components. Thus the "naked breasts" and "glistening" limbs are depersonalized, sexualized objects, while the heavily loaded term "swarming" resonates with the descriptions of envelopment explored in representations of Zululand and Khartoum, suggesting sexual engulfment by a not-quite-human force. The notion of a consuming, cannibalistic wilderness, though, resonates most strongly with fin-de-siècle understandings of the landscape that hosted the Human Leopards and served as a "rapid means of dispersal [of flesh] to the members … after the terrible and mysterious rites have been performed."[75] As we saw in chapter 5, the grotesqueness of the wilderness was figured as both physical and psychic: as one colonial agent put it, "the Sierra Leone bush … makes one's flesh creep."[76] *Heart of Darkness* figures the wilderness as similarly grotesque, but with greater intensity and threat to white bodies: "The reaches opened before us and closed behind, as if the forest had stepped leisurely across the water to bar the way for our return. We penetrated deeper and deeper into the heart of darkness."[77] Thus in Conrad, we see a subtly increasing lack of imperial control: although the white men seem to have all the agency, their penetration is registered as a potentially one-way trip as the forest "bar[s] the way" back; they are now in the hands of the wilderness, and their engulfment intimates the inability of invaders to exert control over the territory. Thus the "little" white man is rendered insignificant by the wilderness, whose grotesqueness is again confirmed by its figuration as a vast current:

> We stopped, and the silence driven away by the stamping of our feet flowed back again from the recesses of the land. The great wall of vegetation, an exuberant and entangled mass of trunks, branches, leaves, boughs, festoons, motionless in the moonlight, was like a rioting invasion of soundless life, a rolling wave of plants, piled up, crested, ready to topple

over the creek, to sweep every little man of us out of his little existence. And it moved not.[78]

Both the forest itself and its silence are figured as a great wave. That the tension between motion and stillness articulates the anticipation of "invasion" rather than its climax suggests that the uneasiness to which Marlow gestures pertains not just to physical but also to psychological reverberations of confronting the site of imperial invasion. This confrontation also includes African people, who, for Marlow, are one other element of the wilderness. As the expedition reaches Kurtz and attempts to return him to the steamer, people emerge from the bush: "as if by enchantment, streams of human beings – of naked human beings – with spears in their hands, with bows, with shields, with wild glances and savage movements, were poured into the clearing by the dark-faced and pensive forest."[79] These partially visible people thickly encircle the party. And, later, when the steamer tries to leave, "the crowd … flowed out of the woods again, filled the clearing, covered the slope with a mass of naked, breathing, quivering, bronze bodies."[80] For the imperial male body, flow is both dangerous and, as Conrad reiterates here, libidinal; segmented and sexualized indigenous people are folded into the larger object of imperial desire that threatens to consume its own zealots. Thus, the prospect of the white male body's consumption in *Heart of Darkness*, whether by the wilderness itself or the human threat within it – not to mention the hungry cannibals in the company's employ – is salient, recurrent, and situated within the broader context of imperial crisis. Recognizing that British metropolitan discourse about African cannibalism was active enough in the 1890s, we can, in consideration of the increasing destabilizations of martial manhood and imperial narrative at the fin de siècle that this study has explored, identify at this historical moment a notable cultural anxiety about both physical and psychic transgression of British boundaries and standards in colonial spaces. What this points to, I argue, is a pervasive concern about imperial integrity and its limitations.

"Hollow at the Core": Engulfment and Complicity

Late-Victorian culture certainly had reason to doubt imperial integrity. As we saw in the archive of turn-of-the-century Sierra Leone, the colonial administration was profoundly inefficacious in curbing Human Leopard and Tongo violence and its own participation in this indigenous violence. Moreover, legal and ethical ideals blatantly disintegrated in colonial practice as the administration contravened the same "civilizing" law used to legitimate its colonization of Sierra Leone and other regions. Finally, the ideal of Western rationalism was compromised as colonial discourse about indigenous superstitions was imbricated by reliance on Tongo judgment and the general presumption of guilt of alleged Human Leopards. Masculine authority, then, was morally vacuous, imperial narrative was dissolving on a range of fronts, and the imperial project and its promises were being recognized as profoundly hollow. Conrad's fiction, recognizing the relationship between limitations to white masculine prowess and imperial greed, expresses metropolitan anxiety about this ideological emptiness through pervasive suggestions of hollowness throughout the novella, particularly manifested in bodies, spaces, and narrative. As aspects of the contact zone transgress the (rather unsound) boundaries of white bodies and territories, the emptiness inside them is underscored. Circling back to Marlow's depiction of flawed imperial masculinity, we see that hollowness abounds. Fresleven, his boundaries mostly hypothetical, dies easily: the "tentative jab with a spear … went quite easy between the shoulder blades."[81] His skeletal remains then embody the void of the imperial project of which he had been a part: "the grass growing through his ribs was tall enough to hide his bones."[82] The wilderness literally penetrates the European; white masculinity is unable to resist the envelopment of the contact zone such that the currents of the threatening force permeate, disable, and ultimately dissolve the invading body. We saw how in *Heart of Darkness* this threat is figured as external through the tropes of water, light, and wilderness. But imperial desire perpetrates its own excavation of the white body: as the station manager puts it, "Men who come out here should have no entrails,"[83] alluding not only to his own emptiness, but also to the imperial imperative of vacuous existence. The brick-maker at the central station exudes a similar emptiness. Of "this papier-mâché Mephistopheles," Marlow imagines "that if I tried I could poke my forefinger through him, and would find nothing inside but a little loose dirt, maybe."[84] Just as for the station manager, the brick-maker's imperial ambitions, which utterly rule his conduct, underpin the hollowness that Marlow identifies.

Signs such as these mark the dissolution of imperial masculine identity and imperial legitimacy. The imagery of hollowness is not limited to human bodies, and imperial enterprise once again underpins such markers of desolation. From Marlow's encounter of "a waste of excavations" at the company's station to the "vast artificial hole somebody had been digging … the purpose of which [Marlow] found it impossible to divine," to the "very narrow ravine, almost no more than a scar on the hillside," into which he nearly falls, to the steamer with its bottom torn out by river rock, the physical world that Marlow inhabits is riddled with voids.[85] Marlow then fixates on stitching up the tears in his "command" – literally his ship, figuratively his project: "What I really wanted was rivets, by Heaven! Rivets. To get on with the work – to stop the hole. Rivets I wanted."[86] The rivets prove to be enough to patch up the steamer, but are insufficient for the recuperation of the problematic figure of Kurtz, who is marked by emptiness: "rivets were what really Mr. Kurtz wanted, if he had only known it" – not simply for his retrieval but because he, too, is full of holes. Marlow's offhanded remark thus casts doubt on Kurtz's solidity before Marlow even sets out on the river toward him. But Kurtz's lack of substance also signifies the emptiness of his precious, supposedly philanthropic "ideas."[87] Marlow notes that "the man presented himself as a voice" rather than as a solid form: "Oh yes ... He was very little more than a voice."[88] In fact, Marlow depicts him as a "phantom," a "shadow," a "shade."[89] Kurtz, along with the ideas he stands for, thus signifies as profoundly hollow. One could further argue that the dissolution of the ideal of "the noble cause" is made manifest mid-quest: "what we could see was just the steamer we were on, her outlines blurred as though she had been on the point of dissolving ... The rest of the world was nowhere, as far as our eyes and ears were concerned. Just nowhere. Gone, disappeared; swept off without leaving a whisper or a shadow behind."[90] The African unknown, as figure for imperial monstrosity, threatens to swallow up the project whose value many Europeans used to legitimize their exploits. In a sense, this example instantiates the ideal of the European quest dissolving in the face of its own baselessness.

While *Heart of Darkness* presents these visible signs of the dissolution of and threats to masculine imperial identity, it also articulates the immaterial threat – also figured as a kind of dangerous flow – of imperial desire. It emerges most potently from within the seductive figure of Kurtz, that supposed "emissary of pity, and science, and progress" who is actually a figure of violent acquisition – "he had collected, bartered, swindled, or stolen more ivory than all the other agents together" – and "monstrous passions."[91] Kurtz is distinguished by his ability to orate: "Of all of his gifts the one that stood out pre-eminently, that carried with it a sense of real presence, was his ability to talk, his words – the gift of expression, the bewildering, the illuminating, the most exalted and the most contemptible, the pulsating stream of light, or the deceitful flow from the heart of an impenetrable darkness."[92] Like Haggard's Ayesha, that other inexplicably persuasive being, Kurtz functions as the logical extension of unchecked imperial aggression and despotic power. He takes without consideration, he "lack[s] restraint in the gratification of his various lusts ... and there is something wanting in him – some small matter which, when the pressing need arose, could not be found under his magnificent eloquence."[93] As Dowling has shown, such a description identifies Kurtz as unmanly in late-Victorian logic, for he utterly lacks self-control.[94] And he remains an incredibly magnetic figure, his "gift" of "the pulsating stream of light" is simultaneously "the deceitful flow from the heart of an impenetrable darkness." Thus, from Kurtz, an "emissary" of empire, flows an engulfing narrative of imperialism:

> He began with the argument that we whites, from the point of development we had arrived at, "must necessarily appear" to them [Africans] in the nature of supernatural beings – we approach them with the might as of a deity, and so on, and so on. "By the simple exercise of our will we can exert a power for good practically unbounded," etc. etc. From that point he soared and took me with him. The peroration was magnificent.[95]

In my reading, Kurtz may have found a literary ancestor in Marsh's Paul Lessingham, that orating empty signifier. Marlow at once manages to be drawn in by "the magical current of phrases" and to distance his audience from Kurtz's seductiveness; he conveys his belief in Kurtz's "magnificen[ce]" but simultaneously undercuts Kurtz's "peroration" by summing up his oration with dismissive fillers such as "and so on, and so on" and "etc. etc."[96] In this way, Conrad brings the seductive narrative of imperialism under critique,[97] using the trope of flow to point at once to its potential power to engulf, and to its utter emptiness. Thus, Marlow's statement, "we penetrated deeper and deeper into the heart of darkness," is actually signalling his approach to Kurtz's darkness: "For me [the steamer] crawled towards Kurtz – exclusively."[98] If Kurtz is the destination, the dark knowledge toward which Marlow's narrative crawls, then the imagery of gloominess and water linking colonial and metropolitan space also constitutes Conrad's irredeemably Eurocentric strategy of using imperial thinking about Africa as a way to confront imperialism itself – and we saw this device in Haggard and Marsh. Whereas the texts previously explored in this study tend to associate flow with a threatening other (such as Zulus, "hordes" of Mahdists, murderous secret societies, and narrative instability), *Heart of Darkness*, through its treatment of Kurtz, articulates more forcefully and undeniably that the most dangerous current threatening to swallow up imperial identity is from the mouth of imperialism itself.

This imperial desire that Kurtz embodies is rooted largely in capital, which threatens in *Heart of Darkness* to wash away the legitimacy of "the idea" and the national identity with which it is associated. The drive for capital also, of course, undergirds the basis of Marlow's journey and narrative. Though muted in comparison to Marlow's focus on the wilderness and the seductive persuasions of Kurtz, the problematic stream of material capital nevertheless underlies the entire narrative. Manifestations of the capital imperative are disordered, which is perhaps Marlow's primary objection: "Everything else in the station was in a muddle, – heads, things, buildings. Strings of dusty niggers with splay feet arrived and departed; a stream of manufactured goods, rubbishy cottons, beads, and brass-wire set into the depths of darkness, and in return came a precious trickle of ivory."[99] The contempt underpinning the racism in this passage intensifies Marlow's scorn for what he understands as chaotic. Here again, the disordered flow is, in a sense, internal – instigated by Western powers, capital underpins every European action in the contact zone. Capital also situates Marlow's fascination with Kurtz; his imagination of the "emissary" as foundational to his "belief" and integral to his "destiny" underscores that Kurtz's narrative is profoundly convenient for grasping Europeans.[100] Kurtz's Intended reiterates the function of Kurtz's narrative of progress, applauding "his example ... Men looked up to him – his goodness shone in every act."[101] The "idea" of philanthropy and "progress," the notion of moral action, serves of course to obfuscate the capitalist desire fundamentally underlying the project.[102] Marlow's problem with Kurtz, however, is that he lacked restraint, which Rawa identifies as a problem of "individual and collective psychosis."[103] Kurtz is an individual representing a collective insanity: after all, "all Europe contributed to the making of Kurtz."[104] The problem of "no restraint" – vicious exploitation, violence, and slave labour – was, even from a fin-de-siècle perspective, notoriously rampant in Leopold's Congo. And in Kurtz, this utter yielding to desire is unchecked. According to the Russian devotee, "He declared he would shoot me unless I gave him the ivory and then cleared out of the country, because he could do so, and had a fancy for it, and there was nothing on earth to prevent him killing whom he jolly well pleased."[105] Noting Kurtz's further resonance with Ayesha in terms of doing what he has a "fancy for," we register his similar dissociation from moral concerns, as Marlow acknowledges: "I had to deal with a being to whom I could not appeal in the name of anything high or low ... He had kicked himself loose of the earth."[106] The object of imperial desire, while it continues to threaten to consume Marlow with its silent currents, has fully overtaken Kurtz: "The wilderness had found him out early, and had taken on him a terrible vengeance for the fantastic invasion. I think it had whispered to him things about himself which he did not know, things of which he had no conception till he took counsel with this great solitude – and the whisper had proved irresistibly fascinating. It echoed loudly within him because he was hollow at the core."[107] As desire for the "immensity" that promises territorial, capital, and libidinal fulfillment is projected onto the foreign othered object itself, the fear of being consumed, of moral grounding being lost, and of male authority dissolving as a result is figured as a "wilderness" that itself extracts "a terrible vengeance" on violently rapacious imperial practice. Marlow's recognition of Kurtz's failings, of his hollowness, is crucial: since Kurtz's narrative, his stream, is morally empty, his authority dissolves.

This relationship between desire and the stability of imperial narrative brings us to the question of the efficacy of *Heart of Darkness* itself. On the one hand, as numerous critics have already noted, Marlow seems to have a sense of his own narrative limitations: "Do you see the story? … It seems to me I am trying to tell you a dream – making a vain attempt, because no relation of a dream can convey the dream sensation … No, it is impossible … to convey the life-sensation of any given epoch of one's existence – that which makes its truth, its meaning – its subtle and penetrating essence. It is impossible."[108] But then, on the other hand, *Heart of Darkness*, as it follows Marlow's narrative, itself attempts to reach Kurtz and his narrative of imperial desire, to "[penetrate] deeper and deeper into the heart of darkness," to work toward illuminating the obfuscated realities of the apparatus of the imperial narrative.

As *Heart of Darkness* highlights the workings of the ideology of imperial desire through Kurtz, it also enacts the expansion of the enfolding darkness he represents, first through Marlow's engulfment in Kurtz's narrative, then through the frame narrator's complicity, and then ultimately through the reader's potential enfoldment into the imperative of imperial complicity as well. Marlow is already fully embedded in empire, even as he is critical of its manifestations in Congo. Rawa has outlined Marlow's material complicity – his employment, his questing – but Marlow himself recognizes this role when confronted by the chain gang: "I also was a part of the great cause of these high and just proceedings."[109] Then when Marlow lets the young brick-maker believe he has powerful friends in the administration, he realizes "I became in an instant as much of a pretence as the rest of the bewitched pilgrims" whose base greed he overtly despises. Crucially, he goes along with this fabrication "simply because I had a notion it would somehow be of help to that Kurtz whom at the time I did not see."[110] Thus, even at this stage, Marlow's susceptibility to Kurtz's seduction is evident. Lawtoo is right in suggesting that Marlow recognizes Kurtz's influence on him, arguing that "non-meditated 'devotion' to a tyrannical leader and to the ideological flame he carries, Marlow now realizes, is 'the most dangerous thing in every way,' as it deprives the subject of ideology of a rational ground to operate basic ethical and political choices."[111] But Marlow submits to Kurtz's narrative anyway, even as he is aware of his own complicity. Importantly, he submits not because he agrees with Kurtz, but because he admires Kurtz's "conviction." For Marlow, it does not matter exactly what "the horror!" was; what matters is that "this was the expression of some sort of belief; it had candour." Marlow is humiliated to realize that, in his own final judgment, "probably I would have nothing to say,"[112] finding himself insignificant for his lack of real conviction. And thus Marlow lays his own critical autonomy aside in favour of Kurtz's passions. This ultimate submission is reiterated in Marlow's lie to the Intended, and he produces the thing he despises with full knowledge of Kurtz's darkness, including the genocidal imperative expressed in his pamphlet: "I had full information about all these things … I was to have the care of his memory. I've done enough for it to give me the indisputable right to lay it, if I choose, for an everlasting rest in the dust-bin of progress… But then, you see, I can't choose."[113] This inability to escape from Kurtz's current necessitates Marlow's stewardship of Kurtz's memory via his narrative. Thus, for Marlow, the greatest terror is perhaps that he chooses to "be loyal to the nightmare," remaining subject to Kurtz and the desires he embodies, with full knowledge of the "taint of death" and "flavour of mortality … like biting into something rotten"[114] suffusing both his own lies and the lies of the "cause."

Marlow is not the sole capitulator to a recognizably problematic narrative; as Baxter has suggested, this submission is echoed in the frame narrator's surrendering to Marlow's language, even though he and the other listeners do not initially give Marlow much credit.[115] Beyond the narrative itself, though, the coterie of listeners is also caught up in the imperial economy and its system of exploitation. This complicity is very simply instantiated when the Accountant casually produces the set of dominoes, made, of course, of ivory. The uneven relationship of power and consumption is laid bare as the frame narrator perceives the Accountant "toying architecturally with the bones":[116] what has been a matter of life and death to Africans and wildlife in the imperial economy becomes for this man an object over which he may idly exercise his authority.

This problem of capitulation to seductive narrative, this loyalty to the nightmare, appears elsewhere in this study: we saw this kind of cover-up of white "regression" in Sierra Leone – lies, violence, and complicity were discursively contained in the confidential archives of the state – and witnessed a similar form of rottenness. What these archives demonstrate, though, is that the complicity affecting individual colonial agents – Captain Soden and Captain Campbell – migrated to higher levels of authority as their role in indigenous violence was whitewashed, and as colonial officials capitulated to the language of colonization; men of empire with the authority to read the archive's narrative were thus consumed by imperial ideology, and tainted, as Conrad puts it, by the "flavour of mortality."

Conrad puts the problem of monstrous colonial complicity that we find instantiated – just as one example – in the confidential archives of fin-de-siècle Sierra Leone into the popular sphere. In a sense, the novella constitutes a litmus test of the public's critical capacities: enfoldment in imperial economy and ideology transcends the pages of Conrad's text, and not just in terms of the capital exchanged to the returned adventurer for his presentation of Africa. As Susan Navarette has suggested, Marlow's abstractions, impressions, similes, his "clusters of images," and his "adjectival insistence,"[117] produce a kind of chaos that "mounts upon its reader a cerebral assault (of the sort produced by Kurtz's mesmeric eloquence) and demands of that reader a degree of complicity in the completion of the text and in the unveiling of the story."[118] Further, Navarette hits on one of the darkest aspects of Conrad's novella when she points out that, "depending upon omissions and silences and the subtly disturbing cadences of a carefully crafted prose, *Heart of Darkness* draws its reader into a complicity that requires that he complete that obscurely-hinted-at 'other' half of the fatal book in which horrors take shape and dark secrets are revealed."[119] While this argument buttresses what I have been saying about the shortcomings of narrative efficacy, what interests me about readerly collusions in the uncovering of horrors that unfold in *Heart of Darkness* is their implications for imperial identity. As when Marsh's Champnell can only imagine the terrors brought upon "a gently-nurtured girl" trapped in the cab with the Beetle,[120] readers of *Heart of Darkness* must go to their own dark mental recesses, recesses that Victorian culture has ascribed to "the Dark Continent," to explain the unspeakable. But it is not just participation in the set of imaginative horrors that are already circulating in Victorian culture with which this text threatens the reader. By being asked to help construct the text – "Do you see the story?"[121] – the reader is invited to entrench in the ideology of the text through necessary reliance on shared cultural references in order to construct meaning, and, in so doing, to capitulate willingly to the voracious imperial ideology that threatens to cannibalize the national identity that cannot abide it. At the same time, the process of narrative enfoldment and dissolution of integrity by the lies of the idea is laid bare for the reader, and the reader has a critical choice to make.

The writing examined in this study undermines imperial legitimacy, even as it remains irretrievably invested in it. That documents tied to the Anglo-Zulu War, Khartoum, and to the violence surrounding Human Leopard activity register martial masculine impotence, penetration, and dissolution of authority at the same time as they articulate martial barbarity underscores the relation of imperial desperation to torture and brutality. Conrad suggests in *Heart of Darkness*, as do Haggard and Marsh in their works, that the crux of narrative authority comes down to the efficacy of reading practice. The novels of each author have, in a sense, tested their readerships, and the frame narrative enables the first "reader" to be contained and presented by the story itself. While Quatermain works to interpret his encounters in the contact zone, the editor assesses them, and then external readers draw critical conclusions about Quatermain's assertions. While Holly works to understand Ayesha and his desire for her, readers have to attend to the process of his moral failings. While the featureless Paul hypnotizes the public with his words, readers register Sydney and Marjorie getting swept into their current. Or at least, maybe they do. Marlow, recognizing fully that the narrative of philanthropy is at its core a lie, that the decay pervading the "work" at the outer and central stations signals the destabilization of the imperial project, nevertheless capitulates to Kurtz's "magical current of phrases." *Heart of Darkness* thus presents the lingering terror of choosing "the nightmare," for the loss of integrity opens up unspeakable "horror" in which moral boundaries have crumbled, identity dissolves, and autonomy is consumed.

Conclusion

Ideological Crises and New Histories

This study has been concerned with how imperialism in Africa fundamentally altered British conceptions of masculinity in the late nineteenth century. Beyond tracking these shifts, it has demonstrated how gendered and racialized power relations became fractured; explored the centrality of space in the maintenance and/or breakdown of male identities; and encountered the futility of narrative authenticity in the zones of intercultural relations. I have argued that narratives that have seemed to champion a triumphant imperial masculinity were in fact not only deeply riddled with doubts about masculine identity but, in some cases, extremely critical of it. Ultimately, the devastating failures in British martial behaviour that were bound up with colonial aggression registered in various facets of the imperial archive, forcing recognitions of the illegitimacy of the British Empire – rendering it a morally hollow project, and thus dissolving British national identity itself.

Importantly, what I have not argued was that the British military was technologically vulnerable in the colonies. While the powers of physical force were certainly asymmetrical, there was nevertheless a *perceived* sense of exposure – as with the Indian Uprising in 1857, the Morant Bay uprising in 1865, the Fenian uprising, the issues of national trade surrounding the Suez Canal and the Cape route, and, as we have seen, the embarrassing loss at Isandlwana. Understanding this perception of vulnerability is crucial for considering how such anxiety influenced imperial motives, cultural discourses surrounding masculinity and the gendered body, the figuration of spaces, and, finally, the representations of Africans and Africa. The other crucial point with respect to imperial power is that the crisis I have identified in this study – a dissolution of legitimate male authority in the writing of history – is rooted not in an inadequacy of force, but in what is at its core an ethical problem. As the institutional writing and the popular fiction I have explored has shown, the reality of imperial oppression was excruciatingly incompatible with the traditional masculine ideal, and, furthermore, fin-de-siècle imperial society recognized this truth and was haunted by it. Correspondence from Zululand was troubled by this failure, Haggard parodied it, Gordon and the newspapers imagined its consequences, Marsh articulated its devastating pervasiveness, the administration in Sierra Leone ultimately became complicit with it, and Conrad despised it. Since male "virtues" were leaky, the body itself grotesque, and narrative authority in turn entirely contrived, those who were invested in the fiction would ultimately be faced with the choice of vehemently countering this truth or finding alternate modes of justifying imperial force. Thus, much more complex, fraught, and critical approaches to imperialism and masculinity were circulating throughout Victorian culture than has heretofore been adequately recognized.

These findings have a number of implications. Reading popular literature more closely and with formal rigour entails a reconsideration of what have thus far been prominent assumptions about authors such as Haggard and Marsh and the political investments of their works. In attending to the contradictory, layered, and complex aspects of male writing, this study points out that, in some cases, quite penetrating critiques came from within the sphere of dominant masculinity itself. If we allow for distinctiveness, attention to contradiction, and precision in our considerations of popular works, then we find that the workings of and reactions to imperialism at the fin de siècle were extremely subtle. Much of the complex critique of imperial power emerges from a careful analysis of gender in this archive. This book has also attempted to address how cultural concerns inhere across genres. Investigating ongoing dialogues between colonial dispatches, wartime reports, private letters, travel writing, newspapers, and fiction establishes the existence of the widely circulating preoccupation with the authority conferred on the bounded male body and its attendant narratives as well as the cultural anxieties and material underpinnings of fin-de-siècle imaginations of Africa. It also foregrounds the relationship between different expressions of print culture. We find in the confidential archives of colonial administration in Sierra Leone the same fear of flow that gets expressed in the private letters (eventually published in newsprint) of British soldiers in Zululand, in Gordon's journals, and in the newspapers reporting on his absence. Haggard's immensely popular texts employed the problematic of narrative flow to parody masculinity; Marsh's Gothic novel used it to evoke fearsome threats of dissolved male bodies, gender stability, and history; and Conrad's novella deployed it to figure devastating but seductive imperial imperatives. Thus, this particular anxiety about a dangerous, enveloping, and consuming force that dissolves bodily integrity and critical autonomy pervaded fin-de-siècle imperial thought.

This study has maintained that imperial masculinity needs to be denaturalized, historicized, and contextualized against a larger web of social, political, and economic relations. In considering late nineteenth-century British narratives about martial masculinity, I have tried to use the fissures highlighted in this book to find ways to access new histories, and to think about how anxieties about vulnerability may have impacted colonial behaviour, violence, and desire. Understanding more precisely how imperialism operated enables more rigorous study into the histories of colonial violence and the underpinnings of representation of Africans – especially African men. The stereotypes about violence in Africa that have persisted from pre-colonial times through to the present day are imbricated with the constitution of the narrators' national identities, at the centre of which I place the question of gender. Knowing more about how colonial confrontations in Africa impinged upon imperial masculinity – its fears, strategies for constitution, and critiques – is crucial in redressing both the construction of these representations and the fantasy of Africa as a testing ground for white masculinity.

I have treated imperial masculinity as a broad concept. Without a doubt, a more nuanced understanding of its varied inflections is imperative, and there are a number of lenses that could inform further investigations about the constitution of imperial masculinity and its vulnerabilities. One such focus is how relationships between men and women influenced the notion of imperial penetrability in the colonies. Women's role in the construction of masculinity was absolutely part of the cultural fabric, and it would be useful to trace alongside the tropes of penetration and dissolution illuminated here how the authority of male writers – metropolitan and colonial – was threatened by the presence of powerful female authors, such as those of the morally weighty triple-decker novel.[1] Equally important is the consideration of women's political groups agitating for rights and social change and their effects on male narratives of impenetrability. Scholarship on women's impact on fin-de-siècle crises in masculinity is strong,[2] but a consideration of the ways in which these dialogues intersect with the pervasive fear of grotesqueness confronted by the British imperial project in Africa would yield new insights into the terms of gender identity. Another imperative question is the impact of class on critiques of martial masculinity and narrative authority. Though class absolutely informs both my focus (for example, the economic conditions of imperial soldiers are foundational, as are the determining factors for which men become colonial figures and need to seek a living abroad; the rise of the New Woman was seen as a threat to men's jobs and masculinities, especially of clerical workers; social status impacts which men are most able to speak and write with authority) and my conclusions, it is not the principal theme of this book. Such a focus, however, would benefit from a nuanced historical tracing of metropolitan and imperial economics, gender dynamics, and metropolitan racial relations, and could yield valuable insights. Critical analysis through the prism of British ethnicity would also tell us something about the formulation of imperial critique. Men of both pen and sword who were involved in African colonial projects came from England, Scotland, Ireland, and Wales. This book subsumes their narratives under the category of Britishness, although my sense is that a nuanced reading of how the spatial divisions between factions within Great Britain and the histories of white ethnicities would deeply inflect the recognition of male vulnerabilities.[3] In my view, however, the most significant gap in this study is an account of African constructions of white and black masculinities in the contexts explored here. Almost certainly such representations informed British understandings of identity and authority in profound ways; this conversation would need to be traced through a range of archives. I believe studies in this area would shed crucial light on the contexts, activities, and aspects of colonial anxiety.

Nevertheless, my hope is that my findings here mark out fresh directions for literary scholarship concerned with how gendered national identity mutated and how empire was critiqued. The concerns this book has explored impact how we might think about other texts in the genres considered here, especially as the First World War approached, and, with it, the beginning of massive and irreversible change for the British Empire.

Ideological Crises and Old Futures

This state of imperial identity on the cusp of modernism bears striking similarities to regulatory fantasies in our own historical period. Our age's imperial giant, the United States, much like imperial Britain, is, for one thing, a nation obsessed with policing its boundaries, both in terms of the fortification of its domestic borders (Trump's proposed border wall is a glaring example) and the regulation of its imperial investments – especially in the Middle East. A second obvious likeness is the use of moral rhetoric – the selling of the crusade against the "Axis of Evil," and that "long-held US claim of moral and cultural exceptionalism, the traditional self-identity ... as the uniquely superior, universal standard-bearer of moral authority," adhering to "a tenacious, national mythology of originary innocence," which is "now in tatters"[4] – and the careful regulation of the circulation and containment of information in order to legitimize war and its corollaries. And third, as I will suggest here, the American military has in some cases come to replicate, as did the British in the Anglo-Zulu War and in the suppression of the Human Leopard Society in Sierra Leone, the same signs of barbarity that it professedly set out to eradicate.[5]

If we understand the proliferation of the US occupation of Afghanistan and Iraq as harnessing the impetus of the 9/11 attacks,[6] then we can discern a pattern among these historical events in the relationship between penetration and brutality. The infiltration of US security and the demonstration of the nation's vulnerability crucially characterized that moment of terror; the perforation of national boundary lines threatened the dissolution of American martial identity. In response, George W. Bush famously reduced the threat from the East to an abstraction, an idea, a radical other, an "evil" – much in the same way the metropolitan press characterized the Mahdist forces after the fall of Khartoum. But, again like Britain after the loss of Gordon, the United States also suffered exposure in the sense that it became the object of international gaze. As Anne McClintock aptly puts it, "it was as if the globe had swung on its axis and the ex-colonized world was now gazing at the West with technologies of vision believed for centuries – by the West – to be under the West's control ... A wounded United States was looked at, watched, and surveyed during a moment of great exposure, devastation, and loss."[7] Quite arguably, the order professedly characterizing the imperial nation's military was once again faced with recuperating masculine prowess. After the American government determined that alQaeda could not have orchestrated the sophisticated attacks without the sponsorship of a state hostile to America, the Bush administration targeted Iraq as the ostensible terrorist backer; the menace had to be found and punished.[8] McClintock argues in "Paranoid Empire" that the need to identify and embody previously unseen enemies has entailed the incarceration of innocent people at military prisons such as Abu Ghraib, Iraq, and Guantanamo Bay, Cuba. Casting back to the vengeful brutality explored in chapter 1, I suggest here that the dehumanizing acts of torture at Abu Ghraib (2003–4) that were photographed and disseminated, and at Guantanamo that have continued to be sanctioned (since 2002), indeed betray a need to reassert a position of dominance that was destabilized. Trump's order to keep Guantanamo open indefinitely reiterates this perception of vulnerability. And yet, although these human rights violations have been laid bare and condemned internationally, they have remained largely unaddressed. As Stephen Eisenman notes, after the physical cruelties, humiliations, and sexual torments of Muslim prisoners at Abu Ghraib came into the public eye,

> The US Congress in 2004 received just twelve hours of sworn testimony … and issued no final reports. Four additional investigations … yielded 150 allegations of torture (euphemistically labelled "abuse"), but only a handful of prosecutions and convictions. The US Army confirmed that at least 27 prisoner deaths at Abu Ghraib were homicides, but the longest sentence received by a soldier convicted of murder was three years. Though journalists, lawyers, and human rights advocates have unambiguously exposed the responsibility of senior military and civilian authorities for policies that condone or legitimize torture, none have been charged with crimes, none have been dismissed, and none demoted or censured.[9]

These acts, while on one level condemned by the upper administration of the invading forces, were in large part sidelined and, just as in Sierra Leone, official complicity in homicides was more or less tolerated. This toleration pervades the pattern of martial masculinity's reliance on brutality to which I keep returning, but the perception of engulfment remains a pivotal feature. McClintock explains that, at ground level in Abu Ghraib, the American military police were considerably outnumbered by Iraqis. While the standard "prisoner-to-guard ratio in the United States is 4:1; at Guantánamo it is 1:1; at Abu Ghraib it was 75:1. Most of the MPs [military police officers] lived in filthy, squalid conditions, many of them sleeping in jail cells themselves. They were exhausted, frightened, undersupervised, and in some cases very depressed and traumatized."[10] This imperial construction of swarming or engulfment has historical precedent: by now, we recognize this pattern of imperial perceptions of both people and landscape from Zululand, Khartoum, and Sierra Leone as encroaching from all sides. As for Guantanamo, like the colonial space in Sierra Leone that the administration so clearly understood as a location where laws and rights could be suspended, the military base remains a space of geopolitical uncertainty, a "non-place," a "legal black hole."[11] If Guantanamo Bay is configured, as Simon Reid-Harvey has suggested, as a quasi-imaginary space, as a place that is not quite real, then, like Africa, it has been appropriated into an imperialist configuration of a "peripheral" geography so as to render it of another world, not subject to the same regulations as the metropole, and its inhabitants/"prisoners" as other, as barbarian. Of course, that Guantanamo is beyond the reach of US law ultimately undermines American leadership in liberatory discourses.

These representations of people and space as non-people, non-spaces, are fundamental in the prevention of cumulative public action, the lack of which is sustained by the ideologies that cultivate a moral ignorance in the case of Abu Ghraib that enables the public, as well as the military police at the prison, as Eisenman puts it, "to ignore, or even to justify, however partially, or provisionally, the facts of degradation and brutality manifest in the pictures" – a complicity often concealed by the rhetoric of imperial narratives that frequently refuse to name it.[12] By "complicity" I mean here a range of relationships that agents may bear to an event or set of events, including the non-discourse-specific notion of criminal involvement in an injustice as well as Jennifer Henderson's understanding of complicity as "implication," being "the effect of discursive entanglements, figurative entailments, and presuppositional thicknesses" of enfolding discourses.[13] Using this spectrum to conceptualize complicity enables us to consider an important relationship between its poles that is characterized by narratives of provisional permission.

Acts of complicity bear a complex and layered relationship to the conditions of torture at Abu Ghraib and Guantanamo Bay. On one level, complicity is manifest in the engagement of military police in acts that were either illegal or would be illegal in the nation state. On another, as we know, the structure of the imperial force remained complicit in the violence – as in Sierra Leone, there followed after the inquiry no serious reprimand of agents on the ground, their supervisors, or the upper administration. Third, the lack of sustained, efficacious critique on the home fronts suggests a disturbing level of complicity. Of course, there are a number of ways that the control of the circulation of information and media managed this. In Sierra Leone, the spectacle of violence was displaced from the Tongo burnings and the government's responsibility in them onto the phantasmagoric elements of Human Leopard cannibalism. In the case of Abu Ghraib, outrage at the brutality in the prison was displaced onto what McClintock identifies as the spectacle of pornography and the shift in focus to "the 'culture wars' within the United States, averting the public gaze away from the calamitous scenes of *imperial misrule* unfolding in Iraq, which fell once more under the administration of forgetting, and pointing the media spotlight instead at the familiar cultural bogeymen of *gender misrule* inside the United States."[14]

Thus, complicity, far from being a static state, is mutable and fluid. Henderson's notion of complicity as a kind of enfoldment – indeed, the Latin *complicare* means "fold together" – thus does not need to exclude legal definitions of implication, since more directly involved agents are also enfolded into larger discourses of assimilation – or, if I may put it another way, are engulfed by surrounding currents and structures of thought.

Thinking about complicity as encompassment helps to situate Eisenman's assessment of metropolitan responses to the Abu Ghraib atrocities. He argues that this brutality and the lack of sustained prosecution resulted from a re-emergence of a behaviour rooted in the Hellenic veneration of victorious conquest. Such martial achievements of course entailed the subjugation of war's victims.[15] Hellenistic artwork depicting capture, torture, and sacrifice celebrated this, and was designed to evoke not pity for the defeated but admiration for the victors. Such a strategy employed the "pathos formula" – that is, the depiction of "passionate suffering" that suggested that those who were subjugated yielded to or even welcomed their fate (hence, some of the photographs from Abu Ghraib featured evidently coerced men posed as if engaged in homo- or auto-sexual activity), ultimately rationalizing basanic practice.[16] Eisenman traces the "*mnemosyne* – the collective memory of images" and the utilization of the pathos formula to rationalize "the subordination of self to authority, hierarchy and doctrine" through to the seventeenth century, illustrating its role in the maintenance of church and state power.[17] However, in the eighteenth century, with the Enlightenment and the questioning of such authority, came a rejection of the subordination that had theretofore been valorized. By the mid-nineteenth century, the physical reality of suffering was being foregrounded in artistic images.[18] But Eisenman also points out that, around the beginning of the twentieth century, global imperialism, the rise of authoritarian regimes, and the extension of clashing capitalist claims began once again to "[fan] new flames from [the] dying embers" of Hellenistic artistic strategy,[19] as empire continued to employ cultural practice in its project of legitimation.

In light of this resurgence, I want to consider the possibility that it is the enfoldment – or the engulfment – in the ideology that posits the necessity of brutality for the maintenance of imperial order that has become, recognized or not, a trans-centurial threat to modern identity and ideas of morality;[20] surely, we do not want to believe that this is who we are. As Colonel Ellis remarked of the colonial agents' implication in the mass burnings in Sierra Leone, the matter was entirely "whitewashed."[21] Eisenman suggests that part of the reason for this same outcome after Abu Ghraib was that the government agents and administration both understood this torture as ultimately crucial to the establishment and maintenance of imperial order – in other words, dominance and imperial power were venerated at the cost of humanity. Thus, the possibility arises that the complicities in Sierra Leone were rudimentary expressions of a shift back toward a widespread acceptance of *basanos* that has again found footing in the twenty-first-century American Empire, and that also, pointing directly to instability, signals imperial decay.

If empire is held together by narratives that permit such violence, then it also requires public complicity in these narratives.[22] If we conceive of complicity as a relation to injustice that is always in flux, always fluid, then, in its integral relationship with narrative, it too becomes a kind of all-encompassing *flow*, an ever-present ideology suffusing modern Western experience. The stories that we are told, and that we tell ourselves, that work to make sense of our local and global positions in relation not only to the kinds of exploitation articulated in the archives explored in this study, but also to those that remain elided, indeed work to obfuscate complicity itself – the acknowledgment of which would threaten conceptions of the self as autonomous, moral, and bounded. In the scenario that the threatening flow of complicity is staved off with powerful illusions of isolation, distance from injustice, and boundaries, the importance of narration – of mediation – becomes crucial to maintaining the moral legitimacy of this position. Crucially, we need to pay attention to narratives that challenge this ideology even as they represent it, that articulate and enact the crumbling of illusions about moral buffering, identity, and authority, because they tell us something about how the dominant order will change.

Notes

Introduction

1 From the full unabridged title of J.W. Buel, *Heroes of the Dark Continent: A Complete History of All the Great Explorations and Discoveries in Africa, from the Earliest Ages to the Present Time* (Freeport, NY: Books for Libraries Press, 1971). James William Buel was a prolific pro-imperialist American author and editor with over fifty titles to his name. He wrote mainly about white conquest and exploration, including multiple publications about the British conquest of Africa.

2 This is the name used by the anonymous author of *The Travels of Sir John Mandeville* for the mythical man with his head in his chest (Buel, *Heroes*, 44). *Travels* emerged in the mid-fourteenth century, claiming to be the travel narrative of a knight from the south of England wandering in the exotic lands of Africa and Asia.

3 Another Mandevillian myth; here, this man reclines in the shade of his single giant foot (ibid.).

4 While the signifiers "penetration" and "engulfment" are not inherently aligned with signs of vulnerability or emasculation, the martial culture in which they are read constructs them as such, and deploys them as sexual encodings of power.

5 Buel, *Heroes*, 20.

6 Ibid.

7 J. Williamson, *The Oak King, the Holly King, and the Unicorn: The Myths and Symbols of the Unicorn Tapestries* (New York: Harper and Row, 1986), 206.

8 See Patrick Brantlinger, *Rule of Darkness: British Literature and Imperialism, 1830–1914* (Ithaca, NY: Cornell University Press, 1988), and Edward Said, *Culture and Imperialism* (New York: Vintage Books, 1993).

9 Klaus Theweleit, *Male Fantasies*, vol. 1 (Minneapolis: University of Minnesota Press, 1987), 24.

10 Jules Law, *The Social Life of Fluids: Blood, Milk, and Water in the Victorian Novel* (Ithaca, NY: Cornell University Press, 2010), 2–3.

11 Mary Douglas, *Purity and Danger: An Analysis of Concepts of Pollution and Taboo* (1966; London: Routledge, 2002), 141.

12 Ibid., 150.

13 Bruce Haley, *The Healthy Body and Victorian Culture* (Cambridge, MA: Harvard University Press, 1978), 4.

14 Gail Bederman, *Manliness and Civilization: A Cultural History of Race and Gender in the United States, 1880–1917* (Chicago: University of Chicago Press, 1995), 7.

15 See also Herbert Sussman, *Victorian Masculinities: Manhood and Masculine Poetics in Early Victorian Literature and Art* (Cambridge: Cambridge University Press, 1995), 8–9; James Eli Adams, *Dandies and Desert Saints: Styles of Victorian Manhood* (Ithaca, NY: Cornell University Press, 1995), 3–6; and Dustin Friedman, "Unsettling the Normative: Articulations of Masculinity in Victorian Literature and Culture," *Literature Compass* 7, no. 12 (2010): 1077–88.

16 For valuable studies on non-normative forms of Victorian masculinity, homoeroticism, and homosexuality, see Eve Kosofsky Sedgwick, *Between Men: English Literature and Male Homosocial Desire* (New York: Columbia University Press, 1992); Christopher Lane, *The Ruling Passion: British Colonial Allegory and the Paradox of Homosexual Desire* (Durham: Duke University Press, 1995); Jonathan Dollimore, *Sexual Dissidence: Augustine to Wilde, Freud to Foucault* (Oxford: Clarendon Press, 1991); and Joseph Bristow, *Effeminate England: Homoerotic Writing after 1885* (New York: Columbia University Press, 1995). Certainly a central premise of this study is Sedgwick's seminal contribution that heterosexuality and homosexuality comprise a range of points on the same spectrum, rather than oppositional orientations (Sedgwick, *Between Men*, 1–2). My discussions of masculinity, which usually employ the qualifications "martial" or "imperial," are generally concerned with the more violent performances of gender identity. While, as ever, multiple forms of contradictory and competing masculinities existed in fin-de-siècle Britain, the brand with which I engage here was constituted through conflict and adventure, the cult of sport, and ideals of chivalry. Central associated concepts such as efficacy, prowess, and power are forged relationally and contextually: because their establishment within the discourse of martial masculinity depends on violence, they are terms inherently bound up with antagonism and dominance.

17 Andrew Dowling, *Manliness and the Male Novelist in Victorian Literature* (Aldershot, UK: Ashgate, 2001), 1; Friedman, "Unsettling the Normative," 1082; J.A. Mangan and James Walvin, eds., *Manliness and Morality: Middle-Class Masculinity in Britain and America, 1800–1940* (Manchester: Manchester University Press, 1987), 1. This last kind of manliness also required what Sussman calls "psychic discipline" (*Victorian Masculinities*, 3).

18 These values were held neither uniformly nor to the same degree, especially across classes. As Mangan and Walvin suggest, ideals of masculinity and femininity "were severely constrained by the overriding effects of social class and economic reality. The ideas of masculinity and femininity were unlikely to prove persuasive, even assuming they reached them, to the untold legions of urban poor who seemed forever beyond the reach (and understanding) of their social superiors ... Nevertheless, determined efforts were made to force those ideals through the barriers of social class. They were set before the proletariat by pedagogues and publishers and pressed on them by charitable organisations and philanthropic activists" (*Manliness and Morality*, 4). Thus, this study uses the notion of hegemonic masculinity in investigating the dynamics of imperialism, while acknowledging that certain class, and ethnic, complexities are not addressed in detail.

19 Joseph Bristow, *Empire Boys: Adventures in a Man's World* (London: Harper Collins Academic, 1991), 58.

20 John Tosh, *A Man's Place: Masculinity and the Middle-Class Home in Victorian England* (New Haven, CT: Yale University Press, 1999), 188–9. Violent energy was an asset: "Self-defence, whether individually or as part of a collective assertion, placed a premium on physical prowess and readiness for combat ... Popular forms of sport, or 'manly exercises,' kept men in a state of alertness and physical fitness, ranging from fox-hunting and cricket to archery and rowing. First impressions of an individual were strongly conditioned by physical indicators – – countenance, voice and hand-clasp could (and should) all be 'manly.' But a manly appearance suggested more than physical health and strength; it indicated virility. In common usage manliness always presumed a liberal endowment of sexual energy, and this feature was commended quite independently of the moral issue of male sexual conduct" (111–12).

21 Dowling, *Manliness*, 13.

22 Sussman, *Victorian Masculinities*, 3.

23 Dowling, *Manliness*, 14. See also Joseph Kestner, *Masculinities in Victorian Painting* (Aldershot, UK: Scolar Press, 1995), 92–140.

24 See also John Kucich, *Imperial Masochism: British Fiction, Fantasy, and Social Class* (Princeton, NJ: Princeton University Press, 2007), 9–10.

25 Kestner, *Masculinities*, 97.
26 Ibid., 98.
27 See also Michael Paris, *Warrior Nation: Images of War in British Popular Culture, 1850–2000* (London: Reaktion Books, 2000), 49.
28 See especially Bradley Deane, *Masculinity and the New Imperialism* (Cambridge: Cambridge University Press, 2014).
29 Mary Louise Pratt, *Imperial Eyes: Travel Writing and Transculturation* (Florence, KY: Routledge, 1992), 4.
30 Deane, *Masculinity*, 26.
31 Merrick Burrow, "The Imperial Souvenir: Things and Masculinities in H. Rider Haggard's *King Solomon's Mines* and *Allan Quatermain*," *Journal of Victorian Culture* 18, no. 1 (2013): 85.
32 Tosh, *Man's Place*, 189.
33 Paris, *Warrior Nation*, 23.
34 Said, *Culture and Imperialism*, 79.
35 Sussman, *Victorian Masculinities*, 10.
36 Kestner, *Masculinities*, 36, quoting Bigelow, *Sexual Pathology* (1875).
37 John Ruskin, "Of Queen's Gardens," in *Sesame and Lilies* (1864; New York: Silver, Burdett, 1900), 84, Internet Archive: California Digital Library, emphasis in original.
38 In *The Social Life of Fluids*, Jules Law explores the troubling of bodily boundaries by the exchange of fluids across bodies and households in Victorian England, and the importance of mastery of these exchanges for identity.
39 Mikhail Bakhtin, *Rabelais and His World*, trans. Helene Iswolsky (Cambridge, MA: MIT Press, 1968), 317.
40 Ibid.
41 Ibid., 317, 316.
42 Ibid., 318.
43 Kucich, *Imperial Masochism*, 15.
44 Christopher Lane, *The Burdens of Intimacy: Psychoanalysis and Victorian Masculinity* (Chicago: Chicago University Press, 1999), 10–11.
45 Ibid., 27.

1 Permeable Boundaries: Violence and Fantasy in Zululand

1 Frank Emery, *The Red Soldier: Letters from the Zulu War, 1879* (London: Hodder and Stoughton, 1977), 16.
2 Michael Lieven, "Heroism, Heroics and the Making of Heroes: The Anglo-Zulu War of 1879," *Albion: A Quarterly Journal Concerned with British Studies* 30, no. 3 (1998): 419–38; John Laband and Ian Knight, *The War Correspondents: The Anglo-Zulu War* (Phoenix Mill, UK: Sutton, 1996).

3 Freud, from "Medusa's Head" (1922), quoted in Theweleit, *Male Fantasies*, 197–8.
4 Theweleit, *Male Fantasies*, 201.
5 Ninety-one million pounds' worth of commercial goods were passing via this route, compared to 65 millions' worth through the Suez. See Ronald Robinson and John Gallagher, with Alice Denny, *Africa and the Victorians: The Official Mind of Imperialism*, 2nd ed. (Houndmills, UK: Macmillan, 1981), 59.
6 Ibid., 60.
7 Ibid., 54, 62.
8 N. Bhebe, "The British, Boers and Africans in South Africa, 1850–80," in *General History of Africa*, vol. 6, *Africa in the Nineteenth Century until the 1880s*, ed. J.F. Ajayi (Berkeley: University of California Press, 1989), 169.
9 Ibid., 171.
10 Joye Bowman, "Reconstructing the Past Using British Parliamentary Papers: The Anglo-Zulu War of 1879," *History in Africa* 31 (2004): 121; Bhebe, "British, Boers and Africans," 172.
11 Bowman, "Reconstructing," 121. While Bulwer wanted to maintain peaceful relations with Cetshwayo, Frere's aim was to subjugate the Zulus because he feared attack, against which ongoing guarding would be costly.
12 Ian Knight, *Zulu Rising: The Epic Story of Isandlwana and Rorke's Drift* (London: Macmillan, 2010), 129.
13 In July, MaMtshali and MaMthethwa, two wives of Chief Sihayo, left their husband and absconded from Zululand with their lovers, taking refuge in Natal and – counting on Sihayo not to risk agitating the British by crossing the national border after them (ibid., 131). However, the jilted chief's son, Mehlokazulu, insulted by the dishonour, led a band of fighters across the border into Natal and violently seized the escapees and took them back to Zululand, where he executed them. Knowing that Sihayo would not condone this, Mehlokazulu had waited until his father was summoned away to Cetshwayo before acting (132). Then, in September, two British surveyors illegally operating in Zululand were briefly detained as trespassers; although roughly handled, they were not injured. Finally, in October, an ex-Swazi chief, Mbilini, who was living in Zululand, crossed the border into Swaziland and the Transvaal and attacked some kraals (Bowman, "Reconstructing," 122; Knight, *Zulu Rising*, 147).
14 Bhebe, "British, Boers and Africans," 174.
15 John Laband, *Lord Chelmsford's Zulu Campaign, 1878–1879* (Dover, NH: Alan Sutton Publishing, 1994), 220.
16 D.C.F. Moodie, *Zulu 1879: The Anglo Zulu War of 1879 from Contemporary Sources. First Hand Accounts, Interviews, Letters, Despatches, Official Documents & Newspaper Reports* (N.p.: Leonaur, 2006), 15.

17 Ibid., 19.
18 John Martineau, *The Life and Correspondence of Sir Bartle Frere*, vol. 2 (1895; American Libraries Internet Archive, last modified 10 Jan. 2008), 251, 244, written in letters to Sir M. Hicks-Beach, 8 Dec. 1878 and 30 Sept. 1878.
19 Moodie, *Zulu*, 15.
20 Martineau, *Life and Correspondence*, 258–9, 265, letters to Sir M. Hicks-Beach, 28 Oct. 1879 and 23 Dec. 1878.
21 Ibid., 249–50, memorandum from 16 Dec. 1878.
22 Ibid., 231, letter to General Ponsonby, n.d.
23 As soon as his report of the British defeat at Isandlwana appeared, however, the public was riveted, and for months afterwards the press fixated on news from Zululand. See Brian Best and Adrian Greaves, *The Curling Letters of the Zulu War* (Barnsley, UK: Pen and Sword, 2001), 80.
24 H. Rider Haggard, *The Days of My Life: An Autobiography*, vol. 1 (London: Longmans, Green, 1926), 117.
25 Stephen Wade, *Empire and Espionage: The Anglo-Zulu War, 1879* (Barnsley, UK: Pen and Sword Military, 2012), 10; quoting from the Lincolnshire Archives, Conyers Papers.
26 Though "distant," the British weapons were by no means quick and painless: "The Martini-Henry bullet, which flattened on impact, caused massive tissue damage and splintered bones lengthwise, with devastating effect." See John Laband, "'War Can't Be Made with Kid Gloves': The Impact of the Anglo-Zulu War of 1879 on the Fabric of Zulu Society," *South African Historical Journal* 43 (2000): 186–7.
27 Ian Knight, "The Zulu Army of 1879," in *Redcoats and Zulus: Selected Essays from* The Journal of the Anglo Zulu War Historical Society, ed. Adrian Greaves (Barnsley, UK: Pen and Sword Military, 2004), 37.
28 Best and Greaves, *Curling Letters*, 94.
29 Chelmsford's column was the central prong of three: Colonel Wood led a mass of soldiers to the north (toward Hlobane), and Colonel Pearson brought in a body of troops to the southeast (toward Eshowe).
30 Described to the assistant adjutant-general for the Court of Inquiry (formed after the disaster), quoted in Emery, *Red Soldier*, 80.
31 "This formation was known as the impondo Zenkomo, 'the beast's horns,' and consisted of a frontal assault by a body known as the 'chest' (isiFuba), comprised of senior or married men, and encircling flanks, the 'horns' (izimpondo), by younger men. A reserve, the 'loins,' was kept some distance away" (Knight, "Zulu Army," 37).
32 As Cochrane attested, "Had the Zulus completed their scheme, by sending a column to the Buffalo River to cut off the retreat, not a man would have escaped to tell the tale" (Emery, *Red Soldier*, 80).

33 Terry Sole, *For God, Queen and Colony: The Colonial, Volunteer and Native Regiments in the Zulu War 1879* (Honiton, UK: Token Publishing, 2011), 295.
34 Emery, *Red Soldier*, 92.
35 Best and Greaves, *Curling Letters*, 106. Howard was a survivor of the stand at Rorke's Drift, but describes Isandlwana presumably as he understood it from an escapee or rumours of the attack.
36 Sole, *For God*, 206–7.
37 For an account of Isandlwana by Mehlokazulu, the same man who crossed the border into Natal to capture the absconded wives of his father, see Emery, *Red Soldier*, 26–7. This account was originally printed in the *Royal Engineer Journal* 10 (1880): 23–4. Emery also provides an account from a warrior named Uguku (86–7), a narrative that was originally printed in Francis E. Colenso and E. Durnford's *History of the Zulu War and Its Origin* (London, 1880), 410–13. For accounts from anonymous Zulu fighters, see Emery, *Red Soldier*, 82–4, and Bertram Mitford, *Through the Zulu Country: Its Battlefields and Its People* (London, 1883), 89–95.
38 In addition to the soldiers in the 80th, also killed were three European conductors, fifteen natives employed with the wagons, and a civilian surgeon (Sole, *For God*, 119).
39 Moodie, *Zulu*, 113.
40 Emery, *Red Soldier*, 159.
41 Sole, *For God*, 121.
42 Laband and Knight, *War Correspondents*, 88.
43 Moodie, *Zulu*, 122; quoting from the *Natal Mercury*, Zulu War Supplement, April 1879: account "from our own Correspondent," dated "Kambula Camp, April 1st, 1879."
44 Moodie, *Zulu*, 139; quoting from *Pearson's Magazine*, "The Bravery of Colonel Buller."
45 While tropes of penetrations are common in martial discourses, the intersection of penetration with imagery of engulfment seems distinct from representations of other European warfare as well as other moments of colonial uprising because of the particular conditions of the Anglo-Zulu War. The rolling landscape in Zululand, the well-practised and efficient battle tactics of the Zulu – the impondo zenkomo, for instance – and imperial unfamiliarity with the territory all contributed to the specific sense of sudden engulfment and penetration appearing here.
46 Published in the *Times* on 12 April 1879; quoted in Laband and Knight, *War Correspondents*, 58.
47 Laband and Knight, *War Correspondents*, 58.
48 Ibid., 58–9.
49 Emery, *Red Soldier*, 88.
50 Moodie, *Zulu*, 47.

51 Sole, *For God*, 321.
52 Anne McClintock identifies all three of these transgressions as the focal points of colonial figurations of vulnerability during exploration into the unknown. Dismemberment signifies "catastrophic boundary loss, associated with fears of impotence and infantilization." See *Imperial Leather: Race, Gender and Sexuality in the Colonial Contest* (New York: Routledge, 1995), 26.
53 Emery, *Red Soldier*, 92–3.
54 "Epitome of Opinion in the Morning Journals," *Pall Mall Gazette*, 12 Feb. 1879, 2.
55 *Morning Post*, 12 Feb. 1879, 4.
56 "The News from Cape Town," *Pall Mall Gazette*, 11 Feb. 1879, 1.
57 *Fun*, 19 March 1879, University of Florida Digital Collections, http://ufdc.ufl.edu/UF00078627/00034/109j. See also Mark Bryant, *Wars of Empire in Cartoons* (London: Grub Street Publishing, 2008), 75.
58 *Fun*, 11 June 1879, University of Florida Digital Collections, http://ufdc.ufl.edu/UF00078627/00034/217j. See also Mark Bryant, *Wars of Empire in Cartoons* (London: Grub Street Publishing, 2008), 77.
59 Laband and Knight, *War Correspondents*, 102; quoting from the *Daily News*, 21 May 1879.
60 Emery, *Red Soldier*, 98.
61 Ibid., 94.
62 Many of the British soldiers sent to South Africa were indeed quite young.
63 This profuse bleeding is analogous with menstruation.
64 Pratt identifies "anti-conquest" strategies as mechanisms by which imperial writers strive to assert their innocence – in this case, as vulnerable – while simultaneously asserting hegemony (*Imperial Eyes*, 7).
65 Emery, *Red Soldier*, 95.
66 Ibid., 96.
67 In response to another case of imperial resistance, Tennyson used the mutiny to argue for harsh punishment for the Morant Bay uprising: "The outbreak of our Indian Mutiny remains as a warning to all but mad men against want of vigour and swift decisiveness." See Thomas R. Metcalf, *The New Cambridge History*, vol. 3, *Ideologies of the Raj* (Cambridge: Cambridge University Press, 2001), 53. Michael Paris notes that "horrendous accounts of Indian atrocities caused a widespread demand for revenge," citing Thomas Macaulay: "The cruelties of the sepoys have inflamed the nation to a degree unprecedented in my memory" (*Warrior Nation*, 38). See also Anna Johnston's suggestion that "righteous outrage" was the response to the perception that British womanhood was under attack during the uprising in *Missionary Writing and Empire, 1800–1860* (Cambridge: Cambridge University Press, 2003), 51, and Christopher Herbert, *War of*

No Pity: The Indian Mutiny and Victorian Trauma (Princeton, NJ: Princeton University Press, 2008), 207–10, for a discussion of the British public's formation of community and unity in response to the insurrection.

68 Jenny Sharpe, *Allegories of Empire: The Figure of Woman in the Colonial Text* (Minneapolis: University of Minnesota Press, 1993), 4.

69 Moodie, *Zulu*, 43.

70 Lauren Berlant argues that, although "the experience of pain is pre-ideological," and is "the universal sign of membership in humanity," and that thus spectators of pain "are obligated to be responsible to it," compassion is also necessarily a choice: spectators "must make judgments about which cases deserve attention." See "Introduction: Compassion (and Withholding)," in *Compassion: The Culture and Politics of an Emotion*, ed. Lauren Berlant (New York: Routledge, 2004), 10–11. In this understanding, participation in compassion requires voluntary social membership – in other words, communities are formed on the basis of who is deemed to be worthy of compassion and its material accoutrements. In the case of Britain circa the Anglo-Zulu War, public compassion and communal affect had the function of strengthening national bonds, on which some leaders drew to call for reparations.

71 Laband and Knight, *War Correspondents*, 150, quoting from the *Natal Witness*, 29 July 1879, Port Durnford correspondent, 20 July 1879.

72 Wade, *Empire*, 31.

73 Best and Greaves, *Curling Letters*, 65–6.

74 Wade, *Empire*, 36.

75 See Catherine Anderson, "Red Coats and Black Shields: Race and Masculinity in British Representations of the Anglo-Zulu War," *Critical Survey* 20, no. 3 (2008): 15.

76 Emery, *Red Soldier*, 132.

77 Ibid., 132, quoting from the *North Devon Herald*, 24 April 1879.

78 Emery, *Red Soldier*, 130.

79 Ibid., 104–5.

80 "The Zulu War," *Birmingham Daily Post*, 1 March 1879, 5. See also Laband and Knight, *War Correspondents*, 54, quoting from the *Natal Mercury*, Zulu War Supplement, January 1879: Report "From the *Times* War Correspondent," Charles Norris-Newman, dated "Pietermaritzburg, Jan. 26th, 1879." This sight and its significance clearly left a strong impression on Norris-Newman, for he writes later, "we began to stumble over dead bodies in every direction … The men were found lying thick and close, as if they had fought till their ammunition was exhausted, and then been surrounded and slaughtered … Within a few hundred yards of the top of the ridge … the large and grotesque form of the Isandwhlana Mountain loom[ed] up in front of us." See *In Zululand with the British throughout the War of 1879* (1880; London: Greenhill Books, 1990), 61.

81 Emery, *Red Soldier*, 107.
82 Ibid., 109.
83 "Epitome of Opinion in the Morning Journals," *Pall Mall Gazette*, 12 Feb. 1879, 2.
84 "The Disasters in Zululand," *Northern Echo*, 12 Feb. 1879, 3.
85 Ibid.
86 Norris-Newman, *In Zululand*, 10.
87 See also Mary A. Favret, *War at a Distance: Romanticism and the Making of Modern Wartime* (Princeton, NJ: Princeton University Press, 2010), especially 73–4.
88 *Lloyd's Weekly*, quoted in Lieven, "Heroism," 423.
89 Lieven, "Heroism," 423, quoting the *Graphic.*
90 Again we see the equation of the Zulus with elements of the landscape.
91 Moodie, *Zulu*, 61–2, quoting the *Bendigo Advertizer.*
92 Best and Greaves, *Curling Letters*, 97.
93 Bowman also argues that correspondence during the war "emphasized the superior quality of the British troops and made them seem like 'super soldiers.' Many reports of actual encounters with the Zulu claimed, for example, that there were often over two hundred times as many Zulu warriors as British soldiers and yet the British were able to hold their line and push the Zulu back. Several reports on the casualties of both British and Zulu forces were written but it is difficult to accept many of the figures because they seem to be rough estimates, intended to make the British army look good." See "Reconstructing," 127.
94 Here, a small body of about a hundred soldiers withheld an attack of three to four thousand Zulus for twelve hours from the evening of January 22nd to the morning of the 23rd.
95 More recently, too, Cy Enfield's 1964 film *Zulu* depicts the attack on Rorke's as a planned, strategic move against British forces, and furthermore replicates nineteenth-century portrayals in British media of redcoat composure.
96 Moodie, *Zulu*, 74. Melton Prior also maintained in retrospect, "Their action [at Rorke's Drift] no doubt saved Natal from invasion by the enemy." See *Campaigns of a War Correspondent* (London: Edward Arnold, 1912), 90.
97 Theweleit, *Male Fantasies*, 244.
98 Ibid., 230.
99 Emery, *Red Soldier*, 131.
100 Ibid., 126.
101 Emery, *Red Soldier*, 127, 129.
102 Lieven, "Heroism," 430.
103 This account was reprinted in Archibald Forbes, *Barracks, Bivouacs and Battles* (London: Macmillan, 1891).

104 Ibid., 144–5.

105 John Hoberman's argument that both war and sport were areas "in which Caucasian men displayed both physical mastery and the masculine qualities of character that established their right to command other races" is particularly relevant here. See *Darwin's Athletes: How Sport Has Damaged Black America and Preserved the Myth of Race* (Boston: Houghton Mifflin, 1997), 100.

106 Ibid., 113.

107 Ibid.

108 Merrick Burrow observes that, "In the case of the imperial souvenir, the killing of an adversary (animal or human) produces its body as a trophy – an object by means of which the adversary's power is projected back onto the gentleman barbarian who takes possession of it" ("Imperial Souvenir," 73).

109 Norris-Newman, *In Zululand*, 138–9.

110 John M. MacKenzie, "The Imperial Pioneer and Hunter and the British Masculine Stereotype in Late Victorian and Edwardian Times," in *Manliness and Morality: Middle-Class Masculinity in Britain and America, 1800–1940*, ed. J.A. Mangan and James Walvin (Manchester: Manchester University Press, 1987), 179.

111 "Penny Wisdom," *Pall Mall Gazette*, 12 Feb. 1879, 1.

112 Emery, *Red Soldier*, 162.

113 Prior, *Campaigns*, 108.

114 Laband and Knight, *War Correspondents*, 132, quoting from the *Natal Mercury*, Zulu War Supplement, 14 July 1879: Report "Compiled by the *Witness* from Mr. Phil Robinson's telegrams to England."

115 Prior, *Campaigns*, 117.

116 Quoted in Moodie, *Zulu*, 56.

117 *Morning Post*, 12 Feb. 1879, 4.

118 Wade, *Empire*, 135, quoting from "Our South African Colonies," *Westminster Review*, April 1789, 187.

119 Quoted in Emery, *Red Soldier*, 101.

120 Sir Bartle Frere, too, in a letter to Sir M. Hicks-Beach on 29 January 1879, described the Zulus in this manner: "Theirs is the courage of maniacs and drunkards, or of wild beasts infuriated and trained to destruction" (Martineau, *Life and Correspondence*, 278).

121 "The Zulu War: The Zlobana Trap and the Kambula Repulse," *Daily Gazette*, 19 May 1879, 3.

122 Laband and Knight, *War Correspondents*, 70.

123 We can consider such observations about Zulu prowess in light of Hoberman's claim that "scientific speculation about what we would call the athletic potential of non-Western people has been a part of the Western racial imagination for at least two centuries" (*Darwin's Athletes*,

103). Europeans were largely obsessed with racialized comparisons of strength, physique, movement, speed, and so on, and evaluating the physical prowess of non-Western men directly impinged on British constructions of Anglo-Saxon manhood.

124 Sole, *For God*, 125.

125 Emery, *Red Soldier*, 171.

126 Ibid., 172.

127 Laband and Knight, *War Correspondents*, x.

128 Emery, *Red Soldier*, 169.

129 Ibid., 173. See Michael Lieven, "'Butchering the Brutes All Over the Place': Total War and Massacre in Zululand, 1879," *History* 84 (1999): 614–32 for a longer discussion of British brutality.

130 Laband and Knight, *War Correspondents*, 91, quoting from the *Natal Mercury*, Zulu War Supplement, April 1879.

131 *Hansard's Parliamentary Debates, Third Series: Commencing with the Accession of William IV. 42° Victoriæ, 1879. Vol. CCXLVI. Comprising the Period from the ninth day of May 1879 to the sixteenth day of June 1879*, Vol. 4 of the Session (London: Cornelius Buck, at the Office for "Hansard's Parliamentary Debates," 22 Paternoster Row. [E.C.] 1879), 1015 (22 May 1789).

132 Emery, *Red Soldier*, 24.

133 "The News from Zululand," *Northern Echo*, 8 May 1879, 3. The quotation in the *Echo*'s story is from an account printed in the *Cape Argus.* In addition to other violations of the rules of war, Zulu envoys were taken prisoner under a flag of truce.

134 "The Peace Society and the Government," *Daily Gazette*, 21 May 1879, 4.

135 "The Peace Society and the Zulu War," *Bristol Mercury and Daily Post*, 13 May 1879, 2.

136 Ibid.

137 See, for example, "Departure of Sir Garnet Wolseley," *Daily Gazette*, 30 May 1879, 3. "Home," *Graphic*, 24 May 1879, 502. *Spectator*, 1 Jan. 1881, 29, review of Waller Ashe and E.V. Wyatt Edgell, *The Story of the Zulu Campaign* (London: Sampson Low, 1880). The Colenso family were also notably outspoken critics of British conduct during this war.

138 This refers to Wolseley's settlement of Zululand, which divided the kingdom among thirteen different rulers so that the colonial office could more effectively control the Zulu nation.

139 Morten Cohen, *Rider Haggard: His Life and Works* (London: Hutchinson, 1960), 41; H. Rider Haggard, *Cetywayo and His White Neighbours; or, Remarks on Recent Events in Zululand, Natal, and the Transvaal* (1882; London: Trubner, Ludgate Hill, 1888), lxxviii.

140 Ibid., 34.

141 Ibid., 78.

2 H. Rider Haggard's Inversions: Vulnerability and the Narrative Volatility of Imperial Romance

1 Haggard, *Days*, 1: 97.
2 Ibid., 2: 104.
3 Cohen, *Rider Haggard*, 28.
4 Ibid., 49.
5 Haggard, *Cetywayo*, 34. This settlement divided the Zulu kingdom into thirteen states, and established as many kings, each with little real power; this resulted in many forms of instability and fighting.
6 Written on 8 June 1881 (Cohen, *Rider Haggard*, 60, quoting John Martineau, *Life and Correspondence*).
7 Haggard, *Cetywayo*, 287.
8 Ibid.
9 Haggard, *Days*, 1: 194.
10 See Eric Hobsbawm, *Age of Empire, 1875–1914* (New York: Pantheon Books, 1987), 35–9.
11 See pages 27–8 in chapter 1 above.
12 Haggard, *Cetywayo*, 23.
13 Ibid.
14 Ibid.
15 Moodie, *Zulu*, 139; quoting from "The Bravery of Colonel Buller,"*Pearson's Magazine*. See also pages 31–2 above.
16 See also Thomas Richards, *The Imperial Archive: Knowledge and the Fantasy of Empire* (New York: Verso, 1993), 6.
17 See Neil Hultgren, "Haggard Criticism since 1980: Imperial Romance before and after the Postcolonial Turn," *Literature Compass* 8, no. 9 (2011): 645–59. For instance, Wendy Katz, in *Rider Haggard and the Fiction of Empire* (Cambridge: Cambridge University Press, 1987), reads Haggard's work in a totalizing way: "Haggard's romances ... illustrate a total mentality, a philosophy of life, an idea of humankind completely in harmony with the imperial ideology" (4). See also readings of Haggard's romances as commending imperialist masculinity in Brantlinger, *Rule of Darkness*, 189–90; Mawuena Kossi Logan, *Narrating Africa: George Henty and the Fiction of Empire* (New York: Garland Publishing, 1999), 146–52; Elaine Showalter, *Sexual Anarchy: Gender and Culture at the Fin de Siècle* (London: Bloomsbury, 1991), 78–89; Bristow, *Empire Boys*, 135–9; McClintock, *Imperial Leather*, 234–48; Deirdre David, *Rule Britannia: Women, Empire, and Victorian Writing* (Ithaca, NY: Cornell University Press, 1995), 161; Stephen Arata, *Fictions of Loss in the Victorian Fin de Siècle* (Cambridge: Cambridge University Press, 1996), 103; and Laura Chrisman, *Rereading the Imperial Romance: British Imperialism and South African Resistance in Haggard, Schreiner, and Plaatje*

(Oxford: Clarendon Press, 2000), 44–6. See also Julia Reid, "'Gladstone Bags, Shooting Boots, and Byrant & May's Matches': Empire, Commerce, and the Imperial Romance in the *Graphic's* Serialization of H. Rider Haggard's *She*," *Studies in the Novel* 43, no. 2 (2011): 152–77 for a concise summary of the "critical consensus [that] cast Haggard's fiction, and the romance revival more generally, as the uncomplicated expression of a crudely jingoist, racist, and misogynist imperialism" (152).

18 See, for example Barri E. Gold, "Embracing the Corpse: Discursive Recycling in H. Rider Haggard's *She*," *English Literature in Transition, 1880–1920* 38, no. 3 (1995): 305–27; Patricia Murphy, *Time Is of the Essence: Temporality, Gender, and the New Woman* (Albany, NY: SUNY Press, 2001), 31–69; Lindy Stiebel, *Imagining Africa: Landscape in H. Rider Haggard's African Romances* (Westport, CT: Greenwood Press, 2001), 75–8; Gerald Monsman, *H. Rider Haggard on the Imperial Frontier: The Politics and Literary Contexts of His African Romances* (Greensboro, NC: ELT Press, 2006), 80–6; Madhudaya Sinha, "Triangular Erotics: The Politics of Masculinity, Imperialism and Big Game Hunting in Rider Haggard's *She*," *Critical Survey* 20, no. 3 (2008): 29–43; Bradley Deane, "Mummy Fiction and the Occupation of Egypt: Imperial Striptease," *English Literature in Transition, 1880–1920* 51, no. 4 (2008): 381–410; and Heidi Kaufman, *English Origins, Jewish Discourse, and the Nineteenth-Century British Novel: Reflections on a Nested Nation* (University Park: Pennsylvania State University Press, 2009), 163–92.

19 *King Solomon's Mines* has been made into five motion pictures: 1937, 1950, 1985, 1986, and 2004. *She*, for its part, has never been out of print since its first serialization. See Andrew M. Stauffer, Introduction to *She: A History of Adventure*, ed. Andrew M. Stauffer (1887; Peterborough: Broadview, 2006), 23.

20 Robert Dixon, *Writing the Colonial Adventure: Race, Gender and Nation in Anglo-Australian Popular Fiction, 1875–1914* (Cambridge: Cambridge University Press, 1995), 8.

21 While Joseph Bristow has suggested that the narrator and editor of *King Solomon's Mines* worked co-operatively to ennoble the deeds of adventure (*Empire Boys*, 136), his argument does not account for the friction and contradictions in the narrator's and editor's voices. I aim to show here that the frame narrative creates dissonance and space for critique.

22 Haley, *Healthy Body*, 4; Dowling, *Manliness*, 13.

23 Bristow, *Empire Boys*, 58. Alan Sandison also notes that by "about 1870 Tom Brown had become a pattern for schoolboys, and [Matthew] Arnold's teaching had given way to a new code in which manliness, animal spirits and prowess at games figure as the attributes most to be admired in a boy." What emerged was "an insistence on … firmness of character, strength of will, sense of duty, reserves of fortitude." See Sandison, *The*

Wheel of Empire: A Study of the Imperial Idea in Some Late Nineteenth- and Early Twentieth-Century Fiction (London: Macmillan, 1967), 14–15.

24 Thomas Hughes, *Tom Brown's School Days* (1857; Oxford: Oxford University Press, 2008), 3–5.

25 Robert Michael Ballantyne, *The Coral Island: A Tale of the Pacific Ocean* (1857; London: J.M. Dent and Sons, 1967), 3–4.

26 Ibid., 333.

27 Robert Michael Ballantyne, *The Gorilla Hunters: A Tale of the Wilds of Africa* (1875; Edinburgh: T. Nelson and Sons, 1901), 52.

28 Ibid., 107.

29 G.A. Henty, *Dash for Khartoum: A Tale of the Nile Expedition* (Glasgow: Blackie and Son, 1892), v–vi.

30 Ibid., 42, 32.

31 Ibid., 102.

32 Ibid., 103.

33 G.A. Henty, *With Kitchener in the Sudan: A Story of Atbara and Omdurman* (London: Foulsham, 1900), 160.

34 Ibid., 163.

35 G.A. Henty, *By Sheer Pluck; a Tale of the Ashanti War* (Glasgow: Blackie and Son, 1897), 32, 33.

36 Ibid., 59.

37 Linda Hutcheon, *A Theory of Parody: The Teachings of Twentieth-Century Art Forms* (New York: Methuen, 1985), 6.

38 Ibid., 53.

39 H. Rider Haggard, *King Solomon's Mines*, ed. Gerald Monsman (1885; Peterborough, ON: Broadview, 2002), 55.

40 McClintock, *Imperial Leather*, 240. Monsman, however, notes that, when Good, Curtis, and Quatermain are "sexually devoured and shat out like lumps of excrement" from the mines, what we have is "an ironic rebirth at best, a parody of renewal" (*Imperial Frontier*, 97).

41 Haggard, *King Solomon's Mines*, 40.

42 Showalter, *Sexual Anarchy*, 76–83; Nicholas Daly, *Modernism, Romance, and the Fin de Siècle: Popular Fiction and British Culture, 1880–1914* (New York: Cambridge University Press, 1999), 18.

43 H. Rider Haggard, "About Fiction," *Contemporary Review*, Feb. 1887, Appendix A in *She: A History of Adventure*, ed. Andrew M. Stauffer (Peterborough, ON: Broadview Editions, 2006), 293. As Stephen Arata notes, Max Nordau's extremely popular *Degeneration* (1895) associated works that "signify promiscuously" (*Fictions*, 29) as degenerate; by contrast, Quatermain's claim to a "blunt way of writing" is a claim to clarity, directness, and what Nordau would come to understand as a healthy sort of writing.

44 Haggard, "About Fiction," 293.
45 Ibid.
46 Arata, *Fictions*, 93.
47 See the discussion on pages 49–52 above.
48 Haggard, *King Solomon's Mines*, 44.
49 Ibid.
50 James Bonwick, *Our Nationalities* (London: David Bogue, 1880), Pt. 1, 59.
51 Ibid., Pt. 4, 92–3. Incidentally, Haggard celebrated his own supposedly Danish origins. See Haggard, *Days*, 1: 1–2.
52 Bonwick, *Our Nationalities*, Pt. 4, 58.
53 Haggard, *King Solomon's Mines*, 183.
54 See Catherine Gordon, "The Illustration of Sir Walter Scott: Nineteenth-Century Enthusiasm and Adaptation," *Journal of the Warburg and Courtauld Institutes* 34 (1971): 297; Annika Bautz, *The Reception of Jane Austen and Sir Walter Scott: A Comparative Longitudinal Study* (London: Continuum, 2007), 75–114; and Cohen, *Rider Haggard*, 87. As Daly notes, the genre of romance "often strived to establish links to Scott" (*Modernism*, 17).
55 Haggard, *King Solomon's Mines*, 49.
56 Ibid., 88.
57 See McClintock, *Imperial Leather*, 3. For McClintock, the restoration of white patriarchy hinges on the argument that the novel attempts to resolve the problems encountered in subduing black female labour by explicitly sexualizing the land through the rendition of a mapping of the feminized landscape "in male body fluids" (3). The writing tool – that is, da Silvestre's cleft bone, McClintock argues, invests the white male heirs to history and fortune "with the authority and power befitting the keepers of sacred treasure" (3). Thus, writing, for McClintock, is equal to the exercise and exertion of male dominance. Haggard, however, was less than venerating toward the subject of writing: "a kind of terror seizes me lest this fair place should be but a scented purgatory where, in payment for my sins, I am doomed to write fiction for forever and a day! … For truly it would be a horrible fate to be doomed from aeon to countless aeon to the composition of romance" (*Days*, 88).
58 Haggard, *King Solomon's Mines*, 108–9.
59 As Laurence Talairach-Vielmas points out, loose hair was frequently associated with unruliness in the Victorian period. See *Moulding the Female Body in Victorian Fairy Tales and Sensation Novels* (Aldershot, UK: Ashgate Publishing, 2007), 79. In *King Solomon's Mines*, this female body is more than ornamental.
60 Bradley Deane, "Imperial Barbarians: Primitive Masculinity in Lost World Fiction," *Journal of Victorian Literature and Culture* 36 (2008): 210; Gerald Monsman, "Introduction: Of Diamonds and Deities in *King*

Solomon's Mines," in *King Solomon's Mines*, ed. Gerald Monsman (1885; Peterborough, ON: Broadview Editions, 2002), 17; Stiebel, *Imagining Africa*, 46; McClintock, *Imperial Leather*, 240.

61 Haggard, *King Solomon's Mines*, 44.

62 A loin-covering; part of traditional Zulu dress.

63 Haggard, *King Solomon's Mines*, 70.

64 Lane, *Ruling Passion*, 4.

65 See Sussman, *Victorian Masculinities*, 3.

66 Haggard, *King Solomon's Mines*, 70.

67 Homi K. Bhabha, *The Location of Culture* (London: Routledge, 1994), 89.

68 Hutcheon, *Theory*, 33.

69 Haggard, *King Solomon's Mines*, 137.

70 The particular readership to whom Quatermain dedicates his adventure story.

71 Haggard, *King Solomon's Mines*, 115.

72 Ibid., 194; Haggard, *Cetywayo*, 78.

73 Haggard, *King Solomon's Mines*, 188.

74 Ibid., 189.

75 Ibid.

76 Ibid., 190.

77 Ibid., 223.

78 See Logan, *Narrating*, 146–7.

79 Ibid., 155, 153, 156.

80 Ibid., 153.

81 Haggard, *Cetywayo*, 237.

82 Haggard, *King Solomon's Mines*, 156.

83 Hutcheon points out that parody is "both a symptom and a critical tool of the modernist episteme" (*Theory*, 2).

84 Ibid., 35–6.

85 Arata, for instance, points out a sense of inadequacy behind the writing of *She* and other texts within the adventure genre: "The theory and practice of the male romance reveals an array of anxieties at once personal, 'racial,' political, and aesthetic: anxieties concerning the dissolution of masculine identity, the degeneration of the British 'race,' the moral collapse of imperial ideology, and the decline of the great tradition of English letters" (*Fictions*, 89). Bristow argues that "everything brutal about British imperialism – the wars, the massacres, the destruction of cultures – is displaced into the very heart of the continent the Victorians sought to conquer" (*Empire Boys*, 140).

86 Criticism, however, has tended to associate Leo with the figure of imperial adventure. See Showalter, *Sexual Anarchy*, 78–88; Arata, *Fictions*, 94–100; Laura Chrisman, "The Imperial Unconscious? Representations of Imperial

Discourse," *Critical Quarterly* 32 (1990): 46; David, *Rule Britannia*, 189, 196; Murphy, *Time*, 34; Deane, *Masculinity*, 186.

87 H. Rider Haggard, *She: A History of Adventure*, ed. Andrew M. Stauffer (1887; Peterborough, ON: Broadview, 2006), 35.

88 Ibid., 39. Andrew M. Stauffer summarizes Leo more bluntly: "he remains a beautiful, empty-headed, flat character who moreover is almost entirely passive, someone hardly worth a two-thousand year wait" (Introduction, 17).

89 Haggard, *She*, 39.

90 Ibid., 52, 35.

91 As Eve Kosofsky Sedgwick points out, homosociality and homosexuality occupy different places on the same spectrum (*Between Men*, 1–2).

92 Haggard, *She*, 50.

93 Stauffer, Introduction, 11 and 15; Showalter, *Sexual Anarchy*, 84; Sandra M. Gilbert and Susan Gubar, *No Man's Land: The Place of the Woman Writer in the Twentieth Century*, vol. 2, *Sexchanges* (New Haven, CT: Yale University Press, 1989), 6; Murphy, *Time*, 58; Sinha, "Triangular Erotics," 35; Bristow, *Empire Boys*, 141.

94 For instance, Arata suggests that *She* is about "the struggle between 'eternal' femininity and male writing," contending that "the power of the pen" is associated with Horace Holly; meanwhile She's femininity and "beauty [is] at once enslaving and destructive" – she is both "the source and negation of life." Furthermore, She is not just an "embodiment of transhistorical femaleness" – she is multifaceted: a representative of a figure of European legends of African tribes tyrannized by white women, a symbol of oriental decadence, and indicative of the Victorian New Woman (*Fictions*, 96–7). As such, Arata submits, She threatens to displace masculine dominance. David, meanwhile, argues that "*She* discloses late-Victorian fear of assertive intellectual women bent upon visibility in the public sphere" (*Rule Britannia*, 197). See also LeeAnne M. Richardson's reading of Ayesha as a punished New Woman who refuses to provide biologically reproductive labour, in *New Woman and Colonial Adventure Fiction in Victorian Britain: Gender, Genre, and Empire* (Gainesville: University Press of Florida, 2006), 67–8, and Rebecca Stott, *The Fabrication of the Late-Victorian Femme Fatale: The Kiss of Death* (Basingstoke, UK: Palgrave Macmillan, 1992), 95–9, for her reading of Ayesha as penetrated colony whose consequent sexual arousal threatens to retaliate against Britain.

95 Deane, for example, in *Masculinity*, has argued that Ayesha represents an Oriental empire that British men aim to possess: as "the perfect imperial bride" (187), the symbol of "enduring power" (198), Ayesha figures as a promise of greatness. In this reading, Ayesha's likeness to the imperial occupiers of Egypt facilitates an imperial fantasy about power (187). Julia Reid, meanwhile, recognizes that *She* "figures dreams of masculine

adventure and unbounded riches as both attractive and repellent," and that "Ayesha is a figure for the colonizer as much as for the colonized 'other'" ("Gladstone Bags," 159). Reid convincingly argues that the novel is uneasy about the primacy of commerce's role in empire. Lastly, Laura Chrisman rightly points out that Ayesha indicates the complex "ambiguities, ambivalences, and indeterminacies" of imperialism ("Imperial Unconscious," 45), and sees the possibility that She figures as the imperialist enterprise itself ("Imperial Unconscious," 49).

96 As numerous scholars have observed, She seems to act as a monstrous double for Queen Victoria; in these readings, Ayesha's imperial prowess is directly linked to Britain's. Crucially, however, my argument here is that the qualities She embodies read as masculine extremes, and Holly, in his desire to possess such forms of dominance and power, produces a narrative with limited integrity. Thus, it is not just the British Empire, broadly, that this romance critiques, but the specific mechanisms of racial control and the narratives of empire produced in contact zones.

97 Jaques Derrida, *Speech and Phenomena and Other Essays on Husserl's Theory of Signs*, trans. David B. Allison (Evanston, IL: Northwestern University Press, 1973), 142–3.

98 Ibid., 147.

99 Ibid., 150.

100 Haggard, *She*, 260.

101 Brantlinger, *Rule*, 195. Within this insight, however, Brantlinger nevertheless does not read She as doubly inverted, as I do; for him, She remains an "archetype of female domination" and suggests that "the New Woman is one of the threats underlying the demonism of Ayesha" (234).

102 Ibid., 195.

103 Similarly, in Robert Stevenson's 1937 Hollywood adaptation of *King Solomon's Mines*, the sexual tension between men in the original text is managed through the addition of a female character in search of her father; in Compton Bennet and Andrew Marton's 1950 production, Sir Henry Curtis is replaced by a female character, "the Lady of the Fire Hair." Eventually, the male triumvirate is disassembled altogether, leaving only Quatermain and the female love interest in J. Lee Thompson's 1985 film starring Richard Chamberlain and Sharon Stone.

104 Haggard, *She*, 74.

105 Ibid., 75.

106 Ibid., 71.

107 Ibid.

108 See also Stott, *Fabrication*, 96–7.

109 Haggard, *She*, 272. This important moment of homosocial devotion is illustrated in *She*'s original periodical publication in the *Graphic*.

110 Ibid., 80–1.
111 See Pratt, *Imperial Eyes*, 7.
112 Haggard, *She*, 81.
113 In Conrad's *Heart of Darkness*, Marlow asks a question highly pertinent to the struggle of Haggard's men of empire, as he, in a similar moment, stares into the African wilderness: "Could we handle that big dumb thing, or would it handle us?" Joseph Conrad, *Heart of Darkness*, ed. Robert Kimbrough (1899; W.W. Norton, 1963), 27.
114 Haggard, *She*, 58.
115 Ibid., 93.
116 Ibid., 141.
117 Ibid., 142.
118 Ibid., 120.
119 Ibid., 146.
120 Ibid., 150.
121 Ibid.
122 Ibid., 152.
123 In *The Origin of Species*, published nearly thirty years previously, Darwin not only equates breeding science with civilization, but also emphasizes that European breeders occupied the apex of the global hierarchy. See Charles Darwin, *The Origin of Species by Means of Natural Selection; or, the Preservation of Favoured Races in the Struggle for Life* (1859; Harmondsworth: Penguin, 1968), 90–4. Haggard's engagement with this problem not only aligns Ayesha with British science here, but also underscores its potential brutality.
124 Haggard, *She*, 232–3.
125 See, for example, Brantlinger, *Rule*, 246; Monsman, *Imperial Frontier*, 195.
126 Haggard, *She*, 153.
127 Ibid., 154.
128 Ibid., 182. Holly also later asserts, "If anybody who doubts this statement, and thinks me foolish for making it, could have seen Ayesha draw her veil and flash out in beauty on his gaze, his view would exactly coincide with my own" (*She*, 222).
129 Ibid., 212.
130 Ibid., 213.
131 Ibid., 221.
132 Ibid., 222.
133 Ibid., 221.
134 Ibid.
135 Reid also draws attention to Holly's willingness to deceive when he shoots the eland buck, "exploit[ing] the Amahaggers' primitive, fetishistic response for his own ends" ("Gladstone Bags," 162).
136 Haggard, *She*, 261.

137 Ibid., 264.
138 See Arata, *Fictions*, 103.
139 Haggard, *She*, 263.
140 Ibid., 265.
141 Ibid., 88.
142 Ibid., 89.
143 Ibid.
144 Ibid., 106.
145 Moodie, *Zulu*, 19. See pages 27–8 above.
146 Haggard, *She*, 106.
147 Ibid., 111–12.
148 Laband and Knight, *War Correspondents*, 58.
149 Haggard, *She*, 152.
150 Ibid., 145. Billali also referred to Leo as "the lion," just as he named Holly "Baboon" and Job "the pig."
151 Ibid., 108.
152 Ibid., 263, my emphasis.
153 Arata, *Fictions*, 92.

3 Transgression and Loss: General Gordon and Gothic Imagination

1 *Daily News*, 6 Feb. 1885, 5. The newspapers cited in this chapter are sourced from the holdings of British Library Newspapers.
2 *Birmingham Daily Post*, 6 Feb. 1885, 5.
3 *Aberdeen Weekly Journal*, 6, Feb. 1885, 5; *Belfast News-Letter*, 6 Feb. 1885, 5.
4 *Manchester Courier and Lancashire General Advertiser*, 6 Feb. 1885, 6.
5 *Western Mail*, 6 Feb. 1885, 3.
6 *Manchester Guardian*, 6 Feb. 1885, quoted in *Freeman's Journal and Daily Advertiser*, 6 Feb. 1885, 6.
7 Buller had headed the battles of Hlobane and Kambula Ridge. *Aberdeen Weekly Journal*, 7 Feb. 1885, 8; *Belfast News-Letter*, 7 Feb. 1885, 5.
8 *Freeman's Journal and Daily Commercial Advertiser*, 6 Feb. 1885, 4.
9 This opportunity arose when the debts that the Egyptian Khedive Ismail (1863–79) accrued to Britain and France reached truly staggering proportions. See Mike Snook, *Into the Jaws of Death: British Military Blunders, 1879–1900* (London: Frontline Books, 2008), 221.
10 Quoted in Ailise Bulfin, "The Fiction of Gothic Egypt and British Imperial Paranoia: The Curse of the Suez Canal," *English Literature in Transition 1880–1920* 54, no. 4 (2011): 413.
11 See also Robinson and Gallagher, *Africa*, 117.
12 The Egyptian landlords resented the increase in land tax while the military resented the cuts to its expenditure. Furthermore, lower ranks perceived and resented the special treatment of Turco-Circassian officers (Snook, *Into*

the Jaws, 222). All of this alienated Egyptian populations from Ismail. See also Robinson and Gallagher, *Africa*, 85–7.

13 Egyptian soldiers were particularly frustrated with receiving low wages, being relegated to lower ranks, and being generally ill-treated by their Turco-Circassian officers. See H.A. Ibrahim, "African Initiatives and Resistance in North-East Africa," in *General History of Africa*, vol. 6, *Africa under Colonial Domination, 1880–1935*, ed. A. Adu Boahen (Berkeley: University of California Press, 1985), 63–5, and Snook, *Into the Jaws*, 222.

14 Robinson and Gallagher, *Africa*, 113.

15 Ibid., 122–4.

16 Charles Gordon, *The Journals of Major-Gen. C.G. Gordon at Khartoum* (London: Keagan Paul, Trench, 1885), 113.

17 Ibrahim, "African Initiatives," 74.

18 William Hicks was a retired British officer who had served in India. The Egyptian Khedive, unable to procure official British military support, hired a number of experienced European officers under contract, including Hicks.

19 By April 1885, the cabinet would recognize that they had overestimated Mahdist intentions to invade Egypt (Robinson and Gallagher, *Africa*, 155).

20 The first public suggestion that Gordon was the man to save the garrison, however, came from Samuel Baker's letter to the editor of the *Times*, printed on 1 January 1884. Subsequently, the *Pall Mall Gazette* published an interview between editor and political journalist W.T. Stead and General Gordon, who spoke about potential strategies in Sudan. Following this, numerous enthusiastic calls for Gordon's involvement appeared in the papers. The cabinet, finding no other appealing solution, and certainly not one so inexpensive, appeased the public and asked Gordon to go to Khartoum.

21 The government directed Gordon to "consider yourself authorised and instructed to perform such other duties as the Egyptian Government may desire to entrust to you and as may be communicated by Sir E. Baring." See Mike Snook, *Beyond the Reaches of Empire: Wolseley's Failed Campaign to Save Gordon and Khartoum* (London: Frontline Books, 2013), 44. In establishing that Gordon was to report to Sir Evelyn Baring in Cairo, Whitehall attempted to distance Britain from the responsibility for Khartoum. See also Charles Chenevix Trench, *The Road to Khartoum: A Life of General Charles Gordon* (New York: Dorset Press, 1978), 248.

22 Gordon recognized that an evacuation of 15,000 people from Khartoum would take about six months, rather than the few weeks his hopeful superiors had allotted (Snook, *Into the Jaws*, 251).

23 Douglas Johnson, "The Death of Gordon: A Victorian Myth," *Journal of Commonwealth History* 10, no. 3 (1982): 300.

24 *Western Mail*, 6 Feb. 1885, 3.
25 See Chenevix Trench, *Road*, 253; Snook, *Beyond*, 93.
26 Chenevix Trench, *Road*, 277.
27 Wolseley refused to use Egyptian boats to navigate the Nile, instead insisting on using Canadian voyageur boats, which, designed for the Red River, were not particularly efficient on the Nile. Furthermore, the boats had to be shipped from Canada, which augmented the delay in the troops' departure (ibid., 274).
28 Ibid., 258, 80; Snook, *Beyond*, xvii.
29 See Johnson, "Death of Gordon."
30 Robinson and Gallagher, *Africa*, 155.
31 *Daily News*, 6 Feb. 1885, 6. In the same vein, the *Western Mail* asserts, "History records no more heroic figure than that of this simple-minded, God-fearing, Christian officer, perched aloft upon his swift-footed dromedary, and riding forth … to confront the wild and barbarous hordes of the Mahdi!" Tennyson wrote an "Epitaph for Gordon" (1885):

> Warrior of God, man's friend, and tyrant's foe,
> Now somewhere dead far in the waste Soudan,
> Thou livest in all hearts, for all men know
> This earth has never borne a nobler man.

A year later, Thomas Archer wrote, "Of this hero – whose noble and simple character, and marvellous personal authority over all those who came within his influence, eminently fitted him for a leader of men … he is still the central figure in the later history of British intervention in Egypt and the Soudan. The attention of the whole civilized world has been fixed upon him, the admiration of people of every nation has been aroused by his simple, unselfish courage and devotion, and men and women throughout Europe and America have mourned his death." See Thomas Archer, *The War in Egypt and the Soudan*, vol. 1. (N.p.: Blackie, 1886), 136.
32 Fergus Nicoll, "'Truest History, Struck Off at White Heat': The Politics of Editing Gordon's Khartoum Journals," *Journal of Imperial and Commonwealth History* 38, no. 1 (2010): 23.
33 *Daily News*, 6 Feb. 1885, 5.
34 *Leeds Mercury*, 6 Feb. 1885, 8.
35 Gordon telegraphed this via Berber to Sir Evelyn Baring in Cairo on 16 April 1884 – an oft-printed message in papers reporting on the fall of Khartoum in February 1885.
36 A. Egmont Hake, "Introduction and Notes," *The Journals of Major-Gen. C.G. Gordon at Khartoum*, by Charles Gordon (London: Kegan Paul, Trench, 1885) x, xxxix.

37 Sir Henry W. Gordon, "Description of the Journal," in *The Journals of Major-Gen. C.G. Gordon at Khartoum* (London: Kegan Paul, Trench, 1885), lxiv–lxv.
38 As Alan Moorehead puts it, "There can seldom have been, at any one time, such a widely read book as [Gordon's] posthumous Khartoum Journals; they were known to every literate adult in England and established a legend which seemed to his contemporaries to be as noble as the classic heroism of St. George." See *The White Nile* (London: Hamish Hamilton, 1960), 300.
39 Hake's book tour was covertly funded by Lord Salisbury's son, Lord Cranborne, who was a Conservative parliamentary candidate and stood to gain from criticism of Gladstone. See Nicoll, "Truest History," 36.
40 Hake, "Introduction," xliii.
41 Ibid., xxxii.
42 Ibid., x.
43 See also Nicoll, "Truest History," 37–9.
44 Gordon, *Journals*, 20.
45 Ibid., 97.
46 Ibid., 390.
47 Both implicitly and explicitly, the imperial government is the primary target of Gordon's sustained attack on British gallantry; Gordon even compares Britain unfavourably with France: "I declare if they had a voice in Egypt the present state of affairs would never have existed. If you can find no chivalry in your own house, you had better borrow it from your neighbour" (*Journals*, 310–11).
48 Snook, *Beyond*, 141.
49 *Daily News*, 6 Feb. 1885, 5.
50 Gordon rounds off this particular rant by mocking his rescuers: "Tired and ill! of course I am tired and ill after bowing and swaying my body to and fro all night, with my eyes pricking like as from so many needles, from desire to sleep … I was between Scylla and Charybdis." This reference to Scylla and Charybdis, as in Haggard, figures difficulty as a fluid, sucking hole; conceptions of difficulty in the African landscape are again figured as both feminine and engulfing. See page 58 above. Gordon, *Journals*, 169.
51 Gordon seems not to hold British soldiers in high esteem generally. On 13 September, he wrote, "I think if, instead of 'Minor Tactics' or books on art of war, we were to make our young officers study 'Plutarch's Lives,' it would be better; there we see men … making, as a matter of course, their lives a sacrifice, but in our days it is the highest merit not to run away" (*Journals*, 26). Referencing the first-century study of Greek and Roman heroism, Gordon finds contemporary martial valour wanting in comparison. The Khartoum journals' continued use of *Lives* as a yardstick for measuring the diminishment of imperial masculinity is symptomatic of a broader cultural fixation on the degeneration of manhood that would become increasingly common in the fin de siècle.

52 Gordon, *Journals*, 90.
53 Ibid., 307.
54 Stewart and Frank Power were killed in an ambush after their steamer ran aground.
55 Gordon, *Journals*, 310.
56 This "pruning" or editing, however, did not happen; according to Henry Gordon, only six or seven pages were omitted. Gordon, "Description," lxv.
57 Gordon was at times convinced that Whitehall wanted to see him fail and to see Khartoum lost so that no reinforcements had to be sent. Nicoll goes on, "In the untidy pages of the original manuscript – written, in the terminal stages of the siege, on the backs of Egyptian Telegraph Service forms and bound in improvised cardboard covers – we find a man endlessly rehearsing arguments for and against retreat, surrender, a British rescue mission, resignation of his commission, an Ottoman mercenary expedition paid for by American millionaires, even suicide." "Truest History," 27.
58 See Richard Davenport-Hines, "Gordon, Charles George," *Oxford Dictionary of National Biography*, 2004; Chenevix Trench, *Road*, 268.
59 Laura Otis, *Membranes: Metaphors of Invasion in Nineteenth-Century Literature, Science, and Politics* (Baltimore, MD: Johns Hopkins University Press, 1999), 5–6.
60 Ibid., 7.
61 Chenevix Trench, *Road*, 239; Snook, *Beyond*, 65.
62 See Gordon, *Journals*, 133.
63 Ibid., 172.
64 Ibid., 33, 47, 63, 110, 134, 158, 268, 270.
65 Ibid., 158.
66 Ibid., 153–4.
67 Snook describes Khartoum's land defences as follows: "Contrary to 'movie history' there were no great city walls sealing off the apex of the *jazīra* [the peninsula between the Blue and White Nile] … Rather, the 6,000 yards of 'South Front' consisted successively of a dry ditch, a berm and an earthen rampart with a firing-step. The ditch was six to eight feet deep, and about 10 feet wide and would not lightly be crossed under a heavy fire. The berm behind it was designed to protect the base of the rampart from artillery fire and was about three feet thick. The main rampart and firing-step had been raised from the spoil of the excavated ditch and was around seven feet high and up to fourteen feet thick. It incorporated three gates and four large protruding bastions to facilitate enfilading fire. In front of the ditch there were successively … a thick belt of broken bottles and spiked iron 'crow's feet,' a minefield of fuse-wire or pressure-initiated explosive charges and a low wire entanglement" (*Beyond*, 68–9).

68 This led imperial authorities to consider "that the Nile route virtually stands condemned, both on account of the length of time occupied in traversing it, and the difficulties to be encountered" (*Birmingham Daily Post*, 6 Feb 1885, 5).
69 Gordon, *Journals*, 196.
70 Theweleit, *Male Fantasies*, 244.
71 Gordon, *Journals*, 117.
72 Ibid., 395. He's berating the government for not investing in spies.
73 Favret, *War*, 65.
74 Gordon, *Journals*, 289.
75 Favret, *War*, 80.
76 Ibid., 74.
77 Gordon, *Journals*, 393.
78 Ibid., 316.
79 Thomas Richards addresses this attempt to supplement gaps in knowledge through the endless recording of census information, statistics, and geographical data; see *Imperial Archive*, 3.
80 For discussions of the complex and yet co-authorizing relationship between empire and the press, see Chandrika Kaul, ed., *Media and the British Empire* (Houndmills, UK: Palgrave Macmillan, 2006), 3–8; John M. MacKenzie, "The Press and Empire" in *Newspapers and Empire in Ireland and Britain: Reporting the British Empire, c. 1857–1921*, ed. Simon J. Potter (Dublin: Four Courts Press, 2004), 23–38; Simon J. Potter, "Empire and the English Press, *c.* 1857–1914," in *Newspapers and Empire in Ireland and Britain*, 43–8; Donald Read, *The Power of News: The History of Reuters, 1849–1989* (New York: Oxford University Press, 1992), 30, 40–69; John M. MacKenzie, *Propaganda and Empire: The Manipulation of Public Opinion, 1880–1960* (Manchester: Manchester University Press, 1984), 3, 6–7, 25–6.
81 Robert Heilman, quoted in Eve Kosofsky Sedgwick, *The Coherence of Gothic Conventions* (1980; North Stratford, UK: Ayer Company Publishers, 1999), 1.
82 See Sedgwick, *Coherence*, 8.
83 For the characteristics of the Gothic, see also Cannon Schmitt, *Alien Nation: Nineteenth-Century Gothic Fictions and English Nationality* (Philadelphia: University of Pennsylvania Press, 1997), 6–7.
84 See Kelly Hurley, *The Gothic Body: Sexuality, Materialism, and Degeneration at the Fin de Siècle* (Cambridge: Cambridge University Press, 1999), 3–16.
85 *Birmingham Daily Post*, 6 Feb. 1885, 5; *Bristol Mercury and Daily Post*, 6 Feb. 1885, 8; *Hampshire Telegraph and Sussex Chronicle*, 7 Feb. 1885, 5; *Ipswich Journal, and Suffolk, Norfolk, Essex, and Cambridgeshire Advertiser*, 7 Feb. 1885, 6; *Liverpool Mercury*, 6 Feb. 1885, 6; *Liverpool Mercury*, 7 Feb. 1885, 6; *Morning Post*, 6 Feb. 1885, 5; *Standard*, 6 Feb. 1885, 5; *Star*, 7 Feb. 1885, 1; *Western Mail*, 7 Feb. 1885, 3; *York Herald*, 6 Feb. 1885, 5.

86 *Pall Mall Gazette*, 5 Feb. 1885, 9; *Aberdeen Weekly Journal*, 6 Feb. 1885, 6; *Aberdeen Weekly Journal*, 7 Feb. 1885, 8; *Leeds Mercury*, 6 Feb. 1885, 8; *Freeman's Journal*, 7 Feb. 1885, 5; *Northern Echo*, 7 Feb. 1885, 3; *Liverpool Mercury*, 6 Feb. 1885, 6.

87 *Western Mail*, 6 Feb. 1885, 3.

88 *Manchester Courier and Lancashire General Advertiser*, 6 Feb. 1885, 6.

89 *Liverpool Mercury*, 6 Feb. 1885, 6; *Northern Echo*, 6 Feb. 1885, 3.

90 *Freeman's Journal and Daily Commercial Advertiser*, 6 Feb. 1885, 6.

91 *Western Mail*, 6 Feb. 1885, 3; *Birmingham Daily Post*, 6 Feb. 1885, 5.

92 *Daily News*, 6 Feb. 1885, 6. In the same spirit, the *Daily News* took the opportunity to announce an exhibition of Sudanese weaponry at the Gallery of National History in Piccadilly.

93 *Aberdeen Weekly Journal*, 6 Feb. 1885, 6.

94 The *Daily News* even described very similar mourning in major cities across the nation in alphabetical order (6 Feb. 1885, 6). Local papers followed suit. See especially *Aberdeen Weekly Journal*, 6 Feb. 1885, 6, and *Belfast News-Letter*, 6 Feb. 1885, 5.

95 For example, Mancunians read that "the editions of the evening papers were sold with astonishing rapidity"; that the news left "a profound impression at Leicester"; and that "a feeling of intense anxiety has been manifested at Chester all day." British alarm was portrayed as communal: the news "caused the greatest possible excitement at Liverpool"; "At Sheffield the news produced a painful impression, and both political parties there regard the disaster as of the gravest character"; "At Aldershot the news was received with mingled feelings of sadness and indignation"; "At Woolwich great consternation prevailed"; "In the Potteries, and at Hanley and Stoke particularly, the information was received amid great excitement, … universal sorrow being expressed at the defeat of General Gordon … At Luton, Dunstable, Exeter, Plymouth, and Ipswich the news created a great sensation" (*Manchester Courier and Lancaster General Advertiser*, 6 Feb. 1885, 6). See also the *Aberdeen Weekly Journal*, 6 Feb. 1885, 5.

96 *Aberdeen Weekly Journal*, 6 Feb. 1885, 6; *Belfast News-Letter*, 6 Feb. 1885, 5.

97 *Liverpool Mercury*, 7 Feb. 1885, 6.

98 Benedict Anderson, *Imagined Communities: Reflections on the Origin and Spread of Nationalism*, 2nd ed. (London: Verso, 2006), 7.

99 *Daily News*, 6 Feb. 1885, 5.

100 *Birmingham Daily Post*, 6 Feb. 1885, 5.

101 *Daily News*, 6 Feb. 1885, 6, quoting the *Soir* (Paris).

102 *Aberdeen Weekly Journal*, 6 Feb. 1885, 6. A report from Alexandria also claimed that "the news of the fall of Khartoum has cast a gloom over the entire European colony" (*Daily News*, 6 Feb. 1885, 6). In St Petersburg,

"The news … has produced a deep and painful impression here. Everyone hopes that the English hero's life is safe" (*Birmingham Daily Post*, 6 Feb. 1885, 5; *Daily News*, 7 Feb. 1885, 5). In Madrid, "The fall of Khartoum and the capture of General Gordon have caused a profound sensation … Great anxiety is expressed by all respecting the General's fate" (*Bristol Mercury and Daily Post*, 7 Feb. 1885, 6). In Rome, "The news of the fall of Khartoum has produced a profound impression among all classes here" (*York Herald*, 7 Feb. 1885, 5).

103 *Glasgow Herald*, 7 Feb. 1885, 5. The article went on: "The *Republique Français* criticises English policy … The *Temps* finds the disaster an unprecedented one, and is doubtful whether the Gladstone Cabinet will not succumb under the pressure of public opinion."

104 *Glasgow Herald*, 7 Feb. 1885, 5.

105 *Leeds Mercury*, 7 Feb. 1885, 3.

106 Ibid., 6.

107 *Morning Post*, 7 Feb. 1885, 5; *Birmingham Daily Post*, 6 Feb. 1885, 4; *Belfast News-Letter*, 7 Feb. 1885, 5; *Dundee Courier and Argus*, 7 Feb. 1885, 3; *Glasgow Herald*, 7 Feb. 1885, 5; *York Herald*, 7 Feb. 1885, 5.

108 See the *Daily News*, 6 Feb. 1885, 6; *Bristol Mercury and Daily Post*, 7 Feb. 1885, 6; and *Western Mail*, 7 Feb. 1885, 3. Similarly, the *Hampshire Telegraph and Sussex Chronicle* and the *York Herald* offered: "Rumours circulated that 2,000 persons were massacred at Khartoum" (*Hampshire Telegraph and Sussex Chronicle*, 7 Feb. 1885, 5; *York Herald*, 7 Feb. 1885, 7).

109 The Egyptian soldiers, Shagiya, and Bashi-bazouks, all serving under Gordon's command, were all massacred. See Chenevix Trench, *Road*, 290. See John Waller, *Gordon of Khartoum* (New York: Atheneum, 1988), 442–4 for a description of the brutal fate of foreigners. Total numbers of people slaughtered in the invasion are estimated at between 4,000 and 10,000. See Moorehead, *White Nile*, 268; Waller, *Gordon*, 444.

110 That is, of the Khedivate. *Birmingham Daily Post*, 6 Feb. 1885, 5.

111 *Manchester Courier*, 6 Feb. 1885, 5; *Aberdeen Weekly Journal*, 6 Feb. 1885, 5; *Belfast News-Letter*, 6 Feb. 1885, 5; *Western Mail*, 6 Feb. 1885, 3.

112 Hurley, *Gothic Body*, 5.

113 *Aberdeen Weekly Journal*, 6 Feb. 1885, 5; *Belfast News-Letter*, 6 Feb. 1885, 5. See also *Berrow's Worcester Journal*, 7 Feb. 1885, 5; *Freeman's Journal*, 7 Feb. 1885, 5; *Ipswich Journal, and Suffolk, Norfolk, Essex, and Cambridgeshire Advertiser*, 7 Feb. 1885, 6; *Lancaster Gazette and General Advertiser for Lancashire, Westmorland, and Yorkshire*, 7 Feb. 1885, 5; *Leicester Chronicle and the Leicester Mercury*, 7 Feb. 1885, 5; *North Wales Chronicle*, 6 Feb. 1885, 5 and 7 Feb. 1885, 5; *Standard*, 7 Feb. 1885, 4; *Star*, 7 Feb 1885, 1; *Western Mail*, 7 Feb. 1885, 3; *Wrexham Advertiser and North Wales News*, 7 Feb. 1885, 7; *Dundee Courier and Argus*, 7 Feb. 1885, 3.

114 *Pall Mall Gazette*, quoted in *Manchester Courier and Lancaster General Advertiser*, 6 Feb. 1885, 6.

115 *Pall Mall Gazette*, 6 Feb. and 5 Feb. 1885, 1. The earlier article even suggested, "It is believed he has his provisions stored there as well as ammunition, and it is known that he has small pieces of artillery there."

116 *Pall Mall Gazette*, 6 Feb. 1885, 8.

117 *Birmingham Daily Post*, 6 Feb. 1885, 5. Other papers also offered some sanguine visions of the state of affairs, stating that "it is still believed by many of the officials at the War-office that there is a great possibility of Gordon having escaped from Khartoum, and that news may at any moment arrive of his safety" (*Morning Post*, 7 Feb. 1885, 5), and that "a strange hope was still cherished that by some supernatural intervention the life of the brave general would be saved" (*Aberdeen Weekly Journal*, 6 Feb. 1885, 5).

118 "The excitement in London during the day grew in intensity, and the utmost eagerness was shown in buying up the numerous editions of the morning and evening papers, but the later editions contained no fresh news beyond that given in the War Office summary of Lord Wolseley's despatch" (*Belfast News-Letter*, 6 Feb. 1885, 5).

119 *Freeman's Journal and Daily Commercial Advertiser*, 6 Feb. 1885, 4. This Dublin paper also took a more critical standpoint than its English counterparts, in part because Ireland's relation to the situation in Khartoum was complex. On one hand, *Freeman's* was very sympathetic to the Nile Expedition in particular, as a number of Irish soldiers were serving on it. On the other, the publication, informed by Ireland's own fraught history with England, recognized the Sudanese as "a people 'struggling to be free'" (6 Feb. 1885, 6). *Freeman's* was critical of Britain's imperial investment in Khartoum, and was attuned to the fragility of imperial ideology: "It is whispered that the letters recently received purporting to be from Gordon were forgeries and stratagems to deceive the British as to the actual crisis at Khartoum. If they were, similar tactics are now pursued in Egypt itself by the British, for we learn that the news of the fall of Khartoum, though known in London, was kept dark in Cairo. The mystery shows how ticklish, so to speak, the British position is all over the principality" (6 Feb. 1885, 4). The issue went on to protest the military's censorship of press correspondents at the front. *Freeman's* was also pointedly less reverent of Gordon than were the English papers, frequently labelling him a "fanatic" (6 Feb. 1885, 4) and criticizing his decision to remain in Khartoum.

120 *Daily Chronicle*, quoted in *Pall Mall Gazette*, 7 Feb. 1885, 8.

121 *Dundee Courier and Argus*, 6 Feb. 1885, 5.

122 The *Ipswich Journal* decided that "England [was] cursed" with the Gladstone government (*Ipswich Journal, and Suffolk, Norfolk, Essex, and Cambridgeshire Advertiser*, 7 Feb. 1885, 4); the *Huddersfield Daily Chronicle* resorted to the abstraction of "evil" in describing the defeat (6 Feb. 1885, 3; see also the *Ipswich Journal, and Suffolk, Norfolk, Essex, and Cambridgeshire Advertiser*, 7 Feb. 1885, 6); and the *Leeds Mercury* suggested that an "evil destiny … for the moment seems to have over taken our great enterprise" (7 Feb. 1885, 6).

123 *Northern Echo*, 7 Feb. 1885, 3; *Bristol Mercury and Daily Post*, 7 Feb. 1885, 5; *Freeman's Journal*, 7 Feb. 1885, 4.

124 *Morning Post*, 6 Feb. 1885, 5, quoting Colonel Walroud, who spoke at Tiverton on 5 February; *Ipswich Journal, and Suffolk, Norfolk, Essex, and Cambridgeshire Advertiser*, 7 Feb. 1885, 4; *Freeman's Journal*, 7 Feb. 1885, 4.

125 *Bristol Mercury and Daily Post*, 7 Feb. 1885, 5.

126 "Ghoul," *Oxford American Dictionary*.

127 The *Pall Mall Gazette* point-blank asserted that Khartoum "fell by treachery on the 26th of January, 1885" (6 Feb. 1885, 4), and even named the supposed traitor: "One Faraz Pasha was the man who opened the gates, and he probably was with Gordon from the first" (6 Feb. 1885, 5). For similar assertions, see the *Birmingham Daily Post*, 6 Feb. 1885, 5; *Daily News*, 6 Feb. 1885, 5; *York Herald*, 6 Feb. 1885, 4; and *Leicester Chronicle and the Leicester Mercury*, 7 Feb. 1885, 5. One exception to the treachery fantasy was Dublin's *Freeman's Journal*'s suggestion that betrayal in Khartoum was "unlikely"; its writer opined (correctly) that, with British reinforcements closing in, the Mahdi abandoned the strategy of starving Khartoum out and executed "a *coup de main*" (6 Feb. 1885, 5). Ireland, being on the periphery of the framework of imperial desire that fabricated the story of double-crossing, did not have the same investment that Britain did in impermeable fortifications of the outpost. One reason for the general assumption of treachery was that the British had received at Metemmeh Gordon's misleading message, scrawled on 29 December, "Khartoum all right, could hold out for years" (Chenevix Trench, *Road*, 284) and concluded that betrayal was the reason for the sudden twist of fate. The *Northern Echo* summed up this perspective, insisting the fall "is indeed inexplicable under any other hypothesis" (6 Feb. 1885, 3).

128 *Preston Chronicle and Lancashire Advertiser*, 7 Feb. 1885, 7.

129 Chenevix Trench, *Road*, 290.

130 *Birmingham Daily Post*, 6 Feb. 1885, 5.

131 *Belfast News-Letter*, 7 Feb. 1885, 5; *Bristol Mercury and Daily Post*, 7 Feb. 1885, 6; *Preston Chronicle and Lancashire Advertiser*, 7 Feb. 1885, 7.

132 "The city is said to have been in possession of the Mahdi who had sent messages in General Gordon's name to lure Wolseley on … it should not be forgotten that proficiency in artifice and stratagem has always been a distinguishing Oriental characteristic" (*Freeman's Journal*, 7 Feb. 1885, 7). This plot thus also othered the Mahdi while emphasizing the danger to Wolseley's men: "It was the wily calculation of the Soudanese Chief to keep General Gordon as an inducement to lure on the British army into a difficult and perilous position" (*Morning Post*, 6 Feb. 1885, 4; *Standard*, 7 Feb. 1885, 5). See also *Morning Post*, 7 Feb. 1885, 5; *Birmingham Daily Post*, 7 Feb. 1885, 5; *Bristol Mercury and Daily Post*, 6 Feb. 1885, 8; and *Leeds Mercury*, 7 Feb. 1885, 3.

133 As Johannes Fabian has shown, this denial that indigenous people were coeval worked to license colonialism. See *Time and the Other: How Anthropology Makes Its Object* (New York: Columbia University Press, 1983), esp. 27–30.

134 *Daily News*, 6 Feb. 1885, 5.

135 Ibid.

136 *Hampshire Telegraph and Sussex Chronicle*, 7 Feb. 1885, 5.

137 See also the *York Herald*, 6 Feb. 1885, 5, which also pointedly gestured to the Sudanese dynasty: "Ruins found in its [Khartoum's] neighbourhood testify not merely to the extent of the power of the Pharaohs, but also to the antiquity of its claims to be considered the most advantageous site for a city."

138 *Berrow's Worcester Journal*, 7 Feb. 1885, 4. Again, there is insistence on treachery.

139 *Manchester Weekly Times*, 7 Feb. 1885, 4; *Wrexham Advertiser and North Wales News*, 7 Feb. 1885, 6.

140 Britons read about "hordes of Islam" (*Times*, reprinted in *Hampshire Advertiser*, 7 Feb. 1885, 7); "hordes of warriors" (*Freeman's Journal and Daily Commercial Advertiser*, 6 Feb. 1885, 5); "hordes of barbarians" (*Northern Echo*, 7 Feb. 1885, 3); "advancing hordes" (*Pall Mall Gazette*, 6 Feb. 1885, 8); "swarming hordes" (*Standard*, 6 Feb. 1885, 5); "hordes of rebels" (*Freeman's Journal and Daily Commercial Advertiser*, 6 Feb. 1885, 5; *Western Mail*, 6 Feb. 1885, 3); "fanatical hordes" (*Aberdeen Weekly Journal*, 6 Feb. 1885, 5; *Belfast News-Letter*, 6 Feb. 1885, 5; *Manchester Courier and Lancashire General Advertiser*, 6 Feb. 1885, 5; *Western Mail*, 6 Feb. 1885, 3; *Bristol Mercury and Daily Post*, 7 Feb. 1885, 5; and *Preston Chronicle and Lancashire Advertiser*, 7 Feb. 1885, 7); "hordes of fanatical rebels" (*Leeds Mercury*, 6 Feb. 1885, 8; *Glasgow Herald*, 6 Feb. 1885, 7); and finally, "immense hordes of enthusiastic fanatics" (*Leeds Mercury*, 6 Feb. 1885, 8), to name only a few. The partial exception that proves the rule is Irish

MP James O'Kelly's article in Dublin's *Freeman's Journal*: "The persistent and absurd newspaper talk of the Arabs as savages has been another element of the want of a correct view of the matter. As a matter of fact, the ordinary Arab is much more of a gentleman in his manners and feelings than most members of the British Parliament" (6 Feb. 1885, 5), although this may also simply be a dig at British MPs.

141 *Leeds Mercury*, 7 Feb. 1885, 3.

142 *Belfast News-Letter*, 7 Feb. 1885, 5; *Freeman's Journal*, 7 Feb. 1885, 5.

143 *Northern Echo*, 6 Feb. 1885, 3.

144 *Aberdeen Weekly Journal*, 7 Feb. 1885, 4; *Huddersfield Daily Chronicle*, 6 Feb. 1885, 4; *Huddersfield Daily Chronicle*, 7 Feb. 1885, 3.

145 *Huddersfield Daily Chronicle*, 7 Feb. 1885, 3.

146 *Daily News*, 6 Feb. 1885, 5; *Hampshire Telegraph and Sussex Chronicle*, 7 Feb. 1885, 5. See also *Freeman's Journal and Daily Commercial Advertiser*, 6 Feb. 1885, 6; *Liverpool Mercury*, 6 Feb. 1885, 5.

147 *Pall Mall Gazette*, 5 Feb. 1885, 1.

148 *Leeds Mercury*, 6 Feb. 1885, 8; *Glasgow Herald*, 6 Feb. 1885, 7,

149 Moodie, *Zulu*, 139, quoting from *Pearson's Magazine*, "The Bravery of Colonel Buller." See chapter 1 above, page 32.

150 *Morning Post*, 6 Feb. 1885, 4.

151 *Standard*, 6 Feb. 1885, 5.

152 *Daily Telegraph*, reprinted in the *Aberdeen Weekly Journal*, 6 Feb. 1885, 5 and 7 Feb. 1885, 8; *Western Mail*, 6 Feb. 1885, 3.

153 Importantly, Gordon's mythologization is bound up with his sacrifice – Gordon the myth is inseparable from the idea of death, and his death was what most strongly ratified his heroic status.

154 *Birmingham Daily Post*, 6 Feb. 1885, 5, reprinted from *Pall Mall Gazette*.

155 *Ipswich Journal, and Suffolk, Norfolk, Essex, and Cambridgeshire Advertiser*, 7 Feb. 1885, 6. The *Pall Mall Gazette* reported the Bishop of Carlisle's address at Marylebone Church: "what made [Gordon's] condition so sad was that he had been practically alone, without any friend with whom he might consult to support him" (*Pall Mall Gazette*, 6 Feb. 1885, 7).

156 *Bristol Mercury and Daily Post*, 7 Feb. 1885, 6; *Northern Echo*, 6 Feb. 1885, 3.

157 *Aberdeen Weekly Journal*, 7 Feb. 1885, 8.

158 *Northern Echo*, 6 Feb. 1885, 3.

159 *Aberdeen Weekly Journal*, 6 Feb. 1885, 5. Invoking such language of saintliness, the metropole often projected this understanding of Gordon as a "holy man" onto the Sudanese's conception of him (*Berrow's Worcester Journal*, 7 Feb. 1885, 5; *Hampshire Telegraph and Sussex Chronicle*, 7 Feb. 1885, 5; *Lancaster Gazette and General Advertiser for Lancashire, Westmorland, and Yorkshire*, 7 Feb. 1885, 5; *Leicester Chronicle and the*

Leicester Mercury, 7 Feb. 1885, 5; *Standard*, 6 Feb. 1885, 5; *Star*, 7 Feb. 1885, 1; *Wrexham Advertiser and North Wales News*, 7 Feb. 1885, 7; *Aberdeen Weekly Journal*, 6 Feb. 1885, 5). Copious papers asserted that "Gordon has been revered by the Soudanis, as a man whose word is truth, … who is inspired by Heaven" (*Daily News*, 7 Feb. 1885, 5) and "whose life and person were sacred" (*Glasgow Herald*, 6 Feb. 1885, 7).

160 *Bristol Mercury and Daily Post*, 7 Feb. 1885, 6, quoting a letter from General Gordon to his sister.

161 *Pall Mall Gazette*, 5 Feb. 1885, 1. "On the 14th of December a letter was received by one of his friends in Cairo from General Gordon, saying, 'Farewell. You will never hear from me again. I fear that there will be treachery in the garrison' … Of the origin of this foreboding nothing is known" (*Pall Mall Gazette*, 6 Feb. 1885, 5).

162 *Liverpool Mercury*, 6 Feb. 1885, 5.

163 *Morning Post*, 6 Feb. 1885, 4.

164 Quoted in *Pall Mall Gazette*, 6 Feb. 1885, 11.

165 *Dundee Courier and Argus*, 6 Feb. 1885, 2.

166 *Dundee Courier and Argus*, 6 Feb. 1885, 5. "Transpontine" refers to the melodramatic and sensational styles of the theatres on the Surrey side of the Thames.

167 *Standard*, 7 Feb. 1885, 5, quoting the *Soleil* (Orléans).

168 *Pall Mall Gazette*, 7 Feb. 1885, 11, quoting the *Economist*.

169 *Daily News*, 7 Feb. 1885, 5, quoting with relish the *Deutsche Zeitung*.

170 *Daily News*, 7 Feb. 1885, 5, quoting from the *National Zeitung* in Berlin.

171 *Morning Advertiser*, quoted in *Pall Mall Gazette*, 6 Feb. 1885, 11.

172 *Pall Mall Gazette*, 5 Feb. 1885, 1. The Sudan traveller Mr O'Kelly asserted, "It would be almost impossible to over-estimate the importance of the capture of Khartoum and the over-throw of General Gordon … No defeat of modern times has been so fraught with danger to the Empire" (*Morning Post*, 7 Feb. 1885, 5).

173 *Leeds Mercury*, 7 Feb. 1885, 6. See also *Pall Mall Gazette*, 5 Feb. 1885, 1.

174 *Glasgow Herald*, 6 Feb. 1885, 7; *Hampshire Advertiser*, 7 Feb. 1885, 4; *Huddersfield Daily Chronicle*, 6 Feb. 1885, 4; *Western Mail*, 7 Feb. 1885, 3; *York Herald*, 7 Feb. 1885, 5; *Hampshire Telegraph and Sussex Chronicle*, 7 Feb. 1885, 1, 5; *Liverpool Mercury*, 6 Feb. 1885, 6; *Northern Echo*, 6 Feb. 1885, 3; *Freeman's Journal*, 7 Feb. 1885, 4; *Birmingham Daily Post*, 6 Feb. 1885, 5; *Dundee Courier and Argus*, 7 Feb. 1885, 3; *Bristol Mercury and Daily Post*, 6 Feb. 1885, 8, and 7 Feb. 1885, 6; *Morning Post*, 7 Feb. 1885, 5; *Daily News*, 7 Feb. 1885, 3; *Pall Mall Gazette*, 7 Feb. 1885, 6.

175 Russia invaded this area of Afghanistan, too closely approaching British interests in India for imperial comfort.

176 See also Brantlinger, *Rule*, and Arata, *Fictions*.

4 Marsh's Perforations: Desire, Imperial Decay, and the Narrative Instability of *The Beetle*

1 An earlier version of the argument presented in this chapter appears in Leslie Allin, "Leaky Bodies: Masculinity, Narrative, and Imperial Decay in Richard Marsh's *The Beetle*," *Victorian Network* 6, no. 1 (2015).
2 John Tosh, *Manliness and Masculinities in Nineteenth-Century Britain* (Harlow, UK: Pearson Education, 2005), 195.
3 Gilbert and Gubar, *No Man's Land*, 26.
4 See Edward Blyden, *From West Africa to Palestine* (1873) in *Black Spokesman: Selected Published Works of E.W. Blyden*, ed. Hollis Lynch (New York: Humanities Press, 1971), especially his call to his "countrymen" to "retake your fame" (152).
5 See Bulfin, "Fiction of Gothic Egypt," 411–43.
6 All three works were incredibly successful commercially and widely read. Haggard's imperial romances sold extraordinarily well: *King Solomon's Mines* sold 31,000 copies in its first year of publication (Monsman, "Introduction," 12), and *She* 30,000 in the first few months (Cohen, *Rider Haggard*, 232). *The Beetle* proved to be a very popular work similarly attuned to its audience's interests, reaching fifteen printings by 1915. See Julian Wolfreys, Introduction to *The Beetle*, by Richard Marsh (1897; Peterborough, ON: Broadview, 2004), 11.
7 J. Tenniel and J. Swain, "In the Desert! Shade of General Gordon (*to* John Bull). 'Remember!'" *Punch* 110, 28 March 1896, 151. Ailise Bulfin, "'In That Egyptian Den': Situating *The Beetle* within the Fin-de-siècle Fiction of Gothic Egypt," in *Richard Marsh, Popular Fiction, and Literary Culture, 1890–1915*, ed. Victoria Margree, Daniel Orrells, Minna Vuohelainen (Manchester: Manchester University Press, 2018), 127.
8 Marsh's focus on topical subjects is well known: "Marsh … constantly referenced Britain's imperial engagements in fictions that probed their significance for 'home'" (Victoria Margree, Daniel Orrells, and Minna Vuohelainen, "Introduction," in *Richard Marsh, Popular Fiction, and Literary Culture, 1890–1915* (Manchester: Manchester University Press, 2018, 14). And as John Höglund writes, "Relying on his sensitivity to popular discourses to sell his novels, Marsh was a writer who kept in close touch with his day and age and who tapped into the many debates of his time" ("Black Englishness and the Concurrent Voices of Richard Marsh in *The Surprising Husband*," *English Literature in History* 56, no. 3 (2013): 277). The "reconquest" of Sudan was no exception. Ailise Bulfin also makes the point that Wadi Halfa and Dongola would have been immediately recognizable to Victorian readerships as sites where British garrisons had been established; Marsh thus explicitly connects events in his novel to events in the Sudan campaign ("'In That Egyptian Den,'" 140).

9 W.C. Harris and Dawn Vernooy, "'Orgies of Nameless Horrors': Gender, Orientalism, and the Queering of Violence in Richard Marsh's *The Beetle*," *Papers in Language and Literature* 48, no. 4 (2012): 369.
10 Arata thus describes the libidinal aspects of reading: the deferral, deciphering, and grasping of textual information (*Fictions*, 68–9).
11 Jennifer McCollum and Victoria Margree read Lessingham in precisely this way. See Jennifer McCollum, "Animation and Reanimation in the Victorian Gothic" (PhD diss., University of Washington, 2012), 180; Victoria Margree, "'Both in Men's Clothing': Gender, Sovereignty and Insecurity in Richard Marsh's *The Beetle*," *Critical Survey* 19, no. 2 (2007): 77.
12 Richard Marsh, *The Beetle*, ed. Julian Wolfreys (1897; Peterborough, ON: Broadview, 2004), 315.
13 For instance, Kelly Hurley adopts an Orientalist reading of *The Beetle*, suggesting that "textual stereotypes that construct the oriental as 'Other' serve a unifying function for the culture that produces them, a culture which, in the service of a coherent and idealized self-definition, denies those qualities that threaten or undermine its own self-image and projects them onto extracultural groups … A paranoiac text like *The Beetle* serves to reflect and feed into British suspicion of contempt for Egyptians during a period of heightened British military activity in Egypt." See "'The Inner Chambers of All Nameless Sin': *The Beetle*, Gothic Female Sexuality, and Oriental Barbarism," in *Virginal Sexuality and Textuality in Victorian Literature*, ed. Lloyd Davis (Albany: New York University Press, 1993), 196–7. See also Margree, "'Both in Men's Clothing.'" Wolfreys is less condemning than Hurley, arguing that "the human-scarab pursues the politician Paul Lessingham, less from some irrational and barbaric Oriental blood-lust, than out of a sense of injustice for the 'barbaric' English defilement of ancient Egypt's sacred locations" (Introduction, 24).
14 Elizabeth Grosz, *Volatile Bodies: Toward a Corporeal Feminism* (Bloomington: Indiana University Press, 1994), 203.
15 As Hurley rightly points out, "the novel even indulges in the traditional comic ending of a triple marriage" ("Inner Chambers," 207) – that is, Paul/Marjorie, Sydney/Dora, and Percy/Dora's bridesmaid form couples.
16 Ibid.; Marsh, *Beetle*, 48, 70, and 293.
17 As Wolfreys explains, "mesmerism is analogous with sexual penetration" (Introduction, 13). Natasha Rebry expands: "Mesmeric practice came to symbolically stand in for a number of social issues ranging from the nature of gender roles to questions of national identity to the strength of individual character." See Rebry's "Disintegrated Subjects: Gothic Fiction, Mental Science and the Fin-de-siècle Discourse of Dissociation" (PhD diss., University of British Columbia, 2013), 139.
18 Marsh, *Beetle*, 53.

19 Ibid., 151.
20 Ibid., 61.
21 Ibid., 140.
22 Ibid., 85.
23 Ibid., 85, 86.
24 Ibid., 183.
25 Wolfreys, Introduction, 19.
26 Ibid.
27 The spectre of the working woman, who took up positions of typist and secretary, and threatened the economic position of men who held those jobs, is implied here. See Daly, *Modernism*, 8; Michael Roper and John Tosh, "Introduction: Historians and the Politics of Masculinity," in *Manful Assertions: Masculinities in Britain since 1800*, ed. Michael Roper and John Tosh (London: Routledge, 1991), 19. As critics have variously noted, Marjorie Lindon, a New Woman, exposes the dissolution of masculinity because she is able to ridicule it, infantilize it, and inhabit it; through her, boundaries of embodied gender, both physical and constructed, deteriorate.
28 McCollum, "Animation," 183.
29 Marsh, *Beetle*, 49.
30 Ibid.
31 Ibid.
32 Ibid., 50.
33 Ibid., 51.
34 Ibid., 52.
35 Ibid., 243–5.
36 Ibid., 52.
37 Ibid., 52, 55.
38 Ibid., 76.
39 Ibid., 84.
40 Roger Luckhurst points out that Holt's demise entails being "sucked dry of his vital juices," and that Holt effectively becomes mummified. See *The Mummy's Curse: The True History of a Dark Fantasy* (Oxford: Oxford University Press, 2012), 172. I think another implication of this desiccation is that the internal regulation of Holt's "innate male energy" (Sussman, *Victorian Masculinities*, 3) – the figuration of his manhood – is fully defunct.
41 Minna Vuohelainen in "'Cribb'd, Cabined, and Confined': Fear, Claustrophobia and Modernity in Richard Marsh's Urban Gothic Fiction," *Journal of Literature and Science* 3, no. 1 (2010): 30–1 makes the point that, in this novel, the city of London seems to shrink around and envelope characters through fog, rain, and wind, thus employing the Gothic motif of spatial transgression, but I would also suggest that these elements work to saturate the body and thus threaten its borders.

42 Marsh, *Beetle*, 49.
43 Ibid., 53.
44 Ibid., 240.
45 Minna Vuohelainen, "'You Know Not of What You Speak': Language, Identity, and Xenophobia in Richard Marsh's *The Beetle: A Mystery* (1897)," in *Fear, Loathing, and Victorian Xenophobia*, ed. Marlene Tromp, Maria K. Bachman, and Heidi Kaufman (Columbus: Ohio State University Press, 2013), 323–5.
46 Marsh, *Beetle*, 240.
47 Ibid., 54.
48 Ibid.
49 Ibid., 105.
50 As Natasha Rebry points out, the dynamics of mesmerism were gendered: the mesmerizer was associated with active masculinity, while the mesmerized was associated with passive femininity. See "Disintegrated Subjects," 145.
51 See Margree, "'Both in Men's Clothing'," 73 for an example of this reading.
52 Marsh, *Beetle*, 102.
53 Ibid., 118.
54 Anna Maria Jones likewise finds Sydney problematic, condemning his propensity for killing street cats at random: "Arguably, a Victorian audience might have been less shocked by Atherton's impromptu animal testing than many twenty-first-century readers; however, given the popularity and visibility of the anti-vivisection movement and of the Royal Society for the Prevention of Cruelty to Animals, which had been instrumental in passing the Drugging of Animals Act (1876) and the Cruelty to Animals Act (1876), it seems likely that many of Marsh's readers would have understood Sydney's actions as at least legally culpable if not morally reprehensible." See "Conservation of Energy, Individual Agency, and Gothic Terror in Richard Marsh's *The Beetle*, or, What's Scarier Than an Ancient, Evil, Shape-shifting Bug?" *Victorian Literature and Culture* 39, no. 1 (2010): 78.
55 Ibid., 79.
56 Marsh, *Beetle*, 250.
57 Harris and Vernooy rightly point out the "homosexual undercurrent" in this and other male relationships in the text, and argue that "*the* unspeakable sin, when read and understood within the larger Victorian milieu, would have been homosexuality" ("Orgies," 352). As I have argued in my discussion of Haggard in chapter 2, the narrative's elision of an unacceptable love indicates its incompleteness, which, in the colonial context, fundamentally undercuts the imperial epistemological imperative.
58 Marsh, *Beetle*, 138, 145.
59 Ibid., 142.

60 Harris and Vernooy, "Orgies," 348–50.
61 Marsh, *Beetle*, 131, 154, 145.
62 Ibid., 146.
63 Ibid., 149–50.
64 See John E. Curran, Jr, *Hamlet, Protestantism, and the Mourning of Contingency: Not to Be* (Aldershot: Ashgate, 2006), 3–7; Ian McAdam, *Magic and Masculinity in Early Modern English Drama* (Pittsburgh: Duquesne University Press, 2009), 1.
65 Marsh, *Beetle*, 194.
66 Ibid., 155.
67 Ibid., 143.
68 Ibid., 245.
69 Ibid., 64.
70 Ibid.
71 Ibid.
72 Ibid.
73 Ibid., 64, 187.
74 Ibid., 97. This anticipates Marlow's description of the brick maker, the "papier-mâché Mephistopheles," in Conrad's *Heart of Darkness*, as hollow: "It seemed to me that if I tried I could poke my forefinger through him, and would find nothing inside but a little loose dirt, maybe" (26).
75 Marsh, *Beetle*, 251.
76 Ibid., 63, 75, 121, 158, 170; "what is known to all the world" (250).
77 Ibid., 76, 75.
78 While Vuohelainen reads Paul as being "positively defined by [his] association with language" ("You Know Not," 321), I read his rhetorical smoothness, set against his absence of substance, as suspicious.
79 Marsh, *Beetle*, 187.
80 Ibid., 87, 115, 292.
81 Ibid., 240, 241, 242.
82 Ibid., 246.
83 Ibid., 249.
84 Ibid., 243.
85 Wolfreys, Introduction, 26.
86 Marsh, *Beetle*, 253.
87 Ibid., 254.
88 Ibid., 292. Arata describes Nordau's notion of hysteria (as explored in his widely read 1895 publication, *Degeneration*) as "the last station on the road to degeneracy" (*Fictions*, 29). Paul's "hysteria," which implies narrative dissolution, thus signals the crumbling of stability.
89 Marsh, *Beetle*, 281.

90 Ibid., 265.
91 Ibid.
92 Ibid., 296.
93 Ibid., 297.
94 Ibid.
95 Ibid., 320.
96 Ibid.
97 Ibid., 319.
98 Ibid.
99 Ibid.
100 Ibid., 321.
101 Ibid., 293.
102 Ibid.
103 Vuohelainen recognizes that "*The Beetle* dwells excessively, even titillatingly, on the unseen horrors that take place inside the train compartment and the public cab" ("Cribb'd," 31); but Champnell's role in their narration is crucial.
104 Marsh, *Beetle*, 298. Given the launch of the "reconquest" of the Sudan and its wide topicality, this focus on metropolitan failure to protect a vulnerable woman resonates with the rekindled memory of Britain's failure to protect its vulnerable hero facing an Eastern African foe, General Gordon. Gordon's feminization in the press in 1885 (see pages 122–3 above) was directly bound up with the onus on Britain's martial capacity to rescue him – and of course, the consequences for both the government in 1885 and Marsh's male characters in failing to fulfill the role of protector is emasculation.
105 Ibid., 149.
106 See Luckhurst, *Mummy's Curse*, 171.
107 Marsh, *Beetle*, 244, 295. Furthermore, their brother's disfigurement signals his inability either to save them or to adequately narrate the story of what happened to them.
108 Ibid., 297.
109 Ibid., 298.
110 Arata, *Fictions*, 68.
111 Particularly in detective fiction, the delaying of conclusions and the deferral of information parallels the experience of reading. Precise details, concrete evidence, and the final climax are all continuously postponed. In this way, it is easy to read *The Beetle* as anti-climactic, with resolution being deferred even beyond the novel's conclusion.
112 Marsh, *Beetle*, 87.
113 Ibid., 80.
114 Grosz, *Volatile Bodies*, 193.

5 Bodily Disintegrations: Forensic Exposure and the Human Leopard Society in Sierra Leone

1 The Leopard Society was not the only one of its kind in West Africa. The Alligator and Baboon Societies were also active in the Sierra Leone protectorate, the Panther Society occupied the Ivory Coast, the Tiger Men Gabon, and the Lion Men Tanganyika. The Human Leopards operated in Nigeria, Liberia, the Congo, French and Portuguese Guinea, the Cameroons, Upper Volta, and Senegal, as well as in Sierra Leone. In each of these societies, members dressed as their totem animal while killing their victims, who would then be shared and eaten. These societies emerged at different times and with different intensities, although there was a marked concentration of activity in West Africa. For a detailed discussion of the regions occupied by the Leopard Men, see Birger Lindskog, *African Leopard Men* (Uppsala, SE: Studia Ethnographica Upsaliensia VII, 1954), 3–7.

2 A contraction of boreh fima, meaning "medicine bag." See K.J. Beatty, *Human Leopards: An Account of the Trials of Human Leopards before the Special Commission Court; With a Note on Sierra Leone, Past and Present* (London: Hugh Rees, 1915), 23. R.G. Berry asserts that "borfimah" comes from the Sherbro words for "bag" (boroh) and "black" (fimah). See Lindskog, *African Leopard Men*, 17.

3 Beatty asserts that the borfimah package "contains, amongst other things, the white of an egg, the blood, fat, and other parts of a human being, the blood of a cock, and a few grains of rice; … it must occasionally be anointed with human fat and smeared with human blood … It is an all-powerful instrument in the hands of its owner, it will make him rich and powerful, it will make people hold him in honour, it will help him in cases in the White Man's Courts, and it certainly has the effect of instilling in the native mind great respect for its owner and a terrible fear lest he should use it hostilely" (*Human Leopards*, 23). See also Lindskog, *African Leopard Men*, 61; D. Burrows, "The Human Leopards of Sierra Leone," *Journal of the Royal African Society* 13, no. 50 (1914): 144.

4 Michael Jackson, "The Man Who Could Turn into an Elephant: Shape-shifting among the Kuranko of Sierra Leone," in *Personhood and Agency: The Experience of Self and Others in African Cultures: Papers Presented at a Symposium on African Folk Models and Their Application, held at Uppsala University, August 23–30, 1897*, ed. Michael Jackson and Ivan Karp (Uppsala, SE: Acta Universitatis Upsaliensis, 1990), 70.

5 Milan Kalous, *Cannibals and Tongo Players of Sierra Leone* (Auckland: M. Kalous, 1974), 16, ellipses in original; Sierra Leone Government Archives, Governor's confidential dispatches, 21.6.1909 80/1909. See also note 3 above.

6 For a discussion of a comparably disruptive colonial problem, see Parma Roy's "Discovering India, Imagining *Thuggee*," *Yale Journal of Criticism* 9, no. 1 (1996): 121–45.

7 "Cannibalism in West Africa," *Sheffield Evening Telegraph*, 1 Nov. 1889, 2. The newspapers cited in this chapter are sourced from the British Newspaper Archive at the British Library.

8 "The Human Leopards," *Bristol Mercury*, 11 Jan. 1896, 3; "How the Human Leopards Originated," *Pall Mall Gazette*, 28 Aug. 1895, 7. I have not encountered any evidence that supports this assertion. Criticism on this subject seems not to have considered the possibility that Sierra Leone Leopard Men used violent cannibalism to deploy terror and fear as defensive mechanisms against the British. Gananath Obeyeskere has argued, of a different historical situation, that Maori in the late eighteenth century employed the discourse of cannibalism as "a weapon to terrify [British sailors] in the context of unequal power, where their real weapons were nothing in comparison to European guns." See "'British Cannibals': Contemplation of an Event in the Death and Resurrection of James Cook, Explorer," *Critical Inquiry* 18, no. 4 (1992): 646. It is distinctly possible that the society in West Africa was using British anxieties about cannibalism to a similar end.

9 "Strange Stories from West Africa: Black Jack the Rippers," *York Herald*, 28 Feb. 1891, 8. The *Northern Echo* published a similar article ("Jack the Ripper in Africa," 26 Feb. 1891, 3), as did the *Dover Express* ("Black 'Jack the Rippers,'" 6 March 1891, 2). "Jack the Ripper" was the "street name" of a notorious murderer of women during 1888 in the impoverished borough of Whitechapel, London. The crimes of Jack the Ripper registered in these reports for both the eviscerative nature of the murders and the fact that the cases, remaining unsolved, resisted closure. Other examples include "Cannibalism in West Africa: Shocking Atrocities," *Sheffield Daily Telegraph*, 3 June 1891, 5; "A Human Leopards Society: Horrors of a Cannibal Feast," *Worcestershire Chronicle*, 18 July 1896, 3; "The Human Leopards: More Horrible Details," *Sunderland Daily Echo*, 30 Aug. 1895, 4; and "Shocking Story of Cannibalism," *Daily Gazette for Middlesbrough*, 28 Aug. 1895, 4. (The story in this article was also printed with only minor variations across England under such various titles as "Cannibalism in a British Colony," *Northampton Mercury*, 30 Aug. 1895, 2; "Horrors of African Life," *Leicester Chronicle*, 31 Aug. 1895, 3; and "Terrible Story of African Cannibalism," *Supplement to the Manchester Courier*, 31 Aug. 1895, 3, among others.)

10 "Strange Stories from West Africa: Black Jack the Rippers," *York Herald*, 28 Feb. 1891, 8.

11 Some examples of the fictional texts include Mary Gaunt's *The Arms of the Leopard* (1923); Hergé's *Tintin in the Congo* (1931); Edgar Rice Burroughs's

Tarzan and the Leopard Men (1935); Jacques Tourneur's 1943 film *The Leopard Man*; the episode "The African Leopard Man" (1944) of the American radio show *The New Adventures of Sherlock Holmes*; Kurt Neumann's 1946 film *Tarzan and the Leopard Woman*; Juba Kennerley's *The Terror of the Leopard Men* (1951); James Shaw's *The Leopard Men* (1953); Willard Price's *African Adventure* (1963); and René Guillot's *Fodai and the Leopard-Men* (1966), to name only a few.

12 See David Pratten, *The Man-Leopard Murders: History and Society in Colonial Nigeria* (Edinburgh: Edinburgh University Press, 2007), 14.

13 Rosalind Shaw, *Memories of the Slave Trade: Ritual and the Historical Imagination in Sierra Leone* (Chicago: University Chicago Press, 2002), 235.

14 Ibid., 237; Pratten, *Man-Leopard Murders*, 10.

15 T.J. Alldridge, *The Sherbro and Its Hinterland* (London: Macmillan, 1901), 153. Other early twentieth-century ethnographers also estimate that the society originated in the 1860s. See A.R. Wright, "Secret Societies and Fetishism in Sierra Leone," *Folklore* 8, no. 4 (1907): 425; A. Gray, "The Human Leopards of Sierra Leone," *Journal of the Society of Comparative Legislation* n.s., 16, no. 2 (1916): 196.

16 Lindskog, *African Leopard Men*, 89–90.

17 Furthermore, English newspapers indicate that London was aware of native courts persecuting alleged Human Leopards: "A native trial on a large scale is proceeding at Tyamah, Mendi country, concerning more than one hundred people charged with cannibalism … The native punishment for this offense is roasting alive, and this barbarous ceremony will take place with fetish rites early in May" ("The West Coast of Africa," *London Standard*, 3 May 1883, 5, referencing correspondence from Sierra Leone, dated 13 April). Parliament displayed little concern over this punishment: "The officer administering the district … sent a letter to the assembled chiefs advising them to end their proceedings; and on the 18th he received a reply from the chiefs that before the arrival of his messenger they had burned 34 persons for witchcraft and cannibalism, but on receipt of the letter they had liberated the rest of the accused, and promised to discontinue the practice in the future. The officer, in reply, thanked the chief for meeting his wishes – (laughter) – and expressed the abhorrence of the British Government for these barbarous customs." See "House of Commons," *York Herald*, 27 July 1883, 5. Perceived racial and geographical distance enabled those at the House to make light of the atrocity. In addition, considering that the Sierra Leonean correspondent knew in April the probable outcome of this trial, it is unlikely that the administrative officer referred to here was unable to anticipate it before May.

18 In other colonized countries such Nigeria and Congo, the Leopard Society continued murdering well into the mid-twentieth century.

19 Ann Laura Stoler, "Colonial Archives and the Arts of Governance," *Archival Science* 2 (2002): 90.
20 Ibid., 97; emphasis in original. As Stoler points out, "From the Latin *archivum*, 'residence of the magistrate,' and from the Greek *arkhe*, to command or govern, colonial archives ordered … the criteria of evidence, proof, testimony, and witnessing to construct moral narrations" (97).
21 For instance, in 1891, Governor Sir James Shaw Hay drew on the Lockean model of colonialism to acclaim "an active interior policy … Not only have trade and farming operations amongst the tribes been made general, but there has been a considerable improvement in their conduct and integrity … the presence of our Frontier Police has made the people feel secure and given them confidence; it has also afforded them an opportunity of farming and becoming a happy and prosperous people … Where two years ago there was no vestige of life or cultivation I found a people who were industrious and happy" (*Sierra Leone Weekly News*, 18 April 1891, enclosed in dispatch to the Colonial Office in London: *Colonial Office and Predecessors: Sierra Leone Original Correspondence*, CO 267/389 5.4.1891, file 175, National Archives at Kew (hereafter NA)). The Frontier Police was composed of West African men and men from the interior, recruited for the purpose of regulating the region. Hay thus purported that British industry and rule of law yielded happier, more civilized indigenous farmers – who could actively support the economy.
22 CO 267/393 16.02.1892, file 77, NA. Bonthe was the location of the key administrative station outside of Freetown.
23 Quoted in Kalous, *Cannibals*, 39; Sierra Leone Government Archives, Minute Papers, Confidential 53/1894.
24 CO 267/419 8.11.1895, file 237, enclosure 2, NA.
25 Richard Strong, ed., *The African Republic of Liberia and the Belgian Congo; Based on the Observations Made and Material Collected during the Harvard African Expedition, 1926–1927* (Cambridge, MA: Harvard University Press, 1930), 100–1.
26 Alldridge, *Sherbro*, 154. Strong also suggests that "the possession of the skin and head of a leopard in one's hut or even its claws or teeth when worn, gives power and strength to the person to whom they belong." See *African Republic*, 94.
27 Alldridge, *Sherbro*, 156.
28 Pratten's *Man-Leopard Murders* analyses the society's activity in colonial Nigeria, which continued into the 1950s. Lindskog's *African Leopard Men*, meanwhile, offers detailed reporting of references in historical archives to locations and dates of big-cat society attacks.
29 Mary Kingsley, *Travels in West Africa*, introduced by Anthony Brandt (1897; Washington, DC: National Geographic Society, 2002), 312.

30 Sir William Brandford Griffith, Preface to *Human Leopards: An Account of the Trials of Human Leopards before the Special Commission Court; With a Note on Sierra Leone, Past and Present*, by K.J. Beatty (London: Hugh Rees, 1915), vi–vii. Griffith was a former chief justice from the Gold Coast.
31 Jackson, "Man Who Could," 71, quoting R.G. Berry.
32 Jackson also concludes that the objective in killing was to activate the borfimah fetish in order to increase strength, wealth, and influence. See "Man Who Could," 71. Burrows meanwhile suggested that "the eating of some of the flesh of the victims is … a means of securing the loyalty of the members and ensuring their unquestioned adherence to the strange cult to which the sacrifice is but an inevitable necessity." See "Human Leopards," 143.
33 "The Human Leopards: More Horrible Details," *Sunderland Daily Echo*, 30 Aug. 1895, 4.
34 Ibid.
35 This story was popular, and repeated in "Human Leopards: Three Cannibals Hanged, More Cannibals Captured," *Hampshire Telegraph*, 31 Aug. 1895, 2; "Terrible Story of African Cannibalism," *Supplement to the Manchester Courier*, 31 Aug. 1895, 3; and "Human Leopards: Three Cannibals Executed," *Nottingham Evening Post*, 27 Aug. 1895, 4, among others. Her status as a "slave girl" and having been tied to a tree is always emphasized, foregrounding her subjugation.
36 Richards, *Imperial Archive*, 3–4, 6.
37 CO 267/384 26.8.1890, file 368, NA. When Human Leopards were "discovered," their property was frequently taken by chiefs.
38 "Cannibalism in West Africa: Shocking Atrocities," *Sheffield Daily Telegraph*, 3 June 1891, 5.
39 "The Human Leopards," *Bristol Mercury*, 11 Jan. 1896, 3.
40 Ibid.
41 "The Human Leopards: Two More Hanged," *Sheffield Evening Telegraph*, 15 July 1896, 3.
42 "The Last 24 Hours," *Bristol Mercury*, 21 Sept. 1896, 5.
43 "This Morning's News," *London Daily News*, 26 March 1896, 5.
44 "Cannibalism in Sierra Leone," *Pall Mall Gazette*, 18 Dec. 1897, 8.
45 "Human Leopards: Three Cannibals Executed," *Nottingham Evening Post*, 27 Aug. 1895, 4.
46 "How the Human Leopards Originated," *Pall Mall Gazette*, 28 Aug. 1895, 7.
47 "Cannibalism in Africa: A Refinement of Gluttony," *Sheffield and Rotherham Independent*, 18 Sept. 1895, 9; "Cannibalism in Africa," *Whitstable Times*, 21 Sept. 1895, 6. In Greek mythology, Thyestes was, by his vengeful brother Atreus, unwittingly served his own murdered sons for dinner.
48 Even so, British print culture was not unaware of its own interest in entertainment: "The moral does not work out quite properly in the story

of cannibalism from Sierra Leone. The good young man who taught in a Sunday school should have been caught by the cannibals, and all that should have been found of him should have been a boot lace, a watch chain, and a diary containing pious reflections … Unfortunately it appears that Mr. Jowe so far fell away from grace as to become a cannibal himself … The 'Human Leopards' is a title fetching enough to grace the cover of a penny dreadful." See "Notes on News," *Sheffield Evening Telegraph*, 27 Aug. 1895, 3. In casting this case as a piece of low-brow fiction, the contributor demonstrates the British public's capacity to read these histories as quite far removed from reality, and through the highly refracted lens of diversion.

49 CO 270/52 25.10.1912, NA.

50 CO 267/393 5.02.1892, file 55, NA.

51 CO 267/384 26.8.1890, NA.

52 Brother Herbert Philip Fitzgerald Marriot, FRGS, "The Secret Societies of West Africa," *Journal of the Anthropological Institute of Great Britain and Ireland* 29, nos. 1/2 (1899): 26.

53 "The 'Human Leopards,'" *Colony and Provincial Reporter*, 30 Aug. 1913, 7.

54 "Human Leopards: Three Cannibals Hanged, More Cannibals Captured," *Hampshire Telegraph*, 31 Aug. 1895, 2.

55 "Cannibalism in West Africa: Shocking Atrocities," *Sheffield Daily Telegraph*, 3 June 1891, 5.

56 MacKenzie, "Imperial Pioneer," 180.

57 MacKenzie suggests the hunting trophy signals "a mastery of environmental signs and knowledge of natural history," ibid., 179.

58 Ibid., 180.

59 CO 267/395 30.8.1892 Conf. 26, NA.

60 CO 267/395 30.8.1892 Conf. 26, NA.

61 Pratten, *Man-Leopard Murders*, 9–10.

62 Lindskog, *African Leopard Men*, 144.

63 Jackson, "Man Who Could," 59.

64 CO 267/383 20.6.1890, NA.

65 CO 267/384 26.8.1890, NA.

66 Into the 1920s, Americans adopted the indigenous use of sasswood concoctions to elicit confessions from alleged Human Leopards in Liberia: "Government officials have employed the trial by ordeal with sasswood successfully … in detecting members of the human leopard society … After undergoing trial by ordeal and being compelled to drink cup after cup of sasswood and after repeated attacks of vomiting, retching, and pain, they finally confessed to their crimes. On recovery from the effects of the poison, they were placed in chains and sentenced to hard labor for life." See Strong, *African Republic*, 102–3. Meanwhile, among British

travellers in West Africa, these practices had been labeled "superstition." See late eighteenth-century and early nineteenth-century writers on Sierra Leone such as John Matthews, *A Voyage to the River Sierra-Leone* (London, 1791); Anna Marie Falconbridge, *Two Voyages to Sierra Leone, during the years 1791–2–3* (London, 1794); and Thomas Winterbottom, *An Account of the Native Africans in the Neighbourhood of Sierra Leone* (London, 1803). See also Buel, *Heroes*, 86, and E.G. Ingham, *After a Hundred Years* (London, 1894). Thus, methods understood to be "uncivilized" were becoming useful to imperial projects.

67 See, for instance, McClintock, *Imperial Leather*, 1–74; David, *Rule Britania*, 168–72, 182, 193–8; Stiebel, *Imagining Africa*, 48; Bristow, *Empire Boys*, 133; and Ania Loomba, *Colonialism/Postcolonialism* (London: Routledge, 1998), 77–81, 152.

68 CO 267/389 19.5.1891, NA.

69 CO 267/384 26.8.1890, NA.

70 CO 267/384 26.8.1890, NA. As Tracey Banivanua Mar points out, by the end of the nineteenth century, the "narrative of the infectious lawlessness and disorder of the frontiers" was "well-established": "British colonialism ... was bound by its own rhetoric of bringing to the savage world benevolent civilisation with impartial and universal rules of government. The language of the Rule of Law, and the application of colonial jurisprudence contributed to the production of an air of moral authority around the British colonial enterprise, which was critical to the manufacturing of consent of both colonisers and colonized." See "Frontier Space and the Reification of the Rule of Law: Colonial Negotiations in the Western Pacific, 1870–74," *Australian Feminist Law Journal* 30 (2009): 24, 38.

71 Banivanua Mar demonstrates that the deployment of the discourse of cannibalism in "opening up" colonial spaces has had a long and global history: "pre-emptive war ... was legal when waged against a people known to live against the Laws of Nature. Anthropophagy, particularly of the cannibalistic variety known to exist amongst natives, was the ultimate unnatural act, and being systemic it condemned entire societies to legitimated and legal conquest." See "Cannibalism and Colonialism: Charting Colonies and Frontiers in Nineteenth-Century Fiji," *Comparative Studies in Society and History* 52, no. 2 (2010): 260. Furthermore, "Cannibalism and savagery" constituted "imperatives for suspending normative moral and judicial standards" (268). We see exactly this manoeuvre in early twentieth-century Sierra Leone when the administration retracted constitutional laws. See pages 191–3 below.

72 CO 267/385 27.10.1890, file 441, NA.

73 Ibid.

74 Ibid. The priority of agricultural production is clear here.

75 The trope of the road as a material imperial vein facilitating trade also signals civilization, but of greater consequence here is the administration's concern with the regulation of the landscape as body. See Roberta J. Park "Biological Thought, Athletics, and the Formation of a 'Man of Character,' 1830–1900," in *Manliness and Morality: Middle-Class Masculinity in Britain and America, 1800–1940,* ed. J.A. Mangan and James Walvin (Manchester: Manchester University Press, 1987), 7–34, for a thorough discussion of how the healthy, muscular, and disciplined body functions as a symbol for moral soundness in the late-Victorian period. Disciplining the landscape attempted to ensure a moral space, maintain psychic hygiene (which, crucially, means policing the body's borders), and regulate internal health.
76 Burrows, "Human Leopards," 143.
77 Ibid., 147.
78 Griffith, Preface, viii–ix.
79 CO 267/401 24.4.1893 Conf. 28, NA.
80 Kingsley, *Travels*, 313.
81 Henry Richard Fox Bourne, *Blacks and Whites in West Africa: An Account of the Past Treatment and Present Condition of West African Natives under European Influence or Control* (London: P.S. King and Son, 1901), 52.
82 This anxiety would have certainly resonated with the discourses surrounding colonial mutiny proliferating after the Indian Uprising of 1857.
83 CO 267/394 7.3.1892 Conf. 14, enclosure 1, NA.
84 In his dispatch, Quayle-Jones called "upon Major Moore to explain how this letter of Sub Inspector Sawyer's came to be suppressed by Captain Lendy, who was Acting Inspector General at the time of its receipt, and why Major Moore, when he ascertained the state of affairs, if he knew of the existence of Sub Inspector Sawyer's letter, did not himself communicate it to the governor … This letter, My Lord, explains what had before seemed inexplicable viz: how the country people in the face of the governor's distinct instructions to the contrary could have supposed that the Tongo play was permitted by the government and would explain Mr. Macfoy's belief that such was the case also." CO 267/394 7.3.1892 Conf. 14, NA.
85 Ibid.
86 CO 267/394 23.4.1892 Conf. 17, NA.
87 Ibid.; emphasis in original.
88 See also Lane's discussion in *The Ruling Passion* of threat of the "contrary interest, or counter allegiance, with the colonized" to empire: "We have only to recall Melville's horror at this possibility in 'Benito Cereno' (1885) to consider its far-reaching consequence: 'Who had ever heard of a white so far a renegade as to apostatize from his very species almost, by leaguing in against it with negroes?'" (4).

89 CO 267/394 23.4.1892 Conf. 17, NA.
90 This imperative to understand the military as a unified body is repeated in the Colonial Office's strikingly similar response to Governor Fleming in a minute dated 27 May 1892: "Constabulary Officers must be made aware that it is in their duty to report fully to the Governor whether they think that the matters to be reported may reflect on the Frontier Police or not, and that neglect to perform such duty will entail serious consequences. It shall also be impressed on every police officer from the highest to the lowest that their attitude must never be one of indifference when brought into contact with crimes of their nature, and that the Queen views with abhorrence all such customs as those which are unhappily practiced in the Imperi." CO 267/394 23.4.1892 Conf. 17, NA.
91 CO 267/395 30.8.1892 Conf. 26, enclosure 2, NA.
92 Ibid. Huggins reported to Fleming: "I visited the village of BOGO where the so-called 'human leopards' were burnt and found that the barré where these unfortunates were 'stocked' is only a yard or two distant from the house the Sergeant lives in – in fact the roofs almost touched each other. The open space cleared of bush especially for the TONGO play can easily be seen by any one in the yard of the Sergeant's house; and it was here that NEPPOH the TONGO man struck the so-called human leopards on the head … It is quite impossible that the Sergeant an[d] Police at BOGO … could live in the Village and not be quite cognizant of what was going on … The evidence of seven persons shows that the constables – not the Sergeant [–] were sometimes dancing the TONGO dance, sometimes looking on while the human leopards were burning." Ibid.
93 CO 267/394 21.4.1892 Conf. 20, NA.
94 CO 267/395 30.8.1892 Conf. 26, NA.
95 Ibid.
96 This was the same Captain Soden mentioned in the *Sheffield Daily Telegraph* above.
97 CO 267/395 30.8.1892 Conf. 26, NA.
98 Ibid.
99 Ibid.
100 Cultural memory of the Coath Trial (1871) and the *Carl* massacre (1871) would have resonated in this situation. "The 'civilized world' was stunned and appalled" at the news of the kidnapping and massacring of Pacific Islanders by British subjects; see Banivanua Mar, "Frontier Space," 35.
101 In Huggins's report, the highly structured narratives, lack of transitions, and occasional repetitiveness indicate that these testimonials were

compiled in response to a series of queries asked by Huggins but not included in the transcriptions.

102 This did not apply directly to disorder in Sierra Leone but nevertheless was a component of the fabric of social anxiety about national identity.

103 CO 267/395 30.8.1892 Conf. 26, enclosure 1, NA.

104 Ibid.

105 Ibid.

106 Ibid.

107 CO 267/401 18.04.1893 Conf. 24, NA.

108 Mr Bramston from the Colonial Office wrote: "It is satisfactory, at any rate, to find that no constabulary officer was concerned in this. The point of course was that the taking of a photograph of the principal persons connected with the 'Tongo Play' would naturally be looked upon by the natives as implying a certain recognition if not condonation of the practice; and this, in the care of constabulary officers who were specially charged to suppress the 'Tongo Play,' could have been a [very] serious matter" (ibid.).

109 In 1890, chiefs had also petitioned the British to allow indigenous methods of hindering Human Leopard attacks, protesting, "1. That in consequence of the prevailing craft or cannibalism in and around our District, preventing free traveling for the purpose of trade, or farming, and especially endangering the lives and safety of our wives and children who dare not move about without a guard of from four to six men, and 2. That these clubs of cannibals taking shelter from the lenient treatment of the British Government in cases brought before their notice are becoming bold, and destructive to our lives, welfare and interest, and therefore 3. That we be allowed and permitted to adopt our native course, in finding out and treating these cannibals as provided by our native polity" (CO 267/385 27.10.1890, file 441, enclosure 2, NA).

110 CO 267/395 30.8.1892 Conf. 26, enclosure 1, NA.

111 Ibid.

112 Ibid.

113 Conveniently for the Colonial Office, by the time of the inquest, Soden was "no longer in the force, so that no action c[ould] be taken with regard to him." As for the other transgressor, Captain Lendy, who had since been promoted, his punishment was to be "censured in the Executive Council by the Govt," and "lectured in this office by ... Mr. Meade." As a result, the secretariat decided not to "go any further with him; on account of his having kept back Sawyer's report" (CO 267/395 30.8.1892 Conf. 26, NA).

114 It was colonial policy not to interfere with country customs outside of British territory. As of 24 October 1890, however, Imperri was proclaimed

imperial jurisdiction. Because this was not sufficiently made known (British communication was grossly inadequate), members of the Frontier Police, such as Sawyer, were unaware of colonial orders to intervene in indigenous customs. Fleming explains Sawyer's lack of intervention: "He stated that in so doing he considered that he was only obeying the strict orders he had received not to interfere in the country customs of the natives and this more especially so as he did not know at the time that the Imperi was under the active jurisdiction of this Colony" (CO 267/395 30.8.1892 Conf. 26, enclosure 3, NA).

115 CO 267/395 30.8.1892 Conf. 26, NA. Bonar and Fahbandeh were constables whom multiple witnesses had identified as participants in the Tongo Play.

116 CO 267/419 23.10.1895, file 216, NA.

117 A number of men of status in the colony offered remarks forwarded to the Colonial Office on the situation, including Colonel Ellis (commander of the West African Troops), C.B. Mitford (acting colonial secretary), Bayldon Walker (acting Queen's advocate), Sam Lewis (a lawyer), and Dr Ross (a surgeon).

118 CO 267/395 30.8.1892 Conf. 26, enclosure 3, NA.

119 The broader public also seemed to share this sentiment. A writer for the *Sierra Leone Weekly News* opined that, regarding the Human Leopard murders, "the interference of the Police and their native officers has hardly ever been satisfactory" (10 Aug. 1895, 4).

120 CO 267/395 30.8.1892 Conf. 26, enclosure 3, NA; emphasis in original.

121 Ibid.

122 Executive Council Minutes; CO 270/32 16.11.1893, NA. The matter in question at this meeting was who to send to investigate and report back on problems the administration was then facing regarding the Sofas. Huggins's name was put forth, and Ellis was contesting this suggestion. Whether in spite of or as a result of Ellis's assessment of him, most at the meeting were in favour of sending Huggins to do the job.

123 CO 267/395 30.8.1892 Conf. 26, enclosure 6, NA.

124 Ibid. The unanswered question of Interpreter Parker's role in communicating whether Tongo Play was sanctioned also troubled the administration. Numerous witnesses testified they heard him say that the administration permitted it; some of the colonial reports denied this suggestion, while some supported it. This question not only implicated the white officers in charge of the region, but also revealed the disruptive liminality of black officers or colonial employees that destabilized the larger imperial system of regulation. For a study of the disruptive role of African intermediaries, see Benjamin N. Lawrence, Emily Lynn Osborn, and Richard L. Roberts, eds., *Intermediaries, Interpreters, and Clerks:*

African Employees in the Making of Colonial Africa (Madison: University of Wisconsin Press, 2006).

125 Lewis noted, "It appears improbable that the chiefs, after their bitter experience suffered in 1890 for employing the TONGO, would have [so] soon called in the TONGO men openly and without some assurance, open or covert, that their act would be supported or allowed." He also pointed out that, "if it was the intention of Captain Soden to prevent the carrying out by the Chiefs of their expressed determination to play, he would have given instructions to at least watch and report to himself at BENDOO, a short distance of 5 hours from BOGO, or when Captain Soden next went to BOGO. I do not believe that any such instructions were given to the Police and this part of the case demands investigation." CO 267/395 30.8.1892 Conf. 26, enclosure 6, NA.

126 Lewis suggested that "Captain Campbell at least passed to and from BOGO after the burnings had commenced. As these atrocities were enacted within a very few feet of the road he passed … it is surprising that he should have failed to see the burning remains of human beings which attracted the attention of Sergeant Sawyer, unless it was a willful determination not to see them." Ibid.

127 Ibid.

128 Ibid., enclosure 5.

129 Ibid., enclosure 7.

130 CO 267/401 10.4.1893, file 125, NA.

131 CO 267/383 20.6.1890, NA; emphasis in original.

132 CO 267/384 28.8.1890, NA.

133 CO 267/383 20.6.1890 File 272, NA.

134 Ibid.

135 CO 267/383 23.7.1890, file 272, NA.

136 CO 267/383 23.7.1890, NA.

137 Haggard, *King Solomon's Mines*, 40.

138 Ibid.

139 Marsh, *Beetle*, 95. A "hasher" is a mangler. A more explicit correlation between writing and British civility exists in Robert Louis Stevenson's *The Strange Case of Dr. Jekyll and Mr. Hyde*. When Utterson brings Hyde's letter to Guest for analysis, Guest is able to tell from the handwriting that Hyde is "not mad" and, when comparing Hyde's letter to an invitation from Jekyll, that, although one hand is more sloping and the other more upright, they are in fact written from the same person. See R.L. Stevenson, *The Strange Case of Dr. Jekyll and Mr. Hyde*, ed. Martin A. Danahay (1886; Peterborough, ON: Broadview, 2003), 53. The underlying graphological implication here is that Jekyll's character – not only Hyde's – is in fact deeply afflicted with the problem of regression.

140 CO 267/384 26.8.1890, NA.
141 CO 267/384 24.9.1890, NA.
142 Governor Fleming summarized: "It appears that [Sawyer] had received strict orders not to interfere in the Country customs of the Natives … I am further disposed to think that, some misapprehension exists among the Frontier Police regarding the Imperri. It was … taken under British Protectionism in 1890, but I question whether this is generally known and it may be that Sub Inspector Sawyer considered that where he saw the Chief Basshi was a part of the country in which he had no authority." CO 267/394 21.4.1892 Conf. 20, NA.
143 CO 267/395 30.8.1892 Conf. 26, NA.
144 Ibid.
145 CO 267/384 26.8.1890; Reports 37 and 38, NA.
146 India Office Records, *Africa*, IOR/L/PJ/6/986, file 379, 5.2.1910, British Library.
147 Ibid.
148 CO 270/52 25.10.1912, NA.
149 Ibid.
150 In other words, conviction could be based on membership, not on a crime. Men could be punished for being Human Leopards without actually having been convicted of murder or being an accessory.
151 Witnesses, to have their evidence admitted in court, previously had to be present during the trial; this ordinance proposed to enable the witness to offer testimony only once, so that the defendant would only have one chance to cross-examine him or her.
152 Governor Merewether referenced special measures that were passed in regards to British suppression of the Chinese Triad Societies. CO 270/52 25.10.1912, NA.
153 Ibid.
154 Ibid. See also page 156 above.
155 In the circuit court, the judge had the final decision, though the claim was that he would theoretically be influenced by indigenous advisers. This decision-making process of course invested all real judicial power in colonial authority. In the proposed special commission court, the decisions of the three panelists would need to be unanimous in order to reach a conviction, but would not be informed by indigenous insight. Mr J.H. Thomas, another honourable member, argued for defendants' right to be tried by "chiefs of experience with their own country and people … rather than three judges who know nothing of the country or lack experience" (CO 270/52 8.11.1912, NA). Shorunkeh-Sawyerr, fearing the judge's opinion would dominate that of the lay assessors, protested that the new court should comprise "legally qualified men" – lawyers

or other people with the requisite experience. This proposal would have enabled indigenous lawyers and chiefs to sit on the tribunal. Again, these arguments were not considered.

156 CO 270/52 8.11.1912, NA. Shorunkeh-Sawyerr refers to the assassination of two government officials in Dublin in 1882 (either he or the stenographer gets the year wrong here) by radical Irish nationalists.

157 Ibid.

158 CO 270/52 25.10.1912, NA.

159 CO 270/52 8.11.1912, NA.

6 Expanding Darkness: Narrative Complicity

1 Chinua Achebe, "An Image of Africa," *Massachusetts Review* 18, no. 4 (1977): 791.

2 Recognizing Conrad's Polish origins, I am considering here his lived experience in Britain and that he was writing for a British audience. It is worth noting that "big-cat" killings were also happening in Congo in the 1890s, but quite far east of where Conrad and Marlow travelled.

3 See Achebe, "An Image."

4 Clement Abiaziem Okafor, "Joseph Conrad and Chinua Achebe: Two Antipodal Portraits of Africa" *Journal of Black Studies* 19, no. 1 (1988): 19.

5 Jim Holstun, "'Mr. Kayerts. He Is Dead': Literary Realism and Conrad's 'Outpost of Progress,'" *English Literature in History* 85, no. 1 (2018): 208.

6 See, most notably, Cedric Watts, "'A Bloody Racist': About Achebe's View of Conrad," *Yearbook of English Studies* 13 (1983): 196–209; Hunt Hawkins, "The Issue of Racism in *Heart of Darkness,*" *Conradiana* 14, no. 3 (1982): 163–71; Robert Hampson, "'Heart of Darkness' and 'The Speech that cannot be silenced'" *English: Journal of the English Association* 39, no. 163 (1990): 15–32.

7 Mongia Padmini, "The Rescue: Conrad, Achebe, and the Critics," *Conradiana* 33, no. 2 (2001): 153–63.

8 Ibid., 158.

9 Hunt Hawkins, "Conrad's Critique of Imperialism in Heart of Darkness," *PMLA* 94, no. 2 (1979): 286–99. Hawkins is, of course, right to argue that it is erroneous to conclude that imperialism "was essentially the same in all areas, varying only according to such subjective factors as the culture and benevolence of the mother country. Actually, imperialism was not monolithic. Important discriminations should be made in terms of imperial aims, systems of administration, degrees of exploitation, and even types of exploitation" (288). Making the point that the central colonial practices under examination in *Heart of Darkness* are Belgian, Hawkins suggests

that, "in judging imperialism according to the criteria of efficiency and the 'idea,' Conrad could appeal to his British readers to condemn Leopold without impugning themselves, since such abuses as forced labour and the absence of currency were not characteristic of British colonies" (292). Conrad meanwhile publicly denounced the use of efficiency as a moral standard and rejected the validity of the philanthropic "idea" (295). Even so, if the more obvious critique of empire is directed toward Belgium, this does not exempt Britain from the implications that the novella brings to bear against British imperial practice.

10 Ian Watt, *Conrad in the Nineteenth Century* (Berkeley: University of California Press, 1979), 141–5; Brantlinger, *Rule*, 267; D.C.R.A. Goonetilleke, Introduction to *Heart of Darkness*, by Joseph Conrad (Peterborough, ON: Broadview, 2003), 11, 26; Maya Jassanoff, *The Dawn Watch: Joseph Conrad in a Global World* (New York: Penguin, 2017).

11 See William Atkinson, "Bound in *Blackwood's*: The Imperialism of 'Heart of Darkness' in Its Immediate Context," *Twentieth Century Literature* 50, no. 4 (2004): 368–93. Atkinson disproportionately values William Blackwood's textual perceptions, suggesting that *Blackwood's Magazine*'s Tory owner and editor's perspective ultimately informed readerly understandings of *Heart of Darkness*'s meaning. Atkinson's argues that Conrad's work was using the paratexts within *Blackwood's* to draw out lessons supporting British colonial practice to be convincing, but, for this to be true, Conrad would have had to have written his story around these other works or, at the very least, would have to have made editorial decisions about their inclusions. In taking Marlow's ostensible praise of "the devotion to efficiency" (quoted at 377) and suggestion that red points on a map of Africa indicate "that some real work is done there" (quoted at 379) at face value, Atkinson misses the frame narrative's critique of Marlow.

12 Ibid., 390.

13 Andrew Michael Roberts, *Conrad and Masculinity* (Houndmills, UK: Macmillan, 2000), 118.

14 Katherine Isobel Baxter, *Joseph Conrad and the Swan Song of Romance* (Farnham, UK: Ashgate, 2010), 7–32.

15 Ibid., 32.

16 Nidesh Lawtoo, "The Horror of Mimesis: 'Enthusiastic Outbreak[s]' in *Heart of Darkness*," *Conradiana* 42, nos. 1–2 (2010): 46.

17 Ibid., 60.

18 Ibid., 46.

19 Sandya Shetty, "Heart of Darkness: Out of Africa Something New Never Comes," *Journal of Modern Literature* 15, no. 4 (1989): 463.

20 J.M. Rawa, *The Imperial Quest and Modern Memory from Conrad to Greene* (New York: Routledge, 2005), 41–2.

21 Ibid., 49.

22 Brantlinger, *Rule*, 268.
23 Roberts, *Conrad*, 125–6.
24 Conrad, *Heart of Darkness*, 29.
25 Here I use Linda Hutcheon and Mario J. Valdés's understanding of nostalgia in "Irony, Nostalgia, and the Postmodern: A Dialogue," *Poligrafías* 3 (2000): 19–20, which suggests that nostalgia expresses desire for a past that is imagined, but never real.
26 Conrad, *Heart*, 6.
27 Ibid., 27.
28 As Holstun points out, Conrad's text fails to name the material consequences of such a counterattack for indigenous Congolese. In reality, Conrad's own job opening occurred when Captain Johannes Freiesleben was killed in the Congo. In retribution, the Belgians "destroyed all the villages between the mouth of the Kasai and Bolobo" and killed scores of villagers. Holstun, "Mr. Kayerts," 205, quoting Robert W. Harms, *River of Wealth, River of Sorrow: The Central Zaire Basin in the Era of the Slave and Ivory Trade, 1500–1891* (New Haven, CT: Yale University Press, 1981), 225.
29 Leslie Heywood's analysis of fat as feminizing further suggests a lack of manliness in this character. See *Dedication to Hunger: The Anorexic Aesthetic in Modern Culture* (Berkeley: University of California Press, 1996), 120.
30 Conrad, *Heart*, 20, 21.
31 Ibid., 22.
32 Ibid., 31.
33 Ibid., 23.
34 Ibid., 53, 46.
35 Ibid., 9.
36 Ibid.
37 Ibid., 21.
38 Ibid., 31.
39 Ibid., 23, 8.
40 Ibid., 5, 7.
41 Ibid.
42 Ibid., 48.
43 Here I disagree with Heywood's suggestion that Marlow's near bodilessness gives him authority (see Heywood, *Dedication*, 127). He is not of the fleshy disposition of some of the other questionable characters (which, as Heywood rightly argues, within the novella signals rapacity and greed), but his physicality does tend toward hollowness, which, within the sign system of the novella, indicates moral groundlessness.
44 Conrad, *Heart*, 48.
45 Ibid.
46 Ibid., 49.
47 Dowling, *Manliness*, 17.

48 Benita Parry, *Conrad and Imperialism: Ideological Boundaries and Visionary Frontiers* (London: Macmillan, 1983), 28.
49 Conrad, *Heart*, 4, 5.
50 Ibid., 20.
51 See Arata, *Fictions*, 107–11.
52 Parry, *Conrad*, 22.
53 Conrad, *Heart*, 5.
54 Ibid., 6–7.
55 Ibid., 7.
56 See Joanna M. Smith, "'Too Beautiful Altogether': Ideologies of Gender and Empire in Heart of Darkness" in *Heart of Darkness: Case Studies in Contemporary Criticism*, ed. Ross Murfin (Basingstoke, UK: Bedford/St Martins, 2011), 199.
57 Holstun, "Mr. Kayerts," 199.
58 Brantlinger, *Rule*, 262.
59 Leslie Heywood reads this pose as a suggestion that "his words are authoritative" (*Dedication*, 121), but, in the context of the criticism of Marlow by the frame narrator and other listeners, Marlow's hypocrisy that is foregrounded.
60 See also Parry's discussion of the "manicheanism of the imperialist imagination" (*Conrad*, 21–3).
61 Conrad, *Heart*, 3, 4, 5.
62 Ibid., 5, 72.
63 Rawa, *Imperial Quest*, 40.
64 Conrad, *Heart*, 14.
65 Ibid., 33.
66 Ibid., 44.
67 See Charles Wesley, "Inscriptions of Resistance in Joseph Conrad's Heart of Darkness," *Journal of Modern Literature* 38, no. 3 (2015): 20–37 for a persuasive discussion of European anxieties about indigenous uprising. While Wesley suggests that "Conrad's language continually reinforces the measures of control and anxieties of enforcement necessary to keep the colonial edifice from crumbling, hinting at the fragility of imperialism's façade, while at the same time denying such weakness exists" (23), I argue that the vulnerability of imperial masculinity and the fragility of imperial identity is precisely what drives the narrative.
68 Conrad, *Heart*, 40.
69 Ibid., 16, 27, 33, 44, 60.
70 Ibid., 44.
71 Ibid., 193.
72 Ibid., 14.
73 Burrows, "Human Leopards," 143.

74 Conrad, *Heart*, 46.
75 Burrows, "Human Leopards," 143.
76 Griffith, Preface, viii. See page 175 above.
77 Ibid., 35.
78 Ibid., 30.
79 Ibid., 60.
80 Ibid., 68.
81 Ibid., 9.
82 Ibid.
83 Ibid., 22.
84 Ibid., 26.
85 Ibid., 15, 17.
86 Ibid., 21, 28.
87 Ibid., 29, 63, 70.
88 Ibid., 48–9.
89 Ibid., 60, 61, 50.
90 Ibid., 40–1.
91 Ibid., 25, 48, 67.
92 Ibid., 48.
93 Ibid., 58.
94 See Dowling, *Manliness*, 1–2, 11.
95 Conrad, *Heart*, 51. As chapter 2 illustrated, Haggard in *King Solomon's Mines* derides this proposition. In *She*, Ayesha embodies Kurtz's perspective on power. Meanwhile, Marlow has already mocked the European narrative of whites appearing as "supernatural" when he examines Fresleven's fragile skeletal remains.
96 Ibid.
97 Brantlinger similarly suggests that on one level, "*Heart of Darkness* offers a devastating critique of imperialist ideology. On another, more general level, however, it offers a self-critique and an attack upon the impressionistic deviousness of art and language." See *Rule*, 273.
98 Conrad, *Heart*, 35.
99 Ibid., 19.
100 Ibid., 48.
101 Ibid., 78.
102 Ibid., 7, 25.
103 Rawa, *Imperial Quest*, 53–4.
104 Conrad, *Heart*, 50.
105 Ibid., 57.
106 Ibid., 67.
107 Ibid., 59.
108 Ibid., 27–8.

109 Ibid., 16.
110 Ibid., 27.
111 Rawa, *Imperial Quest*, 63.
112 Conrad, *Heart*, 72.
113 Ibid., 51.
114 Ibid., 65–6, 27.
115 Baxter, *Conrad*, 32.
116 Conrad, *Heart*, 3.
117 Here Navarette borrows from F.R. Leavis, *The Great Tradition* (Garden City, NY: Doubleday, 1954), 216.
118 Susan J. Navarette, *The Shape of Fear: Horror and the Fin de Siècle Culture of Decadence* (Lexington: University Press of Kentucky, 1998), 220–4.
119 Ibid., 227. Shetty puts the problem this way: "Perhaps underlying the text's adjectival vagueness is the assurance that a Western audience could be counted on to construct the specific 'abominations' if certain familiar, culturally shared, cues were provided" ("Heart of Darkness," 473).
120 Marsh, *Beetle*, 293.
121 Conrad, *Heart*, 27.

Conclusion

1 See Showalter, *Sexual Anarchy*, 76–83.
2 Ibid., 38–44; McClintock, *Imperial Leather*; Lane, *Ruling Passion*; Judith Walkowitz's discussion of the impact of working-class women on metropolitan politics and social authority in *City of Dreadful Delight* (Chicago: University of Chicago Press, 1992), esp. 73–80; Cyndy Hendershot, *The Animal Within: Masculinity and the Gothic* (Ann Arbor: University of Michigan Press, 1998); Tosh, *Man's Place*; Judith Halberstam, "Gothic Nation: *The Beetle* by Richard Marsh," in *Fictions of Unease: Otranto to The X-Files*, edited by Andrew Smith, Diane Mason, and William Hughes (Bath, UK: Sulis Press, 2002), 100–18; Martin A. Danahay, *Gender at Work in Victorian Culture: Literature, Art, and Masculinity* (Aldershot, UK: Ashgate, 2005); Richardson, *New Woman*; and Ben Griffin, *The Politics of Gender in Victorian Britain: Masculinity, Political Culture and the Struggle for Women's Rights* (Cambridge: Cambridge University Press, 2012).
3 This critical conversation would work both ways. For instance, scholarship on the solidarity between nationalist Irish and Boers might be expanded and inflected through an examination of how and why white masculinities are reconfigured during this period, just as scholarship in this area would shed light on the nuances of imperial masculinity across colonial spheres. See, for example, Keith Surridge, "'All You Soldiers Are What We Call Pro-Boer': The Military Critique of the South African War,

1899–1902," *History* 82, no. 268 (1997): 582–600; Julie Cairnie, "Imperial Poverty in Robert Tressell's *The Ragged Trousered Philanthropists*," *The Journal of Commonwealth Literature* 37, no. 2 (2002): 175–91, and "'From the Cradle to the Grave': Bodies, Class, and Masculinities in *The Ragged Trousered Philanthropists*," in *Revisiting Robert Tressell's Mugsborough: New Perspectives on The Ragged Trousered Philanthropists*, ed. Julie Cairnie and Marion Walls (Amherst, NY: Cambria Press, 2008), 79–101; Donal P. McCracken, *Forgotten Protest: Ireland and the Anglo-Boer War* (Belfast: Ulster Historical Foundation, 2003); and Elleke Boehmer, *Empire, the National, and the Postcolonial, 1890–1920: Resistance in Interaction* (New York: Oxford University Press, 2005).

4 Anne McClintock, "Paranoid Empire: Specters from Abu Ghraib and Guantánamo Bay," *Small Axe* 31, no. 1 (2009): 52.

5 Another contemporary eruption of this kind of imperial racial violence was enacted by Canadian peacekeepers in what has come to be known as the Somalia Affair. See Sherene H. Razack, *Dark Threats and White Knights: The Somalia Affair, Peacekeeping, and the New Imperialism* (Toronto: University of Toronto Press, 2004).

6 Drawing on Tara McKelvey's work, McClintock argues that Iraq, although it was not connected with the attacks on September 11th, was "symbolically territorialized" as a space of retribution through the naming of the first camp inside Abu Ghraib after Peter Ganci, a firefighter who was killed during 9/11. See "Paranoid Empire," 58.

7 Ibid., 56–7.

8 Richard Clarke, the national coordinator for security and counterterrorism at the time of the attacks, recalls that factions within the US government, along with President George W. Bush, aimed to use 9/11 to move in on Iraq: "I realized with almost a sharp physical pain that [Secretary of Defense Donald] Rumsfeld and [his deputy Paul] Wolfowitz were going to try to take advantage of this national tragedy to promote their agenda about Iraq … I vented. 'Having been attacked by al Qaeda, for us now to go bombing Iraq in response would be like our invading Mexico after the Japanese attacked us at Pearl Harbor.'" See *Against All Enemies* (New York: Free Press, 2004), 30–1.

9 Stephen F. Eisenman, *The Abu Ghraib Effect* (London: Reaktion Books, 2007), 7–8.

10 McClintock, "Paranoid Empire," 69.

11 Simon Reid-Harvey, "Exceptional Sovereignty? Guantánamo Bay and the Re-Colonial Present," *Antipode* 39, no. 4 (2007): 631.

12 This Eisenman calls the "Abu Ghraib effect" (*Abu Ghraib Effect*, 9).

13 Jennifer Henderson, *Settler Feminism and Race Making in Canada* (Toronto: University of Toronto Press, 2003), 18.

14 McClintock, "Paranoid Empire," 61; emphasis in original.

15 In a reading that similarly echoes Hegel's master-slave dialectic, McClintock suggests that the rationale for the Abu Ghraib photographs is rooted in a paranoid desire to embody and catalogue enemies and the domination of them; "without the barbarians the legitimacy of empire vanishes like a disappearing phantom" (ibid., 55).

16 Eisenman, *Abu Ghraib Effect*, 53, 46. *Basanos* is the Greek word for both "torture" and "touchstone," suggesting a belief in the connection between torture and truth.

17 Ibid., 54, 72.

18 Eisenman analyses, as an example of this, Edouard Manet's *The Mocking of Christ* (1865): "Here, Christ is a pasty-skinned, knobby-kneed Frenchman with a well-trimmed beard; his torturers are a motley group of oddly dressed workers of varied age and pallor, with calloused and bunioned feet, sunburned arms and necks, and uncertain expressions. Torture is shown here to degrade both torturer and victim and to hold no promise of revelation. By the late nineteenth century, the pathos formula in any form – oppressive or redemptive – was only rarely visible in the artistic media and venues for which it had been devised: painting and sculpture exhibited in churches, palaces, salons, academics and museums." See ibid., 88.

19 Ibid.

20 George W. Bush's statement that the prisoners at Abu Ghraib's "treatment does not reflect the nature of the American people," along with Senator John Kerry's that "we cannot let the actions of a few overshadow the tremendous good work that thousands of soldiers are doing every day in Iraq and all over the world" points directly to this anxiety. See Thom Shanker and Jacques Steinberg, "The Struggle for Iraq: Captives; Bush Voices 'Disgust' at Abuse of Iraqi Prisoners," *New York Times*, 1 May 2004. Journalist Thomas Friedman expresses concern that "we are in danger of losing something much more than the war in Iraq. We are in danger of losing America as an instrument of moral authority and inspiration in the world." See "Restoring Our Honour," *New York Times*, 6 May 2004. Meanwhile, Jasbir K. Puar argues that the case of Abu Ghraib is by no means an anomalous example of American depravity. See "Abu Ghraib: Arguing against Exceptionalism," *Feminist Studies* 30, no. 2 (2004): 522–34.

21 Executive Council Minutes; CO 270/32 16.11.1893, NA.

22 Friedman's concern is apposite here: "The war on terrorism is a war of ideas, and to have any chance of winning we must maintain the credibility of our ideas" ("Restoring Our Honour").

Bibliography

Achebe, Chinua. "An Image of Africa." *Massachusetts Review* 18, no. 4 (1977): 782–94.

Adams, James Eli. *Dandies and Desert Saints: Styles of Victorian Manhood.* Ithaca, NY: Cornell University Press, 1995.

Alldridge, T.J. *The Sherbro and Its Hinterland.* London: Macmillan, 1901.

Anderson, Benedict. *Imagined Communities: Reflections on the Origin and Spread of Nationalism.* 2nd ed. London: Verso, 2006.

Anderson, Catherine. "Red Coats and Black Shields: Race and Masculinity in British Representations of the Anglo-Zulu War." *Critical Survey* 20, no. 3 (2008): 6–28.

Arata, Stephen. *Fictions of Loss in the Victorian Fin de Siècle.* Cambridge: Cambridge University Press, 1996.

Archer, Thomas. *The War in Egypt and the Soudan.* Vol. 1. N.p.: Blackie, 1886.

Atkinson, William. "Bound in *Blackwood's*: The Imperialism of 'Heart of Darkness' in Its Immediate Context." *Twentieth Century Literature* 50, no. 4 (2004): 368–93.

Bakhtin, Mikhail. *Rabelais and His World.* Translated by Helene Iswolsky. Cambridge, MA: MIT Press, 1968.

Ballantyne, Robert Michael. *The Coral Island: A Tale of the Pacific Ocean.* 1857. London: J.M. Dent and Sons, 1967.

– *The Gorilla Hunters: A Tale of the Wilds of Africa.* 1875. Edinburgh: T. Nelson and Sons, 1901.

Ballantyne, Tony. *Orientalism and Race: Aryanism in the British Empire.* Houndmills, UK: Palgrave, 2002.

Banivanua Mar, Tracey. "Cannibalism and Colonialism: Charting Colonies and Frontiers in Nineteenth-Century Fiji." *Comparative Studies in Society and History* 52, no. 2 (2010): 255–81.

– "Frontier Space and the Reification of the Rule of Law: Colonial Negotiations in the Western Pacific, 1870–74." *Australian Feminist Law Journal* 30 (2009): 23–39.

Bautz, Annika. *The Reception of Jane Austen and Sir Walter Scott: A Comparative Longitudinal Study*. London: Continuum, 2007.

Baxter, Katherine Isobel. *Joseph Conrad and the Swan Song of Romance*. Farnham, UK: Ashgate, 2010.

Beatty, K.J. *Human Leopards: An Account of the Trials of Human Leopards before the Special Commission Court; With a Note on Sierra Leone, Past and Present*. London: Hugh Rees, 1915.

Bederman, Gail. *Manliness and Civilization: A Cultural History of Race and Gender in the United States, 1880–1917*. Chicago: University of Chicago Press, 1995.

Bennet, Compton, and Andrew Marton, dirs. *King Solomon's Mines*. 1950 (film).

Berlant, Lauren. "Introduction: Compassion (and Withholding)." In *Compassion: The Culture and Politics of an Emotion*, edited by Lauren Berlant, 1–14. New York: Routledge, 2004.

Best, Brian, and Adrian Greaves. *The Curling Letters of the Zulu War*. Barnsley, UK: Pen and Sword, 2001.

Bhabha, Homi K. *The Location of Culture*. London: Routledge, 1994.

Bhebe, N. "The British, Boers and Africans in South Africa, 1850–80." In *Africa in the Nineteenth Century until the 1880s*, edited by J.F. Ajayi, 145–78. Vol. 6 of *General History of Africa*. Berkeley: University of California Press, 1989.

Blyden, Edward Wilmot. *Black Spokesman: Selected Published Works of E.W. Blyden*. Edited by Hollis Lynch. New York: Humanities Press, 1971.

Boehmer, Elleke. *Empire, the National, and the Postcolonial, 1890–1920: Resistance in Interaction*. New York: Oxford University Press, 2005.

Bonwick, James. *Our Nationalities*. London: David Bogue, 1880.

Bourne, H.R. Fox. *Blacks and Whites in West Africa: An Account of the Past Treatment and Present Condition of West African Natives under European Influence or Control*. London: P.S. King and Son, 1901.

– "Natives under British Rule in Africa." *British Africa*. British Empire Series Vol. 2, 195–218. London: Kegan Paul Trench Trubner, 1899.

Bowman, Joye. "Reconstructing the Past Using British Parliamentary Papers: The Anglo-Zulu War of 1879." *History in Africa* 31 (2004): 117–32.

Brantlinger, Patrick. *Rule of Darkness: British Literature and Imperialism, 1830–1914*. Ithaca, NY: Cornell University Press, 1988.

Bristow, Joseph. *Effeminate England: Homoerotic Writing after 1885*. New York: Columbia University Press, 1995.

– *Empire Boys: Adventures in a Man's World*. London: Harper Collins Academic, 1991.

Bryant, Mark. *Wars of Empire in Cartoons*. London: Grub Street Publishing, 2008.

Buel, J.W. *Heroes of the Dark Continent: A Complete History of All the Great Explorations and Discoveries in Africa, from the Earliest Ages to the Present Time*. 1889. Freeport, NY: Books for Libraries Press, 1971.

Bulfin, Ailise. "The Fiction of Gothic Egypt and British Imperial Paranoia: The Curse of the Suez Canal." *English Literature in Transition, 1880–1920* 54, no. 4 (2011): 411–43.

– "'In That Egyptian Den': Situating *The Beetle* within the Fin-de-siècle Fiction of Gothic Egypt." In *Richard Marsh, Popular Fiction, and Literary Culture, 1890–1915*, edited by Victoria Margree, Daniel Orrells, and Minna Vuohelainen, 127–47. Manchester: Manchester University Press, 2018.

Burrow, Merrick. "The Imperial Souvenir: Things and Masculinities in H. Rider Haggard's *King Solomon's Mines* and *Allan Quatermain*." *Journal of Victorian Culture* 18, no. 1 (2013): 72–92.

Burrows, D. "The Human Leopards of Sierra Leone." *Journal of the Royal African Society* 13, no. 50 (1914): 143–51.

Cairnie, Julie. "'From the Cradle to the Grave': Bodies, Class, and Masculinities in *The Ragged Trousered Philanthropists*." In *Revisiting Robert Tressell's Mugsborough: New Perspectives on The Ragged Trousered Philanthropists*, edited by Julie Cairnie and Marion Walls, 79–101. Amherst, NY: Cambria Press, 2008.

– "Imperial Poverty in Robert Tressell's *The Ragged Trousered Philanthropists*." *Journal of Commonwealth Literature* 37, no. 2 (2002): 175–91.

Chamberlain, Joseph. *Foreign and Colonial Speeches by the Right Hon. Joseph Chamberlain*. London: George Routledge and Sons, 1897.

Chenevix Trench, Charles. *The Road to Khartoum: A Life of General Charles Gordon*. New York: Dorset Press, 1978.

Chrisman, Laura. "The Imperial Unconscious? Representations of Imperial Discourse." *Critical Quarterly* 32 (1990): 38–58.

– *Rereading the Imperial Romance: British Imperialism and South African Resistance in Haggard, Schreiner, and Plaatje*. Oxford: Clarendon Press, 2000.

Clarke, Richard A. *Against All Enemies*. New York: Free Press, 2004.

Cohen, Morton. *Rider Haggard: His Life and Works*. London: Hutchinson, 1960.

Colenso, Francis E., and E. Durnford. *History of the Zulu War and Its Origin*. London, 1880.

Conrad, Joseph. *Heart of Darkness*. 1899. Edited by Robert Kimbrough. W.W. Norton, 1963.

Curran, John E., Jr. *Hamlet, Protestantism, and the Mourning of Contingency: Not to Be*. Aldershot: Ashgate, 2006.

Daly, Nicholas. *Modernism, Romance, and the Fin de Siècle: Popular Fiction and British Culture, 1880–1914*. New York: Cambridge University Press, 1999.

Danahay, Martin A. *Gender at Work in Victorian Culture: Literature, Art, and Masculinity*. Aldershot, UK: Ashgate, 2005.

Darwin, Charles. *The Origin of Species by Means of Natural Selection; or, the Preservation of Favoured Races in the Struggle for Life.* 1859. Harmondsworth, UK: Penguin, 1968.

Davenport-Hines, Richard. "Gordon, Charles George." *Oxford Dictionary of National Biography*, 2004.

David, Deirdre. *Rule Britannia: Women, Empire, and Victorian Writing.* Ithaca, NY: Cornell University Press, 1995.

Deane, Bradley. "Imperial Barbarians: Primitive Masculinity in Lost World Fiction." *Journal of Victorian Literature and Culture* 36 (2008): 205–25.

– *Masculinity and the New Imperialism.* Cambridge: Cambridge University Press, 2014.

– "Mummy Fiction and the Occupation of Egypt: Imperial Striptease." *English Literature in Transition, 1880–1920* 51, no. 4 (2008): 381–410.

Derrida, Jacques. *Speech and Phenomena and Other Essays on Husserl's Theory of Signs.* Translated by David B. Allison. Evanston, IL: Northwestern University Press, 1973.

Dixon, Robert. *Writing the Colonial Adventure: Race, Gender and Nation in Anglo-Australian Popular Fiction, 1875–1914.* Cambridge: Cambridge University Press, 1995.

Driver, Felix. "Stanley, Sir Henry Morton." *Oxford Dictionary of National Biography*, 2004.

Dollimore, Jonathan. *Sexual Dissidence: Augustine to Wilde, Freud to Foucault.* Oxford: Clarendon Press, 1991.

Douglas, Mary. *Purity and Danger: An Analysis of Concepts of Pollution and Taboo.* 1966. London: Routledge, 2002.

Dowling, Andrew. *Manliness and the Male Novelist in Victorian Literature.* Aldershot, UK: Ashgate, 2001.

Eisenman, Stephen F. *The Abu Ghraib Effect.* London: Reaktion Books, 2007.

Emery, Frank. *The Red Soldier: Letters from the Zulu War, 1879.* London: Hodder and Stoughton, 1977.

Fabian, Johannes. *Time and the Other: How Anthropology Makes Its Object.* New York: Columbia University Press, 1983.

Falconbridge, Anna Marie. *Two Voyages to Sierra Leone, during the Years 1791–2–3.* London, 1794.

Favret, Mary A. *War at a Distance: Romanticism and the Making of Modern Wartime.* Princeton, NJ: Princeton University Press, 2010.

Forbes, Archibald. *Barracks, Bivouacs and Battles.* London: Macmillan, 1891.

Friedman, Dustin. "Unsettling the Normative: Articulations of Masculinity in Victorian Literature and Culture." *Literature Compass* 7, no. 12 (2010): 1077–88.

Gilbert, Sandra M., and Susan Gubar. *No Man's Land: The Place of the Woman Writer in the Twentieth Century.* Vol. 2, *Sexchanges.* New Haven, CT: Yale University Press, 1989.

Gold, Barri E. "Embracing the Corpse: Discursive Recycling in H. Rider Haggard's *She*." *English Literature in Transition, 1880–1920* 38, no. 3 (1995): 305–27.

Goonetilleke, D.C.R.A. Introduction to *Heart of Darkness*, by Joseph Conrad, 9–48. Peterborough, ON: Broadview, 2003.

Gordon, Catherine. "The Illustration of Sir Walter Scott: Nineteenth-Century Enthusiasm and Adaptation." *Journal of the Warburg and Courtauld Institutes* 34 (1971): 297–317.

Gordon, Charles. *The Journals of Major-Gen. C.G. Gordon at Khartoum*. Edited by Egmont Hake. London: Kegan Paul, Trench, 1885.

Gordon, Sir Henry W. "Description of the Journal." In *The Journals of Major-Gen. C.G. Gordon at Khartoum*, by Charles Gordon, lxiv–lxv. London: Kegan Paul, Trench, 1885.

Gray, A. "The Human Leopards of Sierra Leone." *Journal of the Society of Comparative Legislation* n.s. 16, no. 2 (1916): 196–8.

Griffin, Ben. *The Politics of Gender in Victorian Britain: Masculinity, Political Culture and the Struggle for Women's Rights*. Cambridge: Cambridge University Press, 2012.

Griffith, Sir William Brandford. Preface to *Human Leopards: An Account of the Trials of Human Leopards before the Special Commission Court; With a Note on Sierra Leone, Past and Present*, by K.J. Beatty, v–ix. London: Hugh Rees, 1915.

Grosz, Elizabeth. *Volatile Bodies: Toward a Corporeal Feminism*. Bloomington: Indiana University Press, 1994.

Haggard, H. Rider. "About Fiction." *Contemporary Review*, Feb. 1887. Appendix A in *She: A History of Adventure*, by H. Rider Haggard, 290–99. Edited by Andrew M. Stauffer. Peterborough, ON: Broadview, 2006.

– *Cetywayo and His White Neighbours; or, Remarks on Recent Events in Zululand, Natal, and the Transvaal*. 1882. London: Trubner, Ludgate Hill, 1888.

– *The Days of My Life: An Autobiography*. Vols. 1 and 2. London: Longmans, Green, 1926.

– *King Solomon's Mines*. 1885. Edited by Gerald Monsman. Peterborough, ON: Broadview, 2002.

– *She: A History of Adventure*. 1887. Edited by Andrew M. Stauffer. Peterborough, ON: Broadview, 2006.

Hake, A. Egmont. "Introduction and Notes." In *The Journals of Major-Gen. C.G. Gordon at Khartoum*, by Charles Gordon, ix–liv. London: Kegan Paul, Trench, 1885.

Halberstam, Judith. "Gothic Nation: *The Beetle* by Richard Marsh." In *Fictions of Unease: Otranto to The X-Files*, edited by Andrew Smith, Diane Mason, and William Hughes, 100–18. Bath, UK: Sulis Press, 2002.

Haley, Bruce. *The Healthy Body and Victorian Culture*. Cambridge, MA: Harvard University Press, 1978.

Hampson, Robert. "'Heart of Darkness' and 'The Speech That Cannot Be Silenced.'" *English: Journal of the English Association* 39, no. 163 (1990): 15–32.

Harris, W.C., and Dawn Vernooy. "'Orgies of Nameless Horrors': Gender, Orientalism, and the Queering of Violence in Richard Marsh's *The Beetle.*" *Papers in Language and Literature* 48, no. 4 (2012): 339–81.

Hawkins, Hunt. "Conrad's Critique of Imperialism in *Heart of Darkness.*" *PMLA* 94, no. 2 (1979): 286–99.

– "The Issue of Racism in *Heart of Darkness.*" *Conradiana* 14, no. 3 (1982): 163–71.

Hendershot, Cyndy. *The Animal Within: Masculinity and the Gothic.* Ann Arbor: University of Michigan Press, 1998.

Henderson, Jennifer. *Settler Feminism and Race Making in Canada.* Toronto: University of Toronto Press, 2003.

Henty, G.A. *By Sheer Pluck; a Tale of the Ashanti War.* Glasgow: Blackie and Son, 1897.

– *Dash for Khartoum: A Tale of the Nile Expedition.* Glasgow: Blackie and Son, 1892.

– *With Kitchener in the Sudan: A Story of Atbara and Omdurman.* London: Foulsham, 1900.

Herbert, Christopher. *War of No Pity: The Indian Mutiny and Victorian Trauma.* Princeton, NJ: Princeton University Press, 2008.

Heywood, Leslie. *Dedication to Hunger: The Anorexic Aesthetic in Modern Culture.* Berkeley: University of California Press, 1996.

Hoberman, John. *Darwin's Athletes: How Sport Has Damaged Black America and Preserved the Myth of Race.* Boston: Houghton Mifflin, 1997.

Hobsbawm, Eric. *Age of Empire, 1875–1914.* New York: Pantheon Books, 1987.

Höglund, John. "Black Englishness and the Concurrent Voices of Richard Marsh in *The Surprising Husband.*" *English Literature in History* 56, no. 3 (2013): 275–91.

Holstun, Jim. "'Mr. Kayerts. He Is Dead': Literary Realism and Conrad's 'Outpost of Progress.'" *English Literature in History* 85, no. 1 (2018): 191–220.

Hughes, Thomas. *Tom Brown's School Days.* 1857. Oxford: Oxford University Press, 2008.

Hultgren, Neil E. "Haggard Criticism since 1980: Imperial Romance before and after the Postcolonial Turn." *Literature Compass* 8, no. 9 (2011): 645–59.

Hurley, Kelly. *The Gothic Body: Sexuality, Materialism, and Degeneration at the Fin de Siecle.* Cambridge: Cambridge University Press, 1999.

– "'The Inner Chambers of All Nameless Sin': *The Beetle,* Gothic Female Sexuality, and Oriental Barbarism." In *Virginal Sexuality and Textuality in Victorian Literature,* edited by Lloyd Davis, 193–213. Albany: New York University Press, 1993.

Hutcheon, Linda. *A Theory of Parody: The Teachings of Twentieth-Century Art Forms.* New York: Methuen, 1985.

Hutcheon, Linda, and Mario J. Valdés. "Irony, Nostalgia, and the Postmodern: A Dialogue." *Poligrafías* 3 (2000): 18–41.

Ibrahim, H.A. "African Initiatives and Resistance in North-East Africa." In *General History of Africa*. Vol. 7, *Africa under Colonial Domination, 1880–1935*, edited by A. Adu Boahen, 63–86. Berkeley: University of California Press, 1985.

Ingham, E.G. *After a Hundred Years*. London, 1894.

Jackson, Michael. "The Man Who Could Turn into an Elephant: Shape-shifting among the Kuranko of Sierra Leone." In *Personhood and Agency: The Experience of Self and Others in African Cultures. Papers Presented at a Symposium on African Folk Models and Their Application, held at Uppsala University, August 23–30, 1897*, edited by Michael Jackson and Ivan Karp, 59–78. Uppsala, SE: Acta Universitatis Upsaliensis, 1990.

Jassanoff, Maya. *The Dawn Watch: Joseph Conrad in a Global World*. New York: Penguin, 2017.

Johnson, Douglas. "The Death of Gordon: A Victorian Myth." *Journal of Imperial and Commonwealth History* 10, no. 3 (1982): 285–310.

Johnston, Anna. *Missionary Writing and Empire, 1800–1860*. Cambridge: Cambridge University Press, 2003.

Jones, Anna Maria. "Conservation of Energy, Individual Agency, and Gothic Terror in Richard Marsh's *The Beetle*, or, What's Scarier Than an Ancient, Evil, Shape-shifting Bug?" *Victorian Literature and Culture* 39, no. 1 (2010): 65–85.

Kalous, Milan. *Cannibals and Tongo Players of Sierra Leone*. Auckland: M. Kalous, 1974.

Kaufman, Heidi. *English Origins, Jewish Discourse, and the Nineteenth-Century British Novel: Reflections on a Nested Nation*. University Park: Pennsylvania State University Press, 2009.

Kaul, Chandrika, ed. *Media and the British Empire*. Houndmills, UK: Palgrave Macmillan, 2006.

Katz, Wendy. *Rider Haggard and the Fiction of Empire*. Cambridge: Cambridge University Press, 1987.

Kestner, Joseph. *Masculinities in Victorian Painting*. Aldershot, UK: Scolar Press, 1995.

Kingsley, Mary. *Travels in West Africa*. 1897. Introduction by Anthony Brandt. Washington, DC: National Geographic Society, 2002.

Knight, Ian. *Zulu Rising: The Epic Story of Isandlwana and Rorke's Drift*. London: Macmillan, 2010.

– "The Zulu Army of 1879." *Redcoats and Zulus: Selected Essays from* The Journal of the Anglo Zulu War Historical Society. Edited by Adrian Greaves. Barnsley, UK: Pen and Sword Military, 2004.

Kucich, John. *Imperial Masochism: British Fiction, Fantasy, and Social Class*. Princeton, NJ: Princeton University Press, 2007.

Laband, John. *Lord Chelmsford's Zulu Campaign, 1878–1879.* Dover, NH: Alan Sutton Publishing, 1994.

– "'War Can't Be Made with Kid Gloves': The Impact of the Anglo-Zulu War of 1879 on the Fabric of Zulu Society." *South African Historical Journal* 43 (2000): 179–96.

Laband, John, and Ian Knight. *The War Correspondents: The Anglo-Zulu War.* Phoenix Mill, UK: Sutton, 1996.

Lane, Christopher. *The Burdens of Intimacy: Psychoanalysis and Victorian Masculinity.* Chicago: University of Chicago Press, 1999.

– *The Ruling Passion: British Colonial Allegory and the Paradox of Homosexual Desire.* Durham, NC: Duke University Press, 1995.

Law, Jules. *The Social Life of Fluids: Blood, Milk, and Water in the Victorian Novel.* Ithaca, NY: Cornell University Press, 2010.

Lawrence, Benjamin N., Emily Lynn Osborn, and Richard L. Roberts, eds. *Intermediaries, Interpreters, and Clerks: African Employees in the Making of Colonial Africa.* Madison: University of Wisconsin Press, 2006.

Lawtoo, Nidesh. "The Horror of Mimesis: 'Enthusiastic Outbreak[s]' in *Heart of Darkness.*" *Conradiana* 42, nos. 1–2 (2010): 45–74.

– "A Picture of Africa: Frenzy, Counternarrative, Mimesis." *Modern Fiction Studies* 29, no. 1 (2013): 26–52.

Leavis, F.R. *The Great Tradition.* Garden City, NY: Doubleday, 1954.

Lester, Alan. *Imperial Networks: Creating Identities in Nineteenth-Century South Africa and Britain.* London: Routledge, 2001.

Lieven, Michael. "'Butchering the Brutes All Over the Place': Total War and Massacre in Zululand, 1879." *History* 84 (1999): 614–32.

– "Heroism, Heroics and the Making of Heroes: The Anglo-Zulu War of 1879." *Albion: A Quarterly Journal Concerned with British Studies* 30, no. 3 (1998): 419–38.

Lindskog, Birger. *African Leopard Men.* Uppsala, SE: Studia Ethnographica Upsaliensia. VII. 1954.

Logan, Mawuena Kossi. *Narrating Africa: George Henty and the Fiction of Empire.* New York: Garland Publishing, 1999.

Loomba, Ania. *Colonialism/Postcolonialism.* London: Routledge, 1998.

Luckhurst, Roger. *The Invention of Telepathy, 1870–1901.* Oxford: Oxford University Press, 2002.

– *The Mummy's Curse: The True History of a Dark Fantasy.* Oxford: Oxford University Press, 2012.

MacKenzie, John M. "The Imperial Pioneer and Hunter and the British Masculine Stereotype in Late Victorian and Edwardian Times." In *Manliness and Morality: Middle-Class Masculinity in Britain and America, 1800–1940,* edited by J.A. Mangan and James Walvin, 176–98. Manchester: Manchester University Press, 1987.

– "The Press and Empire." In *Newspapers and Empire in Ireland and Britain: Reporting the British Empire, c. 1857–1921*, edited by Simon J. Potter, 23–38. Dublin: Four Courts Press, 2004.
– *Propaganda and Empire: The Manipulation of Public Opinion, 1880–1960.* Manchester: Manchester University Press, 1984.
Mangan, J.A., and James Walvin, eds. *Manliness and Morality: Middle-Class Masculinity in Britain and America, 1800–1940.* Manchester: Manchester University Press, 1987.
Margree, Victoria. "'Both in Men's Clothing': Gender, Sovereignty and Insecurity in Richard Marsh's *The Beetle*." *Critical Survey* 19, no. 2 (2007): 63–81.
Margree, Victoria, Daniel Orrells, and Minna Vuohelainen. "Introduction." In *Richard Marsh, Popular Fiction, and Literary Culture, 1890–1915*, edited by Victoria Margree, Daniel Orrells, and Minna Vuohelainen, 1–24. Manchester: Manchester University Press, 2018.
Marriott, Brother Herbert Philip Fitzgerald, FRGS. "The Secret Societies of West Africa." *Journal of the Anthropological Institute of Great Britain and Ireland* 29, nos. 1/2 (1899): 21–7.
– *The Secret Tribal Societies of West Africa.* Reprint from *Ars Quatuor Coronatorum*, 12 (May 1899). Margate: H. Keble, 1900.
Marsh, Richard. *The Beetle.* 1897. Edited by Julian Wolfreys. Peterborough, ON: Broadview, 2004.
Martineau, John. *The Life and Correspondence of Sir Bartle Frere.* Vol. 2. 1895. *American Libraries Internet Archive.* Last modified 10 Jan. 2008. https://archive.org/details/lifeandcorrespo01frergoog.
Marzolf, Marion T. "American 'New Journalism' Takes Root in Europe at End of 19th Century." *Journalism Quarterly* 61, no. 3 (1984): 529–36, 691.
Mason, Tony, and Eliza Riedi. *Sport and the Military: The British Armed Forces, 1880–1960.* New York: Cambridge University Press, 2010.
Matthews, John. *A Voyage to the River Sierra-Leone.* London, 1791.
McAdam, Ian. *Magic and Masculinity in Early Modern English Drama.* Pittsburgh: Duquesne University Press, 2009.
McClintock, Anne. *Imperial Leather: Race, Gender and Sexuality in the Colonial Contest.* New York: Routledge, 1995.
– "Paranoid Empire: Specters from Abu Ghraib and Guantánamo Bay." *Small Axe* 31, no. 1 (2009): 50–74.
McCollum, Jennifer. "Animation and Reanimation in the Victorian Gothic." PhD diss., University of Washington, 2012.
McCracken, Donal P. *Forgotten Protest: Ireland and the Anglo-Boer War.* Belfast: Ulster Historical Foundation, 2003.
Metcalf, Thomas R. *The New Cambridge History.* Vol. 3. *Ideologies of the Raj.* Cambridge: Cambridge University Press, 2001.

Miller, D.A. *The Novel and the Police.* Berkeley and Los Angeles: University of California Press, 1988.

Milner, Alfred. *England in Egypt.* London: Edward Arnold, 1892.

Mitford, Bertram. *Through the Zulu Country: Its Battlefields and Its People.* London, 1883.

Monsman, Gerald. *H. Rider Haggard on the Imperial Frontier: The Politics and Literary Contexts of His African Romances.* Greensboro, NC: ELT Press, 2006.

– "Introduction: Of Diamonds and Deities in *King Solomon's Mines.*" In *King Solomon's Mines,* edited by Gerald Monsman, 1–12. 1885. Peterborough, ON: Broadview, 2002.

Moodie, D.C.F. *Zulu 1879: The Anglo Zulu War of 1879 from Contemporary Sources. First Hand Accounts, Interviews, Letters, Despatches, Official Documents & Newspaper Reports.* N.p.: Leonaur, 2006.

Moorehead, Alan. *The White Nile.* London: Hamish Hamilton, 1960.

Murphy, Patricia. *Time Is of the Essence: Temporality, Gender, and the New Woman.* Albany: SUNY Press, 2001.

Navarette, Susan J. *The Shape of Fear: Horror and the Fin de Siècle Culture of Decadence.* Lexington: University Press of Kentucky, 1998.

Nichols, Arthur. "What England Has Done for Egypt." *British Africa.* British Empire Series, Vol. 2, 306–25. London: Kegan Paul Trench Trubner, 1899.

Nicoll, Fergus. "'Truest History, Struck Off at White Heat': The Politics of Editing Gordon's Khartoum Journals." *Journal of Imperial and Commonwealth History* 38, no. 1 (2010): 21–46.

Norris-Newman, Charles. *In Zululand with the British throughout the War of 1879.* 1880. London: Greenhill Books, 1990.

Obeyeskere, Gananath. "'British Cannibals': Contemplation of an Event in the Death and Resurrection of James Cook, Explorer." *Critical Inquiry* 18, no. 4 (1992): 630–54.

Okafor, Clement Abiaziem. "Joseph Conrad and Chinua Achebe: Two Antipodal Portraits of Africa." *Journal of Black Studies* 19, no. 1 (1988): 17–28.

Otis, Laura. *Membranes: Metaphors of Invasion in Nineteenth-Century Literature, Science, and Politics.* Baltimore, MD: Johns Hopkins University Press, 1999.

Padmini, Mongia. "The Rescue: Conrad, Achebe, and the Critics." *Conradiana* 33, no. 2 (2001): 153–63.

Paris, Michael. *Warrior Nation: Images of War in British Popular Culture, 1850–2000.* London: Reaktion Books, 2000.

Park, Roberta J. "Biological Thought, Athletics, and the Formation of a 'Man of Character,' 1830–1900." In *Manliness and Morality: Middle-Class Masculinity in Britain and America, 1800–1940,* edited by J.A. Mangan and James Walvin, 7–34. Manchester: Manchester University Press, 1987.

Parry, Benita. *Conrad and Imperialism: Ideological Boundaries and Visionary Frontiers.* London: Macmillan, 1983.

Potter, Simon J. "Empire and the English Press, *c.* 1857–1914." In *Newspapers and Empire in Ireland and Britain: Reporting the British Empire, c. 1857–1921*, edited by Simon J. Potter, 39–61. Dublin: Four Courts Press, 2004.

Pratt, Mary Louise. *Imperial Eyes: Travel Writing and Transculturation*. Florence, KY: Routledge, 1992.

Pratten, David. *The Man-Leopard Murders: History and Society in Colonial Nigeria*. Edinburgh: Edinburgh University Press, 2007.

Prior, Melton. *Campaigns of a War Correspondent*. London: Edward Arnold, 1912.

Puar, Jasbir K. "Abu Ghraib: Arguing against Exceptionalism." *Feminist Studies* 30, no. 2 (2004): 522–34.

Rawa, J.M. *The Imperial Quest and Modern Memory from Conrad to Greene*. New York: Routledge, 2005.

Razack, Sherene H. *Dark Threats and White Knights: The Somalia Affair, Peacekeeping, and the New Imperialism*. Toronto: University of Toronto Press, 2004.

Read, Donald. *The Power of News: The History of Reuters, 1849–1989*. New York: Oxford University Press, 1992.

Rebry, Natasha L. "Disintegrated Subjects: Gothic Fiction, Mental Science and the Fin-de-siècle Discourse of Dissociation." PhD diss., University of British Columbia, 2013.

Reid, Julia. "'Gladstone Bags, Shooting Boots, and Byrant & May's Matches': Empire, Commerce, and the Imperial Romance in the *Graphic's* Serialization of H. Rider Haggard's *She*." *Studies in the Novel* 43, no. 2 (2011): 152–77.

Reid-Harvey, Simon. "Exceptional Sovereignty? Guantánamo Bay and the Re-Colonial Present." *Antipode* 39, no. 4 (2007): 627–48.

Richards, Thomas. *The Imperial Archive: Knowledge and the Fantasy of Empire*. New York: Verso, 1993.

Richardson, LeeAnne M. *New Woman and Colonial Adventure Fiction in Victorian Britain*. Gainesville: University Press of Florida, 2006.

Roberts, Andrew Michael. *Conrad and Masculinity*. Houndmills, UK: Macmillan, 2000.

Robinson, Ronald, and John Gallagher, with Alice Denny. *Africa and the Victorians: The Official Mind of Imperialism*. 2nd ed. Houndmills, UK: Macmillan, 1981.

Roper, Michael, and John Tosh. "Introduction: Historians and the Politics of Masculinity." In *Manful Assertions: Masculinities in Britain since 1800*, edited by Michael Roper and John Tosh, 1–24. London: Routledge, 1991.

Roy, Parma. "Discovering India, Imagining *Thuggee*." *Yale Journal of Criticism* 9, no. 1 (1996): 121–45.

Ruskin, John. "Of Queen's Gardens." In *Sesame and Lilies*. 1864. New York: Silver, Burdett and Company, 1900. Internet Archive, California Digital Library. https://archive.org/details/johnruskinssesa00ruskgoog.

Said, Edward. *Culture and Imperialism*. New York: Vintage Books, 1993.

Sandison, Alan. *The Wheel of Empire: A Study of the Imperial Idea in Some Late Nineteenth and Early Twentieth-Century Fiction*. London: Macmillan, 1967.

Sawer, Marian. "Gender, Metaphor and the State." *Feminist Review* 52 (1996): 118–34.

Schmitt, Cannon. *Alien Nation: Nineteenth-Century Gothic Fictions and English Nationality*. Philadelphia: University of Pennsylvania Press, 1997.

Sedgwick, Eve Kosofsky. *Between Men: English Literature and Male Homosocial Desire*. 1985. New York: Columbia University Press, 1992.

– *The Coherence of Gothic Conventions*. 1980. North Stratford, UK: Ayer Company Publishers, 1999.

Shaw, Rosalind. *Memories of the Slave Trade: Ritual and the Historical Imagination in Sierra Leone*. Chicago: University of Chicago Press, 2002.

Sharpe, Jenny. *Allegories of Empire: The Figure of Woman in the Colonial Text*. Minneapolis: University of Minnesota Press, 1993.

Shetty, Sandya. "Heart of Darkness: Out of Africa Something New Never Comes." *Journal of Modern Literature* 15, no. 4 (1989): 461–74.

Showalter, Elaine. *Sexual Anarchy: Gender and Culture at the Fin de Siècle*. London: Bloomsbury, 1991.

Sinha, Madhudaya. "Triangular Erotics: The Politics of Masculinity, Imperialism and Big Game Hunting in Rider Haggard's *She*." *Critical Survey* 20, no. 3 (2008): 29–43.

Smith, Andrew. *Victorian Demons: Masculinity, Medicine, and the Gothic at the Fin de Siècle*. Manchester: Manchester University Press, 2004.

Smith, Joanna M. "'Too Beautiful Altogether': Ideologies of Gender and Empire in Heart of Darkness." in *Heart of Darkness: Case Studies in Contemporary Criticism*, ed. Ross Murfin. 3rd ed. Basingstoke, UK: Bedford/St Martins, 2011.

Snook, Mike. *Beyond the Reaches of Empire: Wolseley's Failed Campaign to Save Gordon and Khartoum*. London: Frontline Books, 2013.

– *Into the Jaws of Death: British Military Blunders, 1879–1900*. London: Frontline Books, 2008.

Sole, Terry. *For God, Queen and Colony: The Colonial, Volunteer and Native Regiments in the Zulu War 1879*. Honiton, UK: Token Publishing, 2011.

Spurr, David. *The Rhetoric of Empire: Colonial Discourse in Journalism, Travel Writing, and Imperial Administration*. Durham, NC: Duke University Press, 1993.

Stauffer, Andrew M. Introduction to *She: A History of Adventure*, by Rider Haggard, 11–26. Edited by Andrew M. Stauffer. Peterborough, ON: Broadview, 2006.

Stiebel, Lindy. *Imagining Africa: Landscape in H. Rider Haggard's African Romances*. Westport, CT: Greenwood Press, 2001.

Stevenson, Robert, dir. *King Solomon's Mines.* 1937 (film).
Stoler, Ann Laura. "Colonial Archives and the Arts of Governance." *Archival Science* 2 (2002): 87–109.
Stott, Rebecca. *The Fabrication of the Late-Victorian Femme Fatale: The Kiss of Death.* Basingstoke, UK: Palgrave Macmillan, 1992.
Strong, Richard P., ed. *The African Republic of Liberia and the Belgian Congo; Based on the Observations Made and Material Collected during the Harvard African Expedition, 1926–1927.* Cambridge, MA: Harvard University Press, 1930.
Surridge, Keith. "'All You Soldiers Are What We Call Pro-Boer': The Military Critique of the South African War, 1899–1902." *History* 82, no. 268 (1997): 582–600.
Sussman, Herbert. *Victorian Masculinities: Manhood and Masculine Poetics in Early Victorian Literature and Art.* Cambridge: Cambridge University Press, 1995.
Talairach-Vielmas, Laurence. *Moulding the Female Body in Victorian Fairy Tales and Sensation Novels.* Aldershot, UK: Ashgate, 2007.
Tennyson, Alfred Lord. *The Complete Works of Alfred Lord Tennyson.* New York: Frederick A. Stokes Company, 1891.
Theweleit, Klaus. *Male Fantasies.* Vol. 1. Minneapolis: University of Minnesota Press, 1987.
Thompson, J. Lee, dir. *King Solomon's Mines.* 1985 (film).
Tosh, John. *Manliness and Masculinities in Nineteenth-Century Britain.* Harlow, UK: Pearson Education, 2005.
– *A Man's Place: Masculinity and the Middle-Class Home in Victorian England.* New Haven, CT: Yale University Press, 1999.
Vuohelainen, Minna. "'Cribb'd, Cabined, and Confined': Fear, Claustrophobia and Modernity in Richard Marsh's Urban Gothic Fiction." *Journal of Literature and Science* 3, no. 1 (2010): 23–36.
– "'You Know Not of What You Speak': Language, Identity, and Xenophobia in Richard Marsh's *The Beetle: A Mystery* (1897)." In *Fear, Loathing, and Victorian Xenophobia,* edited by Marlene Tromp, Maria K. Bachman, and Heidi Kaufman, 312–30. Columbus: Ohio State University Press, 2013.
Wade, Stephen. *Empire and Espionage: The Anglo-Zulu War, 1879.* Barnsley, UK: Pen and Sword Military, 2012.
Walkowitz, Judith. *City of Dreadful Delight.* Chicago: University of Chicago Press, 1993.
Waller, John. *Gordon of Khartoum.* New York: Atheneum, 1988.
Watt, Ian. *Conrad in the Nineteenth Century.* Berkeley: University of California Press, 1979.
Watts, Cedric. "'A Bloody Racist': About Achebe's View of Conrad." *Yearbook of English Studies* 13 (1983): 196–209.

Wesley, Charles. "Inscriptions of Resistance in Joseph Conrad's *Heart of Darkness*." *Journal of Modern Literature* 38, no. 3 (2015): 20–37.

Williamson, J. *The Oak King, the Holly King, and the Unicorn: The Myths and Symbols of the Unicorn Tapestries*. New York: Harper and Row, 1986.

Winterbottom, Thomas. *An Account of the Native Africans in the Neighbourhood of Sierra Leone* London, 1803.

Wolfreys, Julian. Introduction to *The Beetle*, by Richard Marsh, 9–34. 1897. Peterborough, ON: Broadview, 2004.

Wright, A.R. "Secret Societies and Fetishism in Sierra Leone." *Folklore* 8, no. 4 (1907): 423–7.

Index